Women in Criminal Law

A PRACTICAL GUIDE FOR INCLUSIVE AND THRIVING WORKPLACES

Maryam Ahranjani

ABA
AMERICAN BAR ASSOCIATION
Criminal Justice Section

Cover design by Mary Anne Kulchawik/ABA Design

Printed in the United States of America.

30 29 28 27 26   5 4 3 2 1

A catalog record for this book is available from the Library of Congress.

Contents

Foreword

"This Task Force . . . brings with it a determination to highlight solutions that will change the conversations, change the way we do things, not only in the [ABA] Criminal Justice Section [(CJS)], but throughout the profession." In the ABA Women in Criminal Justice Task Force's column in the *Criminal Justice Magazine*'s spring 2019 issue, we, the Task Force's founding co-chairs, made a daring prediction that our work would change the profession for criminal legal system practitioners. In developing the plans to achieve that lofty goal, we wrestled with what values and perspectives we should uphold as we confront a legal profession that has caused so many women to experience rejection, disillusionment, and distrust.

While we noted in that spring 2019 column that the Task Force's first logical step was to conduct listening sessions around the nation, our true first step was the creation of the Task Force membership. Unquestionably, countless legal professionals around the nation want a profession that values all its members. To tackle the problem of exclusion, however, we had to be intentional about the skills and lived experiences of those interested in joining the Task Force's long quest.

It is not an accident that we had members who had never taken part in a CJS program, were still in law school, and were vocal critics of the profession. It was also not an accident that we included federal and state court judges, former prosecutors, and lifelong defense lawyers who have practiced in rural, suburban, and urban environments. Our membership had to include the diverse perspectives and demographics our profession often ignores.

Our Task Force consisted of one reporter, two co-chairs, and 12 members:

- Maryam Ahranjani, Reporter—Professor of Law, University of Nevada–Las Vegas William S. Boyd School of Law
- Carla Laroche, Co-Chair—Felder-Fayard Associate Professor of Law, Tulane University Law School and The Murphy Institute
- Tina Luongo, Co-Chair—Chief Attorney, Criminal Defense Practice, The Legal Aid Society of New York City
- Lara Bazelon, Member—Professor of Law and Director of the Racial Justice Clinic, University of San Francisco School of Law
- April Frazier Camara, Member—President & CEO, National Legal Aid and Defender Association

- Barbara Creel, Member—Karelitz Professor of Law Emerita, University of New Mexico School of Law
- The Honorable Bernice Donald, Member—JAMS Mediator and Arbitrator, U.S. Court of Appeals for the Sixth Circuit (retired)
- Daniela Donoso, Member—Gun Violence Intervention Attorney, Legal Services of North Florida
- Maria Carmen Hinayon, Member—Title VI Officer, UCLA
- The Honorable Denise Langford-Morris, Member—JAMS Mediator and Arbitrator, Oakland County Circuit Court (retired)
- Ann Ratnayake Macy, Member—Director of Policy and Government Relations, Victim Policy Institute
- The Honorable Gloria Ochoa-Bruck, Member—Spokane Municipal Court
- The Honorable Rachel Pickering, Member—Kansas Court of Appeals
- Sarah Redfield, Member—Professor of Law Emerita, University of New Hampshire School of Law
- Lieutenant Colonel Susan Upward, Member—Judge Advocate, U.S. Marine Corps

Our determination to make the criminal law profession a more inclusive space guided the Task Force's work. On a more personal level, our respect for each other and the challenges we each have had to overcome fueled our commitment to our goals. We listened, learned, and grew together. Our intense bonding despite our differences served as a microcosm of how the criminal legal profession can be more inclusive, allowing people of diverse backgrounds to be authentic and to work toward justice.

While seeking solutions, we also exposed numerous barriers faced by women across the country that often go unnoticed, including the deeply troubling and unique experiences of Black women criminal law practitioners, the extremely limited resources in rural criminal law agencies and offices, and the persistent discrimination and bias against women with intersectional identities, to name a few. This book, however, sheds light on the untold stories of women criminal lawyers, what the Task Force *did* achieve, and the ways our work has served and will continue to serve as a beacon for the profession at large.

Carla Laroche and Tina Luongo
Women in Criminal Justice Task Force Founding Co-Chairs

Acknowledgments

First and foremost, the editor, authors, and contributors wish to thank the members of the ABA Women in Criminal Justice Task Force. Bonded through intense and time-consuming work, the Task Force members became "sisters in law." We also express appreciation to the brave women who testified before the Task Force, the many ABA Criminal Justice Section leaders and colleagues who support gender equity in criminal law, and our supportive colleagues, family, and friends. The views contained herein are our own and do not reflect the views of our employers.

Introduction

Based on five years of investigation by the ABA Criminal Justice Section Women in Criminal Justice Task Force, *Women in Criminal Law: A Practical Guide for Inclusive and Thriving Workplaces* provides personal insights and research-based suggestions for creating better working environments for women criminal lawyers. Referenced throughout the text, the articles in the appendices provide more information, context, and resources to expand knowledge about the concepts addressed by the authors.

Written for lawyers, law students, and others interested in equitable workplaces by diverse criminal lawyers and judges, the book animates the Ten Principles to Achieve Gender Equity in Criminal Law through first-person narrative. Professor Maryam Ahranjani, editor of the text and reporter of the Task Force, defines the scope of the book in Chapter One (Defining the Problem) by explaining *why* this text is so important—to women criminal lawyers, to criminal defendants and communities, to the legal profession, and to society. Chapter Two (What Are the Ten Principles?) provides the ABA's Resolution 501: Ten Steps to Achieve Gender Equity in Criminal Legal Employment and its accompanying report, which was adopted unanimously by the ABA House of Delegates in 2023.

Passaic County Chief Prosecutor Camelia Valdes is the author of Chapter Three. From her perspective as the first Latina county prosecutor in New Jersey, the first woman prosecutor in Passaic County, and the first lead prosecutor of Dominican ancestry in the United States, she describes in Chapter Three (Getting In and Staying In) how to get and stay in high office. Chapter Four (Navigating Intersectionality: Reclaiming Zeal in the Midst of a Burnout) author Joy Applewhite is an early-career Black public defender in rural New Mexico. She shares with readers her tools for managing the emotional impact of her work. In Chapter Five (Rethinking 9 to 5: Combating the Flexibility Stigma), Lieutenant Colonel Susan Upward (U.S. Marine Corps) explains how providing greater flexibility to employees improves productivity and retention. King County, Washington Senior Deputy Prosecuting Attorney Aubony Burns, a citizen of Choctaw Nation, writes in Chapter Six (Moving Past Survival: Operationalizing Equity Through Transparent Policies, Training, and Support) about her and others' efforts in the Prosecuting Attorney's Office to address a persistent concern of women criminal lawyers: formalizing and advertising office policies about hiring, retention, and promotion.

Chapter Seven (Why Do Judges Matter? And What Can Judges Do?) adopts an interview-style format led by Professor Sarah Redfield with the Honorable Bernice B. Donald (ret., Sixth Circuit Court of Appeals), the Honorable Denise Langford Morris (ret., Oakland County, Michigan Circuit Court), the Honorable Gloria Ochoa-Bruck (Spokane, Washington Municipal Court), and the Honorable Rachel Pickering (Kansas Court of Appeals). The judges reflect on their own experiences as lawyers and judges and the role of judges in promoting gender equity.

Written by Ahranjani, former CJS Chair and Spokane City Prosecutor Justin Bingham, and Judge Ochoa-Bruck, the final chapter (Chapter Eight: Leadership, Mentorship, Sponsorship, and Allyship) amplifies two important next steps—seeking and serving in leadership roles and, relatedly, cultivating mentors, sponsors, and allies. In the final chapter, we seek to share ideas about how *you* can be—and seek—mentors, allies, and sponsors. These steps permeate Resolution 501 and the accompanying report, particularly Principle One (creating culture change by dismantling barriers to hiring, retention, and promotion) and Principle Six (instituting and sustaining opportunities for mentorship, allyship, and sponsorship). Each of us answers how we, in our respective and diverse roles, approach all of these things. As Reporter of the Task Force and a legal academic, Ahranjani contributes her own experiences as a tenured professor who stood and stands on the shoulders of others. As Chair of CJS during the year we introduced and passed Resolution 501 and a longtime chief prosecutor, Bingham shares his experiences as a supervisor and mentor. Finally, Judge Ochoa-Bruck opens her expansive warehouse of tools as a prosecutor, defense attorney, tribal court judge, and state court judge to readers.

CHAPTER ONE
Defining the Problem

Maryam Ahranjani

Key Chapter Points

- Background of involvement in the ABA Criminal Justice Section Women in Criminal Justice Task Force (the Task Force)
- Framing and perspective for the book (why this topic matters for the rule of law)

The failure (again) of the United States to elect a highly qualified woman president—another lawyer, this time a former career prosecutor and woman of color—signals the urgent and long-term need for this text. Some of the critiques of Vice President Kamala Harris during her service in office and in her campaign reflect the need for this book. Just as someone as accomplished as Vice President Harris faces racism and misogyny, thousands of women criminal lawyers go to work every day seeking justice for communities and individuals accused of and harmed by crime, and yet they fight injustices and affronts to their dignity on a regular basis. Those injustices range from microaggressions to pernicious and pervasive institutionalized policies.

When a senior public defender and supervisor in a progressive office in a progressive state found out she was pregnant, she was overjoyed. A woman of color, she had a supportive husband, also a lawyer, and they were excited to grow their family. But the thought of returning to work after her maternity leave felt daunting. She was just over five feet tall, and her daughter was over ten pounds at birth. The birth and recovery were extremely taxing on her body and mind. She loved her work and wanted to get back to defending people accused of crime, but she was concerned that the daily grind of litigation and the structural challenges of the courthouse and jail where she worked would make it impossible to balance pumping milk with running from one courtroom to another.

The years in which we have and raise children are few relative to the span of our careers. But those years have outsized importance because they often coincide with the early part of our careers when we are establishing our professional identities. Also, that same time is critical to our children's long term health. During those years, many feel isolated and struggle just to tread water at work and at home. When challenges arise in terms of scheduling leave, figuring out lactation, identifying high-quality childcare, handling emergencies, and so on, many find it hard to advocate.

Like many women criminal lawyers, the senior public defender's transition back to work was bumpy. Urged by her doctor, hospital staff, and her pediatrician to exclusively breastfeed, she had no idea how to make that work. Despite employing many women, including women who have children while working there, her office *just* opened—in 2024—its first lactation room. The jail where she worked most frequently did not have a dedicated lactation room. All the (inadequate) spaces offered to her at the jail were outside the security line, which would mean that when she needed to pump, every few hours, she would have to go through the long security line each time, making it logistically impossible to be on time to her hearings.

When she respectfully petitioned for a temporary exemption from the requirement that she appear before the judge in person from the jail and instead appear remotely like the judge did, she was denied. All she asked was that she be able to appear remotely, just like the judge. Because it took so long for management to respond to her request, she had to wean her baby from breastfeeding in preparation for going back to work. After carefully considering and consulting with others about the professional risks of doing so, she appealed the denial to her male, childless supervisor. Ultimately her exemption request was granted, but only *after* she returned to work and made the extremely difficult decision to resign. The granting of her request was too little, too late. She felt disrespected and unappreciated. An outstanding public defender and well-regarded supervisor in an office with a revolving door of attorneys, she quit.

This story shines a light on my interest in gender equity in criminal law. One day in 2018 an email arrived in my inbox via a listserv for women law professors. It announced the creation of an ABA task force dedicated to investigating challenges faced by women criminal lawyers and indicated they were seeking a reporter. The email was posted to the list by Professor Sarah Redfield, a longtime friend, mentor, and collaborator. As a relatively new criminal law professor who was preparing students to enter the workforce, I had already heard from some of my former students working in district attorney and public defender offices that they faced some serious and unanticipated identity-related challenges. I was intrigued by the idea that what they faced might be endemic to criminal law and was curious about what this task force might explore and achieve.

I reached out to Sarah Redfield, who was a member of the new task force, and she encouraged me to apply. I interviewed with Professor Carla Laroche, the co-chair, while sitting in the dark in my closet while my then-six-year-old son slept in my bed. I spoke in the lowest possible tone of voice and with the lights off so as not to wake him, and I listened to Carla explain her and Tina Luongo's vision for creating an *intentionally inclusive* task force that would seek to hear from people all over the country with diverse professional and personal experiences in an attempt to figure out why the membership of the ABA Criminal Justice Section (CJS) was only 26 percent women. Was it because this number reflected the percentage of women criminal lawyers? Was it because the dues were too high? Was it because women didn't feel the CJS was an inclusive space? Or was this data point due to a number of factors and not at all reflective of the criminal legal profession at large?

The rest, as they say, is history. Carla and Tina hired me to be the ABA CJS Women in Criminal Justice (WCJ) Task Force Reporter. Much of the past seven years of my life has been devoted to the work of investigating, exposing, and working to improve gender-related challenges to hiring, retention, and promotion of women criminal lawyers. In a nutshell, our research taught us that women *do* face challenges in hiring, retention, and promotion in criminal law, with particular challenges in retention and promotion. Women leave criminal law for gender-related (and other) reasons—sometimes because they are pushed out, sometimes because they jump out, and sometimes because they are pushed to jump out.

It is no secret that in 2025, women continue to face equity challenges in many (most? all?) professional contexts. Inadequate family leave policies; unaddressed and persistent sexual harassment and discrimination; targeting of women in elected roles; prejudice and discrimination based on intersections of race, religion, gender identity, sexual orientation, and other identities; glass ceilings; and other challenges abound. Why the somewhat narrow focus on women criminal lawyers? This initial focus was because that's what we were asked to do as a Task Force. However, many of the themes will resonate with women in any workplace.

Other groups—for example, Women Lawyers on Guard, the ABA's Commission on Women in the Profession (focused on private practice attorneys), and the Legal Accountability Project (focused on judicial clerks)—are dedicated to preventing gender-based discrimination for other women lawyers. The ABA has long been committed to the rule of law and creating a more just and equitable society. The institution recognizes that starting with its own members is a way to move the needle. The ABA is, of course, most interested in the legal profession, and the CJS is most interested in criminal law issues.

As the Reporter of the WCJ Task Force, I conducted a thorough literature review on quantitative data. As a Task Force, we conducted qualitative research through listening sessions, surveys, and focus group meetings. All the findings are described in the two law review articles and the CJS white paper I wrote, which are reprinted in Appendices B, C, and D.

Through the course of our work, we identified the unique aspects of criminal law that may lead to equity challenges. Litigation is notoriously intense and stressful, criminal work takes an emotional toll, jails and prisons require regular and intrusive searches of all visitors, and the stakes are high, sometimes involving life and death. As one judge described in a listening session, while women's ability to empathize makes them ideal advocates for the community and individuals, it also makes the work impossible to leave in the office. The emotional toll is real and heavy.

In addition to the empathy toll, many women, particularly women with intersectional identities, face bias, even from other women. The human brain is wired for bias. There are far too many stimuli—words, sounds, images, thoughts—to process without sorting information into buckets. Our brains sort information based on bias to effectively manage all those constant stimuli. Implicit bias, then, is functional and inevitable. However, it also leads to harmful discriminatory thoughts and behavior. Implicit bias often disadvantages those with less power because the information our brain is fed to create silos is faulty and based on prejudices, or prejudgments.

That bias may lead to harmful conduct. For example, imagine a male elected prosecutor who assumes a junior female prosecutor is unlikely to return to work after maternity leave because of a belief that mothers want to be home with their babies. Based on that prejudgment, he may find it easier to reduce paid leave. Or the judge who assumes the Black woman defender is a family member of a defendant. The judge then firmly instructs the defender to move to the gallery, diminishing her power. Or the lactating women in government offices all around the country who in 2025 still have to fight for adequate (and legally required) lactation room spaces because employers do not concern themselves with lactating people since they are relatively few in number (even though accommodating lactation needs is already required by federal law). Or when a judge requires that shoulders and arms of counsel must be covered in the courtroom, assuming that is not going to cause any harm, but not realizing how uncomfortable this rule is for the women attorneys in menopause who experience extreme and sudden hot flashes. Or when a woman supervising attorney in a boutique firm urges her associate to return to work as soon as possible after having a baby since the supervisor was back within a few days.

This work has not been easy. Listening to challenges faced by good people doing good work invokes empathy and revives painful personal memories for many of the contributors to this book. But the work is important. Each of us has contributed to this effort with an open heart and an earnest desire to build on our successes, provide support to others, and heal ourselves in the process.

We sincerely hope this book will shed light on some wounds and showcase opportunities for growth and inclusion.

Inclusion doesn't just happen. As Tina and Carla insisted, it must be intentional. This book seeks to explain how, in the context of gender equity for criminal lawyers, we can be *intentional* about *inclusion*. We know that the lessons learned through this text will likely apply in many other settings and know we already have inspired and hope to continue to inspire intentional inclusion in other spaces.

CHAPTER TWO

What Are the Ten Principles to Achieve Gender Equity in the Criminal Legal Profession?

Maryam Ahranjani

Key Chapter Points

- The research conducted by the Task Force revealed hurdles for women criminal lawyers, especially those who are racial and ethnic minorities and/or members of LGBTQ+ and other communities
- ABA Resolution 501 passed unanimously and details the Ten Principles to Achieve Gender Equity in the Criminal Legal Profession

Between 2019 and 2023, the ABA Women in Criminal Justice Task Force listened and talked, then brainstormed, pressure-tested, and ultimately wrote and passed Resolution 501: Ten Principles to Achieve Gender Equity in the Criminal Legal Profession. In February 2023, the ABA House of Delegates unanimously adopted the resolution and report. What follows is a reprint of the report and resolution, which is posted on the ABA website. The idea for this book stemmed from a conversation I had with Tina Luongo, Carla Laroche, Judge Rachel Pickering, Judge Denise Langford Morris, Lt. Col. Susan Upward, and Professor Sarah Redfield at an ABA meeting where we discussed how to turn the policy we created into practice. We always hoped to produce a toolkit for employers and employees. This book seeks to animate the Ten Principles that follow.[1]

1. https://www.americanbar.org/news/reporter_resources/midyear-meeting-2023/house-of-delegates-resolutions/501.

1. Create culture change by dismantling longstanding barriers in hiring, retention, and promotion for women practicing law in the criminal legal profession.
2. Acknowledge and address the intersectional challenges of women, particularly those based on historical exclusion from power and access to opportunity, based on racial identity, ethnicity, wealth, rurality, gender identity, sexual orientation, disability, immigration status, religion, and other identities.
3. Integrate ongoing training and continuing legal education on diversity, equity, inclusion, and belonging; gender discrimination; anti-racism; implicit bias; and trauma-informed practices.
4. Assure all recruitment, retention, and promotion policies are transparent, equal in pay and equal in opportunity; and, relatedly, implement individualized, accessible, and ongoing professional development programs that foster advancement.
5. Implement proactive policies and resources to combat the flexibility stigma that is often related to motherhood, family planning, reproductive health care, menopause, gender-affirming health care, and caregiving.
6. Institute and sustain ongoing mentorship, allyship, and sponsorship programs and practices to increase opportunities that contribute to women's advancement, such as business connections, referrals, and networking.
7. Recognize that trauma and secondary trauma are inherent in the criminal legal system and ensure that employers invest in appropriate self-care resources including counseling, therapy, and other supports.
8. Assure that workplaces and courts provide appropriate private spaces and time for lactation, respite, self-care, and wellness.
9. Acknowledge that many women juggle childcare and other caretaking responsibilities with their criminal legal employment and work to improve access to high-quality and affordable childcare, elder care, and care for other dependents.
10. Establish an ongoing, data-driven evaluation system to seek and incorporate feedback from all employees free from retaliation so that gender bias is dismantled.

ADOPTED

AMERICAN BAR ASSOCIATION

CRIMINAL JUSTICE SECTION

REPORT TO THE HOUSE OF DELEGATES

RESOLUTION

RESOLVED, That the American Bar Association adopts the *Ten Principles to Achieve Gender Equity in the Criminal Legal Profession*, dated February 2023:

1. Create culture change by dismantling longstanding barriers in hiring, retention, and promotion for women practicing law in the criminal legal profession.

2. Acknowledge and address the intersectional challenges of women, particularly those based on historical exclusion from power and access to opportunity, based on racial identity, ethnicity, wealth, rurality, gender identity, sexual orientation, disability, immigration status, religion, and other identities.

3. Integrate ongoing training and continuing legal education on diversity, equity, inclusion, and belonging; gender discrimination; anti-racism; implicit bias; and trauma-informed practices.

4. Assure all recruitment, retention, and promotion policies are transparent, equal in pay and equal in opportunity; and, relatedly, implement individualized, accessible, and ongoing professional development programs that foster advancement.

5. Implement proactive policies and resources to combat the flexibility stigma that is often related to motherhood, family planning, reproductive health care, menopause, gender-affirming health care, and caregiving.

6. Institute and sustain ongoing mentorship, allyship, and sponsorship programs and practices to increase opportunities that contribute to women's advancement, such as business connections, referrals, and networking.

7. Recognize that trauma and secondary trauma are inherent in the criminal legal system and ensure that employers invest in appropriate self-care resources including counseling, therapy, and other supports.

8. Assure that workplaces and courts provide appropriate private spaces and time for lactation, respite, self-care, and wellness.

501

9. Acknowledge that many women juggle childcare and other caretaking responsibilities with their criminal legal employment and work to improve access to high-quality and affordable childcare, elder care, and care for other dependents.

10. Establish an ongoing, data-driven evaluation system to seek and incorporate feedback from all employees free from retaliation so that gender bias is dismantled.

REPORT

ABA Criminal Justice Section Women in Criminal Justice Task Force[1]

Ten Principles to Achieve Gender Equity in the Criminal Legal Profession

[1] The views expressed are those of the named individuals in their personal capacities and do not reflect the views of any employer or government agency. Institutional affiliations are listed for identification purposes only. The Task Force includes: Maryam Ahranjani (TF Reporter, Ronald & Susan Friedman Professor of Law, University of New Mexico School of Law), Carla Laroche (TF Co-Chair, Associate Clinical Professor of Law and Director, Civil Rights and Racial Justice Clinic, Washington and Lee University School of Law), Tina Luongo (TF Co-Chair, Attorney in Charge, Criminal Defense Practice, The Legal Aid Society of New York City), Lara Bazelon (Professor of Law, Director of the Criminal & Juvenile Justice and Racial Justice Clinics, University of San Francisco School of Law), The Honorable Gloria Ochoa-Bruck (Spokane Municipal Court), Barbara Creel (Karelitz Professor of Law, University of New Mexico School of Law), April Frazier Camara (President & CEO, National Legal Aid and Defender Association), The Honorable Bernice Donald (U.S. Court of Appeals for the Sixth Circuit (senior status)), Daniela Donoso (Program Wide Immigration Attorney, Legal Services of North Florida), Maria Carmen Hinayon (Compliance and Policy Investigator, University of California Davis), The Honorable Denise Langford-Morris (JAMS Mediator and Arbitrator, Oakland County Circuit Court (retired)), Ann Ratnayake Macy (Adjunct Professorial Lecturer, Department of Justice, Law, and Criminology, American University), Sarah Redfield (Professor of Law (emerita), University of New Hampshire School of Law), and Lieutenant Colonel Susan Upward (U.S. Marine Corps).

Introduction

The ABA Criminal Justice Section Women in Criminal Justice Task Force (TF) created this document to advise and support the criminal law profession, including the employers, institutions, and people that support it. The TF bases the "Ten Principles for Gender Equity" on research, experience, qualitative and quantitative data from women criminal lawyers across the country and on further feedback as it shared its findings.[2]

As gatekeepers of the profession, law schools, bar associations, and arbitration providers play a crucial role in acknowledging and educating students and attorneys about gender-based discrimination. The TF urges law schools to train administrators and faculty on research-based practices to achieve gender equity; to encourage school-wide discussions about challenges in hiring; to provide mentorship, sponsorship, and networking opportunities with local, state, and national bar associations and with the ABA Criminal Justice Section; to host CLEs about/for gender equity in criminal lawyers; and to promote work on gender equity with their alumni.

The TF recognizes that its work may resonate with other practitioners, including, for example, family lawyers and immigration lawyers. Because of the narrow scope of the TF's charge – to investigate and report on the status of women in the criminal law profession – this Report focuses on that slice of the profession. However, we welcome support from those outside criminal law and hope that this work serves as a model for gender equity work in other spaces.

Background

In late 2018 then-CJS Chair Lucian Dervan formed the TF) to investigate gender-based barriers to hiring, promotion, and retention in criminal law. The TF has engaged in original and groundbreaking work to document these challenges. Throughout its work the TF wascommitted to accessing the perspectives of as diverse a variety of women as possible and to crafting workable solutions to reduce barriers and make their work more sustainable.

The TF first conducted a thorough literature review.[3] Second, the TF engaged in qualitative data-gathering through listening sessions and surveys. Third, the TF reviewed its findings with leaders working in the field through focus group meetings and surveys. Throughout its research phase, the TF published and otherwise shared its work and invited a continuous feedback loop.[4]

More specifically, between November 2018 and June 2020, the TF organized twelve listening sessions around the country and online to hear from individuals with diverse lived and professional experiences. The TF also administered a follow-up survey in 2020 after the COVID-19 pandemic began. Participants in the listening sessions and 2020 survey indicated that hiring, retention, and, particularly, *promotion* of women in the criminal justice profession continue to be problematic. The TF identified the following particular challenges: (1) limited flexibility with work schedules; (2) insufficient wellness

---

[2] *See* Appendix A for related Task Force publications to date.
[3] *See* Ahranjani, *"Toughen Up, Buttercup,"* Appendix A, at 106.
[4] *See* Appendix A.

resources; (3) deficient training opportunities, particularly in state and rural criminal law offices; and (4) short supply of meaningful mentorship and transparent policy guidance. According to participants, some employers seem receptive to change, but many do not.

Based on the results of the listening sessions and 2020 survey, the TF designed possible solutions to address these four challenges. The TF invited a diverse group of criminal justice leaders from public and private employment, state and federal government, nonprofit organizations, and law schools to participate in focus groups. Facilitated by TF members, the focus groups pressure-tested proposed solutions and offered additional solutions. The focus groups were held in person in the ABA's Washington, DC, office and online on November 18, 2021 and were supplemented with online surveys from those who were unable to attend.

Reflecting on the lessons learned in its research,[5] the lived experiences of its members and those who participated in the various listening, feedback and focus group sessions,[6] and the insightful writings of its Reporter and Members,[7] TF created the Ten Principles for Gender Equity in Criminal Law Employment. This report includes the Ten Principles and animating information, illustrative sample policies and programs, and other resources for implementation.

Values and reference points: During the TF's listening sessions and online surveys, we heard from cis women, trans women, people who identify as non-binary, gender non-conforming, gender fluid, and some who declined to select a gender identity. In terms of sexual orientation, we welcomed people who identify as heterosexual, homosexual, bisexual, asexual and some who declined to indicate sexual orientation. Listening to their testimony confirmed that their viewpoints, ideas, and experiences had to be reflected in our work. Although we use the term "women" in this document, we firmly acknowledge the diversity of voices we heard, and we use the term "women" based on our expansive and inclusive understanding of sex, gender, gender identity and sexual orientation.

Efforts were made to be inclusive of as many diverse voices as possible, but we acknowledge that we may not have captured all the voices we intended to include. This raises the importance of future, ongoing, and intentional work that our Section and the ABA should engage in to achieve even greater inclusivity.

Terms (for purposes of this report only):

Allyship – An active, consistent and challenging practice of unlearning and re-evaluating in which a person with privilege seeks to show solidarity with a person or group that is traditionally excluded.[8]

---

[5] *See, e.g.*, Ahranjani, *Sprinting a Marathon*, Appendix A; Ahranjani, *"Toughen Up, Buttercup,"* Appendix A.
[6] *See, e.g.*, Ahranjani, *Listening Session Takeaways*, Appendix A; Donoso, *Heavy Purse*, Appendix A; Yeary, *From Sweety to Sisterhood*, Appendix A.
[7] *See, e.g.*, Hinayon, *Who Needs the Old Boys' Club?*, Appendix A; Pickering, *An Awakening and More: How Being Part of the Women in Criminal Justice Task Force Has Provided Me with a Judicial Awareness*, Appendix A.
[8] The Anti-Oppression Network, https://theantioppressionnetwork.com/allyship/ (last visited Aug. 21, 2022).

Counseling versus therapy – Counseling tends to be focused on a particular challenge whereas therapy is longer-term and focuses on exploring a person's characteristics, patterns, and unique responses to stress.[9] Criminal lawyers may benefit from counseling, therapy, or both.

Culture change – The process in which an organization examines its values, goals, and practices to adopt mindsets and behaviors that lead to more equitable outcomes.[10]

Flexibility stigma – Attitudes that punish people who do not fit the "ideal worker" profile—solely devoted to one's job, available 24 hours a day and typically male—such that "even when adaptable work options are available, there is a concealed shame in using them."[11]

Gender – Socially constructed norms, roles, behaviors, and appearance associated with a person's sex and traditional notions of femininity and masculinity. (Views of gender vary through culture and time. For example, Indigenous peoples recognize as a third or fourth gender the "Two Spirits," individuals who embody both the feminine and masculine at the intersection of their gender and spiritual identity).[12]

Implicit bias – Learned associations or preferences, which we absorb from the world around us and which operate outside our direct awareness or control to influence our understanding, actions, decisions. (By comparison, explicit biases are deliberately generated and intentional understandings, actions, and decisions, which we verbally endorse and directly experienced as our own.)[13]

Inclusion—Meaningful involvement of people from different groups into processes and decisions. (By comparison, inclusion connotes quality of participation; *diversity*, quantity of representation.).[14]

---

[9]Joseph Saling, *Guide to Psychiatry and Counseling*, WebMD, https://www.webmd.com/mental-health/guide-to-psychiatry-and-counseling (last visited Aug. 21, 2022).

[10] Steve Denning, *How Do You Change An Organizational Culture?*, Forbes (July 23, 2011, 6:09 PM), https://www.forbes.com/sites/stevedenning/2011/07/23/how-do-you-change-an-organizational-culture/?sh=58e41b5c39dc.

[11]Colleen Flaherty, *Room to Grow*, Inside Higher Ed. (April 1, 2014) https://www.insidehighered.com/news/2014/04/01/work-place-flexibility-stigma-affects-non-parents-too-study-suggests; Greg Orme, *Why the Flexibility Stigma is Making Women Quit*, Forbes (June 9, 2021, 6:44 AM), https://www.forbes.com/sites/gregorme/2021/06/09/why-the-flexibility-stigma-is-making-women-quit/?sh=37a894196eac.

[12] World Health Organization, https://www.who.int/health-topics/gender#tab=tab_1 (last visited Aug. 21, 2022); *Two Spirit Community*, Re: Searching For LGBTQ2S+ Health, http://www.lgbtqhealth.ca/community/two-spirit.php (last visited Aug. 21, 2022); *see also* Meghan DuPuis Maurus, *Sexual Orientation and Gender Identity (SOGI), in* Extending Justice: Strategies to Increase Inclusion and Reduce Bias Ch. 25 (Bernice B. Donald & Sarah E. Redfield eds., 2022).

[13]*See generally* Bernice B. Donald & Sarah E. Redfield, *Framing the Discussion, in* Enhancing Justice: Reducing Bias Ch. 2 (Sarah E. Redfield ed., 2017); Ruta Sevo & Daryl E. Chubin, *Bias Literacy: A Review ofConceptsinResearchonDiscrimination*, https://www.advance.iastate.edu/sites/default/files/Additional%20Resources/BiasLiteracy.pdf.

[14] Jennifer K. Elek & Andrea L Miller, *The Evolving Science on Implicit Bias, in* Extending Justice: Strategies to Increase Inclusion and Reduce Bias Ch. 2 (Bernice B. Donald & Sarah E. Redfield eds., 2022).

501

IDEA – Inclusion, Diversity, Equity, and Access (a more-encompassing variation of DEI—Diversity, Equity, and Inclusion).[15]

Intersectionality – The complex way that a marginalized person's race, gender, class, or other identities or categories combine and overlap to produce compounding effects of oppression, discrimination, or violence.[16]

Mentorship – A relationship between a person giving advice and guidance and another person receiving advice and guidance.[17]

Micromessages– Seemingly small, typically implicit, communications or actions that reflect people's biases for certain groups and against others;[18] when negative, described as microaggressions communicating hostile, derogatory attitudes and leaving the people targeted feeling insulted or uncomfortable.[19]

Role model – A person, often not an actual acquaintance, who may serve as an example and inspiration.[20]

Sex – Categories of being male, female, or intersex assigned at birth and associated with biological and physical characteristics such as anatomy and chromosomes.[21]

Sponsorship – Spending one's social capital or using one's influence to advocate for a protégé. A sponsor is someone who uses their power to boost (usually behind the scenes) a traditionally excluded person, usually behind the scenes. Sponsorship may include, inter alia, recommending them for a promotion or award, granting them a promotion or award, speaking highly of them during a review process, and defending them against unfair critiques.[22]

SOGI – An acronym for Sexual Orientation and Gender Identity. It is important to note that sexual orientation and gender identity are two separate identities.

---

[15] *See, e.g.,* ABA, Diversity, Equity, and Inclusion FAQ *available through link at* https://www.americanbar.org/groups/diversity/; Exec. Order No. 14035, 86 FR 34593 (June 25, 2021) (Executive Order on Diversity, Equity, Inclusion, and Accessibility in the Federal Workforce).

[16] Professor Kimberlé Crenshaw introduced the theory of intersectionality in 1989 to describe the multiple social forces, social identities, and ideological instruments through which power and disadvantage are expressed and legitimized. *See* Kimberlé Crenshaw, *Demarginalizing the Intersection of Race and Sex: A Black Feminist Critique of Antidiscrimination Doctrine, Feminist Theory and Antiracist Politics*, 40 U. CHICAGO LEGAL F. Article 8 (1989), *available at* https://chicagounbound.uchicago.edu/uclf/vol1989/iss1/8.

[17] Janice Omadeke, *What's the Difference Between a Mentor and a Sponsor?*, ASCEND (Oct. 20, 2021), https://hbr.org/2021/10/whats-the-difference-between-a-mentor-and-a-sponsor.

[18] *See, e.g.,* Kevin Burke, *Confronting the Hurricane*, *in* EXTENDING JUSTICE: STRATEGIES TO INCREASE INCLUSION AND REDUCE BIAS (Bernice B. Donald & Sarah E. Redfield eds., 2022); Mary Rowe, Micro-affirmations & Micro-inequities, 1 J. INT'L OMBUDSMAN ASS'N 45 (2008).

[19] *See, e.g.,* Derald Wing Sue, et al., *Racial Microaggressions in Everyday Life*, 62 AM. PSYCHOLOGIST 271 (2007).

[20] Ruth Gotian, *Why You Need a Role Model, Mentor, Coach and Sponsor,* FORBES (Aug. 4, 2020, 9:10 AM) https://www.forbes.com/sites/ruthgotian/2020/08/04/why-you-need-a-role-model-mentor-coach-and-sponsor/?sh=66c9d467c489.

[21] CENTER FOR DISEASE CONTROL AND PREVENTION, https://www.cdc.gov/healthyyouth/terminology/sexual-and-gender-identity-terms.htm (last visited Aug. 21, 2022).

[22] Rosalind Chow, *Don't Just Mentor Women and People of Color. Sponsor Them.*, HARVARD BUS. REV. (June 30, 2021), https://hbr.org/2021/06/dont-just-mentor-women-and-people-of-color-sponsor-them.

Sexual orientation – A person's identity based on the enduring patterns of romantic and/or sexual attraction to another person/s of the opposite gender (heterosexual), same gender (homosexual), both or other genders (bisexual, pansexual), or to none (asexual).[23] LGBTQIA+ is a collective acronym for lesbian, gay, bisexual, transgender, queer, questioning, intersex, and asexual people.[24] The "+" holds space for the inclusion of other identities as our understanding of gender and sexual orientation continues to expand.[25]

Gender identity – A person's individual sense and experience of gender.[26] There are people whose gender identity does not conform to their sex assigned at birth (transgender), do not conform to either masculine or feminine (nonbinary), conform to their sex assigned at birth (cisgender), or have no gender identity (agender).[27]

Trauma-informed lawyering – This approach aims to reduce re-traumatization and recognize the role that trauma plays in criminal justice settings, particularly in the lawyer-client relationship.[28]

TEN PRINCIPLES OF GENDER EQUITY IN CRIMINAL LEGAL EMPLOYMENT

The ensuing text includes the Ten Principles and more details, examples, ideas, links, and other information to animate each one. These recommendations promote greater gender equity in four areas of interest to employers: hiring, retention, promotion, and equitable practice. Each section describes the Principle with reference to the TF findings and experience. Additional resources for implementing the Principles are provided in Appendix A.

1. Create Culture Change

Create culture change by dismantling longstanding barriers in hiring, retention, and promotion for women practicing law in the criminal legal profession.

Meaningful and sustained change begins with a reckoning with the current climate.[29] Therefore, employers who wish to adopt these principles should start with a values assessment that focuses on IDEA data-gathering with particular reference to diversity,

---

[23] PSYCHOLOGY TODAY, https://www.psychologytoday.com/us/basics/homosexuality (last visited Aug. 21, 2022).

[24] GENDER SEXUALITY RESOURCE CENTER, https://www.gsrc.princeton.edu/lgbtqia-101 (last visited Aug. 21, 2022).

[25] *Id.*

[26] *Id.*

[27] PSYCHOLOGY TODAY, https://www.psychologytoday.com/us/basics/gender (last visited Aug. 21, 2022).

[28] Lorilei Williams, *An Antiracist Approach to Trauma -Informed Lawyering*, SHRIVER CENTER FOR POVERTY LAW (June 29, 2021), https://www.povertylaw.org/advocacy-network/racial-justice-institute-network/; Sarah Katz & Deeya Haldar, *The Pedagogy of Trauma-Informed Lawyering*, 22 CLINICAL L REV. 359 (2016).

[29] We recognize that DEI and DEI strategy and training are large areas for concern as we seek to gain the benefits of diversity. For our purposes here we focus on points highlighted in our own work listening to those in the field.

inclusion, and equity focused on SOGI, race, ethnicity, religion, and disability.[30] Once the current IDEA climate is reviewed, employers should provide regular trainings geared to issues that have been identified as problematic—likely including trainings on intersectionality, implicit bias, creating inclusive workplaces that combat feelings of invisibility, and having difficult conversations. Employers should also review promotion practices through an equity lens and correct practices that do not align with equity goals. To earn trust and respect, employers should publicize their promotion policies in a transparent way so that employees know what it takes to be promoted. For example, the TF heard many times that women put off having children to comply with a tacit expectation of certain types of experience required for promotion.

2. **Acknowledge and Address Intersectional Challenges**

Acknowledge and address the intersectional challenges of women, particularly those based on historical exclusion from power and access to opportunity, based on racial identity, ethnicity, wealth, rurality, gender identity, sexual orientation, disability, immigration status, religion, and other identities.

Women with intersectional identities experience amplified discrimination, which heightens the need for supervisors and all employees to be aware of equity challenges. Scholars have documented the challenges faced by women who identify with other groups who have been historically underrepresented and excluded from power. The TF heard from many women with intersectional identities and those stories illuminated the particular stressors for women criminal lawyers. To mitigate the effects of discrimination based on intersectional identities, employers should institute trainings and policies targeted to the particular identities of their attorneys.

3. **Implement DEI Training**

Integrate ongoing training and continuing legal education on diversity, equity, inclusion, and belonging; gender discrimination; anti-racism; implicit bias; and trauma-informed practices.

Numerous actors in the criminal legal system – clients, survivors, and attorneys – have experienced racism, bias, and trauma. These experiences shape how we interact with others and contribute to our identity-formation. To be compassionate colleagues and better serve clients, *all* criminal lawyers benefit from ongoing training on anti-racism, bias, trauma-informed lawyering and related IDEA topics.

Based on the TF's research, it is critically important for employers to do a better job of training *all* staff on anti-racism, bias, and trauma-informed lawyering. This training will benefit the staff and the organization and will also benefit clients and victims.[31] Women –

---

[30] *See generally, e.g.*, Ass'n of Corp. Couns., *DEI Resources*, https://www.acc.com/resource-library/interest-area/diversity-and-inclusion.

[31] *See, e.g.*, Kristine Hamann, et al., *The Empathetic Prosecutor Reducing Bias When Working with Victims, Survivors, and Witnesses*, Extending Justice: Strategies to Increase Inclusion and Reduce Bias Ch. 8 (Bernice B. Donald & Sarah E. Redfield eds., 2022).

particularly those who are BIPOC – regularly experience microaggressions and belittling of their professional identities,[32] making training on these points especially critical.

Successful training will have as its goals providing requisite vocabulary, data, and science background; providing practice- and evidence-based strategies to change habits and norms; enlisting participants as active players in the process; and focusing forward for setting an ongoing agenda with accountability measures.[33] Successful training is not a *once and done* exercise but rather a planned and sustained effort to address problems identified systemwide and within a particular institution.[34]

Well-constructed training works.[35] A number of resources exist in this space. For example, TF members Judge Bernice Donald and Professor Sarah Redfield have long been leaders in the anti-racism, implicit bias, and DEI space and have published and presented widely in the field.[36] The Women's Bar Association of the District of Columbia, which is the largest women's bar association in the country, has collected hundreds of anti-racism and career-related resources that are available to members on their web site (https://wbadc.org/). The Shriver Center on Poverty Law and its Racial Justice Institute (https://www.povertylaw.org/advocacy-network/racial-justice-institute-network/) offer excellent advice and training on anti-racism in trauma-Informed lawyering. The Trauma-Informed Law Project offers its own extensive list of additional sources and networking (http://www.traumainformedlaw.org).[37] It is also critical that these topics be integrated into legal education. Law school clinics and elective courses are fertile ground for this kind of education as is general curricular revision.[38]

4. Create Transparent Policies and Opportunities for Professional Development

---

[32] Ahranjani, *"Toughen Up, Buttercup,"* Appendix A.

[33] *See generally* Patricia G. Devine, Et Al., *Long-Term Reduction in Implicit Bias: A Prejudice Habit Breaking Intervention*, 48 J. EXPERIMENTAL SOC. PSYCHOL. 1267 (2012).

[34] *See generally, e.g.,* Hon. Reba Ann Page & Hon. Benes Z. Aldana, *Judicial Education on Implicit Bias: Instilling a Lifelong Pursuit of Fairness,* Ch. 11; Hon. Bernice B. Donald, Justin Levinson & Sarah E. Redfield, *Diverse Voices: A Critical Conversation About Bias both, in* EXTENDING JUSTICE: STRATEGIES TO INCREASE INCLUSION AND REDUCE BIAS (Bernice B. Donald & Sarah E. Redfield eds., 2022).

[35] *See, e.g.,* Sarah E. Redfield et al., *Implicit Bias is Real, Implicit Bias Training Matters: Responding to the Negative Press*, SOCIAL SCIENCE RESEARCH NETWORK (2020), http://dx.doi.org/10.2139/ssrn.3686762; Patricia G. Devine et al., *Long-Term Reduction in Implicit Bias: A Prejudice Habit-Breaking Intervention,* 48 J. Experimental Soc. Psychol. 1267 (2012).

[36] *See e.g.,* EXTENDING JUSTICE: STRATEGIES TO INCREASE INCLUSION AND REDUCE BIAS (Bernice B. Donald & Sarah E. Redfield eds., 2022); ENHANCING JUSTICE: REDUCING BIAS (Sarah E. Redfield ed., 2017); Sarah E. Redfield, Professor, UNH, Presentation to Leadership, ABA Civil Rights & Social Justice, *Training Toward Intentional Equity* (April 2022), https://www.americanbar.org/content/dam/aba/administrative/crsj/webinar/april-2022/implicit-bias-sara-redfield.pdf.

[37] THE TRAUMA-INFORMED LAW Project, http://www.traumainformedlaw.org/ (last visited Aug. 21, 2022).

[38] *See, e.g.,* Teri A. McMurtry-Chubb, *Strategies and Techniques for Integrating Diversity, Equity, and Inclusion into the Core Law Curriculum* (2022): The Honorable Bernice B. Donald, Sixth Circuit Court of Appeals; Professor Patty Ferguson-Bohnee, Pointe-au-Chien, Director, Indian Legal Clinic, Sandra Day O'Connor College of Law; Beth Kransberger, DEI Consultant; Commissioner, City of San Diego Citizen's Equal Opportunity Commission; & Professor Sarah Redfield, University of New Hampshire; Presentation, Conversation with the Faculty, Albany Law School (2021) (on file with the authors).

<u>Assure all recruitment, retention, and promotion policies are transparent, equal in pay and equal in opportunity; and, relatedly, implement individualized, accessible, and ongoing professional development programs that foster advancement.</u>

The TF intentionally "went where the ABA traditionally does not go" by seeking participation and input from attorneys in rural and underfunded areas. The TF heard from Native American attorneys practicing in rural New Mexico and small-town solo criminal defense attorneys in Florida and Washington State.

TF listening session participants and survey respondents all over the country shared concerns about the lack of transparency about pay and assumptions about promotion.[39] Employers ought to report not only average and individual salaries but ought to report salaries by gender identity.

A second common theme was that while big-city public defenders and prosecutors have access to networking, support, training, and opportunities, there is a big gap in access to professional development resources. The lack of access makes attorneys feel isolated and alone.[40]

Principle Six encourages employers to consciously connect employees to existing free resources through their state and local bar associations, local law schools, affinity associations such as the National Hispanic Bar Association and National Bar Association, and others. One example of professional development that was raised during the focus groups was training on how to set up Zoom backgrounds (e.g., lighting, touch-up features, mic, etc.).[41]

Another common request, especially by first generation lawyers, is access to webinars and other information about how to run for public office such as judgeships, District Attorney and Public Defender.

5. **Eliminate the Flexibility Stigma**

<u>Implement proactive policies and resources to combat the flexibility stigma that is often related to motherhood, family planning, reproductive health care, menopause, gender-affirming health care, and caregiving.</u>

Criminal legal employers should normalize gender-related planning and decision-making. People of all gender identities report that there is a cost to making personal choices about family planning. That cost has been described as a flexibility stigma. If a woman dares to mention she wants to have children or talks about her children's activities at work, she is perceived as not being serious about her job. And this stigma may cause women to

[39] Ahranjani, *"Toughen Up, Buttercup,"* Appendix A, at 142.

[40] Greg Orme, *Why the Flexibility Stigma is Making Women Quit*, FORBES (June 9, 2021), https://www.forbes.com/sites/gregorme/2021/06/09/why-the-flexibility-stigma-is-making-women-quit/?sh=37a894196eac.

[41] FOUR-DAY WORKWEEK, www.Fourdayweek.com (last visited Aug. 21, 2022) (describing how most Americans want a four-day workweek even if they are four longer days because this schedule allows workers to have one day for errands, doctors' appointments, and other personal matters so that they can truly enjoy and disconnect on the weekends).

question whether they should continue working in an environment in which they have to hide their true selves.[42]

To normalize flexibility, employers are turning to four-day workweeks,[43] sabbatical programs,[44] job sharing, and remote work. However, employers should keep in mind that one size does not fit all. For example, remote work sometimes makes life even harder for many women.[45]

6. **Offer Multi-Layered, Individualized Support**

<u>Institute and sustain ongoing mentorship, allyship, and sponsorship programs and practices to increase opportunities that contribute to women's advancement, such as business connections, referrals, and networking.</u>

Individual support through mentorship, allyship and sponsorship leads to success with equity goals. However, one size does not fit all. Therefore, the TF recommends individualized, multi-layered support for employees. Leadership must ask each lawyer what she/they need and ought to institutionalize support. Women reported in listening sessions and through our surveys that their needs change over time. Those who felt "listened to" at different stages of life reported feeling less likely to leave or think about leaving.

The Women in White Collar Defense Association (https://www.wwcda.org/home) serves as a powerful model of how to boost members and colleagues. They regularly spotlight their members' successes on their website, social media, and email blasts. Similarly, the National Bar Association (www.nationalbar.org) exemplifies support for its members by eliminating barriers to participation and recognizing members' excellence through awards and other recognition. The TF held a listening session at the 2019 NBA Annual Convention and discovered the organization always provides on-site childcare at its annual meetings.

Even offices with limited budgets may amplify existing in-person and online resources through local, state and national bar associations, the ABA Criminal Justice Section, and affiliation groups. Of course, where gaps exist, employers may create new opportunities through intention-setting and partnership-building. Allyship/mentorship/sponsorship training leads to more supportive environments. Women who feel supported at work are more likely to remain in their jobs.[46]

7. **Provide Low- or No-Cost Therapeutic Support**

---

[42] Ahranjani, *Sprinting a Marathon*, Appendix A, at 250 (One focus group participant explained how his office allowed prosecutors to take one-month sabbaticals and reported that morale and retention was high at least in part because of the sabbatical program).
[43] Ahranjani, *Listening Session Takeaways*, Appendix A.
[44] Ahranjani, *Sprinting a Marathon*, Appendix A, at 250.
[45] Anne Helen Petersen, *The Work-From-Home Revolution is also a Trap for Women*, BLOOMBERG (Aug. 10, 2022, 7:00 AM), https://www.bloomberg.com/news/features/2022-08-10/work-from-home-jobs-haven-t-made-things-easier-for-women.
[46] Ahranjani, *Pulling Back the Curtain*, Appendix A.

501

Recognize that trauma and secondary trauma are inherent in the criminal legal system and ensure that employers invest in appropriate self-care resources including counseling, therapy, and other supports.

Lawyers who work with people experiencing poverty, homelessness, addiction, abuse and other serious challenges absorb the pain of others. Those who are especially empathic are especially prone to internalizing the suffering of others. TF listening session participants shared that more therapeutic support would be appreciated.[47] One listening session participant went so far as to say she would not be able to do her job as an assistant district attorney if she didn't have regular therapy, which she could not really afford on her salary.

Some suggestions for therapeutic support include on-site therapy, wellness rooms for employees to decompress, and compassion fatigue training.

8. **Provide Private Spaces**

Assure that workplaces and courts provide appropriate private spaces and time for lactation, respite, self-care, and wellness.

All employees benefit from private spaces that allow for rest, reflection, and self-care. Federal law requires break time for people who are nursing and a private space that is shielded from view (other than a bathroom).[48] The ABA passed a resolution urging employers to go much further than required by federal law.[49]

Despite these requirements, we heard during listening sessions that many employers, including government employers, do *not* provide adequate space *or* time.[50] Employers sometimes transform closets, file rooms, and other inappropriate spaces into lactation rooms. We heard from women who did not need lactation rooms that having a quiet space for contemplation and decompression before and after trial and at other stressful times would go a long way to signal employers' focus on their mental wellness. The National Legal Aid and Defender Association (NLADA) has a policy on wellness rooms.[51] Additionally, the TF recommends that employers ensure employees can use facilities based on their gender identity; having gender-neutral facilities; and respecting employees' lived names and pronouns notwithstanding the information on their legal identity documents.

9. **Support Caretaking**

---

[47] Christina Rainville, *Understanding Secondary Trauma: A Guide for Lawyers Working with Child Victims*, A.B.A., https://www.americanbar.org/groups/public_interest/child_law/resources/child_law_practiceonline/child_law_practice/vol-34/september-2015/understanding-secondary-trauma--a-guide-for-lawyers-working-with/ (last visited Aug. 21, 2022).

[48] U.S. DEP'T OF LABOR, BREAK TIME FOR NURSING MOTHERS, https://www.dol.gov/agencies/whd/nursing-mothers.

[49] A.B.A. RESOLUTION 501 ADOPTED BY THE HOUSE OF DELEGATES 2022 MIDYEAR MEETING (Feb 14, 2022), https://www.americanbar.org/content/dam/aba/directories/policy/midyear-2022/501-midyear-2022.pdf.

[50] Ahranjani, *"Toughen Up, Buttercup,"* Appendix A, at 141.

[51] NAT'L LEGAL AID AND DEF. ASS'N, https://www.nlada.org/defender-standards (last visited Aug. 21, 2022).

Acknowledge that many women juggle childcare and other caretaking responsibilities with their criminal legal employment and work to improve access to high-quality and affordable childcare, elder care, and care for other dependents.

Without affordable and high-quality childcare and preschool options (especially in places where public preschool is limited or nonexistent), gender equity is an elusive goal. The United States lags behind almost all other countries in the world with regard to paid parental leave.[52] Adding insult to injury, childcare costs have skyrocketed in recent years, and in many places in the United States public preschool options are limited.[53] World Population Review reports that even though some states have subsidized care, the costs are substantial (an average of $14,000 per child per year). The high cost of care, low salaries of early childhood workers and concerns about quality of care cause stress for families and for society as a whole.

During the TF listening sessions, many women reported the financial burden of childcare caused them to delay having children, have fewer children, and consider leaving criminal law for higher-paying work.[54] Financial forces cause women to leave public service for private practice or leave work altogether. Employers may alleviate the tensions by partnering with childcare, senior care, and other providers to arrange employee discounts. For example, many federal employees in Washington, DC receive discounts with KinderCare locations throughout the area.

10. **Continual Evaluation and Adjustment**

Establish an ongoing, data-driven evaluation system to seek and incorporate feedback from all employees free from retaliation so that gender bias is dismantled.

Ongoing evaluation and adjustment lead to more inclusive work environments. Many employers already utilize annual review systems. These systems often involved gender dynamics and implicit expectations that are harmful to women and other gender minorities.[55] The TF recommends that employers review their evaluation systems to scrub for gender bias and to regularly identify gender-based challenges. There are straightforward ways to reduce or eliminate bias.[56]

---

[52] Claire Cain Miller, *The World 'Has Found a Way to Do This': The U.S. Lags on Paid Leave,* N.Y. TIMES (Nov. 3, 2021), https://www.nytimes.com/2021/10/25/upshot/paid-leave-democrats.html (explaining that only six other countries in the world do not have national paid leave).

[53] Jane Thier, *The Cost of Child Care Has Risen by 41% During the Pandemic with Families Spending Up to 20% of their Salaries,* FORTUNE (Jan 28, 2022, 7:51 AM), https://fortune.com/2022/01/28/the-cost-of-child-care-in-the-us-is-rising/#:~:text=Across%20the%20U.S.%2C%20parents%20are,from%20a%20recent%20LendingTree%20report.

[54] Ahranjani, *"Toughen Up, Buttercup,"* Appendix A, at 142.

[55] Paola Cecchi-Dimeglio, *How Gender Bias Corrupts Performance Reviews and What to Do About It*, HARVARD BUS. REV. (Apr. 12, 2017), https://hbr.org/2017/04/how-gender-bias-corrupts-performance-reviews-and-what-to-do-about-it; Virginia Valian, Gender and Evaluation, *in* EXTENDING JUSTICE: STRATEGIES TO INCREASE INCLUSION AND REDUCE BIAS Ch. 15 (Bernice B. Donald & Sarah E. Redfield eds., 2022)

[56] Andrea Rivera and András Tilcsik, *One Way to Reduce Gender Bias,* HARVARD BUS. REV. (Apr. 17, 2019), *https://hbr.org/2019/04/one-way-to-reduce-gender-bias-in-performance-reviews* (describing how using a 6-point scale instead of a 10-point scale yields equitable results); Tannera Gibson & Terrence Reed, *Addressing Underrepresentation in the Legal Profession, in* EXTENDING JUSTICE: STRATEGIES TO INCREASE

501

Conclusion

No workplace is perfect, and change is inevitable. However, many criminal lawyers spend more time working than doing anything else. To the extent that workplaces strive toward and achieve gender equity, they will do a better job of serving their clients, their communities, and the justice system at large. As front-line advocates, criminal lawyers deserve respect, dignity, and equity regardless of their gender identity. When our workplaces are diverse, inclusive, and equitable, we can fight for justice with clear minds.

Appendix A: Task Force Publications

Maryam Ahranjani, *Sprinting a Marathon: Next Steps for Gender Equity in Criminal Legal Employment*, 106 MINN. L. REV. 228 (2022).

Maryam Ahranjani, *Women in Criminal Justice Task Force Concludes Research Phase and Moves into Action* CRIM. JUST. MAG. (July 28, 2022).

Maryam Ahranjani, *"Toughen Up, Buttercup" versus #TimesUp: Initial Findings of the ABA Women in Criminal Justice Task Force*, 25 BERKELEY J. CRIM. L. 99 (2020).

Maryam Ahranjani, *Listening Session Participants Express Feelings of Isolation—and Demonstrate Resilience*, CRIM. JUST. MAG. (Nov. 1, 2019), https://www.americanbar.org/groups/criminal_justice/publications/criminal-justice-magazine/2019/fall/listening-session-participants-express-feelings-isolation-demonstrate-resilience.

Maryam Ahranjani, *Pulling Back the Curtain: A Follow-Up Report from the ABA Criminal Justice Section Women in Criminal Justice Task Force*, ABA, https://www.americanbar.org/content/dam/aba/administrative/criminal_justice/tf-women-report.pdf (last visited Jan. 10, 2022).

Maryam Ahranjani, *Looking Back, Looking Forward*, CRIM. JUST. MAG. (Oct. 29, 2020), https://www.americanbar.org/groups/criminal_justice/publications/criminal-justice-magazine/2020/fall/looking-back-looking-forward.

Joy Applewhite, *Brave, Bold, Booked, and Balanced*, CRIM. JUST. MAG. (July 20, 2021), https://www.americanbar.org/groups/criminal_justice/publications/criminal-justice-magazine/2021/summer/brave-bold-booked-and-balanced.

Lucian E. Dervan, *Undefined Vision: An Ally's Journey*, CRIM. JUST. MAG. (Jul. 15, 2020), https://www.americanbar.org/groups/criminal_justice/publications/criminal-justice-magazine/2020/summer/undefined-vision-allys-journey.

Daniela Donoso, *Heavy Purse: A Law Student's Reflection on the CJS Women in Criminal Justice Task Force's NYC Listening Session*, CRIM. JUST. MAG. (Apr. 20, 2020), https://www.americanbar.org/groups/criminal_justice/publications/criminal-justice-magazine/2020/spring/heavy-purse-law-students-reflection-the-cjs-women-criminal-

---

INCLUSION AND REDUCE BIAS Ch. 17 (Bernice B. Donald & Sarah E. Redfield eds., 2022) (offering strategies all along the pipeline to achieve inclusion and equity).

justice-task-forces-nyc-listening-session (last visited Jan. 10, 2022).

Maria Carmen Hinayon, *Who Needs the Old Boys' Club? Let's Make Our Own—Highlights from the WCJ Bay Area Listening Session*, CRIM. JUST. MAG. (Jan. 21, 2020), https://www.americanbar.org/groups/criminal_justice/publications/criminal-justice-magazine/2020/winter/who-needs-old-boys-club-lets-make-our-ownhighlights-the-wcj-bay-area-listening-session.

Carla Laroche & Tina Luongo, *Task Force Launches*, CRIM. JUST. MAG. (Spring 2019), https://www.americanbar.org/groups/criminal_justice/publications/criminal-justice-magazine/2019/spring/task-force-launches.

Ann Ratnayake Macy, *From Mad Men to Times Up and Beyond: What We Must Do to Ensure Workplace Parity for Women in Criminal Justice*, CRIM. JUST. MAG. (May 24, 2022), https://www.americanbar.org/groups/criminal_justice/publications/criminal-justice-magazine/2022/spring/from-mad-men-times-what-we-must-do-ensure-workplace-parity-women-criminal-justicea-women-criminal-justice-taskforce-members-perspective/.

Hon. Gloria Ochoa-Bruck, *The Call for the Rise of the Modern Prosecutor*, CRIM. JUST. MAG. (Jan. 11, 2021), https://www.americanbar.org/groups/criminal_justice/publications/criminal-justice-magazine/2021/winter/the-call-the-rise-the-modern-prosecutor.

Hon. Rachel Pickering, *An Awakening and More: How Being Part of the Women in Criminal Justice Task Force Has Provided Me with a Judicial Awareness*, CRIM. JUST. MAG. (May 1, 2021), https://www.americanbar.org/groups/criminal_justice/publications/criminal-justice-magazine/2021/spring/awakening-how-being-part-women-criminal-justice-task-force-provided-me-judicial-awareness.

Yaamini L. Rao, *Voice Lessons,* CRIM. JUST. MAG. (Jan. 12, 2022), https://www.americanbar.org/groups/criminal_justice/publications/criminal-justice-magazine/2022/winter/voice-lessons/.

Jessica J. Yeary, *From Sweetie to Sisterhood: A Public Defender's Listening Session Reflection*, CRIM. JUST. MAG. (Oct. 20, 2021), https://www.americanbar.org/content/dam/aba/publications/criminal_justice_magazine/fall-2021/criminal-justice-v036n03-fall-2021.pdf.authcheckdam.

Respectfully submitted,

Justin Bingham
Chair, Criminal Justice Section
February 2023

501

GENERAL INFORMATION FORM

Submitting Entity: Criminal Justice Section

Submitted By: Justin Bingham, Chair

1. Summary of the Resolution(s).

   This resolution urges the ABA to adopt the report of the Criminal Justice Section's Women in Criminal Justice Task Force ("TF") on ten principles to advance the goal of gender equity among employers, institutions and people who are part of the criminal legal profession. The T bases the Ten Principles for Gender Equity on research, experience, and, most importantly, over three years of collecting qualitative and quantitative data from women criminal lawyers across the country and on further feedback as it shared its findings.

2. Indicate which of the ABA's Four goals the resolution seeks to advance (1-Serve our Members; 2-Improve our Profession; 3-Eliminate Bias and Enhance Diversity; 4-Advance the Rule of Law) and provide an explanation on how it accomplishes this.

   The resolution advances Goals 1, 2, and 3. It serves our members and improves our profession by promoting equity for men and women, and it eliminates bias and advances diversity by making the legal profession attainable for all individuals who wish to make the practice of law their profession.

3. Approval by Submitting Entity.

   The Criminal Justice Section's Council approved this resolution at its fall meeting on November 19, 2022.

4. Has this or a similar resolution been submitted to the House or Board previously?
   Many have been adopted to advance the goal of gender equity since 88A121 in 1988, but this is the first resolution with specific steps for lawyers in the criminal legal profession. Some other examples include 22M501 (on lactation rooms), 19A106 (pay equity), 18M302 (sexual harassment and retaliation), and 21M300B (childcare).

5. What existing Association policies are relevant to this Resolution and how would they be affected by its adoption?

   Existing resolutions would not be impacted by this resolution, but instead will be advanced through work of the task force in collecting qualitative and quantitative data from women criminal lawyers across the country and reporting on its findings.

6. If this is a late report, what urgency exists which requires action at this meeting of the House?

Not applicable

7. Status of Legislation. (If applicable)

   Not applicable

8. Brief explanation regarding plans for implementation of the policy, if adopted by the House of Delegates.
   The report will be publicized both by the ABA and CJS, and will be sent to state bar associations, specialty bar associations, practitioners in the Criminal Justice Section and other related ABA entities, and other institutions with the goal of informing and enacting the ten principles.

9. Cost to the Association. (Both direct and indirect costs)

10. Disclosure of Interest. (If applicable)

    Not applicable

11. Referrals.

    Referrals are being made to the following ABA entities:
    Administrative Law and Regulatory Practice
    Antitrust Law
    Business Law
    Center for Public Interest Law
    Civil Rights and Social Justice
    Commission on Women in the Profession
    Dispute Resolution
    Government and Public Sector Lawyers Division
    Governmental Affairs Office
    Health Law
    Judicial Division
    Labor and Employment Law
    Law Practice
    Law Students
    Legal Services
    Litigation
    Science & Technology Law
    Solo, Small Firm & General Practice
    State and Local Government Law
    Taxation
    Torts, Trial and Insurance Practice
    Young Lawyers Division
    Commission on Domestic and Sexual Violence

12. Name and Contact Information (Prior to the Meeting. Please include name, telephone number and e-mail address). *Be aware that this information will be available to anyone who views the House of Delegates agenda online.*)

Justin Bingham, Section Chair
Phone: 1 (509) 835-5994
Email: jbingham@spokanecity.org

Kevin Scruggs, Section Director
Phone: 1 (202) 662-1503
Email: kevin.scruggs@americanbar.org

13. Name and Contact Information. (Who will present the Resolution with Report to the House?) Please include best contact information to use when on-site at the meeting. *Be aware that this information will be available to anyone who views the House of Delegates agenda online.*

Steve Saltzburg
2000 H St NW
Washington, DC 20052-0026
Phone: (202) 994-7089
Email: sasaltz@law.gwu.edu

Neal Sonnett
1581 Brickell Avenue Suite 1804 Miami, FL 33129
Phone: (305) 3582000
Email: nrslaw@sonnett.com

EXECUTIVE SUMMARY

1. Summary of the Resolution.

   This resolution urges the ABA to adopt the report of the Criminal Justice Section's Women in Criminal Justice Task Force on ten principles to advance the goal of gender equity among employers, institutions and people who are part of the criminal legal profession. The Ten Principles for Gender Equity on research, experience, and, most importantly, over three years of collecting qualitative and quantitative data from women criminal lawyers across the country and on further feedback as it shared its findings.

2. Summary of the issue that the resolution addresses.

   The resolution addresses longstanding differences in the criminal legal profession between men and women lawyers, and urges the ABA to adopt the report of the Women in Criminal Justice Task Force.

3. Please explain how the proposed policy position will address the issue.

   The principles provide very practical and impactful solutions to create a working environment for men and women that is more equitable, diverse and inclusive. These principles focus on the criminal legal profession, but other areas of the law should undertake similar studies as well.

4. Summary of any minority views or opposition internal and/or external to the ABA which have been identified.

   We are not aware of any views in opposition to this Resolution.

CHAPTER THREE
Getting In and Staying In

Camelia M. Valdes, as told to Maryam Ahranjani

Key Chapter Points

- One woman's firsthand account of her appointment and reappointment as Passaic County, New Jersey County Prosecutor in the face of gender-based, racial, and other attacks
- How and why to stay in high office

Introduction

When she became the Passaic County Prosecutor in New Jersey in 2009, Ms. Camelia M. Valdes became the first Latina county prosecutor in New Jersey, the first woman prosecutor in Passaic County, and the first lead prosecutor of Dominican ancestry in the United States. She has successfully served in the role for over sixteen years and will share advice based on her journey about how to enter and how to stay in the male-dominated role.

Maryam and Camelia first met at an ABA Criminal Justice Section (CJS) meeting at which Camelia received the Norm Maleng Minister of Justice Award. Tina Luongo, co-chair of the CJS Women in Criminal Justice Task Force, suggested we appoint her to the Task Force's Board of Advisors, and Maryam had the pleasure to reach out and make that invitation in an initial conversation that lasted hours and led to Maryam's desire to include Camelia's powerful voice in this book. This chapter developed from several conversations over the span of more than a year, between 2024 and 2025. We start with how Camelia earned her current role, progress to how she managed to stay in the role for so long in the face of challenging circumstances, and end with her advice for others interested in similar roles.

On Getting In . . .

What is your connection to this topic of gender equity in criminal law, Prosecutor Valdes?

I am a Dominican American born in the Bronx and raised in Newark who "wasn't supposed to be here," meaning the chief law enforcement official in my county. Now I have 16 years as the Passaic County Prosecutor in NJ, 28 years in public service (was an AUSA (Assistant United States Attorney) prior to my current role), mom of two young women with autism, and typically the only woman in the room. Women leaders get labeled, and common narratives (in the media and elsewhere) include presumed incompetence and/or being sexualized and/or gendered. I remain interested in telling the story of once you're in it, how do you stay in it, interested in telling the truth and exploring ways in which we can make things better. I want my contribution to speak to upper and middle management or women inspired to become a County Prosecutor or District Attorney. Motivated by my faith and a commitment to serve, as well as active life membership in Alpha Kappa Alpha Sorority, Inc., whose motto is "service to all mankind," I want to give a support lifeline to sisters who are already in the seat and who want to serve the public.

You once told me about a presentation you gave to a group of young women college students. Can you recount why you were so inspired by them?

They wanted to know about why law. What drew me to the law? As a daughter of immigrant parents, the role of advocate came early when I used to translate for everyone in our building. Even as a child, I understood the power of being a voice for those who didn't have the language or understand the systems that impacted their lives. I saw the power in that. The message is that there is power in being able to translate and interpret for others and advocate on their behalf. Law was a natural vehicle for advocacy and my career choice.

You decided to go into public service right after law school. Why did you choose to be a prosecutor rather than a defense attorney?

Prosecutors are dealing with individual cases *and* policy. You can have a greater impact as a prosecutor than as a defense attorney whose responsibility is to an individual client. Prosecutors have a broader reach because they experience facets of criminal law that can help them pursue justice by ensuring the system is fair and rights are protected.

In your experience, what are some of the skills that are necessary to be a good prosecutor?

Being able to understand and argue both sides. Analytical thinking. Clear and concise writing. Displaying honesty, integrity, and courage about the facts of the case and what must be done in the interest of justice. I tell students to study anything that's analytical, critical, and thoughtful about the human condition. Critical thinking and clear writing skills are important. Detailed grasp and objective analysis of fact and law. The written and spoken word are very important as an attorney and advocate, especially if you want to be a trial attorney.

What are your views on balance?

Balance is a goal; I strive for balance. I do not have balance at times. Had to learn to make peace with the fact that some days, I am a great mom but just a good prosecutor and other days, I'm a great prosecutor and just a good mom. It depends on the day. Life is doing a number of things at once, and it's about how to navigate your time and priorities. It's about purpose management. I think that's how the personal and the professional blend. Remembering to extend myself grace and practice self-care is a daily to-do, in one shape or form. Caretakers, like me, deserve care too.

What advice do you have about building a resume and gaining the "right" experience?

Sometimes you have to go sideways to go forward. For example, when I was a NJ Deputy Attorney General (DAG), I wanted to become an Assistant United States Attorney (AUSA). I knew that I would have to distinguish myself from every other DAG that had similar aspirations. I accepted an opportunity to serve as Assistant Governor's Counsel. I learned a completely different skill set and immersed myself in a different environment to achieve my goal and distinguish myself. Although I yearned to be a trial lawyer, mastering the legislative process added to my skill set. Two of my greatest accomplishments were working on the bills that created the NJ Drug Court, now known as Recovery Court, and the NJ Sex Offender Internet Registry. As Prosecutor, I can appreciate the profound impact of these two pieces of legislation in my daily role as a full circle moment.

On Staying In . . .

How do you do the difficult cases?

You have to be very clear about the rule of law and the facts of your case as a practical matter. The impact to the victim of the crime helps shape advocacy and who you are fighting for. The burnout rate is high, depending on what you're working on. If all you're doing is one type of case, especially violent crimes or child abuse cases, after a while it's taxing to the soul. I think about the victims that my staff and I are serving and how helping them helps the community at large. I'm talking to them at the worst time of their life—when they've committed or experienced crime.

How do you deal with trauma and disappointment? How about when you're dealing with victims?

Faith, family, and my purpose anchor me.

It's important to spend time understanding the impact of crime on victims. It's about seeking justice, it's creating spaces for victims to be heard and seen within the parameters of law. Some of them have never been in court—they don't *want* to be in court. You have to be the one to guide them through a daunting process. Often there's a misunderstanding of our criminal justice system and frustration when processes are different than those seen on TV or in movies. Understanding victimology, sometimes they're not sympathetic at all because they are angry or lash out out of fear or frustration. They might be angry at you. They're displacing their grief. As a good prosecutor, you must learn to compartmentalize facts, evidence, emotion, psychology and community pressure.

How do you find and serve your purpose?

Your purpose will change as your life changes. When I was younger, my purpose was to prove "them" wrong. By "them" I meant anybody who doubted my greatness or belonging. By "them" I meant anybody who wanted to put me in a box because I was a girl, a brown girl from Newark who wanted better for myself and my family and chose to pursue a nonstereotypical path. I was taught I was supposed to get married and have children because that is what my mom did and her mom before her. While the greatest privilege of my life has been to be a mother to my daughters, Isabela and Elsa, I have done and will do so much more to contribute to the betterment of the world.

At this age and in my 28th year in public service, the purpose is to serve and leave whatever spaces I occupy better and always speak truth to power. Last year, I suddenly lost my mom due to a devastating fall. I lost my dad to renal failure eight years ago. Going through those challenges and heartbreak, while working a very public and serious job and taking care of my daughters with autism, reminded me that our time is limited and unpredictable. I want to serve and do the best I can in the time that I have while leaving a solid legacy for my daughters and the world and the law.

With life comes personal and professional loss. How do you go on with a broken heart?

Grief is something you don't get over, you learn how to navigate and work through. When it visits, you have to let it visit until the healing is slowly done. Embracing grief as a natural process is essential in the healing process. Navigating a world without my parents is a new experience. Some days, it feels like I'm floating through space, untethered.

I talked about being the only one and how to navigate that. I may be the only or first one in that space, but I labor to ensure that I am not the only one or the last one. Creating spaces for others is a responsibility I do not take for granted.

What advice do you have about finding mentors?

Look around and find people whose work and resilience you admire and who would be willing to guide you on your journey. They may not always look like you, and that is okay too, perhaps even better.

I have professors who introduced me to programs and talked to me, but they did that because I was very serious about my work and committed to my self-improvement. Being a serious student and professional will draw attention to you and opportunities will come to you. Never too early to establish your brand and reputation. And once the opportunities arrive, pause before saying "no." The world already tells us all the reasons a dream may not work. Be bold and courageous enough to go for it anyway.

The good book says that "a man (or a woman's) gifts will bring you before great men." Start thinking about what your legacy is going to be. Were you fearless? Resilient? Brave? Did you make way for others?

What are the biggest obstacles to "getting in and staying in"?

Presumed incompetence (and corresponding narratives in the media, courtrooms, and elsewhere), being sexualized and/or gendered, especially when fulfilling familial caretaker roles or when advocating for better opportunities.

Can you tell me more about your work and experience with the media in your role?

Because of the proximity to the NYC media market, my office's work is covered in the media almost daily. With the near extinction of print media, coverage can seem more like clickbait than objective journalism. Therefore, our message must be clear, basic, and factual. Sometimes reporters do not take kindly to being told they have to wait for information and have made their coverage more sensational and personal, unnecessarily so, while covering a story. There was a period of time, not too long, where I became the story. Weathering through unfair and incorrect coverage takes faith, discipline, and patience. It is natural to want to defend against inaccurate and slanted media coverage. Best to litigate your case in court. Ultimately, the legal truth prevails.

You have served for over 15 years in your role. How have you managed to successfully stay in office when that role usually has a lot of turnover?

I maintain an open and transparent line of communication with stakeholders, my staff of over 165 attorneys, detectives, agents, and support personnel. I try hard to listen and support while reconciling the needs of the office. I try to be flexible and creative when crafting viable solutions because life happens, and it impacts our work. Sometimes life can be really life-y. We don't just work. We work and we live. And we must balance the two. Happy people tend to be happy lawyers and members of law enforcement. I'm also a straight shooter, and people know they can rely on me to tell them the truth, especially when it's hard or unpopular. I also try to keep the community apprised of our role as prosecutors and work so they know what we're doing to keep them safe and the roles they play in the process. As a result, the work of the office has spoken for itself for the past 16 years.

In *"Toughen Up, Buttercup" versus #TimesUp,* I identify a dynamic of different expectations for the workplace among women who have graduated from law school more recently compared to the more seasoned attorneys. Have you noticed that in your office?

Generationally, it's very different. I'm impressed by the new generations' confidence and boldness. After three months they think they should be running the place. They don't know what they don't know, but they strongly believe that they should lead because of how special they are.

I am very conscious about giving new prosecutors nontraditional roles. I want them to just try new things. I think it rounds them out better. Cross-training is vital for individuals and the organization as a whole.

You're going to try things that you think people want, and it isn't going to work.

Sometimes progress is individualized to the organization. What works for you might not work for someone else. A lot of that has to do with where you are in your life cycle and the individual community you are serving. If you're adopting, or have a child with special or medical needs, or when you're losing a parent, you need flexibility from leadership. If you don't get flexibility, you may not be able to continue working for the organization. You need to strike that balance with people who want to work but their ability to give you more is temporarily hindered by being ill, losing a child, having a child, or assuming caretaker responsibility for an elderly or sick parent.

As a leader, how do you maximize the workforce that you have, not the one that you thought you were going to get?

I don't know if there is a blueprint for leadership. It's ever evolving and calls for creative thinking.

Something has to anchor you, whether it's faith, family, or personal mission. Motivation changes over time with life experiences.

What would make you stay past retirement?

What would make me stay is experience, I'm not afraid of anything anymore, doing the unfamiliar, breaking new ground, legacy work, and enhanced, wider mentorship.

In New Jersey, you're appointed every five years. A lot of prosecutors don't do more than one term. I have been honored to serve as Prosecutor for three different governors, both Democratic and Republican, and nine different NJ attorneys general. Because of them, I have served in the role of a lifetime.

Advice and Next Steps . . .

Do you have any regrets?

Naturally, I made mistakes, but I don't have any regrets. Everything that I learned, especially the hard things, led me to you! You're going to make mistakes. It's learning the lessons and applying them next time. Important to keep your circle positive. You have to believe in your dream first, and then surround yourself with people who support your dreams. Do you feel encouraged or deflated after you talk to people? Then make a change! That makes a big difference! Humility, integrity, empathy, and accountability are important character traits to zealously guard at all times throughout the course of your career and life. Do not let the challenges change you at the core. And never forget the why, your why.

In terms of gender-related reflections, anything to add?

As professional as we are, be conscious of what the gender roles are—the ones you might have for yourself and the ones other people might put you in. You have to come to a place where you reconcile that for you. I remember when my daughters were sick, I felt as their mother I had to take care of them. It was the unspoken expectation that I adopted as a belief that it was going to be me as their mother. There's a perception that women are more emotional than men. It has been my observation that some women have a better handle on their emotions because we typically juggle more responsibilities because we are expected to. Some men and women—especially law enforcement officers—feel entitled to the assignment, to the work car, to the promotion; rules do not apply to them because they are authority figures, and they stomp around when things do not go their way. There is nothing more telling than to witness an adult temper tantrum, women and men, exhibit passive-aggressive or aggressive behavior and then have to manage all of that in order to not impact the very hard work of investigating and prosecuting cases and advocacy for victims and communities.

It hasn't been my experience that women are encouraged to be emotional. I see it in the trap of wanting to be liked. Some women may not want to be assertive because then you're called a b**** or other derogatory names outside of our names. Somewhere along the way, I reasoned that it is not what they call me. It is what I call myself that matters.

We're supposed to be well-behaved, but as the popular saying goes, "Well-behaved women seldom make history." The best supervisors know that to be respected is more productive than to be liked.

You see that in the context of sports. When the legendary Serena Williams showed her frustration or disappointment, she was labeled as out of control, but if a male player did the same, he was passionate.

There's a lot of overt and covert messaging about how we're supposed to behave.

As a leader, it's also about assignments and how I ensure assignments will benefit the individual and the office. I'm mindful about how to create opportunities for everyone, particularly women and people of color who may be boxed in because they either are too good or are perceived to need more support. I'm very conscious about who gets assigned to what cases and opportunities. I make adjustments every chance I get. I have a perspective that is helpful to people. Everyone should have the opportunities, plum and challenging, to develop the necessary skills to be successful. I do not subscribe to the limiting belief that women are only meant to do certain tasks, nor do I believe men should not be exposed to assignments that are traditionally reserved for women. For example, our domestic violence, special victims (child abuse), trial, and narcotics units, to name a few, each consist of women and men. I do not stand for pigeonholing or boxing in, on any level for our assistant prosecutors, detectives, or support staff.

While I have endeavored to make the office as accommodating as I can, especially to new parents, by implementing lactation rooms and planning for paternity bonding leaves, there is much we can accomplish when we listen to each of our staff members and the practices that can help them succeed at work and at home.

What are you most worried about in terms of the future of women criminal lawyers?

I am concerned that women will hesitate to enter or will exit criminal practice, especially on the government side, because there are more lucrative areas of practice to enter. Once in it, the demands and the burnout rate are high, and there is no intentionality about growth and wellness.

What are you most hopeful about in terms of gender equity in criminal law?

My greatest hope is that employers recognize life realities and do their level best to practice empathetic leadership to attract and maintain women criminal lawyers. Speaking with lawyers about the practice and life while practicing is a critical and instructive exercise.

What is next?

Who's to say? I'm just getting started! I have a body of work that only God knows what or where it will bring me. But I know that I have the skills to do whatever is next. I can speak. I can write. I can think and I can withstand the challenges of a high-profile role with dignity and integrity. If you have those three things, you can do anything. And I am not afraid. Whatever it is, I can make it through because I have survived everything that I have been through in this high-profile role, the highest highs and the lowest lows.

What advice do you have for those whom you inspire to follow in your footsteps?

What got me into the criminal justice field is what has kept me in. Here are a few of my key takeaways from the past 16 years:

Passaic County Prosecutor's Office (PCPO) Best Practices

1. Pipeline programs from college to law school through legal and investigative internships that are flexible, tailored to the student's availability and interests. This feeder system allows the organization to observe and develop the student's development and it allows the student to gain real insight into the available roles, support staff, agent, detective, or assistant prosecutor. We make it a point to engage the two universities in our county and the three law schools in our state, as early as the student's freshman or first year in law school. We participate in career fairs, criminal justice programs, and criminal justice events as often as possible. Students get to engage with my staff and me personally, and we get to recruit for the future. It's important for me to be seen and have a real conversation with them about criminal practice. I never saw or interacted with a Latina lawyer until I got to law school. I do my best to give students the opportunity to experience as much of work as possible as early as possible. Our office has support staff which includes victim advocates, agents which are a nonsworn hybrid between a detective or an assistant prosecutor. We have hired directly from college. Many of the agents have successfully become sworn county investigators because of their successful pipeline program.
2. Cross-training of all personnel is invaluable. I intentionally rotate staff through our office units. It is my desire to see that everyone learns how to take a statement, investigate a case, try a case before a jury, write an appeal. It has been a long-standing practice to ensure everyone has the exposure to different areas of the practice, including night and weekend work, regardless of gender.
3. Because of the emphasis on cross-training, we plan for life events, such as medical leaves, and familial situations that require flexibility. We manage intermittent leaves as a matter of course and are sensitive to necessary accommodations when the staff member returns to the office. Unless absolutely unavoidable, and then in consultation with the impacted member, we do not transfer personnel while on leave without taking into account the person's wishes.
4. Leadership development is a serious focus for my administration. Every member of the PCPO is encouraged to participate in community service by way of teaching or presenting educational programs to the community on such topics as cyber-bullying, bias incidents, mental

health considerations, and substantive topics such as domestic violence, use of force, or financial crimes. Observing and working with staff allows me the opportunity to gauge a person's leadership abilities, beyond how they handle their individual cases. Passaic County is a diverse county in terms of geography and population. We strive to have assistant prosecutors, investigators, and advocates reflect the populations we serve. It has made a difference to defendants, victims, and witnesses.

5. With regard to promotions, I am clear and vocal about how promotions work and provide as many opportunities as we can to have staff showcase their abilities. We seek out trials and other multi-faceted investigations, especially uncommon fact patterns. We emphasize effort over result. As a matter of practice, we assign appellate lawyers to work with the trial team, and we provide opportunities to try at least a few cases for the experience and appreciation for what trial lawyers are tasked to do. The bottom line for me is that the work is paramount. No other factor matters more than the commitment to the work. The more diversity of thought and perspective from within the staff, the greater the outcomes.
6. One of the most rewarding aspects of my experience is creating opportunities to develop new leaders. Whenever we sit down to discuss promotions, the entire staff is up for discussion for the immediate needs and future. Sometimes in organizations, the most problematic employees receive the most attention, while the ones that toil quietly are overlooked. We intentionally seek out unlikely candidates for new challenges. I have not subscribed to heirs apparent. It keeps the organization motivated and the leadership styles fresh.
7. One of the most important retention vehicles is that of employee collective bargaining agreements. Policies are important but contract terms are immediately tangible, black-and-white factors that reflect priorities. Contract terms like salaries, educational incentives, and work schedule flexibility that were not previously available now are.
8. Frank discussions with staff members about their professional aspirations and their current life experiences have led to a greater understanding of the operation of the office as a whole.

For all of the above and more, I am eternally proud and grateful to and for the policies, work, and legacy of the past 16 years. And that's what has kept and keeps me in.

CHAPTER FOUR

Navigating Intersectionality: Reclaiming Zeal in the Midst of a Burnout

Joy Applewhite

Key Chapter Points

- Burnout of a public defender working in the rural Southwest
- Imposter syndrome, work-related insomnia
- Recovery and wellness—finding a therapist who understands her identity

For years, I knew that I wanted to be a public defender. As a child, I loved helping others. That passion for helping others continued to grow in the capacity of serving my rural Mississippi community through community service, mentoring the youth, and serving in leadership. As a child and teenager, I was not immune to the realities of racism and white supremacy that continued to plague our nation before, during, and after its founding. Witnessing the senseless murders of Black people, particularly the youth, at the hands of the police was devastating. People would search for reasons for their untimely deaths, and I knew that there was always a story behind it all. I had a curiosity in figuring out the reasons that may get us closer to the reason why that more than likely stemmed from my interest in criminal cases since I was an itty bitty child watching live court TV and crime shows with my Nana.

All of these things led me to realize that everyone deserves someone to tell their story, and I knew that I wanted to help people to do that. But I did not see myself becoming a prosecutor. It never felt right to me to be a part of the system that helped to create and sustain the mass incarceration system that starkly incarcerates Black and Brown people. I wanted to advocate for those who were oftentimes and unfortunately ignored by society and amplify their voices to help tell their stories—stories that some people did not want to hear, stories that made people realize our system is still rife with inequities that continue when we collectively ignore the realities, stories that made people feel for the people accused of the most simple crimes to even the most egregious, and stories that made the people accused of those crimes feel heard, seen, and worthy of being defended, especially for people who may have never or rarely had anyone fight for them in their lives.

Entering college at Alcorn State University, I knew I was on the pathway to becoming a lawyer and studied psychology to have a greater understanding of the human mind and behavior. One of the most pivotal concepts I studied was that "change is inevitable." There is no way to avoid change because it is bound to happen, whether we want it to or not and especially despite whether we are ready or not. Because of this, I realized that change is going to always be a part of my life, and I have to learn to adjust to it, but that did not mean I would be immune to the challenges, as I learned later in life as a practicing public defender who had finally achieved her dreams.

In August 2021, I started my career with the New Mexico Law Offices of the Public Defender (LOPD). After what seemed like forever and a lifetime, but what was in reality only about three months, I had survived bar study and the exam that was the last barrier to achieving my dream. I began work as a Law Practitioner, essentially a law clerk, where I learned the foundational concepts of defense practice. It was what drew me to LOPD because I had not seen many public defense offices that provided an opportunity where you could start as a law clerk and learn what you needed before becoming an attorney and having your own caseload. It helped to alleviate the concerns and "what ifs" as a new attorney. Once I passed the bar and entered into the official ranks of being a public defender, I was placed in a magistrate and district court because our District Defender, Ibukun Adepoju, began her career as a public defender with the other attorneys in the office in similar fashion. It was a learning experience that I am grateful to have been chosen for, but it came with many challenges, heartaches, and dark days that led me to grow into a more mindful, wellness-focused attorney (and continue to flourish as today).

Being a Black woman in America is tough enough. We are one of the most educated groups in recent years, yet we are perpetually mislabeled and misunderstood when we have historically tapped into our Black Girl Magic to lead movements and embark on change and continue to do so today. The realities of being a Black woman with a Juris Doctorate and a license to practice in rural New Mexico shined a light on what I knew was still an issue but was still shocking to my core in the aftermath of 2020. Being raised in Mississippi and attending law school at American University Washington College of Law in Washington, D.C., I had grown accustomed to being surrounded by Black people in most of the spaces where I traveled and having access to outlets highlighting Black excellence, protests for social change, and just simply safe spaces to be in as a Black woman when police brutality, white supremacy, and white fragility reared their ugly heads. There was comfort in knowing we had each other and could exchange those glances in spaces like the subway or the sidewalk that said, "It's okay. We will get through this," or "I see you, girl. You go."

But moving to southeastern New Mexico, a state that does not have a high Black population, unlike my home state and second home in my mid-20s, was an adjustment. Not only was I starting my career in a profession with only 2 percent Black women, but I was also beginning a new chapter of my life—moving to a new state where I did not know anyone locally, officially.

When I began practicing as a public defender, I began by taking over and covering magistrate cases. At first, my initial hearings were simple ones: pretrial hearings where I was only getting dates to perform tasks that included checking to ensure we received discovery, conducting pretrial interviews, and motions. Then came the day of my first preliminary hearings in what became my assigned magistrate court. Despite being nervous, I was ready and excited. I had succinctly prepared my script that would become my standard practice. But nothing could prepare me for the challenges of how my tone or questions would be handled by opposing counsel, law enforcement, judges, and at times even my own clients.

During one of my first preliminary hearings, I was cross-examining a detective who seriously asked me, "Are you okay?" Mind you, in the new normal of life during COVID, most hearings were being done over Google Meet. I had my video on, but this detective did not. In my mind, my question was simple. During cross-examination, I am typically looking for a yes or no answer. So when this detective asked me if I was okay during this cross-examination, I was taken aback as a new attorney. I had to pause a moment before responding because I know I am fully capable of reading a person to where all their edges and soul are gone. In this professional setting, I had to bite my tongue to not snap back, "I am very well indeed, but clearly you are not asking me that question." The imposter monster made me wonder if I was a white male asking the exact same question, would it have been answered or met with the same energy. After my momentary pause to process and think of a professional response, I indicated that I have my camera on and although she could not see me I was fine and attempted to clarify my question since the detective had issues understanding or did not want to understand to avoid answering the question. Once court was complete, I was able to go vent and get it off my chest with like-minded individuals who would see and hear me.

At this point in my career, I had only had my bar license for a little over a month and had a rollercoaster of more experiences to come.

In my first few months of practice, the main focus was learning how to practice what I was educated on and theoretically trained to do. But the good thing was that our office was fully staffed with some senior attorneys who had learned from their own practice and had advice and mentorship to share. Everyone's door was always open if a new attorney had a question, and a benefit to joining LOPD as a legal practitioner was having the opportunity to attend new attorney training before being assigned to a courtroom. What made the office even better, and bearable in times where my identity stood out, was tried, and was even questioned, was the diversity that I had never encountered in a public defender's office. Those first couple of months felt full and supportive because our office was fully staffed with attorneys, making representing indigent clients across four district courts and five magistrate courts easier.

Then the summer hit, and rumors of people leaving the office spread like wildfire. Law school did not just teach me the black letter law and the foundations of advocacy; it also introduced me to anxiety and seasonal depression. The winter blues and questioning my capabilities in a law school environment where all are brilliant in their unique way did not leave me in the adult world where I was now licensed to practice. What began as a slight numbness eventually grew into detachment that became a debilitating state of depression, so much so that even getting out of bed was a task. I found myself taking on more responsibility in my newly assigned courts as I transitioned to handling the cases primarily on my own because my supervisor had taken over another district court in another office for the district. I had also discovered that I was an empath and started to feel the overwhelm of "what ifs" as I represented indigent people, people who are our most vulnerable and who often face other barriers like mental health challenges, poverty, and limited to no access to healthcare.

I would find myself waking up in the middle of the night, thinking about a case, walking myself through all the things that could happen or that I could do to get my client to a better outcome, talking myself through the arguments I could make to the court, prosecutor, and jury if the case went to trial. My bouts of insomnia soon started to interfere with my ability to function because six to eight hours of sleep is what gets me through the day because of my body's strong aversion to caffeine. But what was even more taxing were the days when I preferred to sleep my worries away and would stay in bed as long as I possibly could to avoid the realities of life and the law. My passion for public defense drove me to get the care I would suggest that a loved one get.

When I began therapy through the Cerebral app, I did not know what to expect, but I knew the goal was to get and feel better—to feel like my full self in this new era of my life. Attending teletherapy rebuilt the strength and coping skills that I needed to thrive in a profession where I witnessed clients at their lowest lows, in their toughest times, and during their saddest stories. I realized

I could not erase the trauma that they had experienced, but that I could help them by listening and telling their stories. I learned many coping skills through therapy to bring my tiger back to the good fight and realized that with them, medication—that made me feel better but like a robot on autopilot—was not a necessity when I take the time to fill my cup, saying no to the things that do not matter and yes to the things that do.

I was coping and working like I did before the deep dive into depression when the senseless murder of Tyre Nichols occurred in January 2023. The murder of a young Black man in the wake of 2020 was painful. The Black community had borne witness to the terrors of policing that resulted in brutality and killings of Black men, women, and children that made society as a whole stop and march in Black Lives Matter protests in the summer of 2020. Progress and demands had been made. People banded together for a pivotal moment in history that considered what Black people unfortunately were enduring and warning their loved ones about. The murder of Tyre Nichols struck me to my core, and unlike my days in Washington, D.C., and Mississippi, there were no protests to attend in my rural New Mexico community and no safe space to just go be and mourn another Black American tragedy. In addition to joining the 27 club that presented the segue to true adulthood and personal life lessons, work and grieving the killing and brutality against Black bodies brewed the perfect storm for burnout that led to the darkest tunnel of depression and anxiety-filled gloom.

In February 2023, I knew I needed to return to therapy, but I could not return to Cerebral. For my next therapist, I required someone who looked like me and could understand the racial trauma I was experiencing from police brutality, being Black in America, and being a Black professional in rural America in a state that did not have anywhere close to the Black population I was accustomed to.

The challenge for me was finding a Black woman therapist in New Mexico in general. It took months to find a Black woman therapist, and the delay increased the burnout I kept denying that I treated like my typical bout of depression and anxiety. But it was not. Most days I felt numb and detached from work because I felt like what I was doing was not enough. I felt like I was losing everything. I also felt like I was not as good as my counterparts because realistically I could not work beyond eight- to ten-hour days with my energy only. Negative self-talk was my new normal, and the imposter monster became my best friend. I felt bad for my clients as they battled through their cases, even when they were at fault, because for some, trauma had led them to where they were. Knowing the history of our country, I was aware that a large reason for these life experiences was the lack of resources and inequities throughout society. Feelings of inadequacy in the workplace and the inherent trauma from working in public defense in addition to the pressures of everyday life and the racism that continues to infect our society, both firsthand and secondary, brought me to a breaking point. I no longer wanted to exist and thought about how death would be so much better for myself and everyone else. Although I was not dealing with suicidal ideation, death ideation was a scary reality that I was sinking into day by day. Unfortunately, court and working in an environment where opposing counsel was not empathetic and understanding of my clients' plights only intensified the burnout that was brewing.

During these dark days, I experienced opposing counsel yelling in court during a change of plea over paperwork that I communicated via email that felt like a moment back in 1619; having my tone checked by a judge while I was advocating on behalf of a client; and sometimes unknowing clients doubting my capabilities. I attempted to find temporary fixes until I could find the right therapist for me, but many of the resources for Black women were far beyond the boundaries of where I was located. But somehow, I kept going. I took the mental health days that I needed. Most importantly, I was seen and heard. Both of my supervisors realized I was struggling and supported me when I needed to take time off and later encouraged me to take a wellness sabbatical to reset and recharge. My partner also did what he could to provide support, even when he did not quite understand the extent of my work and the amount of time and energy it can take.

Despite the burnout, depression, and anxiety, my commitment and zealousness for my clients remained a top priority. I took the time I needed for my mental health while taking the time I needed to prepare for my trials set later in June. I found a therapist in early May that had an opening in the beginning of June. I continued to swim, although it felt like I was drowning nearly every day, overwhelmed with the lack of understanding for my clients, the lack of resources in our communities, and the lack of progress in equality and equity for every individual in our society. I was the it girl for faking it 'til I make it, and I was going to carry on despite the weapons formed against me.

Ironically, I began therapy the same day I presented at a training session on wellness and burnout for our annual training. To live through what you are speaking on as it is happening is an interesting experience because I found myself providing advice on scenarios I had been struggling with. That is when it hit me that what I was experiencing the last couple months was burnout. Throughout the next couple months, my therapist guided me through burnout recovery and learning how to cope with a job as demanding as mine. Every day brings new challenges, but I take it as a work in progress that is part of my healing and growth as a Black woman in public defense, reclaiming not just her time but her zeal.

CHAPTER FIVE

Rethinking 9-to-5: Combating the Flexibility Stigma

Lieutenant Colonel Susan E. Upward, USMC[1]

Key Chapter Points

- Roots of the flexibility stigma
- How the flexibility stigma harms workers, especially caregivers
- What we learned from COVID-19 about the value of flexibility
- How organizational policies can address the flexibility stigma
- What leaders can do to promote flexibility

In 1980, Dolly Parton released "9 to 5," the theme song for a movie of the same name. It became an instant hit , rocketing up both the country and pop charts, and has endured to become what some call "one of the most socially impactful songs *ever*," an anthem for women's empowerment and the fight against "white patriarchal control structures" of the workplace.[2] Yet, the song's longevity has just as much to do with its catchy melody as it does with the fact that more than 45 years later, professionals continue to combat those traditional constructs, especially outdated notions of business hours and toxic work environments the song's name and lyrics allude to.

It is in that context that the flexibility stigma exists and thrives—the stereotypes and biases, both explicit and implicit, that accompany any deviation from the long-held, socially accepted definition of the "normal" workday or, in

1. The views presented are those of the author alone and do not represent the views of the Department of Defense or the U.S. Marine Corps.

2. Marcus K. Dowling, *"9 to 5," 40 Years Later: Dolly Parton's Movie Theme Remains One of the Most Socially Impactful Songs Ever*, The Boot (Nov. 3, 2020), https://theboot.com/dolly-parton-9-to-5-song-legacy/.

other words, the 9-to-5. But under further scrutiny, what emerges is that how society defines work, both in location and in time, is an evolving concept, not a static principle. The COVID-19 pandemic forced both employers and employees to rethink flexibility and work, showing that flexible work options could have positive effects on individuals' well-being without sacrificing an organization's productivity. Nevertheless, the stigma that attaches to those who avail themselves of remote work or nontraditional working hours remains, and the allure of going back to the "old" ways of doing business is powerful. Companies that were already reluctant to implement and skeptical of remote work have been bolstered by federal return-to-office mandates and have quickly and completely retreated to 9-to-5 norms.

Despite this regression, organizations should still seek to evolve and need a comprehensive strategy to combat the flexibility stigma, couched in the realization that it is a leadership issue more than a logistical challenge—while it requires practical solutions, it also requires leaders to combat their own attitude and their team's mindset to reframe how they think about work, separate from the choke chain of old-fashioned beliefs about the workplace and the workday.

The Roots of the Flexibility Stigma Run Deep

To combat the stereotypes and stigmas that surround flexible work scenarios, it is important to understand the underpinnings of these thought processes in a historical context. Like other biases, the flexibility stigma is based on our own experiences, both collectively and individually, that have shaped how we see the world. The result is a tendency to look less favorably not only at employees who request and utilize flexible work options, but also at the managers who are apt to grant flexible work requests to those individuals.[3]

Traditional philosophies of the workday are directly tied to concepts of the Protestant work ethic dating back to the 17th century. Farming and harvesting crops using manual labor and crude instruments required working outside from sunrise to sunset. When that reality was coupled with the religious ideology that promoted working long and arduous hours at one's vocation, the combination was believed to set the nation apart from others around the globe, making "hard work" an American virtue.[4]

---

3. Victoria L. Brescoll, Jennifer Glass & Alexandra Sedlovskaya, *Ask and Ye Shall Receive? The Dynamics of Employer-Provided Flexible Work Options and the Need for Public Policy*, 69 J. Soc. Issues 367, 367–88 (2013).

4. *Truth v. Myth: The Protestant Work Ethic*, The Historic Present (Sept. 12, 2008), https://thehistoricpresent.com/2008/09/12/truth-v-myth-the-protestant-work-ethic/; *see also*

It was during the Industrial Revolution of the late 18th century that capitalists began to exploit that work ethic with deplorable working conditions for workers, including workweeks that exceeded 80 hours. Such conditions endured for decades until workers began to bend the ears of political and industry leaders. As a result, Teddy Roosevelt campaigned in 1912 on the promise of establishing a national eight-hour workday, and in 1914, Henry Ford voluntarily reduced the workweek at his automobile production plants from 48 to 40 hours because he "believed that too many hours were bad for workers' productivity."[5] However, a national standard for defining the workweek did not come until 1938, when Franklin Delano Roosevelt signed into law the first Fair Labor Standards Act, setting the benchmark at a 44-hour workweek, which was amended and reduced two years later to the current standard of 40 hours.[6] But what is missing from FDR's original legislation to the current version of the law is any mention of *when* those 40 hours actually occur; the act does not mandate that the working day occur between the hours of 9-to-5 or even Monday through Friday.[7]

Contrary to popular belief, the extreme schedules of some working professionals that are commonplace today were frowned upon just 50 years ago. In her book *Bias, Interrupted*, Joan C. Williams discusses the evolution of "the 1960s paradigm of work, with a fixed time and place, fixed roles, fixed beliefs about who does what when," to the 1970s when "Americans signaled social class by displaying their leisure: think bankers' hours (9 a.m. to 3 p.m.)."[8] Williams's research shows a sharp distinction between that generation, when employees "who worked more than fifty hours a week suffered a wage *penalty* of almost 10 percent," to just 30 years later when the pendulum swung back toward increased working hours such that "40 percent of managerial men work more than fifty hours a week, and they enjoyed a 10 percent wage premium."[9]

Sean Illing, *Why Work Is So Miserable in America*, Vox (Feb. 11, 2024, at 6:00 EST), https://www.vox.com/the-gray-area/24034358/gray-area-work-labor-miserable-protestant-ethic.

5. Eric Ortiz, *Where Did the 40-Hour Workweek Come From?*, NBC News (Sept. 1, 2014, at 6:31 EDT), https://www.nbcnews.com/news/us-news/where-did-40-hour-workweek-come-n192276; Carl Seaver, *The 9 to 5 Workday: A Brief History*, Hist. Defined, https://www.historydefined.net/the-9-to-5-workday-a-brief-history/#:~:text=The%20idea%20of%209%20to%205%20being%20a,lunch%20being%20counted%20as%20part%20of%20the%20workday (last visited Aug. 15, 2025); Erin Blakemore, *How America Settled on a 5-Day Workweek*, Nat'l Geographic (Mar. 24, 2023), https://www.nationalgeographic.com/history/article/american-workweek-history-explained.

6. Fair Labor Standards Act of 1938, 29 U.S.C. §§ 201–219.

7. Seaver, *supra* note 5.

8. Joan C. Williams, Bias, Interrupted: Creating Inclusion for Real and for Good 130, 132 (2021).

9. *Id.* at 134.

At a more basic level, most working adults today grew up in a school system that perpetuated the show-up and show-your-work philosophy. Perfect attendance awards incentivized and celebrated the mere act of just going to school every day as a grand achievement worthy of recognition. But while the act of sending a child to school even if they are sick might be in line with the traditional gritty work ethic, it is increasingly frowned upon in a post-COVID world where taking care of yourself also shows that you are taking care of those around you—an increasingly accepted practice.[10] In another context, we all had math teachers growing up who made us show our work—it was never enough to just state the right answer; we also had to show the steps of applying the right mathematical equation that got us to the right answer. Undoubtedly, there is value in that stage of early development to ensure that students understand the concepts to get to correct solutions, but the byproduct of such methodology is that we unconsciously become programmed to prefer to see the work behind solving the problem on an equal footing with the solution itself.

COVID-19: The Great Forcing Function

Until January 2025, the greatest catalyst for change in how we think about work came about in a necessary response to the COVID-19 pandemic. Seemingly overnight, managers and companies were forced to adapt and overcome the challenges of fully remote telework that previously was thought impossible. Yet, employers came to realize that remote work not only was feasible but also had tangible benefits, including statistically measured increases in performance, productivity, creativity, and innovation.[11] For instance, a 2022 survey conducted on behalf of the American Bar Association (ABA) found that almost 60 percent of lawyers work more than the standard 40 hours a week, and 22 percent work over 50 hours a week.[12] However, most lawyers reported that during the period of total or hybrid remote work required by the pandemic, the quality and quantity of their work did not suffer; in fact, women especially thrived in that environment, with 56 percent stating that it "increased their ability to balance work and family obligations."[13] The time

---

10. Caitlynn Peetz, *Are Perfect Attendance Awards Fundamentally Flawed? Some School Leaders Say Yes*, EDUC. WEEK (Dec. 23, 2022), https://www.edweek.org/leadership/are-perfect-attendance-awards-fundamentally-flawed-some-school-leaders-say-yes/2022/12.

11. WILLIAMS, *supra* note 8, at 136.

12. ROBERTA D. LIEBENBERG & STEPHANIE A. SCHARF, AM. BAR ASS'N, WHERE DOES THE LEGAL PROFESSION GO FROM HERE? 9 (2022), https://www.americanbar.org/content/dam/aba/administrative/law-practice-division/practice-forward/2022-practice-forward-report.pdf.

13. *ABA Survey: Most Lawyers Want Options for Remote Work, Court and Conferences*, AM. BAR ASS'N (Sept. 28, 2022), https://www.americanbar.org/news/abanews/aba-news-archives/2022/09/aba-survey-lawyers-remote-work/?login.

saved on commuting to and from the office alone made a significant difference, considering the average commute time was seventy-two minutes a day, and even more (101 minutes) for employees who take public transit.[14]

In post-pandemic practice, some law firms changed their old-school mentality about client interaction, which research shows was helped, not harmed, by the remote meetings that COVID-19 mandated.[15] But, more importantly, the legal profession found that flexibility is an essential part of comprehensive wellness programs that are essential to recruiting new employees.[16] Other employers have also realized that the pandemic normalized and legitimized flexible options like remote work, to the point where employees have become accustomed "to taking time off during the day to attend to family matters and working flex time as needed."[17] As a result, on its 2024 List of the Best Companies to Work For, *Fortune* magazine found that "only two of 100 firms said that they required workers to be on-site four days a week or more."[18] In another study, 33 companies in the United States, Ireland, and Australia tested a 32-hour workweek. At the end of the six-month trial period, the companies reported increased revenue, while the employees reported a marked "improvement in stress, burnout, work-life balance and physical health" and, as a result, "zero of the participating companies said they were leaning toward stopping or switching back."[19]

Of course, that research predated the January 2025 Inauguration Day order by President Donald Trump that summarily terminated all remote work arrangements and ordered the entire federal workforce to return to the office immediately, with essentially no room for exceptions.[20] Even before that federal precedent was set, companies like BlackRock, Amazon, and Farmers

---

14. Alana Semuels, *As People Return to Offices, It's Back to Misery for America's Working Moms*, Time (Feb. 2, 2023, at 6:30 EST), https://time.com/6251465/return-to-office-working-moms-pandemic/; *see also* Maryam Ahranjani, *"Toughen Up Buttercup" versus #TimesUp: Initial Findings of the ABA Women in Criminal Justice Task Force*, 25 Berkley J. Crim. L. 99, 145 (2020).

15. Michael Alvarez et al., *The Post-COVID Law Office: Attorney Viewpoints*, 59 Ariz. Att'y 20 (2022).

16. Danielle Braff, *Warm Welcome: Law Firms Are Using Wellness Programs to Recruit New Lawyers*, ABA J. (Aug. 1, 2022, at 2:20 CDT), https://www.abajournal.com/magazine/article/warm-welcome-law-firms-are-using-wellness-programs-to-recruit-new-lawyers#google_vignette.

17. Williams, *supra* note 8, at 136.

18. Chloe Berger & Irina Ivanova, *"Gen Z Doesn't Live to Work. They Work to Live": The Paradox That Defines the Best Companies to Work For in 2024*, Fortune (Apr. 4, 2024, at 7:00 EDT), https://fortune.com/2024/04/04/gen-z-millennials-2024-best-companies-to-work-for-remote-balance/.

19. Alix Martichoux & Nexstar Media Wire, *33 Companies Test a 4-Day Workweek. None Are Planning to Switch Back*, The Hill (Dec. 1, 2022, at 11:08 ET), https://thehill.com/homenews/nexstar_media_wire/3756058-33-companies-tested-a-4-day-workweek-none-are-planning-to-switch-back/?ipid=promo-link-block1.

20. Return to In-Person Work, 90 Fed. Reg. 8251 (Jan. 28, 2025).

Insurance had already started to move away from entirely or mostly remote work.[21] Ironically, even Zoom—one of the companies that made remote work possible during the pandemic—had also reinstituted in-person requirements "in what the company is calling a structured hybrid approach."[22] In the legal profession, while there was some evidence "that the stigma associated with teleworking as an attorney has started to fade," there was similar backlash and an increasing push to return to the office to "the pre-pandemic norm" of normal business hours.[23]

Whom the Flexibility Stigma Affects

While the flexibility stigma is not gender specific, the phenomenon has historically affected women at a higher rate than their male counterparts. Some of this is attributable to the maternal wall bias: the stereotype that women professionals who become mothers are not only less competent, but also "less committed—and in fact *shouldn't* be as committed to their careers now that they have a kid."[24] As a result, mothers are often subjected to "higher performance and punctuality standards" than their counterparts without children or fathers.[25]

Caregiving, which is still predominantly handled by women in American households, is intrinsically tied to the need for flexibility and the biases that come with it. This point was reiterated in the research conducted by the ABA's Women in Criminal Justice Task Force, which found that the flexibility stigma "is often related to motherhood, family planning, reproductive health care, menopause, gender affirming health care, and caregiving."[26] In listening sessions held across the United States, women repeatedly testified that not only was limited flexibility with work schedules an ongoing and persistent challenge, but also an organizational culture shift was required to collectively acknowledge that flexibility does not equate to ineffectiveness.[27]

Yet, while caregiving is the most cited reason for schedule flexibility, "it's not the only reason that, over the course of a lifetime people need time

21. Andrea Hsu, *Remote Work Is Harder to Come By as Companies Push for Return to Office*, NPR (Sep. 1, 2023, at 5:19 ET), https://www.npr.org/2023/09/01/1196731284/return-to-office-rto-hybrid-remote-work-from-home-zoom.

22. *Id.*

23. Alvarez et al, *supra* note 15, at 23.

24. Williams, *supra* note 8, at 8.

25. *Id.* at 114.

26. Resolution 501, Am. Bar Ass'n (Feb. 6, 2023), https://www.americanbar.org/content/dam/aba/directories/policy/midyear-2023/501-midyear-2023.pdf.

27. Ahranjani, *supra* note 14; Maryam Ahranjani, *Sprinting a Marathon: Next Steps for Gender Equity in Criminal Law Employment*, 106 Minn. L. Rev. 228, 244 (2022).

off—others could be divorce, or poor health, or any number of life events."[28] More simply put, a single man is just as likely as a married woman to need an appliance repair or oil change—errands that are simply made easier if there is more flexibility in an individual's work schedule. Accordingly, the Task Force concluded that while increased flexibility would "improve the likelihood of recruiting and retaining talented women," it would also positively affect their male counterparts.[29]

But in a quest to understand the nature of the flexibility stigma, it is important to recognize that the foundations of its stereotypes and biases are often found in office environments that devolve into "masculinity contest cultures," where four characteristics are prized in its members: (1) showing no weakness; (2) stamina and strength; (3) work devotion; and (4) a dog-eat-dog mentality.[30] Research shows that this ideology, which expects employees to spend "extreme hours at the office" and "define[s] commitment as always being available," creates a toxic work environment and actually decreases company effectiveness, much to the chagrin of bosses who mistakenly assume the opposite.[31] In fact, such cultures increase the likelihood of bullying, social humiliation, and racial and sexual harassment, as well as "burnout, turnover, illness, and depression among both male and female employees."[32] As a result, it would be a mistake to consider the flexibility stigma as a women-only issue; although it is applied disproportionately between the genders, its detrimental effects are felt by men and women alike, as well as the organization as a whole.

The New Norm?

Before January 2025, a departure from the daily 9-to-5 and five-day workweek was increasingly becoming more of an accepted practice. In a 2022 study by McKinsey & Company, researchers found that more than half of a nationwide pool of respondents from both blue-collar and white-collar professions reported having the opportunity to telework from home at least one day a week.[33] In the wake of the pandemic, the workforce had come to expect flexibility as a necessity, not just a perk—a flexible work schedule ranked behind only greater pay and better career opportunities as one of the top reasons

28. Williams, *supra* note 8, at 127.
29. Ahranjani, *Sprinting a Marathon*, *supra* note 27, at 235–36.
30. Williams, *supra* note 8, at 94–95.
31. *Id.* at 95.
32. *Id.* at 95–97.
33. André Dua et al., *Americans Are Embracing Flexible Work——And They Want More of It*, McKinsey & Co. (June 23, 2022), https://www.mckinsey.com/industries/real-estate/our-insights/americans-are-embracing-flexible-work-and-they-want-more-of-it.

employees are motivated to look for a new job.[34] This is especially true of the younger generations of employees. Millennials rate work-life balance as the second most valued benefit in the workplace behind only training and development.[35] Gen Z, whose early professional careers came of age in the uncertainty of the pandemic, unsurprisingly values stability above all else but also places a high premium on flexibility and an employer's "healthy respect for individuality."[36]

Given these desires and the ever-increasing prevalence of remote technologies, and considering that flexible working arrangements reduce turnover while also increasing employee health and productivity, the traditional 9-to-5 no longer makes sense.[37] In fact, research shows that a mandate for a complete return to office during normal business hours does not increase productivity and that a more balanced and flexible approach to both location and time might be a middle ground that results in a win-win for employees and employers alike.[38]

Nevertheless, it remains to be seen if the recent push back to fixed working hours in office spaces is merely a temporary regression or a further entrenchment into the relative safety of the status quo. While some requirements to return to the office were expected in both the public and private sectors in the wake of the pandemic, it remains to be seen whether organizations will stay with an all-or-nothing approach. If companies can begin to see flexible work schedules as a win-win for both employers and employees, and such schedules become less of an exception to outdated concepts of normal business hours, the stigma that accompanies flexibility should proportionally diminish. But the battle against the flexibility stigma is a war of attrition that requires efforts on two fronts—changing policies and changing mindsets.

Progressive Policies

Ensuring that policies are in place to support flexible work schedules is the low-hanging fruit in the fight to suppress the flexibility stigma. Increasing opportunities for remote work, decreasing the number of days in the office, and allowing nontraditional work hours outside the normal 9-to-5 and Monday to Friday have already been discussed and should be liberally employed. Even the

34. *Id.*

35. WILLIAMS, *supra* note 8, at 209.

36. Berger & Ivanova, *supra* note 18.

37. Seaver, *supra* note 5; Madeleine Gyory, *Legislating Flexibility in the Post-Pandemic Workplace*, 69 VILL. L. REV. 209, 215 (2024).

38. Taylor Telford & Danielle Abril, *Companies' Hard-Line Stance on Returning to the Office Is Backfiring*, WASH. POST (Feb. 2, 2024, at 17:35), https://www.washingtonpost.com/technology/2024/02/02/return-to-office-punishments-remote-hybrid-work/.

military has had to rethink its telework policies during COVID-19. The U.S. Space Force, which has prided itself on not being tied to legacy systems or traditional notions of how the other armed forces do business, announced that it is working on, and getting closer to, enabling employees to work on classified tasks at home.[39]

Organizations should also plan for employees to take longer absences from the office, whether it be for maternal/paternal leave, professional sabbaticals, or other circumstances. One mitigation strategy is to create work cohorts—partners or small teams collectively working on similar cases or projects that can easily flex and cover for an individual who is absent from the office for any period of time. The fortunate byproduct of such small cross-functional teams, if managed correctly, is that they can combat single points of failure and silo thinking that stifle the creativity necessary for organizations to tackle complex problems.[40]

Legally speaking, leaders need to note that because "research indicates a strong link between workplace flexibility and maternal wall bias," there is a colorable argument that penalizing a woman under such conditions could be considered actionable as gender discrimination.[41] That might seem extreme, but at the very least, this is an area ripe for new legislation.[42] In 2023, lawmakers reintroduced legislation to reduce the federal government's definition of the standard workweek from 40 to 32 hours.[43] Ironically, the original draft of the Fair Labor Standards Act back in 1932 called for a 30-hour week, but, like flexibility options now, it met with virulent backlash.[44] Nevertheless, some argue that the current proposed legislation does not go far enough—beyond limiting the workweek, future proposed bills could provide for comprehensive flexible workplace laws to provide flexible work arrangements to benefit not only caregivers but also a broad spectrum of workers, regardless of age, income, education, race, and gender.[45]

---

39. Lauren C. Williams, *Space Force Inches Closer to Classified Remote Work*, DEF. ONE (May 24, 2024), https://www.defenseone.com/defense-systems/2024/05/space-force-inches-closer-classified-remote-work/396900/.

40. *See* GEN. STANLEY MCCHRYSTAL, TEAM OF TEAMS: NEW RULES OF ENGAGEMENT FOR A COMPLEX WORLD (2015).

41. 29 C.F.R. § 825 (2013); WILLIAMS, *supra* note 8, at 117 n.9 (citing in endnote Bostock v. Clayton Cnty., 139 S. Ct. 2049 (2019); Back v. Hastings on Hudson Union Free Sch. Dist., 365 F.3d 107 (2nd Cir. 2004)).

42. Stephanie Bornstein, *The Legal and Policy Implications of the "Flexibility Stigma"*, 69 J. SOC. ISSUES 389, 390–91 (2013).

43. Thirty-Two Hour Workweek Act, H.R. 4728, 117th Cong. (2021).

44. Gillian Brockell, *That Time America Almost Had a 30-Hour Workweek*, WASH. POST (Sep. 6, 2021), https://www.washingtonpost.com/history/2021/09/06/40-hour-work-week-fdr/.

45. Gyory, *supra* note 37; *see also* Bornstein, *supra* note 42.

Intentional Leadership

However, even the greatest policies cannot attack the flexibility stigma alone. To create an inclusive workplace culture, organizations have to also change the mindset associated with requesting, granting, and utilizing flexible work options or otherwise risk theoretically useful policies being undermined by biases in practice.[46] Intentionally engaged and empathetic leadership can address all five of the flexibility stigma's myths: the loss of (1) control; (2) culture; (3) collaboration; (4) contribution; and (5) connection.[47] By using basic leadership principles, leaders can reframe how their teams think about work.

First and foremost, effective leaders should provide clear expectations to their teams and reprioritize efforts to focus on the work produced, not on where or when it is produced. This includes taking the time to set performance objectives at the outset of superior-subordinate relationships, regularly scheduled and in-stride evaluations to review expectations and either validate or redirect an employee's efforts, and then periodic, holistic performance reviews that focus on "the quality of their work and their ability to meet clearly defined performance objectives, rather than on time spent in the office."[48] Supervisors then must also provide the right environment and structure for each individual, and the team collectively, to succeed. This starts with knowing your people and having a genuine concern for their welfare so you can properly set them and your organization up for success. Learning about their goals, concerns, personal preferences, et cetera, will help you understand their challenges and whether there are simple adjustments that could be made to make employees happier, healthier, and more productive.[49]

In that context, leaders cannot overlook the power of setting the example. Even if managers generously grant flexible working arrangements to others, the sentiment might ring hollow if they do not utilize the same policies themselves. The old-school nose-to-the-grindstone mentality might lead some to believe they must be the first in and last out of the office, must always be available for telephone calls, or must reply to emails during vacation time or in the middle of the night. But the negative consequence is that followers will assume not only that the leader prioritizes work above all else but also that

---

46. Bornstein, *supra* note 42, at 391; Tony Schwartz, *Leaders Focus Too Much on Changing Policies, and Not Enough on Changing Minds*, Harv. Bus. Rev. (June 25, 2018), https://hbr.org/2018/06/leaders-focus-too-much-on-changing-policies-and-not-enough-on-changing-minds.

47. Manar Morales & Ivan Misner, *5 Myths About Flexible Work*, Harv. Bus. Rev. (June 3, 2021), https://hbr.org/2021/06/5-myths-about-flexible-work.

48. *Id.*

49. *See* Christine Ro, *How Overwork Is Literally Killing Us*, BBC (May 19, 2021), https://www.bbc.com/worklife/article/20210518-how-overwork-is-literally-killing-us (discussing the health risks of not having a balance between home and work life).

they should follow suit, and flexible work options are not for anyone who aspires to be successful or advance in the organization. Such practices just add fuel to the flexibility stigma fire, where the goal becomes simply being seen at work instead of actually working.

Yet, while actions speak louder than words, the latter still must accompany the former. The only way to mitigate biases is to acknowledge, discuss, and discredit them. Leaders must be prepared to have open conversations and group training that ensure that individuals and teams have meaningful connections with one another and counter the otherwise harmful narratives that accompany the flexibility stigma.[50] A suggested starting point would be to debunk the notion that any time a person is not in the office is equivalent to time off. For example, parental leave is anything but a vacation, as anyone who has had to deal with a newborn baby at all hours of the night and day while simultaneously either recovering, or helping a significant other recover, from childbirth will tell you. One way to reframe how a team thinks about maternal or paternal leave is to offer a different point of view: consider that the individual has new or heightened skills to offer the organization, with "new expertise at handling many different demands at once on little sleep."[51] Finally, the organization needs to send a strong message that both men and women are not just allowed but *expected* to take the full duration of the allotted parental leave.[52]

Conclusion

In the end, combating the flexibility stigma takes a healthy corporate culture built on a strong relationship of trust between the leader, the follower, and the organization to build cohesive and productive teams that are impervious to its deleterious effects.[53] This starts with sensible policies that equitably treat each employee with fairness and are visibly supported throughout the organization. But, more importantly, it requires a fundamental shift in the attitudes individuals have toward using those flexibility policies. Understanding the historical context and the ebbs and flows that have already occurred in defining the workday helps to demonstrate that business hours and workplaces are simply artificial constructs that have changed before and can change again. Effective leaders must see flexible working options as an opportunity to strengthen

50. Alvarez et al., *supra* note 15.
51. Williams, *supra* note 8, at 123.
52. *Id.* at 125.
53. Francoise Contreras, Elif Baykal & Ghulam Abid, *E-Leadership and Teleworking in Times of COVID-19 and Beyond: What We Know and Where Do We Go*, 11 Frontiers in Psych. (Dec. 2020).

workplaces, not as a burden to be borne. We should define the value of employees' performance not by when or the amount of time they spend in the office, but by the quality of the work they produce.

Change is possible, but change is hard. COVID-19 did not just shift how we thought about the workplace; it also prompted Dolly Parton to rework the lyrics of her hit song to reflect the changing times. In an homage to a new generation of "entrepreneurs who keep unorthodox hours," she created a new version of the classic tune called "5 to 9" for a 2021 Super Bowl ad.[54] If the timeless Dolly Parton can change her iconic song to reflect the times, then so too should we change how we work and how we think about work to meet the needs of the modern-day working professional.

54. Jordan Hoffman, *Dolly Parton Tells Jimmy Fallon How "9 to 5" Became "5 to 9"*, VANITY FAIR (Feb. 6, 2021), https://www.vanityfair.com/hollywood/2021/02/dolly-parton-tells-jimmy-fallon-how-9-to-5-became-5-to-9.

CHAPTER SIX

Moving Past Survival: Operationalizing Equity Through Transparent Policies, Training, and Support

Aubony Burns

Key Chapter Points

- How to listen first to create culture change in a place where people report they are "surviving the organization"
- How King County, Washington's Prosecuting Attorney's Office created transparent pay policies
- Intentional leadership, outside consultants, pay analyses that are regularly reviewed
- Using research to support policy changes
- Practicing criminal law is a calling
- The critical importance of supervisors modeling good behavior and work/life balance
- How to move past "surviving the organization" to thriving

Introduction

This chapter discusses, from the vantage of a female criminal trial attorney in a large metropolitan prosecutor's office, the challenges, successes, and barriers of an office moving toward a more equitable work environment for similarly situated attorneys. The chapter will discuss why transparency is important, the movement toward transparent policies and training, and the related continued challenges. The purpose of this chapter is to show a snapshot of some policies that a prosecutor's office has taken toward creating a more equitable workplace.

1. Why the Need for Transparent Policies Regarding Gender Equity?

This is a well-researched topic in the larger world, the legal world, and corporate America. Any internet search on "gender pay equity," "transparent pay policies," or similar phrases will result in plenty of source material and white papers describing the changes in pay equities when policies are made transparent. The Biden White House National Strategy on Gender Equity and Equality highlights the importance of strengthening women's economic security and labor force participation and notes that it is not just essential to advancing gender equity and equality but that our nation's economy and the global economy cannot reach their full potential when women are left behind in the workforce.[1]

Prosecutors are by nature concerned about their commitment to the community served and the trust the community has in the Prosecutor's Office. Women employees play a key role in that trust. According to *Toughen Up Buttercup* (TUB), the Women in Criminal Justice Task Force's first report[2] on the statistics of women in the criminal justice field, many studies indicate that the presence and leadership of women in criminal justice reduce corruption. This is incredibly important in a time when community trust in our legal systems is actively degraded on a national scale. TUB further identifies how female and child victims often feel more comfortable with female attorneys. Further, TUB details through its research that victims, defendants, and jurors from marginalized groups are more likely to participate in the system in a positive way when they perceive that the attorneys reflect their own social identities and believe that the attorneys can understand their experiences and empathize with them.[3]

---

1. *National Strategy on Gender Equity and Equality*, The White House (2021), https://bidenwhitehouse.archives.gov/wp-content/uploads/2021/10/National-Strategy-on-Gender-Equity-and-Equality.pdf.

2. Maryam Ahranjani, *"Toughen Up, Buttercup" versus #TimesUp: Initial Findings of the ABA Women in Criminal Justice Task Force*, 25(2) Berkeley J. Crim. L. 100 (2020).

3. *Id.* at 104.

2. Movement Toward Transparent Policies, Training, and Support

Since 1935, the King County Prosecuting Attorney's Office (KCPAO) has had only seven elected Prosecuting Attorneys, including the current elected prosecutor, Leesa Manion. Prior to Prosecutor Manion, Dan Satterberg held the position for sixteen years, taking over when his predecessor, Norm Maleng, died in office. Satterberg was Maleng's Chief of Staff, and Maleng served the community as the elected prosecutor for twenty-eight years, one of the longest tenures in Washington State. Prior to being elected, Manion was Satterberg's Chief of Staff. In government offices, this type of consistency in leadership over time is rare. Manion, who is Asian American, is the first woman and person of color elected to the position and worked in the office her entire career before being elected as Prosecutor. The introduction of equity trainings and policies began during her time as Chief of Staff and have continued to evolve as she has taken over. This chapter is informed by conversations with Prosecutor Manion and Carla Lee (Manion's Chief of Staff), HR Director Hazel Johnson, Senior Deputy Prosecuting Attorneys Jina Kim, Ann Summers, Samaneh Alizadeh, and many current and former criminal Deputy Prosecuting Attorneys (DPAs).

Gender equity is seen by office leadership as one of many issues where an equitable lens needs to be applied. Trainings on unconscious bias, inequities in the justice system, historical trauma, and the like have been offered for going on ten years now, some optional, most mandatory. These trainings are part of what Prosecutor Manion and Chief of Staff Lee describe as a necessary part of culture change toward an equitable work environment. Trainings have provided employees with a vocabulary they did not have before, a vocabulary that allowed them to describe issues and concerns employees should be aware of as public servants serving our community. For instance, the term "microaggression" was a new term for many. Understanding terms and learning to identify them not only makes for a more insightful office but also develops skills in criminal trial attorneys that aid them in jury selection and connecting with juries from the community we serve.

In 2019 the KCPAO hired an outside consultant to assess whether it was paying its DPAs consistently among the (then) four Divisions, or even within any given Division.[4] The consultant was assigned to work with office leadership

4. The KCPAO employs hundreds of attorneys in several Divisions focusing on different types of law, in both criminal and civil courts; represents the county in legal matters; and provides legal guidance to county agencies and administrators. In 2019 there were four Divisions: Criminal, Juvenile, Civil, and Family Support. There are now six: Mainstream Criminal Division (criminal practice), Gender Based Violence Division (criminal practice), Juvenile Division (criminal practice), Economic Crimes and Wage Theft Division (criminal practice), Civil Division, and Family Support Division.

to conduct a pay analysis and review of DPA pay structure and practices. The goals of the consultant's analysis were to

- review the DPA pay structure for consistency throughout the office,
- establish criteria and expectations for each of our Senior DPA levels (which did not exist prior to the analysis), and
- determine if there were pay adjustments to be considered within the KCPAO.

The consultant's analysis revealed that there were inconsistencies within the KCPAO's DPA pay practices. Leadership then took steps to share the results of the analysis, to implement more consistent criteria, and to identify DPAs who, based on the criteria, deserved a pay adjustment. The KCPAO implemented those pay adjustments in 2022.

The analysis also led to the KCPAO establishing criteria for promotional movement to Senior DPA levels, clarified and improved communication regarding the movement between Senior DPA levels by creating a rubric to guide these decisions, and created the Talent Review and Opportunity, Performance, Pay, and Evaluations (OPPEN) committees, whose purpose is to annually review all senior DPAs and make recommendations to the elected Prosecutor regarding potential merit pay and promotions. Salary decisions are now made with committee input and recommendations. The analysis also led to the establishment of a tool, process, and timing for DPA coaching and professional development and created a Senior DPA self-evaluation form and process that provides additional input for the committee to review.

While the analysis and adjustments were being finalized in 2022, then-Chief of Staff Manion and then-Deputy Chief of Staff Carla Lee assigned senior female attorneys from a noncriminal division to conduct a listening tour of current and former women DPAs in the Criminal Division in response to many senior women DPAs departing from or rotating out of the Criminal Division. It was important to have attorneys from outside of the Criminal Division conduct the sessions to have a more impartial view of the issues raised in the division. While the number of women leaving KCPAO criminal roles was of great concern, this may have been part of a national trend explored in depth by author and then-University of New Mexico law professor Maryam Ahranjani in her 2021 report summarizing the initial findings of the ABA Women in Criminal Justice Task Force.[5]

I participated in the Task Force's listening tour and had briefed then-Chief of Staff Manion on my involvement. When Ahranjani and the Task Force came out with their initial findings, I provided them to both Manion and Lee. Manion sought to learn at an office level what was having an impact on women

5. Ahranjani, *supra* note 2.

criminal lawyers and why they were leaving the practice locally. The purpose for the tour as described by Manion was to learn whether there are cultural or institutional challenges within the KCPAO that were contributing to the exodus of women from the Criminal Division and, if so, to better understand those challenges.

Soon after Manion took office, a report was released to all KCPAO employees. The internal report included anonymized comments relayed by a wide variety of women from the Criminal Division about their lived experiences. Reading the internal report was hard for many, including me. It was jarring, heartbreaking, and rage inducing in many ways. After reading it, however, many felt a new sense of camaraderie because of the shared experiences of inequality and negativity. Of note to many was the written acknowledgment by Prosecutor Manion that many women experienced unfair pay and opportunity while working in the Criminal Division. Manion noted that she hoped sharing the information would be a first step in healing the deep hurt and pain that many women experienced in a path toward restoration, remedy, and repair.[6]

2023 Pay Analysis Project

When Manion left her role as the Chief of Staff to begin her first term as the elected prosecutor in January 2023, she and her team immediately began another pay analysis project, the "2023 Pay Analysis Project." That project was described to employees as part of KCPAO's ongoing efforts to adjust and modernize our office's DPA pay structure.

Prosecutor Manion and Chief of Staff Lee were clear when we spoke and in the materials provided about the 2019 outside analysis that resulted in 2022 leveling of pay for many employees who were underpaid that the analysis was not a "one and done." They stated that the KCPAO must, from time to time, review its pay structure and practices to pay its employees consistently throughout all parts of the office. To conduct the 2023 Pay Analysis Project, leadership pulled together a team of KCPAO leaders, including Human Resources and representatives from different Divisions, to engage in the next phase of our pay analysis review. The team included the Chief of Staff, the Director and Deputy Director of Human Resources, an Assistant Chief from the Civil Division with 30-plus years of employment law experience, the Chief of Criminal Operations, and the Director of Budget and Finance. The team sought input and review from each of the now six Division Chiefs and Assistant Chiefs and the adult criminal practice Talent Review Committee.

That team gathered the salary information for every DPA in the KCPAO. They organized this data into "cohorts" by using bar admission date because it was an

6. *Id.*

easy and objective way to sort the data. Sorting the data this way also allowed them to more easily identify and consider a DPA's total length of service as an attorney, particularly for those who had prior experience in another jurisdiction, in private practice, or in another legal context, such as a judicial clerkship.

When they examined the data, the team discerned that most (but not all) DPAs were paid within a consistent range for each bar admission year/cohort. Our pay analysis team identified some outliers. Those outliers generally fell into three main categories:

- DPAs whose prior legal experience may not have been recognized,
- DPAs who worked part-time for some portion of their career and returned to full-time work (**a majority of these were mothers**), and
- DPAs whose body of work or practice area was especially complex or required a special expertise not previously recognized.

When the pay analysis review team was finished, they provided a summary of their work to the KCPAO in both written and presentation formats. Employees learned through that transparent reporting that the team met weekly for most of 2023 to identify ways to value the depth of experience DPAs (from all Divisions) bring to the KCPAO. Prior to providing the summary, the team met with impacted DPAs individually to share with them how they would be impacted. Once the work was presented to the office, the team also offered to meet with DPAs not impacted who were interested to learn where they were situated compensation-wise. The team advised employees that the following are some of the principles that guided their analysis and work:

- Addressing the themes and values identified in the 2021 Women's Listening Tour:
  - Valuing part-time work
  - Valuing committee work[7]
- Valuing Race Equity and Social Justice (RESJ) work
- Acknowledging all leadership roles
- Acknowledging DPAs' prior legal experience, including experience in other jurisdictions or private practice
- Adjusting pay to acknowledge a DPA's expertise, leadership, work accomplishments, and other work-related criteria

7. The KCPAO has for several years now, since before the pandemic, engaged in committee work to highlight equity and social justice issues, criminal practice issues, and caseload concerns. Committee work has been unpaid and voluntary and has been done by DPAs and legal service professionals alike to find better ways to serve the community. Many practice and policy changes come from committees, but historically participation in these committees has not been officially assessed for promotional opportunities or pay.

The PAO pay structure and compensation practices will be reviewed on a two-year cycle. The team advised that as a result of the 2023 work, 43 DPAs were identified who will receive an upward pay adjustment, of whom **30 were women.**

PAO Diversity Report Card

During the 2020 pandemic, the KCPAO established Equity Action Groups (EAGs), committees to focus on issues identified in a Deputy Prosecuting Attorney Association letter and memo as potentially impacting justice and service to the community. One such group was a "Diversify PAO" group that raised concerns about the KCPAO not representing the community it serves through employee representation. In addition to the concern of senior experienced women leaving the criminal division, the EAG raised concerns about recruitment and retention of women and people of color. In January 2022, after performing an analysis of available data on the then-current makeup of attorneys and legal service professionals across all divisions broken down by gender, race, age, salary, and years with the office, the Diversify the PAO EAG Data Collection & Reporting subgroup recommended to the leadership team that the office hire a professional with expertise in data analytics to develop an Annual Report Card. The purpose of the Annual Report Card is to measure the impact of Diversity, Inclusion, Equity & Belonging (DIEB) efforts within the KCPAO and identify and remove barriers to the recruitment, hiring, promotion, and retention of diverse candidates from historically excluded communities.

The KCPAO hired a different consultant than the 2019 analysis consultant with the goal of developing a model RESJ Report Card that the office can use to measure progress on an annual basis. The information will be used to identify and ultimately focus on sustainable policies and practices to promote a healthy and productive work environment. The consultant is a small, Native American–owned and –operated consulting group with extensive experience in data analytics and a history of being a pro-equity and anti-racism equity and belonging group.

Senior DPA Jina Kim, a DPA in our Civil Division, described the objective of the consultant's work is to produce a dashboard and report that will serve as the basis for an annual survey and report card that measures how effective our equity practices are in reaching the desired outcome. The consultant will provide guidance about identifying the type of data to collect, how to engage employees, and how to plan for changing practices to improve equity outcomes. The consultant will also make recommendations to create a more inclusive environment for everyone at the KCPAO. The work is ongoing, updates are periodic, and employees have been provided with multiple opportunities to engage with the consultant.

Women's Listening Session

The aftereffects of the 2022 Women's Listening Tour report have been widespread. The report affected women who took part in deep, painful ways. It also served to bring together women in the criminal division in a more cohesive way than before, both officially and unofficially. Officially, Carla Lee, the current Chief of Staff, and her HR team hosted additional opportunities to share, listen, and learn.

The Women's Listening Session (WLS) team reviewed TUB and Ahranjani's subsequent Task Force reports. They also spent much time with the resulting ABA Resolution 501: Ten Principles to Achieve Gender Equity in the Criminal Legal Profession included in Chapter Two. In April, the WLS announced the adoption of the Ten Principles, modified for the KCPAO to reflect the needs and desires of the office and acknowledge progress already made. The WLS announced the Ten Principles as tools that will establish clear guideposts to focus the WLS's ongoing work on gender equity at the KCPAO. The adopted principles were shared at an officewide presentation in early June 2024.

The WLS is also currently developing ways to reduce barriers and ensure more women apply to and serve in leadership roles. WLS is working in conjunction with office leadership to identify leadership training and coaching opportunities for women (not just attorneys) to enhance support and to promote innovative practices to encourage women to pursue professional development opportunities. RESJ trainings are constantly being sought and developed for employees and are highlighted by WLS updates as well as advertised to a broader officewide audience.

3. Support: Continued Challenges and the Future

I have spoken with several senior women as well as Prosecutor Manion and her Chief of Staff, Carla Lee, about the changes we've experienced together at the office since 2020. One concern I inquired about was how the budget concerns and loss of COVID funding would impact equity goals. Chief Lee and Prosecutor Manion were clear that continued work on gender equity issues was always going to be a priority. Manion, who has spent decades in the office working her way up through the civil division from a line prosecutor, described wanting to turn the office from a place where women are simply "surviving the organization" to get to retirement into a place where they are thriving and leading.

Hearing Manion say "surviving the organization" hit me incredibly hard. So many of the women I spoke to about the office's pay analysis and pay structure changes are still reeling from the listening tour. The reality of decades of inequity is not lost on them. The compounding effect of pay disparity on women was not something fixed by the leveling related to the consultants or the 2023 Pay Analysis. We know that those women who did receive pay adjustments to level them up did not also see their retirement plans adjusted or increased. It has been hard on many to learn just how impactful the disparities over the decades have been to our sisters, especially in the criminal division. Knowledge gained during the process has in some instances changed trajectories and career choices women make.

This is compounded by hurt and exhaustion. Learning we were not alone in our experiences through the listening tour was enlightening. We learned we all had experienced very similar, very bad, gender-based acts over the years that went unaddressed and unacknowledged. We discovered a shared trauma. In the Criminal Division specifically, the challenges are great. Women continue to feel spoken down to by male judges and attorneys and even male colleagues with less experience. When such behaviors are reported to line supervisors, excuses are often made for the individual rather than addressing the harm caused, even when the individual is a judge or opposing counsel. There are known bad actors in our local courts who have treated female judges, defense attorneys, and DPAs disrespectfully over the years. Rather than address the behavior head on, there is a "that's just who he is" attitude that prevails. These men are avoided, and warnings are given about them. Female prosecutors and defense attorneys have often found themselves being witness to poor behavior and coming up with ways to help each other navigate. A common navigation technique includes not going into the courtroom without opposing counsel present to be a witness. Safety in numbers is a strategy for women that exists in King County beyond just walking to and from a parking garage.

The post-pandemic caseload is crushing, and the KCPAO, like offices across the country, is having to make hard choices to keep the system from imploding. All this equity work highlighted what women in the KCPAO already know, that criminal law is more than just a job. For most it is a calling, a desire, and a compulsion to serve others. The work itself is personality shaping. The current situation, which is arguably worse than before the pandemic, highlights that exhaustion. The ownership and care women DPAs have toward this calling of a career results in unequal work-life balance. That lack of work-life balance can and does fuel feelings of discontent.

So what do senior women criminal attorneys who have survived and thrived for decades in the office before the positive changes and transparent policy shifts of the current administration think will help support women? Resoundingly they want to see supervisors model good behavior and work-life balance. Supervisors should support line DPAs by actively encouraging work-life balance. Supervisors should be pushing DPAs to use their leave, to get space away from the secondary trauma that permeates every criminal practice division. Leadership should be encouraging qualified women to apply for supervisory positions. Long term change will require a true culture change, and many feel we are on the path.

I spoke with a senior woman attorney about "surviving the organization" versus thriving. She has been a mentor of mine for a decade now and has watched over me like a mother hawk since I was a "baby deputy." She said that only we can make healthy choices for ourselves and that we need to. She clarified that these healthy choices are necessary for the culture change we seek. By making these choices, we not only are modeling good behavior but also are changing expectations for the less senior women coming up behind us. For example, encouraging women to push back on bully judges when supervisors will not address concerns. Like attorneys across the country, female attorneys here have experienced judges who force pregnant attorneys to skip prenatal doctor appointments and will not work around childbirth schedules despite agreed continuances; these attorneys have had less than positive results from KCPAO supervisors when issues are raised. Having broad goals of equity without support from middle management can make for a frustrating environment.

The KCPAO has just developed a Women's Equity Action Group (WEAG), helmed by Samaneh Alizadeh and Ann Summers, two senior attorneys who recently returned to the adult criminal practice divisions after many years.[8] Their stated goals are to share experiences and insights, support and uplift the experience of women/femme identifying employees, and use those experiences and insights to inform advocacy for increased transparency, equity, and inclusivity in the office. Support is communication. Support is modeling good behavior. Support is kindness. By supporting each other, we support our leaders who have often been overlooked because of gender. This is necessary for culture change—support empowers women leaders to continue to make strides to dismantle the structures and practices that have left women behind.

8. While the KCPAO continues to lose senior attorneys, like all prosecution offices, of note are recent returns beyond the two mentioned. We have had multiple senior women attorneys return to the criminal practice divisions from civil divisions but have also had several recently return or lateral in from various other government agencies (other county prosecutor offices, Western District of U.S. Attorney's Office, Washington Attorney General Office, and the City of Seattle).

CHAPTER SEVEN

Why Do Judges Matter? And What Can Judges Do?

the Honorable Bernice B. Donald, the Honorable Denise Langford Morris, the Honorable Gloria Ochoa-Bruck, the Honorable Rachel Pickering, and Sarah Redfield

Key Chapter Points

- Isolation felt by judges
- Resilience and hard work are keys to success
- The more things change, the more they stay the same
- The power of women supporting women
- Reflections on the Ten Principles
- Path to judgeships
- More women in law school likely means more women judges one day
- Advice for would-be judges

Introduction: Maryam Ahranjani

In 2016, a criminal defendant appeared in Judge Amber Wolf's courtroom in Louisville, Kentucky, for shoplifting.[1] The woman's female attorney told Judge Wolf that her client was denied pants and feminine hygiene products during the entire three days she spent in jail. Outraged, Judge Wolf made national headlines and a video capturing the hearing went viral. Judge Wolf, who served

1. Lindsey Bever, *"She Has No Pants and She Is in Court": Judge Outraged over Inmate's Appearance*, Wash. Post (Aug. 1, 2016), https://www.washingtonpost.com/news/morning-mix/wp/2016/08/01/am-i-in-the-twilight-zone-a-judges-reaction-to-a-bare-legged-defendant-in-court/.

as both a defense attorney and a prosecutor prior to her election to judge, demanded an explanation from the Louisville Metro Department of Corrections and released the woman with a $100 fine and time served. Less than a week later, a second video in Judge Wolf's courtroom went viral when she temporarily suspended a no-contact order so a defendant could hold his newborn child for the first time before he went back to jail.[2]

Judges play a critical role in promoting equity and compassion in the criminal legal system. We learned this through our various listening sessions. They possess the power to manage the court schedules, set the tone and mood in the courtroom, set and maintain decorum rules, sanction attorneys and other criminal system actors such as law enforcement officers who engage in disrespectful behavior, and blow the whistle on discrimination, among other levers.

We also learned in our listening sessions that women judges of color and women judges with other identities such as LGBTQ+ face more complex challenges. Not only did many of them experience familial obligations, overcome financial burdens, and manage other complications related to entry into the profession, but they also entered a profession filled with bias and inequity. Women judges with layered identities occupy an important place of power in that they often relate to the women appearing before them, but have the power to do something about the systemic barriers to equity.

When I decided to create this book, I knew that hearing from judges would be critical to telling the story of how we get to gender equity in criminal law. And I knew that Professor Sarah Redfield would be the perfect person to facilitate the storytelling. Professor Redfield was a member of the ABA Criminal Justice Section (CJS) Women in Criminal Justice Task Force, and she is an expert in, among other things, implicit bias. She and another Task Force member—Judge Bernice Donald—are editors of *Extending Justice: Strategies to Increase Inclusion and Reduce Bias*. In that book, they employ an engaging format of interviewing high-level experts in several chapters. Inspired by their approach, I asked Professor Redfield to adopt the same one with this chapter.

A Note from the Interviewer

I was honored and privileged when Professor Ahranjani asked me to interview these jurists and contribute a chapter to this important book. I was part of the CJS's Women's Task Force that inspired this work—and all of us. Preparing for this interview, I reflected again on what we had heard across the country

2. Alysia Santo, *Kentucky Judge Amber Wolf on Her Newfound Internet Stardom*, The Marshall Project (Aug. 10, 2016), https://www.themarshallproject.org/2016/08/10/kentucky-judge-amber-wolf-on-her-newfound-internet-stardom.

in the Task Force listening sessions. Then, by talking with the women interviewed here, I reflected again on my experience in the profession, in the academy, in the public sector—and in life writ larger as the mother of a fabulous son and daughter.

The women I interviewed for this chapter are Judges Bernice Donald (U.S. Court of Appeals for the Sixth Circuit, retired), Rachel Pickering (Kansas Court of Appeals), Gloria Ochoa-Bruck (Spokane, Washington Municipal Court), and Denise Langford Morris (Oakland County, Michigan Circuit Court, retired). They are all women of color with significant experience as both criminal lawyers and judges, and we all served on the ABA Women in Criminal Justice Task Force together.

I find that I am both saddened and encouraged. I am saddened because many of our stories today are the same stories I could have told when I first started working more than fifty years ago. I am encouraged because they are not exactly the same. There are many more women in law schools and in the profession now, and their impact is both visible and significant. I am also encouraged by the enormous trend I see of women supporting other women. Judge Donald observes in this interview that she did not have a mentor, nor did I. I know that Judge Donald has gone on to mentor many women, as have I.

Looking to the future, now not only for my daughter but also for my granddaughters, this picture of mutual accomplishment and growth gives me hope. I invite our readers to be in touch with me or any of us to learn more about our work and our so-called work-life balances, or just to hear a friendly voice.

The Interview

The Path to Judgeship

Professor Sarah Redfield: I want to welcome you all to this opportunity to talk about the chapter entitled "Why Do Judges Matter? And What Can Judges Do?" This chapter and this book grew out of our work together on the American Bar Association Criminal Justice Section Women in Criminal Justice Task Force. The work for this Task Force brought us together with each other and with women across the country to share our learned and lived experience about the practice of law. I know I speak for all of us when I observe that the work of the Task Force was inspirational—perhaps even transformational—as we found common ground and common purpose in advancing the roles of women in the criminal legal system. These roles are many and changing. Here we are going to focus on one part of the profession, the judiciary. I very much look forward to your sharing your wisdom with me and our readers.

We begin with a question about how you all came to be judges. As we all know, judges become judges in a variety of ways, and I'm hoping each of you could talk about two points: first, about how you got your positions, and, second, about how your particular pathway has influenced what you do and what you think you can do and achieve as a judge in terms of promoting better and more equitable opportunities for women.

Judge Bernice Donald: Thank you for the opportunity to participate in this project. I was inspired to become a judge in response to an individual—a woman, as a matter of fact—whom I thought was being abused and basically denied her dignity in court. At that time, I was a Public Defender in Shelby County, Tennessee, and I represented a population that was really underserved—people who otherwise had no voice, people who were poor. I was in court one morning, waiting for my opportunity to talk to the prosecutor, and the judge was interviewing a woman in another case to see whether she qualified for representation by a public defender. This was an indigency determination. The woman was very pregnant, and she was somebody who obviously was not a regular in the court system. She had what appeared to me to be reverence and respect for the process and also an appropriate measure of fear and skepticism. The charge was shoplifting, by the way.

The judge began, as a lot of judges do, by asking for her name and for her source of income, and the woman replied, "Either welfare or AFDC." The judge then said, "I see that you are pregnant. How many children do you have?" The woman answered, and then the judge said, "Are you having more children so you can get a bigger welfare check?" At that point it got my full attention because that question had no legitimate place in that kind of determination. But the judge continued, asking the woman, "Do any of these children have the same father?" At that point, the assumptions and stereotypes were simply leaping into the fore. This was a woman who was probably about 4 foot 10 and pregnant and just seeking representation for this misdemeanor offense. The judge continued this line of questioning, asking, "Who is the father of this child?" At this point, the bailiff went over and hovered over the woman and said, "You heard the judge, who's the father of this child?"

At that moment, even though it was not my client, I was paying real attention. I thought, this can't be required. We know the Constitution and the laws provide that a person is innocent until proven guilty and has the right, when they're criminally accused, to have an attorney appointed to represent them. No one should have to sacrifice their dignity in order to get that attorney, to get justice. That experience, even though it wasn't my client, left me so moved and so angered that I decided that I would run for judge. I was a very young lawyer, but what I saw did not conform to anything I had learned in law school or in any of my readings about the law. I took this notion seriously—that every individual stands equal before the law and one's socioeconomic status, one's gender, one's race, none of that is supposed to matter in the cause of justice.

I saw this episode played out time and time again. Not those exact same questions, but I saw people without means who stood there before the court seeking justice, but often they were abused or denied dignity in the process. I decided that I could do better than that, because my belief was that every individual is presumed by the law to be innocent. Innocent or not, even when they come in saying "I'm guilty," they should still be accorded basic respect and human dignity. This is what caused me to run.

When I ran, it gave me an enormous opportunity to go into the community, to talk about justice, not to talk about that incident, but to talk about my hope for our justice system, my hope for what people could expect when they stood before the bench, what people could expect from judges. Judges are there to do a job. It's a difficult job by every measure. But it can be done well by judges who recognize that the people in their courtroom were hoping to receive a measure of justice based on their individual case and the law applied, based on the facts as found, not based on their socioeconomic, racial, or gender status. Running for this position gave me an opportunity to present myself as someone who looked a lot like the people in the community, who spoke to them, who saw them so that they were no longer cloaked with the veil of invisibility. I could and did see them in living color, see them as people who wanted to understand the law and who had hopes for the law.

My first position was an elected one. I made the commitment there that I would honor that pledge of respect and dignity for everyone, and I have done that for the length and breadth of my career.

Professor Redfield: Thank you, Judge Donald. We all know that you have done exactly that. I think I've already heard a likely theme in this interview, which is that women become judges, just as they enter many other professions, to give voice to others, to take our education—we are all very well educated in this group—and use it to benefit our communities. Judge Pickering?

Judge Rachel Pickering: Yes, my becoming a judge does go along with the same theme. I have served on both the District Court and Court of Appeals, and both are merit selection.

The reason I wanted to put in for judge is because I had a decade of criminal defense experience followed by years as a prosecutor. I had trial and appellate experience. I thought that with those perspectives I would be able to do a good job on the bench. I could use my experience to make sure that trials are done in a way that preserves a person's right to a fair trial. I had worked on appeals raising *Batson* issues, Fourth Amendment suppression issues. Because I was so keyed into these essential due process questions, I thought I could offer a lot to the bench. Also, I was encouraged to seek this office by people who approached me and said, "Maybe you should think about putting your name in." While it wasn't something I had been planning—I'm sure others have had that happen where others approached you—I put my name in.

For the District Court, I had a nominating committee of three judges and three laypeople. It's merit selection, so I was judged on my work. I was judged on how I spoke to others, including members of the bar. When the reviewers have the application, they contact attorneys who have been on the opposite side of cases from you. They talk to people about your temperament. They talk to people in the community. The nominating committee is just looking for good judges. This is helpful for women because it puts us on an equal footing with all the other candidates, and so that helped a lot.

It's the same with the Court of Appeals. Before the nominating committee sends three names to the governor, they look at the work that you've done with those in the bar, and they look at your experience and what you could offer to the bench. I think I've benefited from being in a merit selection process.

Professor Redfield: It's great that you put your name forward, and I applaud your state for having a system about which you can say you benefited from a merit selection process. It certainly doesn't surprise me to hear that in a merit system your merit would have been recognized. Still, it will come as no surprise that not all women are reviewed so fairly.

Judge Donald: At the end of the story, I did run for election, and I was successful. At that time in Shelby County, which was probably the most populous county in the state, there had only been two women judges before me, two White females. When I came along, I was the first African American female. I really believe it would have taken a very long time in Shelby County for us to have gotten to the bench had it not been for the electoral process, where we could take our case to the people. I respect the nominating process and have gone through a couple of selection processes since then. Judge Pickering, you are of course much younger than I am. Back during the time I came along—slightly after the Flintstone era—it was really difficult for women to break into the circle of judges.

Judge Pickering: Yes, we also have an election process for District Court judges, where men and women are both successful.

Professor Redfield: I think what we are seeing is that different processes provide different kinds of opportunities, and perhaps different kinds of difficulties, for women. Judge Ochoa-Bruck, is this in line with your experience?

Judge Gloria Ochoa-Bruck: I knew early in my career that someday I wanted to be a judge, and I knew I had to put my time in. I was very diligent. Like Judge Pickering, I was a prosecutor first, and then I did criminal defense, staying in federal courts. I also had the opportunity to work with the tribes around Spokane as a tribal court judge. I did some policy work for six years in criminal justice. Altogether, I felt that I did all the groundwork to be very well rounded and to be able to run competitively. In Washington, judges are all elected, but if there's a vacancy that comes open, then there's an appointment process with mayors. The Superior Court and appellate court positions are all gubernatorial appointees.

I had heard that it's a lot easier to get appointed and then run to retain your seat. Knowing the process is political in nature, I actually tried getting appointed seven times. I was either a closet Republican, or a raging Liberal, depending on the committee makeup. Even though I thought that I was showing myself as a balanced person, I didn't get an appointment. Then I had an opportunity to run for a seat that I had tried, and failed, to be appointed to three years prior. Now the person who had been appointed had to run to retain that seat. Since it was open, I decided, *the time is now*. I'd done all this work. I prepared myself. I ran in a contested election against the appointee, and I won. I'm very proud of myself. I was the first Latina judge in Spokane County history to be elected to the bench.

My inspiration was very similar to Judge Donald and Judge Pickering. I am a first-generation high school graduate in my family. My parents were undocumented farmworkers, and they did not speak English. As a little girl, I was their interpreter, and I saw injustices happen to our family because of language barriers. One thing that I bring to the bench is the commitment to make sure that there is accommodation for different education levels, different languages, different backgrounds and experiences.

Judicial practices and justice systems in different countries vary. For example, the justice system, as my parents describe it, is very different in Mexico. I started my career learning about other judicial or justice systems in other parts of the world. We have a lot of immigrants and refugees in our area. I'm very cognizant of possible differences between our system and theirs. I make sure that as a judicial officer I take the time to educate them about the differences so that they know what our system is, and they can navigate it.

These are the reasons I am where I am. I think it's a privilege to do this job. I'm sure my colleagues here can attest that it is a privilege and gives us great opportunities to really make sure that people have procedural justice and are treated with dignity and respect.

Professor Redfield: Judge Langford Morris, I'm going to have you close the circle on this question, but before I do, I'd like to add a layer for you to address and maybe others will chime in as well. I am struck once again by the extraordinary commitment you have all made to doing good for your communities, to using your experience and education to bring about a more fair, more just, more equitable system of justice for the communities you serve and for all of us. I'm wondering: if you can imagine for a minute if we were doing this interview with four men judges of about your own age and race/ethnicity, would I be hearing the same really strong voice for others that I'm hearing from you all? Judge Langford Morris, you're next. Maybe you can weave that into your answer.

Judge Langford Morris: Thank you, Professor. I appreciate the opportunity to respond to these in-depth questions and serve on this panel with these fantastic, amazing female jurists. This conversation is so important because the rule of law is so important. The independence of the judiciary is critical to the rule of law. We know the ABA and judges are under attack, and the ABA has stood up for our independence. All judges are being scrutinized and attacked and MUST support one another, as their importance in our democracy has never been greater in my humble opinion!

I started out not as an attorney, but an investigative social worker. My mother is the person who really encouraged me from the time I was a little girl to be involved in my community. I marched with Dr. King when I was ten years old. My mother took me to National Organization of Women meetings in downtown Detroit. I attended the Women's Conference of Concern with my mother. I became a joiner of certain organizations.

Before law school I had worked for six and a half years as an investigator focused on cases of child abuse and neglect, adult abuse and neglect, and mentally and physically challenged seniors. I had done thousands of home calls throughout the city of Detroit and Wayne County, where Detroit is located. I was very close to the legal system, and when I worked there, we actually presented the cases in court before they had prosecutors doing it. The social worker did the investigation and then presented the case. I met so many great lawyers and judges and referees, and people encouraged me to go to law school. I earned my masters in adult counseling and then went right to law school.

I, like all of these ladies, had a lot of experience as a litigator in my first full-time job as a prosecutor in Oakland County, where I ultimately served as the first Black judge. But when I walked into the office at the prosecutor's office, there wasn't an African American there. No one—no bosses, no secretaries, no attorneys, nothing. A hundred and ten people worked there, and I walked in and was the only Black employee. I was treated fairly. I had an opportunity to really get great experience. I handled every kind of criminal case you can think of. I think that it was the experience that I had and the culmination of that with the input from my parents that made me always care about people, and I viewed being a judge as public service.

People called me when a judge, the first woman judge on the Oakland Circuit Court, abruptly quit to run for Congress. There were hardly ever any judicial openings. There had never been an African American. I started getting phone calls because I served on the panel that made recommendations to the governor for judicial appointments. I wasn't really thinking about applying, because I had no clue how you could become a judge. I had been an investigative social worker, assistant prosecutor, private practitioner doing civil trial work at a law firm, and then Assistant United States Attorney in the Civil

Division. I loved my job in federal court where there were great judges that I appeared in front of all the time.

Twenty-seven people applied for the opening. I was the last person. I applied on the last day because I didn't think I had a chance. Not that I didn't want to be a judge, but I was encouraging other people to apply. As a founder of the Black Bar Association in Oakland County, I was encouraging other Black lawyers to apply. We had five out of the 27. I was the fifth. What I'm saying is that I knew that there was a strong need for an African American judge on that bench, and I knew that there were so many Black defendants in the criminal cases. I handled so many criminal cases, 55 jury trials in one year in Oakland County as a prosecutor. It was really a lot of work, but you saw the pain and suffering in defendants' eyes.

When I started, there was no diversity, not on the bench. Nor was there much diversity in the pro bono area where lawyers were appointed to represent criminal defendants. So I applied. I never dreamed that I would be appointed, but I was. I was appointed by Governor John Engler, who was one of the most conservative governors in the world. The governor shocked everyone when he appointed me. But I had a lot of experience. I had done about a hundred trials, state, federal, civil, and criminal. It was truly an honor.

I have to say that there are still not enough women and not enough minorities. I continue to work on this. Even though I'm recently retired as a jurist, I'm still very active in many ways, and I work hard to encourage young lawyers, young women in particular, to apply and run for judge, for all the reasons that have been said by these great jurists that are here in this conversation.

Judge Donald: Professor Redfield, you asked the question, if you were interviewing a panel of men, would you be likely to hear similar answers as to their motivation for serving on the bench and their approach, if you will, or their concern really about the human level of justice.

Let me preface this by saying on the front end that I don't believe that justice depends on any particular race or gender, sexual orientation, or socioeconomic status. I believe that every individual, from all races and ethnic backgrounds and genders, if they have a commitment to justice, they can do excellent work. For a case in point, there were no women or people of color on the United States Supreme Court when they decided *Brown v. Board of Education*, one of the most celebrated decisions in our history. In the exchange that I relayed earlier about what motivated me to become a judge, the person violating all of those standards and values that I hold dear was a woman.

You can have great judges who are male or female; you can have bad judges who are male and female. Still, I think you would have a different conversation, because the barriers that we faced getting there have not been there for most men. People have seen men as they came forward to this position almost as having a presumption of competence, a presumption of leadership and an excellent work ethic. Until you repaint the picture, until you break the ceiling, there's not that easy expectation for women. I think we're seeing more women on the bench now because our numbers in the profession are greater. Still, I believe you would hear men talking more about adherence to the rules. They might celebrate with pride their going through the selection process. But it's almost as if *judge* is synonymous with *male*, and we are comfortable with that focus from men. Not that they wouldn't care about the issues we've been discussing, but I don't believe that would be the lead in the story. That's one woman's perspective.

Isolation, Resilience

Professor Redfield: Thank you all. I'm going to pursue some of the themes that you've raised already and move on to another question. As you all know, we're doing this interview as a chapter of [*Women in Criminal Law: A Practical Guide for Inclusive and Thriving Workplaces*] to follow on the work of the Criminal Justice Section Task Force on Women in Criminal Justice.

The Task Force was concerned with why women lawyers leave the practice of criminal law. One of the things the Task Force did to answer this question was to conduct a series of listening sessions across the country. One of the very common themes in those listening sessions was what it was like for women practitioners when they're new and don't know their way around, don't know what the path is to step forward in their professions to a promotion or to a judgeship. A second very common theme was their isolation, not knowing who to ask and not knowing how to find the support that might be useful to them. To these I add my own layer of something I see in all of you, something I see in all of the professional women that I know and honor, and that is you have tremendous resilience. You have tremendous ability to not be pushed aside or pushed over or silenced.

I see all these things somehow coming together and hope you can speak about the isolation of your work, the need to have mentors, the call to be mentors. I consider your work to be extraordinarily important and difficult and your commitments to be extraordinarily courageous. It's clear you haven't forgotten your roots. How have you managed to stay centered? These are big questions, but I know you can do it. Judge Ochoa-Bruck, could we start with you?

Judge Ochoa-Bruck: I'm the first one, that is the first Latina that was elected in Spokane County. I'm the first person of color elected to my bench. I'm the first person that comes from outside the usual system. Everybody else has come in from either the city prosecutors or from the public defenders. I'm a complete and total outsider. One of the things that I have discovered is that when you're the first—and I stand on the shoulders of a lot of people who are in this position—when you get there, when you've worked so hard to break so many barriers to get there, when you do arrive, you're all alone. You have no one to support you.

One of the things that has been extremely valuable for me is that I've always appreciated having strong women friends in my social circles and in my life. They have just been an incredible source of support, so I can't emphasize enough how important it is for women entering this profession. The job itself is already inherently isolating, just with the nature of the job. This makes it important to have a really strong support system outside of court, perhaps with other women, other women lawyers who don't practice in your area and won't come before you. It's also been important to me to be able to reach out to other judges in other jurisdictions. For me, having spent years networking at the local and state level, and being involved with the Latina/Latino Bar Association and other bar opportunities, I have been able to find help when I needed a lifeline or advice. I have other women and other people that I can reach out to. Some of the most helpful people, honestly, have been White men, who have been allies, who have come in and been a champion for me. To sum up, I'd emphasize how important it is to be very broad and invest in your relationship building. That's just been invaluable.

Judge Pickering: The isolation certainly is there. Someone was kind enough to give me a membership in the National Association of Women Judges, a nationwide group of women judges. Isolation is addressed when we get together and talk. We get to share issues, get to share concerns that we have, share ways we've overcome a problem or obstacle. That has helped. Then your colleagues also help. For me, I practiced in front of the judges that I now work with. Already there was a respect there, and now I get to be their colleague. I just enjoy that relationship so much, to be able to exchange ideas like that. At the Court of Appeals, we judges are known for our collegiality.

In terms of resiliency, resiliency is necessary to serve on the bench. It's also important that we support others because we all get our batteries worn out and worn down. Yes, we are resilient, but sometimes we need to take a bit of a break and recognize that for ourselves and our colleagues.

Professor Redfield: Well, just when I thought you were all operating at 200 percent, all of the time.

Judge Langford Morris: I certainly relate to what's been shared thus far. I also had a different type of isolation in that I was a very young mother. When I graduated from high school, I had a six-month-old daughter. I missed two days of school, my senior year, and the only reason I missed those two days was because I believed the doctor when he said the date she'd be born, and I stayed home to wait for her to come. She didn't come that day, or the day after, but rather that weekend. So at any rate, I missed two days, but that isolation stuck with me.

All through law school I was going to school full time and working full time. I'd rush to pick my daughter up. She'd be in the backseat sometimes with some of the victims who had been abused or abandoned. My daughter became a big part of what I had to do in order to get through law school and become a lawyer, a trial lawyer, and then the first African American judge in Oakland County, a county that at that time was about 90 percent Republican and 95 percent White.

I had a mentor who was a fabulous Jewish woman. She was the first woman chair of the American Bar Association National State Trial Judges Conference. Her name was Hilda Gage. She was a remarkable woman. She had actually been in a law firm in Detroit with some great Black lawyers who themselves ultimately became judges. So thank God for Hilda, because there were so many times when I didn't have a clue.

My first six months on the bench, I had a case where my former boss, the prosecutor who had hired me as an assistant prosecutor, appeared in his last trial before taking over as the county executive. He was representing the son of a Democratic mayor. He was a phenomenal trial lawyer. He was trying this case in front of me as a new judge. The trial was done in days, but the jury deliberated for weeks. They never sent one note out. I called Hilda, who was my chief at the time, and admitted I didn't know what to do. You can't ask them what they're doing in there. They haven't sent out a note, and they're in there. I can hear them laughing. I don't know what's going on. They won't reach a verdict, and it's December. I had promised them that they would go on their Christmas vacations. The bottom line is, Judge Gage helped me so much with trying to stay strong and do that job. I appreciated the support. I was in an extremely busy court. At that time, I was getting 1,800 cases a year, family cases, civil and criminal, and appeals from the District Court and state agencies. So I was very, very busy and just thrown into it. But women helped me. To Judge Ochoa-Bruck's point, there were some men who stepped up to help me as well. They knew me because I had practiced in front of them, and they helped me. The isolation didn't feel nearly as bad as it could have because I had good people that cared.

Professor Redfield: I know you have all gone on to be great mentors yourselves, and I want to acknowledge that before we go on.

Judge Pickering: I think Judge Langford Morris brought up something really important that everyone has alluded to. Our caseload is so high. We are very busy. We are isolated. When we have private time, we're very selective about who we spend time with. It's important to be around people who are very supportive. I just think that high caseload also adds to the mix of the resiliency that you need because you are going to have to work that weekend to get that order out or work that weekend to be ready for that jury trial on Monday.

Judge Donald: As I listen to each of you all, there was a sense of loss in my own self because I did not have anyone encouraging me to run for judge. I can't say that I had a mentor at that time. I ran in a reaction to my own outrage over what I witnessed. Instead of supporting me, people said to me, basically, "Not now, you're too young, you don't have enough experience." And so, I ran against a lot of opposition.

I'm not saying that as I went along, there weren't a couple of judges who helped me. The first woman judge in Shelby County, I would talk to her, and she would give me some advice. But had I known at the time I started what that journey was, that I was going to have to take a leave without pay from my job, I probably wouldn't have done it. Maybe deep down, I had not made the commitment. People accused me of getting in the way of other candidates, of being a self-promoter, of being an upstart.

When I won the race, I had not heard about *impostor syndrome*, but I felt that I was the ultimate impostor. I didn't have a circle of people around me that Judge Ochoa-Bruck described. But I was elected, and I went to the ABA where women judges were meeting. I found there this community of women I could talk to. I'm not saying that we were all that close, but at least there were women there who had experienced years on the bench. I met Hilda Gage early on during that time.

Still, I had what I consider a multi-sided burden. I wasn't able to dismiss those voices who said I shouldn't be there, not now. They were still in my head, and I had some doubt about whether I could do this. I also had the fear that I didn't want to mess this up because I thought my performance could actually impede somebody else's opportunity. I had a wonderful large family that worked hard for me. My mother actually fasted without food or water for seven days, praying that I would make it. I had the burden of expectation.

Because I did not have the mentors, allies, or sponsors that the others have described in my own county, one of the things I did was to develop groups of people that I could talk to around the country. If I had a problem in the morning, I could call somebody on the East Coast. If I had an issue that afternoon, I could call the West Coast. My network became sort of a national network.

I also found that sometimes people who have not grown up with you, people that you don't work with every day, they can celebrate you and affirm you. As I started my early career, I got that affirmance from this national network of people who didn't live in Shelby County, who didn't know that I wasn't supposed to be there. To channel President Obama, these were people who said, "Yes, you can, and I will help you."

You all have said that men were often very helpful to you. When I got on the bench and after I'd served for a while, there were men on the court who were exceedingly supportive and helpful. As I navigated my way through my own 40-year judicial career, many men, especially White males, played a key role in terms of letter writing and of being advocates for me.

I just want to make this point on resiliency. One of the problems I think we still face, as women, is when we manifest characteristics that are stereotypically attributed to men. Sometimes we can be penalized for this. People have said to me that I was too aggressive. Even though I mentor lots of people, and I'm always in there trying to get others in there, people said to me that I came off as a self-promoter. I am so vocal and out front and sometimes people feel that maybe I'm too much out front. But, you know, I made it 40 years and four courts. And I'm okay with that now.

Professor Redfield: And we're all okay with you now and always.

Judge Pickering: We're grateful for your perseverance, Judge Donald. I'm glad you did not listen.

Judge Langford Morris: Judge Donald, thank God you didn't listen to those people. I wouldn't be here.

Professor Redfield: Women in many professions know the impostor syndrome even though we didn't always know this name for it. I know that when Judge Donald and I talk to other women, we sometimes title our talk "If I'd Known Then What I Know Now." If I'd understood that the biases I saw at play were implicit biases, if I'd understood that people of good faith maybe weren't responding to me in a personal way as an individual, if I'd understood that the impostor syndrome was a common thing, and that I wasn't one, wasn't an impostor—all those things would have been helpful to me. I think it's what you're all saying in different ways in this conversation.

Advice for Would-Be Judges

Professor Redfield: What advice might you offer others who might want to pursue similar career paths?

Judge Donald: I would say this. If they want to do that—first of all be the best lawyer, leader, bar person that you can be. Also understand that you can't do everything, and, you know, don't put more on yourself than you need to.

Strive for excellence in your career. When I listen to these women and their backgrounds, I mean amazing backgrounds, I am sure that if you're willing to work hard and you are prepared, you are enough. Go after what you want to, whether you have people cheering you on and encouraging you or not; bet on yourself. But also don't go for it if you're not willing to put in the work and be great in that position, because you're sure to be scrutinized. People are going to measure you against what their assumptions are. But as long as you're willing to do the work, go for it now. We recently had somebody in Shelby County who was elected and was not prepared to do the work, has really just sort of messed up a lot of things, so much so that we lost a judgeship as a result. This was a woman.

If you're not willing to do the work, don't go forward. But if you do go for it, make a commitment to yourself and to the profession that you are going to adhere to the rules, that you're going to have an ethic of excellence, that you're not coming in with an agenda other than being the best judge you can be, a judge who is really committed to justice for all.

Judge Ochoa-Bruck: I would like to piggyback on what we've been discussing. I think it's really important to understand that when you're entering into these kinds of positions, especially in situations where you run for election with open seats, even when you win and you get in there, not everybody likes you. I think that's one of the things we have to understand and know that's okay. Mostly women are seen as having to be nice and agreeable. But sometimes, no, we have to self-advocate, and we have to be okay with that. Perhaps not everyone's going to like us, and that's okay. We have plenty of other people in our lives that do.

Professor Redfield: I think that's terrific advice.

Judge Donald: Yes, it certainly is.

Professor Redfield: That would not be advice that my mother would have given me. My mother taught me that if you were polite and worked hard, everything would be fine. I've always been polite, and I've always worked hard. But not quite everything has always been fine. Judge Ochoa-Bruck, I think your point is really well taken as lawyers go forward. Perhaps, despite the advice of their mothers. I'm not sure.

Judge Pickering: I'd add, *Get out of your comfort zone*. I went from appellate work to trial work. In appellate defense, we get to argue in front of the Court of Appeals. But in a trial court, I knew it was going to get messy. I knew I would make mistakes and stumble. But I told myself that this is what I had to do to get experience as a trial lawyer. I'd say the number one point is to be diversified and balanced. This is what you are hearing from all of us here. We all didn't have just one job for years. We had many jobs and many experiences before the bench. The other thing is that you're going to be surprised who will support you, and you'll be surprised who doesn't support you.

Judge Donald: Agreed. Good point.

Judge Ochoa-Bruck: This is really true in my experience as well.

Judge Pickering: You do not learn that until the end. There will be people who quietly support you, and you may never know. People who will make a call on your behalf, and you have no idea who they might be. This is why how you behave as an attorney now is so important. I'm just going to applaud the point about being the best attorney you can be because that's when your supporters come out to support you. They may never say anything to you now or in the future. Ever.

Professor Redfield: Another really good point.

Judge Donald: Yes, excellent.

Judge Langford Morris: I would ditto everything that's been said by these great jurists, and I would add that your job as a judge does not end at five o'clock. You're going to be working, but you also need to be involved in your community. One thing that I always did, I got involved in the bar associations and the nonprofits. I was seen and heard in the community. So when I ran for election, people weren't just seeing me once every six years. In Oakland County we had big elections, and it cost a lot of money to run. The first time I got appointed by the governor, but I had to run after that, and I raised $400,000. I had to do commercials.

Today, when I'm speaking to mentees—I'm working with young people who are running for judge right now in Oakland County—I share this with them. I also talk about something that I didn't have to worry about, but that's important today, and that's social media. You've got to be careful about what you say and do when you are a judge. You're a judge, and people are watching you everywhere you go, whether you're out on social media or at a restaurant.

If you're having a glass of wine, they're going to be watching you as an active sitting judge. And now they are videoing you, taking your picture, and they can post it. Anyone can run against you, anyone who's not a sitting judge, and they can talk about what they will do when they are a judge. When they're on the bench, no one's ever going to have to wait to have their trial, they'll always be on time on the bench. But they're not likely to talk about the things that really happen, that you've got 1,800 cases, and you can't do 1,800 trials in one year. You've got to do settlement conferences. You've got to work with the lawyers. You've got to hear all the motions before you get to the trial. There's so much more to being a judge besides just the work in the courtroom. It is a lot. I would say, as Judge Donald said, if you don't want to put in the work, don't go there because you're making us as women, as minorities, as people, look bad.

Judge Donald: I would embrace everything everybody else has said, but I would also remind people to engage in self-care. Take care of yourself because you can't pour from an empty glass. I know people are pulling us from all directions, but don't be embarrassed, and don't be ridden with guilt because you take some time for yourself. We can be there for other people, but we have to take care of ourselves.

Judge Pickering, Judge Langford Morris, Judge Ochoa-Bruck: Excellent point, thank you.

Judges as Caregivers

Professor Redfield: Commitments to our communities—and to ourselves—are points that everyone has really wanted to drive home for us. This leads me to one of the other questions I want to get to, even if just for a short time with you. I'd like to ask about your thoughts on the role that we all play as caregivers of some kind, of our children as Judge Langford Morris already talked about, or of our parents, our partners, or others in our communities. We are expected to be and are caregivers, and that is a big piece of our life's work and love. But so often during our work on the Task Force, we heard about something called the *flexibility stigma*—talk about words that we didn't know then, but we know now. In fact, one of the Ten Principles in Resolution 501 addresses the flexibility stigma, and Lieutenant Colonel Susan Upward was asked to write a chapter about it for this book!

The idea is that when women (and I say women based on the data that statistically speaking it is mostly women who do this work) need the time to do these kinds of work, there is a stigma attached. Their careers are sometimes stymied or set on hold or hurt in some way, explicitly or implicitly. Would you talk about your own experiences as caregivers and also about the ways you, as judges, may have the ability to reduce the flexibility stigmas for other professionals that you work with and for other people who might come before you?

Judge Pickering: When I found out we were going to have a baby, I took a pause in my legal career and left the intellectual property law firm where I was working. I basically left the practice of law. That was a time when I didn't think I could have flexibility, and so I took a year off to raise our son, and then I went back to find a job that gave me flexibility. I certainly thought there was a stigma. Now, though, as I mentioned, the pandemic showed that more flexibility is possible. We see that people can work from home, work remotely. This offers a bit more flexibility in terms of being a caregiver. If I had to do it all over again, I don't know if I would have had to pause.

In terms of the present day, as a judge, I work with attorneys who help us get our work done. If they're also caregivers, I'm very mindful of that and don't want to prevent them from having flexibility. In other words, if I know that an attorney is available in the afternoons because they have childcare issues in the morning, I am going to work with that. I'm leaning into everybody's schedule. I think that's what you have to do. Similarly, as a judge, there are certain cases I wouldn't start until 9:30 because I knew that some of the women were dropping off their kids at school.

Judge Langford Morris: I would agree the best thing that came out of COVID, I'd say the only good thing, is Zoom court and Zoom classes for students. It's an opportunity for those who have children to be able to stay home with the young children. It really has benefited many of my mentees. Still, I know some that have children and face childcare costs that are absolutely outrageous compared to when I was in law school. It is a lot to pay, and I had my mom to help me. But some people don't have a relative that can help. One of my mentees at the University of Detroit Mercy was a young police officer, and she has children. She is remarkable. I don't know how she does it. I have worked with some women and help them to think about helping to care for each other's children when they don't have a babysitter. If they can work together and get classes at a different time, and then carpool, and have the kids together, it's a way to save on costs.

I was a sandwich mom in that I had a young child when I was in law school and then my dad was very sick. My mom had always helped me, and I helped her. My father was sick for nine years with Alzheimer's, and my mother didn't like to drive at that time, so I had to go back and forth doing the driving. People that I worked with supported me, but I didn't get any time off. I had to do it after or before hours or on weekends. I just worked like a dog to help make sure that my father was okay. He stayed home with my mom for five years, but it was killing her. So, the last four years, I couldn't quit my job and stay with them that last four years, but I went to the nursing home every single day.

I encourage young people who have these situations, whether they're at work or in school, to find people to help work with them and to not drop out. Don't give up, no matter what. Persevere, work full time, go to school full time, bachelor's, master's, law degrees. It's not that I'm brilliant. I just persevered. I took off from work to study for exams. I took vacation time to study. I did what I had to do to get it done. I tell my mentees, "If I could do it, you could do it."

Professor Redfield: Persevere is perhaps the word of this segment. Judge Ochoa-Bruck, do you want to add to this point?

Judge Ochoa-Bruck: One of the things that I have found really fascinating is just how rigid the criminal justice system is. It's been done this way forever, and that's the way it's always going to be, and we're not going to question it. Then one of the things that we found during COVID was a great opportunity for change. COVID required us to think differently about things. Is it really necessary for everybody to have to show up at nine a.m.? All 50 people at nine, all 50 people at 1:30 p.m.?

It turns out things could be done differently. There are three women on our bench. When COVID restrictions lifted, we brought work back, but we left the Zoom option open so that unless it's a bench warrant recall or a jury trial, you can appear by Zoom. You're authorized to do that by court rule. Also, during COVID, we had to break up the dockets. We staggered them for one, two, and three o'clock in the afternoon, and nine, ten, and eleven in the morning. We decided to do this permanently and just keep them staggered, but now at half-hour increments. Now we ask if you prefer morning or afternoon. And then we ask your time preference. When people have a choice, they'll mention things like, "If I can drop my daughter off at school, I can be here by ten." Or they'll say, "I work, and I can get off early at the end of my shift and be there at 2:30." I think that, especially as women judges, we have the ability to really be thoughtful and creative and understanding about time needed for caretaking functions. We knew we could be more flexible, and I think that COVID has allowed us the permission to do things differently.

Judge Pickering: One thing that made me a better judge on the bench was serving on the CJS Women's Task Force. I was able to hear about the flexibility issues. I was able to learn from that and apply it on the bench. Because of the CJS sessions, my own awareness of issues women faced increased, and this allowed me to have a better understanding of what other attorneys were juggling in terms of their workday.

Judge Donald: Coming from my own background working for legal services and having to run for judge, I realize the role that poverty and family play in the choices that people have to make. This made me very sensitive to exercising some modicum of flexibility. As I and others have mentioned, COVID helped us to explore new dimensions of flexibility.

When I was on the District Court, I thought about why I was requiring a criminal defendant who's on bond to come to court every 30 days for a report date when there's been no allegation of a violation, and the attorneys were just going to come in and ask for more time. That person was working at the margin and may have had to take time off from work, as others have said, to come to court for a ten-minute hearing where, really, we're not going to accomplish anything. Why, why do that? I started letting the attorney appear on behalf of the client unless there was some indication of trouble and then letting some attorneys, women and men, just handle their Rule 16 scheduling conferences by telephone, or by getting together outside and submitting something and then being available if I had questions.

We judges can do this more often. We can recognize, as we age and as our family members age, that the amount of responsibility that each of us is required to undertake may increase. We need some flexibility and accommodation. The population of people who are appearing before us likewise will need some accommodation. We can be more open to that. I don't mean allowing people to abuse the system, but just being open. As Judge Ochoa-Bruck said, we should ask ourselves whether we are doing what we are doing because we've always done it that way, or whether there is something that can better accommodate and still serve the cause of justice.

Judge Langford Morris: And I just wanted to add, it's so important as a judge that you are kind, civil, and professional at all times in working with the lawyers and your colleagues. Even before COVID, if I had a lawyer that needed a different date, I would grant their request. I had plenty of cases that I could maneuver around to accommodate a lawyer that had a prepaid vacation or something came up where a lawyer needed to deal with a child or an issue with their family. You can accommodate these people just like Judge Donald is saying. You have a defendant. What is he coming for? You don't have to get the

Black Robe disease where you're just ordering people to show up just for the heck of it, because you *can* order it.

This kind of consideration is so important because reputation, reputation, reputation goes with you, no matter where you go as a judge.

CJS Women's Task Force Ten Principles

Professor Redfield: I'd like to circle back around to where we started and pick up on Judge Pickering's point acknowledging the work of the Criminal Justice Section's Women's Task Force. As you all know, that Task Force came to recommend ten key approaches that it thought could improve the practice of law and create an environment where women would be less inclined to leave the profession. Could you reflect on those recommendations and also on the title of our chapter, "Why Do Judges Matter? And What Can Judges Do?" I'd like to do a round robin and give you all the chance to say a final word on the Task Force recommendations.

Judge Langford Morris: I would highlight the importance of encouraging law firms, law schools, and various practices, whether it's arbitration or otherwise, to engage in DEI [Diversity, Equity, and Inclusion].

> {Principle 3. Integrate ongoing training and continuing legal education on diversity, equity, inclusion, and belonging; gender discrimination; anti-racism; implicit bias; and trauma-informed practices.}

In corporations, oftentimes there's no direct DEI officer separate and apart from human resources, if you will. It needs to be an independent, focused position that will really strive to encourage DEI. DEI is not a bad word. DEI is a good thing, and it benefits all people. When we're talking about helping women and helping others to gain from the profession—whether you're prosecuting white-collar crimes or you're in a big firm handling white-collar cases or you're a sole practitioner—it's always important to help people to be heard and seen, help them get promoted or advanced when they deserve it. Lawyers work really, really hard, and women lawyers sometimes work harder if they don't have a wife at home to take care of the kids or the like. All this makes the equitable inclusion of DEI so significant.

Judge Ochoa-Bruck: I would say *Principle 5: Eliminate the Flexibility Stigma.*

> {Principle 5. Implement proactive policies and resources to combat the flexibility stigma that is often related to motherhood, family planning, reproductive health care, menopause, gender-affirming health care, and caregiving.}

I think that as women judges we can work on this. We heard a lot about the need for flexibility at all the listening sessions, especially from private attorneys who are in court. We can be creative to support them. Going back to the earlier discussion of COVID giving us permission to say, "Oh, it doesn't have to be this way." We can find ways to be more accommodating for the women that work in the court system. Having influence as a judge, we can get changes made like the docket example that I gave. That's something that can be done through a policy change. I strongly encourage judges to find ways like this where we can get involved in the core processes, to work with your court administrators to infuse more flexibility where possible.

Judge Pickering: Mine is really a mix of 3 and 4.

> {Principle 3. Integrate ongoing training and continuing legal education on diversity, equity, inclusion, and belonging; gender discrimination; anti-racism; implicit bias; and trauma-informed practices.}

> {Principle 4. Assure all recruitment, retention, and promotion policies are transparent, equal in pay and equal in opportunity; and, relatedly, implement individualized, accessible, and ongoing professional development programs that foster advancement.}

As a judge who practiced in Shawnee County, I encourage attorneys to come and practice in our county. I encourage them to practice in Topeka. I begin with telling them how professional the judges were when I was practicing there. That's a selling point for law students and new lawyers to set up a practice in Topeka, and it's something we can all do as judges. This professional atmosphere goes not only with the principle of ongoing training but also with the principle concerning promotion and retention.

I remind law students and new attorneys that we're at the state capitol. This is the place where you want to work. There are government agencies, so many opportunities and benefits. But what I emphasize is that the judges set a professional tone in the courtroom. They're respectful to the attorneys, they're approachable, they do not degrade you, they support you. Creating that very positive courtroom experience, as judges on the bench and as part of bar activities, makes our community inclusive and equitable. Judges who are the kind of judges that attorneys want to practice in front of contribute to ensuring a community where young attorneys will be able to have those four things, fair recruitment, retention, promotion, and equal opportunity.

Judge Donald: I agree and concur in the comments of everybody else. But I think a couple of general things are really important, and people have alluded to them already. As judges, what can we do? We can make certain that we ourselves are treating women with the same respect and authority as we treat men, that we are appointing them when we have opportunities, with the same frequency as we appoint male lawyers. We need to see women in different spaces and places and support them getting there.

When we have authority, we need to exercise that in a way that extolls equal justice and equal treatment. If I have an opportunity to appoint somebody to a big-time case that's going to give them exposure and recognition and an opportunity to demonstrate what they are, I do. I know what women can do, and I want to open the way for them to do that. We often go to the people who've always gotten those appointments, people we may know. But we need to be expansive in our thinking and be better allies and mentors and supporters when it comes to women as well as their male counterparts. We need to be the best allies, sponsors, and mentors we can be.

Professor Redfield: We are pretty close to the end of our time. I am going to leave our questions there and just take a minute to say what a pleasure it's been for me to listen to and learn from all of you. I consider you all to be both my colleagues and my friends, but also I know you to be exceptional contributors to the role and image that judges have in society. I'm going to end this interview with my huge and sincere gratitude for all that you do. But I see Judge Pickering has something to add. That's the trouble with being the only nonjudge in the group. You all don't listen to my directions.

Judge Pickering: I have to say this before we close. Judge Donald, you have been mentoring all of us judges. You have kept me interested in the practice of law and in how to do it right. I want to thank you. Even within our small group here, we have somebody helping us women judges.

Judge Donald: Thank you. I want to thank all of you. You talk about what I give, but I also take from you and that keeps me going. And for our interviewer, our leader, Professor Redfield, what an amazing, amazing woman! I feel honored to have been here to have this conversation with you. You never stop. You're selfless to a fault. You make us all better, and you make us appreciate our role and the opportunities we have to do what we do. So, thank you so much.

Professor Redfield: It has been my honor and joy. My enduring thanks to you all.

CHAPTER EIGHT

Leadership, Mentorship, Sponsorship, and Allyship

Maryam Ahranjani, Justin Bingham, and the Honorable Gloria Ochoa-Bruck

Key Chapter Points

- What are mentors, sponsors, and allies?
- Finding—and serving as—a mentor, sponsor, and ally is fulfilling and critical to healthy workplaces

This book focuses on just some of the aspects of gender-related challenges faced by women criminal lawyers. Lawyers with intersectional identities face even more nuanced and complicated challenges. Maryam Ahranjani defined the scope of the book in Chapter One. In Chapter Two, she included Resolution 501: Ten Principles to Achieve Gender Equity in the Criminal Legal Profession and its accompanying report. Prosecutor Camelia Valdes, the voice of Chapter Three and a long-serving county prosecutor, described how to get and stay in office from her perspective as the long-serving lead prosecutor in Passaic County, New Jersey. Joy Applewhite, a Black public defender in rural New Mexico, wrote about how to navigate intersectionality and related burnout in Chapter Four.[1] In Chapter Five, Lieutenant Colonel Susan Upward (USMC) describes the flexibility stigma. Aubony Burns writes in Chapter Six about her and others' efforts in the Prosecuting Attorney's Office in Seattle to operationalize equity through transparency.

1. Alisa Smith, *Stress and Public Criminal Defense: Comparing Male and Female Defender Experiences and Coping Strategies*, 61 Idaho L. Rev. 1 (2025) (presenting the results of her study of burnout and the different ways men and women cope).

Professor Sarah Redfield led a discussion with the Honorable Bernice B. Donald (retired, Sixth Circuit Court of Appeals), the Honorable Rachel Pickering (Kansas Court of Appeals), the Honorable Gloria Ochoa-Bruck (Spokane, Washington Municipal Court), and the Honorable Denise Langford Morris (retired, Oakland County, Michigan Circuit Court) in Chapter Seven about their own experiences as lawyers and judges and the role of judges in promoting gender equity.

In addition to the need for structural and systemic reform goal-setting, confidence, persistence, resilience, and community-building—even in the face of bias and mistreatment—are common threads throughout the book.

In this final chapter, we hope to describe and amplify two important next steps—seeking and serving in leadership roles and, relatedly, cultivating mentors, sponsors, and allies. We seek to share ideas about how *you* can be—and seek—mentors, allies, and sponsors. These steps permeate Resolution 501 and the accompanying report, particularly Principle One (creating culture change by dismantling barriers to hiring, retention, and promotion) and Principle Six (instituting and sustaining opportunities for mentorship, allyship, and sponsorship). Each of us answers how we, in our respective and diverse roles, approach all of these things. As the TF Reporter and a legal academic, Ahranjani contributes her own experiences as a tenured professor who stood and stands on the shoulders of others. Justin Bingham, a longtime chief prosecutor and the CJS Chair the year we introduced Resolution 501, shares his experiences as a supervisor and mentor. Finally, Judge Ochoa-Bruck opens her expansive warehouse of tools as a prosecutor, defense attorney, tribal court judge, and state court judge.

Maryam Ahranjani

I never dreamed of becoming a law professor. I made the mistake of attending law school right after undergrad when I was just 21 years old and had very little context for what I was studying. With little prior exposure, law school was quite difficult. One bright spot was serving as a Marshall-Brennan Constitutional Literacy Project Fellow, which gave me the opportunity to co-teach constitutional law at a public high school in Washington, DC. Then, just two years after law school, I had an opportunity to teach as an adjunct professor because one of my professors—Jamie Raskin—recommended me to cover his upper-level constitutional law seminar for Marshall-Brennan Fellows while he took a sabbatical.

Because people listen to now-Congressman Raskin, the doors opened for me. Jamie saw something in me that I didn't see in myself. I absolutely loved every minute of teaching at my alma mater that year. When Raskin returned, he was pulled in other directions, so I kept teaching two to three courses a year as an adjunct professor in addition to full-time employment. It took some time for the dream to crystallize—almost 11 years, to be precise—but once I realized teaching full time was something I felt called to do, I knew it would take a village to help me get there. I didn't have the traditional "pedigree" that is still, unfortunately, the norm. But I had a vision.

I proactively and eagerly made sacrifices to achieve my dream. One sacrifice was commuting to another city to "cure" my law degree with an Ivy League LLM degree while working full time and pregnant. It took me three years to complete my LLM at the University of Pennsylvania Carey Law School, but when Dean Ted Ruger let me walk across the commencement stage with my handsome toddler in my arms, it created a watershed moment. Another sacrifice was moving to New Mexico, a state where I knew no one, to accept an incredible opportunity as a visiting professor and ultimately to take my dream job as a tenure-track law professor. Dean David Herring hired me at the University of New Mexico and welcomed me and my young son with open arms.

As one of just three criminal law professors at the only law school in the state, I felt an obligation to expose my students to what gender equity and other identity-related challenges lie ahead. Even now that I have moved on to the University of Nevada–Las Vegas Boyd School of Law, a large percentage of my students will practice criminal law in-state, some in rural towns. Many scholars have described the ways in which misogyny harms us all. Gender-based expectations limit everyone. I hope that by leading discussions, helping students to anticipate and brainstorm ways to handle gender-based challenges, bringing in well-respected members of our legal community to inspire and offer support, and implementing other interventions, I am equipping all of them to handle the challenges ahead and, for those who will not directly experience gender-related challenges, teach them what allies do.

In *Sprinting a Marathon*, included as Appendix D, I write about mentors, sponsors, and role models. Also, on pages 2, 4, and 9, as well as in citations 17, 20, and 22 of Resolution 501 in Chapter 2, I refer to allyship, mentorship, role models, and sponsors. Judge Bernice Donald, whom we affectionately refer to as the lifetime mayor of the American Bar Association, first presented this framework at one of our many Task Force dinners on the road. In Judge Donald's view, **mentors** actively interact with us to help us develop personally and professionally.

Sponsors speak our names in spaces where we may not even be present. They nominate us for awards, promotions, and opportunities. They're thinking about us and inviting others to think about us when perhaps we don't even know it and didn't ask them for support. In fact, we may never know the ways in which a sponsor moves behind the scenes to get us noticed, promote us, and boost us. We earn sponsors by earning a strong professional reputation for excellence.

Role models inspire and motivate us. They often are people we don't know and may never know. People like Justices Sonia Sotomayor and Ketanji Brown Jackson might be role models to diverse women lawyers. Finally, **allies** are people who stand shoulder to shoulder with us, who agree with us in public spaces, and who bring attention to our concerns when we may not be able to or won't be taken seriously. In his article in Appendix I, Lucian Dervan, the CJS chair who created the Women in Criminal Justice Task Force, writes about how he leveraged his leadership role for allyship. In my daily work, allies may be faculty colleagues who vote together, support petitions, and advocate for fairness in all aspects of our lives as employees. They are leaders in legal education who are willing to moot me for interviews (often without much notice), who brainstorm scholarship ideas, who are willing to read and offer edits on my writing, and who identify professional opportunities for me and nominate me for things.

All of these special people in our lives serve as sources of support, and the roles often overlap. Sometimes mentors, sponsors, and role models look just like us. As the authors of Chapters Three and Seven point out, many times, they don't. For example, a mentor also may be an ally and a sponsor. One law school dean, a white male who started as a mentor to me, forwarded a posting for a leadership position in a city he knew I wanted to live in, called up the former dean to sing my praises, mooted me when I was made a semifinalist, and lent a supportive and constructive ear when I was not advanced as a finalist. Thanks to the support I have received over the years—and observed others receiving to get to where they want to go—I strive to help others and ask for help when I need it.

I strive to serve as a mentor, ally, and sponsor to many students and aspiring students, colleagues, community members, and others over the years. I often reflect on the words of Cassandra Sneed Ogden, former executive director of the Council on Legal Education Opportunity (an organization dedicated to diversifying the legal profession for over 50 years), who instructed aspiring law students that every time they receive a hand up, they should extend the other hand to bring along another.

Serving as a mentor, ally, and sponsor for talented pre-tenure colleagues whenever possible is also very important to me. I recommend talented pre-tenure scholars for panels and speaking engagements, review their draft articles, help them brainstorm teaching strategies, and share my class notes, slides, and exams. I also help them think about how and where to place their law review articles to maximize their goals at various stages of their careers, whether the goal is placing in the highest-ranked journal or galvanizing support for social justice advocacy.

I feel a strong duty to pay forward all the energy that others have poured into me. As a first-generation American whose parents came to the United States seeking freedom of thought, religion, and opportunity, I take nothing for granted and appreciate all the support from those in my garden.

Justin Bingham

As chief prosecutor, my job has many challenges. Most of those challenges are fairly typical of any prosecutor's office, but sometimes a challenge appears that really confounds you. I never thought lactation rooms would be one of the most unsolvable of challenges I would face as a manager, but that turned out to be the case. My office has many young attorneys in their late 20s and early 30s. Having babies has become a regular occurrence for the people I employ. This wasn't always the case. Previously, our staff was mostly male and mostly middle-aged. Lactation rooms were not high on the list of priorities. As we have become more intentional about diversity in our hiring, our staff looks much different than it did when I arrived in the office. Diversity may require you to face new challenges and find unique solutions. Thus, lactation rooms have entered the conversation at my office.

In 2018, multiple attorneys in our office welcomed babies into their families. These joyous arrivals brought with them a not-too-pleasant reality . . . our office was wholly unprepared to welcome new mothers back to the office. We had no permanent lactation rooms and no ability to temporarily modify existing spaces into lactation rooms. In the past, new mothers discreetly used the bathroom for their lactation needs. This was an unacceptable solution, but no one questioned it. We were facing multiple new mothers returning to the office at the same time with a similar need for appropriate lactation space. Something had to be done. One of the mothers approached me with her concerns. I immediately reached out to human resources for assistance. Human resources wanted to help, but they were met with resistance from upper management because of the expense needed to create a dedicated lactation room for my office. Management suggested we create a shared lactation space in a file room located downstairs in the public defender's office. My attorneys would need to walk downstairs to the front desk at the public defender's office to ask for the key to the file room. They would then lactate in a room that contained files for clients that were being prosecuted by my office. I quickly raised the ethical and logical issues this arrangement created. Regardless of how loudly I protested, I was unsuccessful. It seems upper management believed their solution met the minimum standards required by law. If any of my employees didn't agree, they could challenge the accommodation that was provided. I assumed someone would challenge the accommodation. Sadly, that never happened.

I have wondered for a long time why my young attorneys decided to remain silent. My hunch is that being a young parent returning to the workplace is hard enough. Adding an emotional fight with management over the quality of an ADA accommodation might be too much to bear. So, the decision to accept the unacceptable seems to be the easiest thing to do. This whole episode still bothers me. I wasn't able to provide an acceptable solution to my employees. I felt like I let them down. My conversations with them after the fact indicated that they appreciated that I was willing to put up the fight. The lack of an unacceptable lactation room doesn't adversely affect me on a personal level, but it greatly affects individuals who work for me. Being an ally is sometimes the most important thing you can do as a supervisor. You fight for those who can't fight or fear recriminations if they do speak out.

We will never attain gender equity in the practice of law unless men stand up for issues that impact women's work conditions. Equity and inclusivity are not only the right thing to do, but they also make a stronger workforce. When people feel they are part of an organization that values and supports them, they are more productive and have a greater sense of loyalty. When we do the right things for our employees, we are building stronger and more resilient organizations. Allyship is not just about being empathetic. Allyship is also an integral part of being a strong leader. Leadership requires us to set a course of action and provide support for everyone so they can make it to the goal successfully. I don't see allyship and leadership as two separate ideas. They are interlinked. I wish I had understood this more keenly when I was fighting for my employees back in 2018. I wasn't being empathetic to their needs as women; I was fulfilling my obligations as leader of their office. Equity, inclusion, and allyship are all parts of being a successful leader!

The Honorable Gloria Ochoa-Bruck

The mentorship, sponsorship, and allyship from so many people over my 25-year career in the legal profession have played a significant role and are a factor in my professional success. I have served as a Deputy Prosecuting Attorney, contract Public Defender in both state and federal court, owned and managed a private practice law firm, served as a Tribal Court Judge and a member of the City of Spokane Mayor's cabinet, and most recently was elected Spokane Municipal Court Judge. However, the powerful impact of mentors, sponsors, and allies did not begin in law school and in my legal career.

My parents immigrated to the United States from Mexico when I was four months old. My father went to school until the second grade, and my mother was allowed to attend school for two months. I was the first person to graduate from high school in my family, and there was no one in our family or social network who had a college degree, let alone a law degree. I share this part of my background because I would not have made it to college were it not for a high school teacher that helped me map out an alternative route to earning a bachelor's degree, as going on to a college or university right out of high school was not an option for me. Then it was a counselor at my community college who encouraged me to stay the course and not switch pathways to the paralegal program when working a full-time job, while attending classes, and raising my oldest son made it seem impossible. These are just two examples of the many mentors, sponsors, and allies that have been instrumental in shaping the trajectory of both my life and legal career.

I have invested much time and energy over the years educating myself on how to be an effective mentor, sponsor, and ally by both reading and learning from others who have modeled strategies and practices. Regardless of where we are in our careers, we can all serve in one or all of these roles to others. Whether someone is a law student, intern, first-year associate, or well into their legal career, there are always opportunities to uplift and support others to succeed in achieving their goals. Following are brief and unexhaustive ways we can all serve in these roles.

Mentorship—Being a mentor is the most readily available method of making a positive impact. Making it a practice to welcome and introduce ourselves to incoming 1L students, new hires, or new members of boards and associations we belong to is something we can all do. Offering to get together for lunch or coffee and scheduling a time to get to know them and learn about their goals and interests help us map out a plan on how we can best serve as a mentor. A mentorship plan can include things such as suggesting who else they should meet, offering support and advice on what action they can be taking now to prepare for any opportunities that come up, and offering to be available and being someone they can trust to come to for any issues or situations that come up.

Being a mentor doesn't have to be a commitment that requires a formal plan and an ongoing time commitment. We can serve as mentors in smaller but equally impactful ways such as serving as a guest speaker, being on the lookout for organic and in-the-moment ways to offer advice and counsel, or simply developing a reputation as someone with an open door that is accessible and willing and able to set aside a few minutes to walk through something with others. The best aspect of being a mentor is how creative and flexible you can be in this role.

Allyship—Being an ally has different definitions in various settings. In this discussion, I will focus on the role of being an ally as someone that supports others in professional settings where their voices are being silenced, where their ideas and input are being minimized, or where they have a project or initiative the ally also supports.

Being an ally in this context can present itself in a variety of ways. One of the most common ways is when someone with less experience, time in the organization, or agency due to who they are and where they come from makes a valuable contribution in a meeting but is ignored, and someone else makes the same or a similar contribution but theirs is embraced and moved forward. This example came up, time and time again, in the listening sessions of the Women in Criminal Justice Task Force. Immediately speaking up and echoing or piggybacking on their comment, naming them, and giving them credit for the contribution is an impactful way to serve as an ally.

Sponsorship—Aside from someone's experience and qualifications, one key factor that I have found to be critical to not only learning about potential opportunities, but also more importantly being given an opportunity, is who someone has in their professional and social network that can advocate and serve as a supporter and a reference. I realized early on in my career that I was someone that, due to my life's circumstances, would need to build my own social and professional network. I have dedicated the last 19 years of my 25-year legal career to volunteering both in the legal profession and in my community. What I have learned over the years is that through the process of genuinely and sincerely supporting and uplifting others, and engaging in organizations that align with my values, I have built a network of friends, colleagues, and established professional relationships that in turn allow me to serve as an impactful and effective sponsor.

If someone already has an established network, this makes it much easier to connect others and offer to serve as a sponsor. Helping someone establish a connection, serve as a reference, or coordinate a meeting and connection are so valuable and helpful to someone that doesn't have access. If you are like me and were not or are not in that position, you can build and establish a social and professional network on a foundation of genuine and sincere support and sponsorship of others. I find sponsorship to be the most rewarding of the three roles. As a sponsor, you can open doors that would otherwise have remained closed, you can assist in making valuable and instrumental connections someone may not have been able to make on their own, and your support and sponsorship of someone you know and have worked with can give them the credibility and confirmation that can make a difference.

Serving in these roles as mentors, sponsors, and allies is both deeply impactful and personally rewarding. I highly encourage all of us to invest in doing what we can, with where we are, to make an impactful difference.

* * *

We hope the information shared in this chapter and throughout the book, including in the appendices, has made the case for gender equity in criminal law and beyond. Ethical lawyers, an independent judiciary, and the rule of law are critical to our democracy. Intentional inclusion of all voices truly benefits everyone. Transparent, equitable workplaces lead to happier and healthier lawyers who better serve their clients and communities. The macro effect of intentional inclusion is a more stable rule of law, a system that recognizes and celebrates the unique contributions of us all. We hope the information shared in this book catalyzes individual and collective action. Please share the ideas you learned here with others and seek changes in your own workplaces. Each of us can take big and small actions that cumulatively will have a positive impact.

Conclusion

A criminal legal system that prevents, treats, and punishes behavior that violates community norms improves everyone's freedom. If those holding up the system quiver, the system—and all of us—suffers. Born of a concern that women criminal lawyers and judges experience challenges in hiring, retention, and promotion, this book weaves together the inspiring stories of high-achieving criminal lawyers and their advice for creating inclusive and thriving workplaces.

Based on their own leadership experiences, the authors operationalize ABA Resolution 501: Ten Principles to Achieve Gender Equity in the Criminal Legal Profession. The Ten Principles are

- creating culture change,
- acknowledging and addressing intersectional challenges,
- implementing diversity, equity, and inclusion training,
- creating transparent policies and opportunities for professional development,
- eliminating the flexibility stigma,
- offering individualized support,
- providing low- or no-cost therapy,
- developing private spaces in the workplace,
- supporting caretaking, and
- engaging in continual evaluation and adjustment.

While the Ten Principles specifically address criminal legal employment, the takeaways from the book are universal. To create *inclusion*, we must be *intentional*. To achieve greater gender and other equity, we must honestly assess our current workplaces and build both individualized and systemic responses to the challenges. This book offers a guide and further resources such as articles, websites, and leading voices.

APPENDIX A
Bibliography

Poignant personal accounts of being a woman criminal lawyer first published in *Criminal Justice* magazine

- Being mistaken for court staff or relative of a defendant
- What education debt load means for women criminal lawyers
- Running for office
- Why allyship, sponsorship, and mentorship matter
- Findings from the Task Force
- The need for the ABA to promote policy changes

Published some of the research related to hiring, retention, and promotion of women criminal lawyers

- Helpful for educational purposes
- Gives stakeholders a roadmap for change

Maryam Ahranjani, *"Toughen Up, Buttercup" versus #TimesUp: Initial Findings of the ABA Women in Criminal Justice Task Force*, 25 Berkeley J. Crim. L. 99 (2020).

Maryam Ahranjani, *Pulling Back the Curtain: A Follow-Up Report from the ABA Criminal Justice Section Women in Criminal Justice Task Force*, ABA (2021).

Maryam Ahranjani, *Sprinting a Marathon: Next Steps for Gender Equity in Criminal Legal Employment*, 106 Minn. L. Rev. 228 (2022).

Carla Laroche & Tina Luongo, *Task Force Launches*, Crim. Just. Mag. (Spring 2019).

Maryam Ahranjani, *Listening Session Participants Express Feelings of Isolation—and Demonstrate Resilience*, Crim. Just. Mag. (Nov. 1, 2019).

Maria Carmen Hinayon, *Who Needs the Old Boys' Club? Let's Make Our Own—Highlights from the WCJ Bay Area Listening Session*, Crim. Just. Mag. (Jan. 21, 2020).

Daniela Donoso, *Heavy Purse: A Law Student's Reflection on the CJS Women in Criminal Justice Task Force's NYC Listening Session*, Crim. Just. Mag. (Apr. 20, 2020).

Lucian E. Dervan, *Undefined Vision: An Ally's Journey*, Crim. Just. Mag. (July 15, 2020).

Maryam Ahranjani, *Looking Back, Looking Forward*, Crim. Just. Mag. (Oct. 29, 2020).

Honorable Gloria Ochoa-Bruck, *The Call for the Rise of the Modern Prosecutor*, Crim. Just. Mag. (Jan. 11, 2021).

Honorable Rachel Pickering, *An Awakening and More: How Being Part of the Women in Criminal Justice Task Force Has Provided Me with a Judicial Awareness*, Crim. Just. Mag. (May 1, 2021).

Joy Applewhite, *Brave, Bold, Booked, and Balanced*, Crim. Just. Mag. (July 20, 2021).

Jessica J. Yeary, *From Sweetie to Sisterhood: A Public Defender's Listening Session Reflection*, Crim. Just. Mag. (Oct. 20, 2021).

Yaamini L. Rao, *Voice Lessons*, Crim. Just. Mag. (Jan. 12, 2022).

Ann Ratnayake Macy, *From Mad Men to Times Up and Beyond: What We Must Do to Ensure Workplace Parity for Women in Criminal Justice*, Crim. Just. Mag. (May 24, 2022).

Maryam Ahranjani, *Women in Criminal Justice Task Force Concludes Research Phase and Moves into Action*, Crim. Just. Mag. (July 28, 2022).

Lieutenant Colonel Susan E. Upward, *#NoRetreat: The Women in Criminal Justice Task Force Takes the Road Less Traveled to the ABA House of Delegates*, Crim. Just. Mag. (Apr. 19, 2023).

Honorable Denise Langford Morris, *Reflections by a Sister in Law: 40 Years in Practice and Counting*, Crim. Just. Mag. (July 15, 2023).

Sarah Redfield, *Listening Authentically, Extending Inclusion*, Crim. Just. Mag. (Oct. 1, 2023).

Melba V. Pearson, Rachel A. Silverthorn & Tierra Fulwood, *Black, Female and Elected: The Long Road for Black Women as Top Prosecutors*, Crim. Just. Mag. (Oct. 18, 2023).

APPENDIX B

"Toughen Up, Buttercup" versus #TimesUp

Maryam Ahranjani

"Toughen Up, Buttercup" versus #TimesUp: Initial Findings of the ABA Women in Criminal Justice Task Force

Maryam Ahranjani*

"Practicing criminal law as a woman is like playing tackle football in a dress." Andrea George, Executive Director of the Federal Public Defender for Eastern Washington and Idaho, began her testimony to the American Bar Association's Women in Criminal Justice Task Force with that powerful observation. In the wake of the #MeToo movement, the ABA has focused on ways to enhance gender equity in the profession and in the justice system. The Criminal Justice Section of the ABA has invested significant resources in the creation of the Women in Criminal Justice Task Force (WCJ TF), which launched its work in January 2019. Written by the WCJ TF Reporter, this Article describes the current status of women criminal lawyers by situating the Task Force's research within the larger literature on gender equity in the legal profession and in criminal law in particular, sharing unique original qualitative data from the project's listening sessions, and proposing solutions and next steps for supporting women who choose the important societal role of criminal attorney.

DOI: https://doi.org/10.15779/Z386D5PB95

* Associate Professor and Don L. & Mabel F. Dickason Professor, University of New Mexico School of Law. I express my deepest gratitude to my fantastic research assistants Kristen Edwards and Nat Saing, former faculty assistant Sila Manahane, the co-chairs and members of the Women in Criminal Justice Task Force for their individual and collective support, and colleagues Nathalie Martin and Marc-Tizoc González for their thoughtful edits and enthusiasm for this project. The piece also benefitted from feedback following presentations to CJS's 2019 Fall Institute in Washington, D.C. and to faculty colleagues at a January 2020 colloquium. I also am grateful to the BJCL student editors and staff who worked on this piece while juggling the unique challenges presented by the global COVID-19 pandemic. Finally, I express immense respect for the brave women who participated in our listening sessions.

INTRODUCTION

Like many mothers, Marta wants to provide breast milk for her baby and needs to pump that milk at work. For Marta, current policy has her leaving her office in the district attorney's office on the third floor and going through a series of steps to be able to get to the secure second floor room designated the lactation room. Marta is a young prosecutor in an urban area who recently returned from parental leave after having a baby. Mothers who are lactating have the right to use the file room on the second floor of a building that is leased by both the district attorney's office and public defender's office. The file room is located inside the public defender's office. To access the room, Marta must notify security, walk outside (sometimes through rain and snow) and around the building, and then wait for the security guard to let her into the room, which contains locked client files.

The room used to be a clerk's office, so although there are blinds, there is a glass window with an opening at the bottom. People walking by the office hear the whirring of Marta's pump. While the head prosecutor has worked to improve the situation, the administrative office for the state government said there is no other room available to convert into a lactation room. The head public defender did not object to prosecutors using the space.

Marta's story is just one among many stories shared with the American Bar Association Criminal Justice Section Women in Criminal Justice Task Force (ABA CJS WCJ TF). Marta's story exemplifies the institutional barriers that women criminal lawyers face. The ABA CJS is dedicated to telling these stories in order to expose and eliminate such barriers.[1]

The ABA is the world's largest voluntary professional association, with a membership of 365,000 attorneys.[2] It plays an important role in the profession and in society. It accredits law schools, promotes fairness in the profession and society, and weighs in on high-impact issues such as judicial appointments, lawmaking, and systemic reforms in the U.S. and abroad.[3]

One of the behemoth organization's four core goals is to eliminate

---

[1] Past chairs Lucian Dervan and Kim Parker, as well as current chair April Frazier Camara have all pledged to and actually offered critical support.

[2] *ABA Timeline*, AM. BAR ASS'N, https://www.americanbar.org/about_the_aba/timeline (last visited Jul. 12, 2020).

[3] *See Rule of Law Initiative*, AM. BAR ASS'N, https://www.americanbar.org/advocacy/rule_of_law (last visited Dec. 11, 2020); *see also American Bar Association*, WIKIPEDIA, https://en.wikipedia.org/wiki/American_Bar_Association (last visited Jul. 12, 2020).

bias and enhance diversity in the justice system and in the legal profession.[4] The ABA defines diversity broadly, and recent efforts include the creation of new professional groups such as the Coalition on Racial and Ethnic Justice, Commission on Disability Rights, Commission on Hispanic Legal Rights & Responsibilities, Commission on Racial and Ethnic Diversity in the Profession, Commission on Sexual Orientation and Gender Identity, Commission on Women in the Profession, Council for Diversity in the Educational Pipeline, and ABA Diversity and Inclusion Advisory Council.[5]

When CJS staff member Emily Johnson discovered that only 26% of the approximately 16,000 members of the CJS are women, she wondered whether that number reflected the total population of criminal lawyers or merely the Section membership. She raised her questions with CJS Director Kevin Scruggs and Section Chair Professor Lucian Dervan. Given the organization's core goal of eliminating bias and enhancing diversity, Lucian created the TF to investigate Emily's question. He appointed Carla Laroche, a clinical professor at Florida State College of Law, and Tina Luongo, chief defender at the Legal Aid Society of New York City, to co-chair the TF. The WCJ TF[6] was charged through the TF with exploring issues related to hiring, retention, and promotion of women in criminal law.[7] Carla and Tina envisioned—and created—a vibrant Task Force of women with diverse lived and professional experiences.[8] This TF engaged in an eighteen month-long series of listening sessions.[9] The Section's magazine dedicated a regular column to the TF to share its progrcss.[10]

---

4 AM. BAR ASS'N, *supra* note 3.

5 *Id.*

6 While the Task Force recognizes that its name reinforces a false binary gender identity, it has strived to be inclusive of gender non-conforming individuals by inviting "women and gender non-conforming people" to testify. The Task Force has narrowed its scope to women and gender non-conforming lawyers who either work in traditional criminal litigation roles (prosecutors, defense lawyers, judges at the state and federal levels) or those who work on criminal justice issues through non-profit organizations, government (legislatures, city and municipal government, etc.), and private foundations.

7 *See infra* Part II.

8 *See infra* Appendix A for a list of Task Force members.

9 *See infra* Part IV.

10 *See* Carla Laroche & Tina Luongo, *Task Force Launches*, CRIM. JUST. MAG., https://www.americanbar.org/groups/criminal_justice/publications/criminal-justice-magazine/2019/spring/task-force-launches (Spring 2019); Maryam Ahranjani, *Listening Session Participants Express Feelings of Isolation—and Demonstrate Resilience*, CRIM. JUST. MAG. (Nov. 1, 2019),

Through the simple, but incredibly powerful, qualitative methodology of providing safe spaces for women to talk and for TF members to listen, in 2019 and 2020 the Task Force heard from women all over the country about institutional and individual barriers. The reported barriers included challenges related to re-entry to work after giving birth, lack of transparency around promotion, significant secondhand trauma, inadequate training of supervisors regarding race and gender issues in the workplace, objectification, and more.[11]

This article reports on the original data that came from these listening sessions and is the first to report on actual conditions for women criminal lawyers in the United States. Part II describes why gender (and other) diversity matters in the legal profession, why it matters in criminal law in particular, and how the TF set up its listening sessions. Part III situates the research on women in criminal justice in the context of relevant literature. Part IV describes the original qualitative findings from the WCJ TF's listening session tour. Part V explores next steps to promote systemic reforms that will better protect women criminal lawyers.

I. THE ROLE AND VOICES OF WOMEN CRIMINAL LAWYERS

There are a number of reasons why it is important to have a well-trained, well-supported body of women criminal lawyers. The first major reason is to promote the rule of law. Many studies indicate that the presence and leadership of women in criminal justice reduce corruption.[12] Female victims often feel more comfortable with female attorneys.[13] Child victims feel more comfortable with female attorneys.[14] When

---

https://www.americanbar.org/groups/criminal_justice/publications/criminal-justice-magazine/2019/fall/listening-session-participants-express-feelings-isolation-demonstrate-resilience/; Maria Carmen Hinayon, *Who Needs the Old Boys' Club? Let's Make Our Own—Highlights from the WCJ Bay Area Listening Session*, CRIM. JUST. MAG. (Jan. 21, 2020), https://www.americanbar.org/groups/criminal_justice/publications/criminal-justice-magazine/2020/winter/who-needs-old-boys-club-lets-make-our-ownhighlights-the-wcj-bay-area-listening-session.

[11] *See infra* Part IV.

[12] *See generally* The American Judicature Society, *Different Voices, Different Choices? The Impact of More Women Lawyers and Judges on the Justice System*, 74 JUDICATURE 138 (1990).

[13] *See generally* Debbie Leecock, *Professional Females: Are There Enough Available? Gender Bias of Female Victims*, 6 MOD. PSYCHOL. STUD. 18, Article 4 (1998), https://scholar.utc.edu/mps/vol6/iss2/4.

[14] Telephone Interview with Kyle T. Nayback, Head of the Indian Country Crimes

people feel more comfortable with their attorneys, they are likely to feel more confident in the system and in the rule of law.

Representation matters to the rule of law. It also matters to people's perceptions of and buy-in to the justice system.[15] Representation matters to victims. It matters to defendants. It matters to jurors. Victims, defendants, and jurors from marginalized groups are more likely to participate in the system in a positive way when they perceive that the attorneys reflect their own social identities and believe that they can understand their experiences and empathize with them.[16]

Second, achieving gender equity and equality[17] is important because women have worked incredibly hard—in many cases against societal and familial expectations—to earn their rightful, equal space in the field.[18] If we want such victories as increased enrollment in law school and increased participation in the highest levels of the profession to remain and expand, we must expose the obstacles and work together—those affected and allies[19] alike—to eliminate them.

There are different ways to assess the current landscape. On the one hand, there are signs of progress. Progressive prosecutors, including women of color, have been elected all over the country.[20] There are more

---

section of the Criminal Division in the U.S. Attorney's Office, District of New Mexico (February 2019).

[15] *See generally* Robert J. Aalberts et al., *Do Race/Ethnicity and Gender Influence Criminal Defendants' Satisfaction with Their Lawyers' Services? An Empirical Study of Nevada Inmates*, 2 NEV. L.J. 72 (2002).

[16] Jill L. Cruz, Melinda S. Molina & Jenny Rivera, *Hispanic National Bar Association Commission on the Status of Latinas in the Legal Profession, Study on Latina Attorneys in the Public Interest Sector, La Voz De La Abogada Latina: Challenges and Rewards in Serving the Public Interest*, 14 CUNY L. REV. 147, 190–91 (2010) (discussing Spanish-speaking clients favorable response to Latina attorneys who resemble them and also speak Spanish).

[17] Gender equality refers to equalizing *access* to the same opportunities to people of all gender identities whereas gender equity refers to widespread changes in *outcomes* that uplift historically marginalized people. *See* Agnes Binagwaho, *The Difference Between Gender Equity and Equality—and Why It Matters*, FORTUNE (Mar. 25, 2020, 12:30 PM), https://fortune.com/2020/03/25/gender-equality-and-equity-iwd-womens-education/.

[18] *See* Jane R. Wettach, *Women in the Practice: The Struggle Continues*, 37 N.C. ST. B. Q. 18 (Summer 1990) (discussing the various obstacles women lawyers have overcome striving for equal treatment).

[19] Allyship is a major focus of the Task Force. While the early stages have involved primarily women—and, to a lesser extent, gender non-conforming individuals—there has been a recognition since the beginning of the importance of building allies, including men.

[20] *See* Lauren-Brooke Eisen, *The Big Winners in DA Races: Women and Black*

female judges on the federal bench than any other time in American history.[21] Women have outnumbered men in law school classrooms across the country for the past four years in a row.[22] Dynamic new groups such as the Black Public Defender Association, co-founded and chaired by CJS chair and TF member April Frazier Camara, are gaining traction and influence.[23]

Both state and federal legislation and policies also show signs of hope. For example, although the future of the Equal Rights Amendment is uncertain, Virginia recently became the thirty-eighth state to ratify it.[24] The Florida Supreme Court recently passed a new rule creating a presumption that attorneys arguing lawsuits are entitled to continuances to accommodate parental leave when they give birth or adopt.[25] The federal government recently announced paid family leave for federal workers, which certainly will influence private employers and more states to follow suit.[26]

On the other hand, despite these signs of progress, progress seems

---

Candidates, BRENNAN CTR. FOR JUST. (Nov. 12, 2018), https://www.brennancenter.org/our-work/analysis-opinion/big-winners-da-races-women-and-black-candidates.

[21] *40 Years Later, Pioneering Women Judges Savor Place in History*, U.S. CTS. (Aug. 14, 2019), https://www.uscourts.gov/news/2019/08/14/40-years-later-pioneering-women-judges-savor-place-history.

[22] *Where Do Women Go to Law School? Here Are the 2018 Numbers*, ENJURIS: BEFORE THE BAR BLOG, (Feb. 28, 2019), https://abaforlawstudents.com/2019/02/28/where-do-women-go-to-law-school-2018-numbers/.

[23] *See* Press Release, National Legal Aid & Defender Association, *NLADA Announces New Section-Black Public Defenders Section* (Oct. 29, 2018), http://www.nlada.org/node/20886.

[24] Bill Chappell, *Virginia Ratifies the Equal Rights Amendment, Decades after the Deadline*, NPR (Jan. 15, 2020), https://www.npr.org/2020/01/15/796754345/virginia-ratifies-the-equal-rights-amendment-decades-after-deadline.

[25] Michael Moline, *A Change in Florida's Rules of Court Just Made Work Life Easier for Women*, FLORIDA PHOENIX (Feb. 3, 2020), https://www.floridaphoenix.com/2020/02/03/a-change-in-floridas-rules-of-court-just-made-work-life-easier-for-women/.

[26] *See* Joe Davidson, *Federal Workers Will Get 12 Weeks of Paid Family Leave. Should Everyone?*, WASH. POST (Dec. 20, 2019), https://www.washingtonpost.com/politics/federal-workers-will-get-12-weeks-of-paid-family-leave-should-everyone/2019/12/19/b9e9c502-228b-11ea-9c2b-060477c13959_story.html; *Family Medical Leave*, NAT'L CONF. OF STATE LEGISLATURES, https://www.ncsl.org/research/labor-and-employment/state-family-and-medical-leave-laws.aspx (last visited Dec. 1, 2020) (including a comparison of family medical leave laws by state).

stalled.[27] Barriers stubbornly persist, particularly for women with intersectional identities. In recent years women lawyers and law professors have filed numerous lawsuits against major law firms, law schools and other legal employers alleging unequal pay and discriminatory treatment.[28] Part II examines these lawsuits as part of a larger analysis of the research related to hiring, retention, and promotion of women criminal lawyers.

II. SITUATING QUALITATIVE DATA AMONG (LIMITED) RELEVANT LITERATURE

While there is no clear source showing how many women criminal lawyers are in the United States and the unique challenges they face, this section attempts to situate the oral accounts within the existing research. After a brief overview of women in the legal profession, this section describes five major sources of data: ABA/CJS data, the Women of Color study done by NALP and the Center for Women in Law, the Canadian Bar Association Study, the LAPIS study, a report issued by the ABA Commission on Women in the Profession, and research from other professional fields traditionally dominated by men.

A. Overview of the Relevant Literature on Women in the Law and in Criminal Law

As a general matter, women face barriers in the workforce. Black and Hispanic[29] women face even greater barriers. The Bureau of Labor Statistics provides valuable annual information regarding unemployment rates, types of work, salaries, disparities across racial/ethnic groups, and legal protection for workers' caregiving responsibilities. With regard to

---

[27] *See Equal Pay & the Wage Gap*, NAT'L WOMEN'S L. CTR. (last visited Feb. 14, 2020), https://nwlc.org/issue/equal-pay-and-the-wage-gap/.

[28] *See* Rebecca Sha, *The Persisting Gender Pay Gap: Recent Developments in the Law that Address Gender Pay Disparities*, ABA J. (May. 16, 2019), https://www.americanbar.org/groups/litigation/committees/diversity-inclusion/articles/2019/spring2019-gender-pay-gap-recent-developments/; Stephanie Francis Ward, *Recent Equal Pay Lawsuits Filed by Female Law Professors has Shined a Light on Academic Compensation Process*, ABA J. (Oct. 1, 2020), https://www.abajournal.com/magazine/article/a-recent-spate-of-gender-discrimination-and-equal-pay-lawsuits-filed-by-female-law-professors-has-shined-a-light-on-the-otherwise-opaque-academic-compensation-process. *See also infra* Part II, Section G.

[29] While recognizing the relevant sensitivities, for simplicity, the author primarily uses the terms "Black" and "Hispanic." To the extent that "African American," "Latino" or "Latinx" are used in the text, they are used interchangeably with "Black" or "Hispanic," respectively, because of the outside source's usage.

unemployment, Hispanic women and Black women have much higher rates than Asian and white women.[30] Asian and white women are more likely to work in higher paying management, professional, and related occupations (53 percent and 45 percent, respectively) than were Black (36 percent) and Hispanic women (27 percent). Hispanic (31 percent) and Black women (28 percent) were more likely than Asian and White women (21 percent and 20 percent, respectively) to work in lower paying service occupations.[31]

Women who work full time in wage and salary jobs earn 81 cents for every dollar earned by men.[32] Asian and white women earn significantly more than Black and Hispanic women.[33] More women workers than men live below the official poverty level.[34] Again, Black and Hispanic women are "much more likely to be among the working poor than white or Asian women."[35]

In terms of working women who are mothers, Black and Hispanic women—who are more likely to work in hourly and low-wage jobs covered by the law—are more likely than White and Asian women to be protected by the Nursing Mothers law. However, more than 1 million Black women and nearly 1 million Hispanic women are not covered.[36] Also, the Center for WorkLife Law, which monitors laws and cases related to gender discrimination, reports that family responsibilities discrimination is compounded by race/ethnicity and/or national origin. For example, Black caregivers report that compared to white co-workers, they are more often denied leave, given schedules incompatible with childcare in retaliation for complaining about race discrimination, and disciplined when family responsibilities make them late or require them to miss work.[37]

---

30 *Women in the Labor Force: A Databook*, U.S. BUREAU OF LAB. STAT. (Dec. 2019), https://www.bls.gov/opub/reports/womens-databook/2019/home.htm (providing data from 2018, the most recent year for which data is available).

31 *Id.* at Table 12.

32 *Id.*

33 *Id.*

34 *Id.*

35 *Id.*

36 LIZ MORRIS, JESSICA LEE & JOAN C. WILLIAMS, UNIV. OF CAL., HASTINGS COLL. OF THE LAW, EXPOSED: DISCRIMINATION AGAINST BREASTFEEDING WORKERS, https://www.pregnantatwork.org/wp-content/uploads/WLL-Breastfeeding-Discrimination-Report.pdf.

37 CYNTHIA T. CALVERT, UNIV. OF CAL., HASTINGS COLL. OF THE LAW, CAREGIVERS IN THE WORKPLACE: FAMILY RESPONSIBILITIES DISCRIMINATION LITIGATION UPDATE 2016, https://worklifelaw.org/publications/Caregivers-in-the-Workplace-FRD-update-

Moving from workers in general to lawyers in particular, discrimination against women in the practice of law is a relatively well-studied area. Since Arabella Mansfield became the first woman admitted to the bar in 1869, observers have tracked women's representation in the law.[38] The roots of the "toughen up, buttercup" mentality for women as lawyers run deep. In the 1920s, the President of the Women's Bar Association reportedly told recently admitted women to never let anyone refer to them as a "woman lawyer" because that in and of itself is an obstacle to practice.[39] The idea was to mimic men as much as possible in order to fit in. Both men and women adopted and adopt the "toughen up, buttercup" mindset.[40] The use of the term in this article refers to the idea that women criminal lawyers must mimic masculine norms to be successful in the field.

When men went off to fight in World War II, new opportunities for women to self-actualize and support themselves and their children arose. There was a significant increase in female law student enrollment during the war.[41] After the war, however, female enrollment in law schools dropped. In the 1950s, many law schools enrolled only one female student.[42]

Enrollment again increased during the civil rights era of the 1960s. The Women's Law Caucus was created during this period, and the organization advocated not only for equal treatment and pay for women practicing law, but also for the Equal Rights Amendment.[43] Although women still accounted for less than 10% of law students in 1970,[44] increases in women's enrollment in law schools during this era

---

2016.pdf.

[38] *See generally* Doris L. Sassower, *Women in the Law: The Second Hundred Years*, 57 AM. B. ASS'N J. 329, (1971); *see also* Catharine V. Waite, *Admission of Women to the Bar*, 1 CHI. L. TIMES 76 (1887), http://wlh.law.stanford.edu/wp-content/uploads/2011/01/waite-adminssiontobar1887.pdf.

[39] Evelyn H. Larson, *Women in the Law*, 6 STUDENT L.J. 21, 22 (1960).

[40] Jim Tankersley, *How Sexism Follows Women from the Cradle to the Workplace,* N.Y. TIMES (Aug. 19, 2018), https://www.nytimes.com/2018/08/19/business/sexism-women-birthplace-workplace.html; Fiona Kay & Elizabeth Gorman, *Women in the Legal Profession*, 4 ANN. REV. OF LAW. & SOC. SCI. 299, 315–20 (2008) (describing the dangers of internalized misogyny).

[41] Larson, *supra* note 39.

[42] *Id.*

[43] Sassower, *supra* note 38.

[44] SUSAN E. MARTIN & NANCY C. JURIK, DOING JUSTICE, DOING GENDER: WOMEN IN LEGAL AND CRIMINAL JUSTICE OCCUPATIONS 113 (SAGE Publications, 2nd ed. 2006). According to Los Angeles-based civil rights lawyer Mia Yamamoto, ten percent of her

were viewed as a major accomplishment of the feminist movement.[45]

A broad summary of the studies done during the 1980s and 1990s is that while women, almost exclusively white, were entering law school in higher numbers, they failed to thrive in the profession. Entry may not have been as much of a challenge in the same way that it was in earlier decades,[46] but during this period, women still faced challenges in pay equity, promotion opportunities, and other opportunities to excel in the legal profession.[47] The studies often cautioned that if some of the obstacles were not addressed, women would not achieve true equality of representation and retention.[48]

Despite the civil rights era increases in women's enrollment in law schools, later in their careers women left the profession at very high rates. The phenomenon of women's "flight from law" garnered much notice and was the subject of numerous studies in the late 1980s and early 1990s.[49] One such study was done by the Gender Bias Task Force (GBTF) created by the Ninth Circuit to uncover data relating to women in the federal court system.[50] This study showed that, of all practice areas, women were least represented in the area of private criminal law, accounting for only 11% of the practicing attorneys in that area.[51] The GBTF report discussed explanations for this low number:

> We heard from many Federal Public Defenders that male defense attorneys operate a "closed, 'old boy' network" described by one woman as "a glass wall around the federal criminal defense bar that excludes women." This exclusive "old boys club" attitude results in not referring cases to women attorneys; not seeking the advice of women Public Defenders; and not treating women defense lawyers with any respect unless they are extraordinarily talented (whereas men of ordinary talent are respected). As one

UCLA class in 1971 was women, and this percentage was the highest enrollment of women of any law school in the country that year (notes on file with the Author).

45 Mabel C. McKinney-Browning, *Don't Call Me Madam - The Personal Side of the Law, from Women Who've Made it to the Top*, 5 UPDATE ON L. RELATED EDUC. at 27 (1981).

46 MARTIN & JURIK, *supra* note 54.

47 *Id.*

48 *See generally* JOAN C. WILLIAMS, UNBENDING GENDER: WHY FAMILY AND WORK CONFLICT AND WHAT TO DO ABOUT IT (Oxford University Press, 2000).

49 *See generally* Fiona M. Kay et al., *Undermining Gender Equality: Female Attrition from Private Law Practice*, 50 LAW & SOC'Y REV. 766 (2016).

50 Judith M. Bilings & Brenda Murray, *Introduction to the Ninth Circuit Gender Bias Task Force: The Effects of Gender in the Federal Courts*, 67 S. CAL. L. REV. 745 (1993).

51 *Id.* at 778.

male respondent reported, he was at an advantage by being male in the "macho world of criminal defense work." As jobs themselves gain gender attributes, women become perceived as "naturally" unable to perform as well as men.[52]

Similarly, the State Bar of New Mexico commissioned a task force to investigate gender bias in 1987. Publishing its findings in 1990, that task force identified issues with pay equality, child-care responsibility, the struggle for a flexible, stigma-free work schedule, and partnership opportunities.[53] This study examined whether certain practice areas were predominately male or female. It found that only general civil practice, family law, and plaintiff's personal injury practice areas showed discrepancies among genders. Notably, the study found a relatively equal percentage of male and female attorneys practicing criminal law.

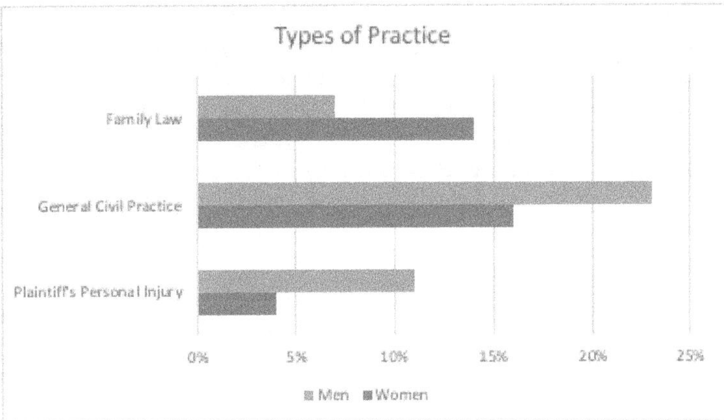

In terms of law school enrollment, in the 2000s, the number of female law students eventually grew to make up roughly half of all law students. However, women have not caught up to men in terms of representation in the highest spheres of influence, salary, and equal treatment. In 2016 and every year since, women represented a slight majority of entering law students in the United States.[54] However, women

[52] *Id.* at 807–08.

[53] SARAH M. SINGLETON, TASK FORCE ON WOMEN AND THE LEGAL PROFESSION, FINAL REPORT OF THE NEW MEXICO STATE BAR TASK FORCE ON WOMEN AND THE LEGAL PROFESSION 7–16 (1990).

[54] Elizabeth Olson, *Women Make Up Majority of U.S. Law Students for First Time*, N.Y. TIMES (Dec. 16, 2016), https://www.nytimes.com/2016/12/16/business/dealbook/women-majority-of-us-law-

still represent a small percentage of leaders in the profession. For example, less than 20% of all law firm partners are women.[55] Some data indicate that even the women who make partner at large firms earn much less than their male counterparts.[56]

Even among rank-and-file attorneys, women's attrition rates have been a concern for some time. Women start out strong, representing nearly half of recent law school graduates, but many studies, including another one released in December 2019, show that the percentage of working female attorneys declines significantly with time in practice.[57] Also, notably, nationwide roughly 31% of law students are people of color but 85% of lawyers are white.[58]

More studies address the issue of women leaving the practice of law in general than specifically address women leaving the practice of criminal law.[59] The Task Force members wanted to know early on what data exists on what percentage of criminal lawyers are women, what percentage of those in senior positions in criminal law are women, and whether there are gender representation differences in various types of criminal law (e.g. public defense offices versus district attorney offices). Unfortunately, that data does not currently exist. However, a few recent studies provide some insights shaping the Task Force's efforts to gather its own data.

students-first-time.html.

55 Jacqueline B. Helfgott et al., *BADASSES: The Rise of Women in Criminal Justice*, 28 WOMEN & CRIM. JUST. 235, 237 (2018).

56 ROBERTA D. LIEBENBERG & STEPHANIE A. SCHARF, WALKING OUT THE DOOR: THE FACTS, FIGURES, AND FUTURE OF EXPERIENCED WOMEN LAWYERS IN PRIVATE PRACTICE, 1 (Am. Bar Ass'n., 2019), https://www.americanbar.org/content/dam/aba/administrative/women/walkoutdoor_online_042320.pdf.

57 *Id.* at 3.

58 *Compare* AM. BAR ASS'N, ABA LAW SCHOOL DATA: JD TOTAL FY CLASS ENROLLMENT DATA, AGGREGATE, FALL 2019 (2019), *with* AM. BAR ASS'N, ABA NATIONAL LAWYER POPULATION SURVEY (2019), https://www.americanbar.org/content/dam/aba/administrative/market_research/national-lawyer-population-demographics-2009-2019.pdf.

59 *See* Joan C. Williams, *Canaries in the Mine: Work/Family Conflict and the Law*, 70 FORDHAM L. REV. 2221 (2002) (discussing the issues facing women in the practice of law generally, such as parental leave and need for flexible schedules); *see also* Deborah L. Rhode, ABA COMMISSION FOR WOMEN IN THE PROFESSION, BALANCED LIVES: CHANGING THE CULTURE OF LEGAL PRACTICE (2001) (discussing how women in the profession brought the issues of work-life balance to the surface).

B. ABA and CJS Data Provide Insights but Research Gaps Remain

While more research is needed into the area of women in criminal law, the American Bar Association recently provided some insightful data on the diversity of the profession generally in the 2020 *ABA Profile of the Legal Profession*.[60] This report is a lengthy compilation of statistics and trends related to the demographics of lawyers, women lawyers, pay, legal education, federal judges, legal technology, lawyer well-being, and lawyer discipline, and includes data from the early 1900s up through 2020.[61] The report noted that while in the past few years the number of women lawyers has barely increased, the overall population of female lawyers increased by 6% between 2010 and 2020.[62] In 2019, 53.3% of law students were women,[63] and about 37% of all lawyers in the United States were women.[64]

By comparison the number of lawyers who identified as a person of color only increased 3% in the past decade, from 11.4% to 14.1%.[65] While no reliable data about LGBTQ lawyers across the entire profession are available, from the over 900 law firms that participated in a 2018 survey, less than 3% of lawyers identified with the LGBTQ community.[66] Interestingly, nearly 6% of summer associates identified as LGBTQ.[67]

It is encouraging that the overall percentage of women federal judges has increased to 27.6% in 2020.[68] The number of minority judges appointed to the federal bench has also increased but remains very low. It appears that the overwhelming majority of sitting federal judges confirmed by the Senate are still white men.[69] Even though men federal judges still greatly outnumber women federal judges, the number of women federal judges has steadily increased, including at the United States Supreme Court, where three of the nine justices have been women

---

[60] AM. BAR ASS'N, ABA PROFILE OF THE LEGAL PROFESSION (2020), https://www.americanbar.org/content/dam/aba/administrative/news/2020/07/potlp2020.pdf.

[61] *Id.* at i–ii.

[62] *Id.* at 32.

[63] *Id.* at 58.

[64] *Id.* at 32.

[65] *Id.* at 33.

[66] *Id.* at 39.

[67] *Id.*

[68] *Id.* at 66.

[69] *Id.*

since 2010.[70] In 2020, 41% of law school deans are women.[71] The percentage of women in the role of general counsel for Fortune 500 companies increased to one-third in 2019.[72]

However, even with the increase of women enrolled in law schools, in the profession, on the bench, and in some leadership positions, pay equity remains a challenge, and law firms struggle with gender diversity. In the past fifteen years, women partnership in law firms has only increased by 5%, and the percentage of female associates has remained fairly stagnant.[73] Also, women associates, non-equity partners, and equity partners earn significantly less than their male colleagues.[74] While all of this information illuminates the current state of the legal profession, it does not specifically address the drop in women from the practice of criminal law.

While only a percentage of criminal lawyers in the U.S. are members of the ABA, CJS senior public relations specialist Emily Johnson provided the TF with relevant CJS data. There is a total of 116,704 women within the ABA's Sections, Divisions, Forums, etc.[75] CJS appears to be one of the entities with the lowest number of women, as its 1,704 women members make up just 1.46% of all women in the ABA.[76] The entity with the highest number of women is the Young Lawyers Division with 36.02% (42,035 women) and the entity with the least amount of women is JD National Conference of Specialized Court Judges with .09% (101 women) of all women in the ABA.[77]

Additionally, under the leadership of then-ABA President Hilarie Bass, the ABA has been focused on how to retain more women in the profession.[78] The ABA Commission on Women in the Profession

---

[70] Linda Lowen, *Meet the Female Supreme Court Justices*, THOUGHTCO. (last updated Oct. 2, 2019), https://www.thoughtco.com/history-of-women-on-the-supreme-court-3533864.

[71] AM. BAR ASS'N, *supra* note 60, at 140.

[72] *Women Held a Third of Fortune 500 GC Spots in 2019*, *Law360* (Jan. 22, 2020), https://www.law360.com/articles/1236839/women-held-a-third-of-fortune-500-gc-spots-in-2019.

[73] AM. BAR ASS'N, *supra* note 60, at 140.

[74] *Id.* at 80.

[75] Provided by CJS Staff Emily Johnson.

[76] *Id.*

[77] *Id.*

[78] *See Why Women Leave the Profession*, AM. BAR ASS'N (Dec. 2017), https://www.americanbar.org/news/abanews/publications/youraba/2017/december-2017/aba-summit-searches-for-solutions-to-ensure-career-longevity-for/.

recently published two studies on the topic.[79] However, the focus on a small slice of the legal profession (i.e. women in large law firms) is a major limitation to their work.

In December 2019, the Commission released *Walking out the Door*, which reported that 50% or more of experienced women lawyers cited caretaking commitments, level of stress at work, emphasis on marketing or originating business, and number of billable hours as "very" or "somewhat" important reasons for leaving private practice.[80] As for caretaking commitments, the study found striking differences between how women and men lawyers perceive their caretaking duties. Experienced women lawyers are more likely than experienced men lawyers to arrange for childcare, leave work for childcare and tend to their children's extracurricular activities.[81] These responsibilities adversely impact the time and effort needed to maintain a successful law practice.[82]

A recent article pointed out that while the issue of women in leadership positions in the legal profession receives attention, the issues facing women of color in similar positions are glossed over.[83] Attempting to address this critique, in June 2020, the Commission released *Left Out and Left Behind: The Hurdles, Hassles, and Heartaches of Achieving Long-Term Legal Careers for Women of Color. This study—which gathered information from focus groups and online surveys from 103 self-identified women of color working in the large firms across the United States.* Women of color continue to experience barriers and bias, resulting in isolation within an infrastructure that refuses to acknowledge the influence of stereotyping of women of color, which is then exacerbated by microaggressions.[84] For one Black participant, the "black tax" was an immovable barrier, whereby one has to demonstrate outsized achievements in order to obtain the same opportunities as everyone else

---

[79] *See, e.g.*, LIEBENBERG & SCHARF, *supra* note 56, DESTINY PEERY, PAULETTE BROWN, & EILEEN LETTS, *Left Out and Left Behind: The Hurdles, Hassles, and Heartaches of Achieving Long-Term Legal Careers for Women of Color* (2020), https://www.americanbar.org/content/dam/aba/administrative/women/leftoutleftbehind-int-f-web-061020-003.pdf.

[80] LIEBENBERG & SCHARF, *supra* note 56, at 11.

[81] *Id.* at 12.

[82] *Id.*

[83] Andrea L. Sanders, *Alawfultruth: Black Girl Magic and the Toll it Takes*, PHILA. SUNDAY SUN (May 10, 2019), https://www.philasun.com/commentary/alawfultruth-black-girl-magic-and-the-toll-it-takes/ (describing her own experiences and those of other Black women leading organizations of two people to five hundred or more people).

[84] PEERY, BROWN, & LETTS, *supra* note 79, at 7.

(i.e. Black associates having two Ivy League degrees).[85] There continues to be a persistent preference for white men, who monopolize access to prime work, the best mentors or sponsors, and insider information in typically male-dominated spaces (i.e. the golf course).[86] While the women of color in this study largely considered leaving the legal field, most decided to stay because they enjoy the work, it makes financial sense, and their personal and familial lives require or encourage it.[87]

C. The National Association of Law Placement and Center for Women in Law Study Provides Important Insights into Law Student Experiences[88]

In June 2020, the National Association of Law Placement (NALP) and the Center for Women in Law at the University of Texas School of Law released a study called *Women of Color: A Study of Law School Experiences* that explores the experiences of women students of color. Below are some relevant highlights and charts.

- A total of 4,084 students from 46 law schools across the United States participated including 2,682 women, of whom 773 were women of color;[89]
- Only 82% of women of color report that they are "satisfied" with their law school experience, compared to 89% of white women;[90]
- Likewise, 31% of women of color considered leaving law school compared to 24% of white women and 22% of white men;[91]
- About 52% of women of color reported comments or interactions with other students or faculty that negatively impacted their academic performance, compared to 21% of white men;[92]
- While over 50% of women of color seek help from the Career Services Office, a lower percentage of women of color seek out guidance on judicial clerkships from the Career Services Office;[93]

---

85 *Id.* at 13.

86 *Id.* at 9–10.

87 *Id.* at 13.

88 *See* THE NALP FOUND. FOR L. CAREER RSCH. & EDUC., THE CTR. FOR WOMEN IN L., WOMEN OF COLOR: A STUDY OF LAW SCHOOL EXPERIENCES (2020), https://www.nalpfoundation.org/uploads/products/WomenofColor-AStudyofLawSchoolExperiencesReport.pdf.

89 *Id.* at 17.

90 *Id.* at 28.

91 *Id.* at 18.

92 *Id.* at 47.

93 *Id.* at 95.

- A higher percentage of women of color report considering work in public interest than men of color, white women and white men;[94]
- Students of color are far less likely to apply for judicial clerkships;[95]
- A higher percentage of women of color report considering work in legal services or as a public defender than all other groups.[96]

CHART 3: OVERALL SATISFACTION WITH LAW SCHOOL EXPERIENCE AMONG WOMEN OF COLOR

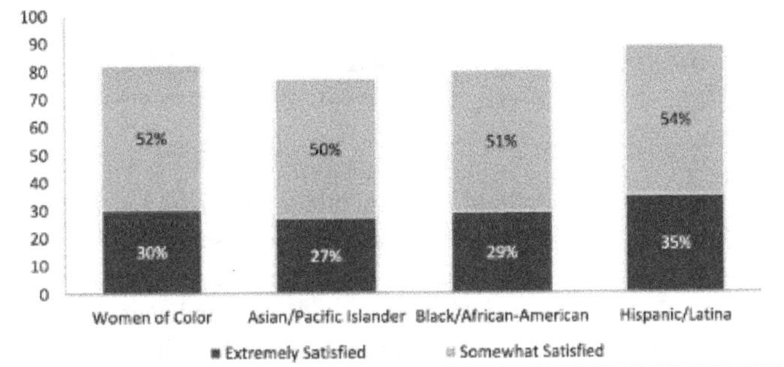

Note: On a 5-point scale where 5 equals "extremely satisfied" and 1 equals "extremely dissatisfied."

CHART 4: OVERALL SATISFACTION WITH LAW SCHOOL EXPERIENCE BY YEAR IN SCHOOL

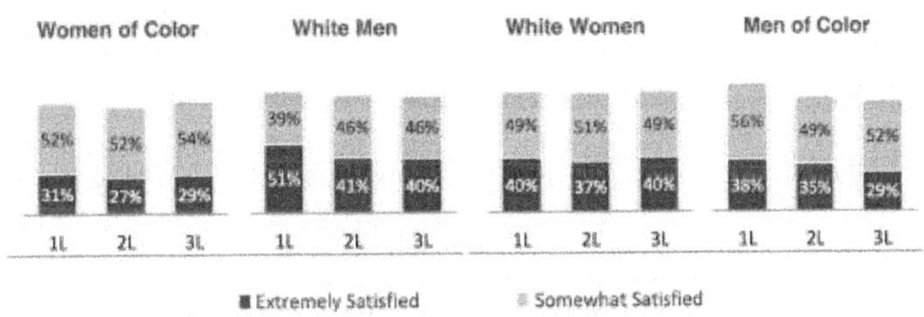

Note: On a 5-point scale where 5 equals "extremely satisfied" and 1 equals "extremely dissatisfied."

94 *Id.* at 127.

95 *Id.* at 64.

96 *Id.* at 127.

CHART 30: STUDENTS WHO APPLIED FOR A POSTGRADUATE JUDICIAL CLERKSHIP
– By Year in School

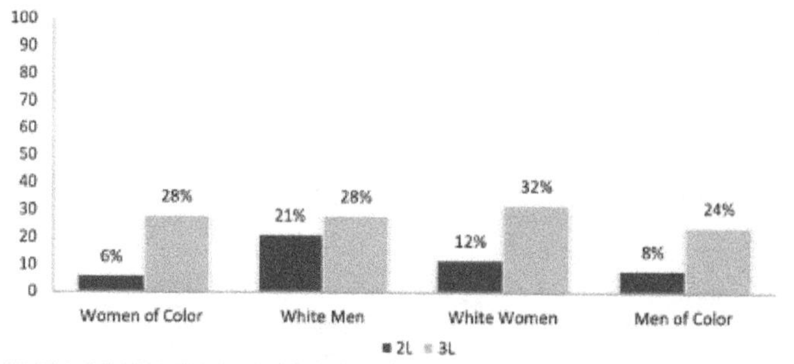

There are some significant limitations of the study. In terms of methodology, it is not clear which schools were surveyed. The study explains that most of the schools surveyed are small (less than 500 students total) or mid-sized (500–900 students), and that 42% of the schools are private and 58% are public.[97] It is not clear whether any Historically Black Colleges and Universities and/or Hispanic Serving Institutions participated, where students of color likely report very different experiences. Also, indigenous women were excluded from the survey,[98] which created an immediate outcry.

Further, important terms such as "of color" and "multi-racial" are not described in detail. A higher percent (6%) of the women of color respondents are F-1 visa holders compared to white men (<1%), white women (1%), and men of color (5%),[99] but no explanation was provided about how their experiences compare to those of the other women of color.

Another omission was the opportunity to explore intersectionality. For example, women of color who also identify as LGBTQ may report exacerbated challenges. Along the lines of student identity and intersectionality, there does not seem to be any attempt to

[97] *Id.* at 156.

[98] Angelique W. EagleWoman (Wambdi A. Was'te Winyan), *Native Women Law Students Excluded From So-Called "Women of Color in Law Schools" Study*, INDIAN COUNTRY TODAY (Jun. 26, 2020), https://indiancountrytoday.com/opinion/native-women-law-students-excluded-from-so-called-women-of-color-in-law-schools-study-lCrOQBx3UEux6kqr2kGxbw.

[99] THE NALP FOUND. FOR L. CAREER RSCH. & EDUC., THE CTR. FOR WOMEN IN L., *supra* note 88, at 155.

identify how such factors as socioeconomic backgrounds, parents' income and education levels, first generation college graduate and immigration status might affect responses. In terms of addressing root issues, exploring intersectionality would be helpful.

Finally, the survey attempted to assess students' interest in different areas of practice, but the categories were both overinclusive and underinclusive. The work categories included: solo practitioner, private law firm-small/medium, private law firm-large, academic, business/corporation, judicial clerkship, government, legal services, public defender, and public interest. These are awkward categories for criminal law. For example, students may have checked "government" or "public interest" who did not check "public defender" because they thought one or both categories included "public defender."[100] Additionally, there is a lack of clarity as to why certain categories were included or left out. For example, if "public defender" was a separate category, seemingly "prosecutor" should have been an option. So, in fact, the study is not conclusive in terms of what percentage of white women and women of color are interested in criminal law as a practice area.

D. Canadian Criminal Lawyers' Association Study Foreshadows Listening Session Reports

A study commissioned in 2016 by the Criminal Lawyers' Association of Canada appears to be the most recent comprehensive study regarding women leaving the practice of criminal law.[101] The study is relevant and instructive to the Task Force's work, but its applicability is limited since it surveyed women in Ontario, Canada, there *have* been some positive changes in terms of federal leave in Canada since the study was completed,[102] and it only included women engaged in the private practice of criminal law. However, there is no parallel study done to date in the United States, so its findings provide some useful insights that ultimately mirror what the Task Force has heard in its listening sessions.

With regard to whether women are leaving the practice of criminal

[100] *See generally id.* at 128–29.

[101] NATASHA S. MADON, PH.D., THE RETENTION OF WOMEN IN THE PRIVATE PRACTICE OF CRIMINAL LAW: RESEARCH REPORT, CRIM. LAWS.' ASS'N (Mar. 2016), https://criminallawyers.ca/wp-content/uploads/2016/03/CLA-Womens-Study-March-2016.pdf.

[102] *See* John Paul Tasker, *Parental Leave Being Extended 3 Months Earlier Than Planned*, CBC (Sept. 26, 2018, 12:54 PM), https://www.cbc.ca/news/politics/parental-ei-leave-benefit-march-2019-1.4839097.

law, the study suggests that women experience unique gender-based challenges and do appear to be leaving the practice of criminal law at higher rates than are men, demonstrating that "there does appear to be an issue in the retention of women in this area of law."[103] Women were 141% more likely to leave the private practice of criminal law than women working in other private practice areas.[104] The Canadian study indicates that women are leaving the practice of private criminal law due to pay and benefit inequities as well as lack of respect.[105] This study also showed that while working in criminal law had a major effect on the attrition of women, it did not have this impact on men.

The gender-based obstacles reported by study participants include financial and logistical difficulties associated with taking time off to have a child, the financial challenge associated with being in private defense practice, the unpredictability of income and the difficulties of building a business on one's own, heavy reliance on "legal aid certificates" (the equivalent of court-appointed cases in the U.S.), and gendered differences in treatment by judges and other court actors which "make an already challenging career all the more difficult."[106]

In terms of sex-based differences respondents reported that judges appear more amenable to men than women when asking to leave court for family purposes such as getting a child from school.[107] Further, men take the lead with some client interactions, "presuming that their female counterparts would not want to and/or would have difficulties dealing with male clients."[108] Senior lawyers (usually male) do not refer clients to female lawyers unless the clients need a "softer" approach and "hand-holding."[109] Women are sometimes viewed as assistants or students rather than lawyers, and given work commensurate with those views.[110] Also, subjects reported that male clients often asked personal and inappropriate questions of their female counsel, or broached subjects they would never discuss with male lawyers.[111]

In terms of the pipeline to criminal law practice, similar to the

---

[103] MADON, *supra* note 101, at 9.
[104] Kay, *supra* note 49, at 787 (providing an update to the previous research on Canadian women criminal lawyers' experiences).
[105] MADON, *supra* note 101, at 8.
[106] *Id.* at 7.
[107] *Id.* at 12.
[108] *Id.* at 13.
[109] *Id.* at 15
[110] *Id.* at 13.
[111] *Id.*

body of work done in the United States in the 1980s and 1990s,[112] the study warned that "there may be a number of women who are making the decision during law school or articling[113] not to go into the practice of criminal law because of their concerns over balancing growing a career with starting/caring for a family."

In terms of support and retention, women who participated in the study shared ideas for improving retention, including:[114]

- Continued and expanded mentorship from senior female lawyers;
- Fixed court end times to ease the stress of uncertain work hours;
- Greater financial support for maternity leave;
- Promotion of collectives of defense lawyers working together;
- Improved financial support for women to take maternity leave;[115] and,
- Greater education of the judiciary to minimize gender-based differences in the courtroom.

The Canadian study's findings and recommendations closely align with those of the TF's recommendations.[116]

E. Latina Attorneys in the Public Interest Sector Study (LAPIS) Bridges Some Gaps in Data

Another important piece of the puzzle is the Hispanic National Bar Association ("HNBA")'s research on the issue of Latina attorneys working in the public sector.[117] Since most criminal law jobs would be considered public sector jobs and women of color are a major focus of the TF's work, this study—coupled with the findings from the CLA study—provides important context and grounding for the TF's work.

The HNBA Commission on the Status of Latinas in the Legal Profession ("Commission") was initiated in January of 2010 to study the

---

[112] *See supra* Part III, Part A.

[113] Articling refers to the experiential component of legal education in Canada where law students are placed at a firm or organization to learn the substantive and practical aspects of being a lawyer. *See Articling and Law Practice Program*, LEGALLINE.CA (last visited Jul. 17, 2020), https://www.legalline.ca/legal-answers/articling-program/.

[114] MADON, *supra* note 102, at 9.

[115] Notably, maternity leave for women in Canada is far more robust than in the United States. *See* Angie Mohr, *U.S. v. Canada: Maternity Leave Differences*, INVESTOPEDIA (updated May 7, 2019), https://www.investopedia.com/financial-edge/0512/maternity-leave-basics-canada-vs.-the-u.s..aspx.

[116] *See infra* Part IV.

[117] Cruz, et al., *supra* note 17, at 151.

challenges facing Latina public interest lawyers.[118] This effort was an extension of the 2009 HBNA report on Latina attorneys in different areas of legal practice.[119] The 2010 study is referred to as the study on Latina Attorneys in the Public Interest Sector ("LAPIS"). This study was done in response to the lack of research on retention of Latina attorneys in the public sector practice of law.[120]

The LAPIS study used both qualitative and quantitative data.[121] For the qualitative data, focus groups were held wherein Latina attorneys were interviewed based on questions raised by the 2009 HNBA study.[122] For the quantitative data, a series of surveys were sent out across the nation.[123] However, by the authors' own admission, the information obtained was limited because there is no national information on the number of Latina attorneys in the public sector and therefore all conclusions and recommendations are based on the surveys returned.[124] Furthermore, based on U.S. Census data from 2008, while the U.S. population was roughly 15% Latinx, only 1% of practicing attorneys were Latina.[125]

The LAPIS study found that Latina attorneys work in public interest because of a strong commitment to social and economic justice, particularly in Latino communities.[126] Participants reported that their employers are more accommodating of family commitments than law firms.[127] Latina lawyers face negative stereotypes due to their gender and ethnicity despite having qualifications that are equal to or better than the qualifications of other lawyers.[128] The study also reveals that Latina lawyers express frustration because even though their employers express a commitment to diversity, they experience discrimination.[129] The low pay of public sector jobs creates concern that young Latina lawyers will not enter public sector practice given their high student loan debt.[130]

---

[118] *Id.*
[119] *Id.*
[120] *Id.* at 152.
[121] *Id.* at 154.
[122] *Id.*
[123] *Id.*
[124] *Id.* at 156.
[125] *Id.* at 159.
[126] *Id.* at 183.
[127] *Id.* at 188.
[128] *Id.* at 193–94.
[129] *Id.* at 196–97.
[130] *Id.* at 199.

According to participants, there is little room to move up as supervisory positions are limited and the turnover is very low for those leadership positions.[131] However, the study did note that mentorship, support from leadership within the attorney's respective organization, and support from community organizations such as local bar associations, positively affect the retention of Latina attorneys in public sector positions.[132]

The study emphasized the importance of public sector work and the concern that inadequate pay creates a larger gap between legal need and available assistance.[133] While there was some research on the pay disparity between public and private sectors being a cause for attorneys leaving the public sector, there was not research on the other factors affecting Latina attorneys' decisions to leave the public sector.[134]

The study did note that research shows that of all areas of law, female attorneys make up the majority of public sector attorneys.[135] The study further noted that Black and Latina/o/x attorneys worked in public sector jobs at a higher rate than white attorneys.[136] Some characteristics of respondents include:

- Women generally around age 40 and under, most were married, but most did not have kids living at home.[137]
- While over half of the participants never practiced in the private sector, over 75% of those who did left after less than five years for the public sector.[138]
- Of the public sector jobs, the survey participants reported mostly working for non-governmental public sector employers with legal services accounting for 35.4% of the current employers.[139]
- In terms of supervisors, 36.9% of the respondents reported having white male supervisors, and 29.8% reported having white female supervisors.[140]
- Similarly, Latino attorneys made up 12.1% of the supervisors while

[131] *Id.* at 198.
[132] *Id.* at 200–01, 208.
[133] *Id.* at 160-61.
[134] *Id.* at 159–60.
[135] *Id.* at 158–59.
[136] *Id.* at 159.
[137] *Id.* at 162, 166–68.
[138] *Id.* at 176.
[139] *Id.*
[140] *Id.* at 178.

Latinas made up only 8.6%.[141]

- Most participants also reported a great disparity in the number of attorneys of color in their offices.[142] Notably, half of the participants reported five or fewer of the total employees in their offices were attorneys of color.[143]
- Close to a third of participants reported earning between $50,000 and $69,000 annually while over a quarter of their supervisors earned over $100,000.[144]
- Most participants did not have parents who were attorneys or went to law school.[145] However, several participants shared that they were inspired by a mentor either in school or in a work setting that led them to law school to make a change in communities in need.[146]
- Many participants reported that they worked in the public sector because of a commitment to social justice and a strong family moral upbringing.[147]
- Respondents also noted the importance of giving back to their communities by providing a familiar face and language to someone in need who may not speak English.[148] However, they also noted that this motivation places a burden on them to provide translation services generally for their employer and other attorneys and staff.[149]

In terms of the substantive findings, respondents reported facing outright discrimination and harassment.[150] They noted mistreatment

---

[141] *Id.*
[142] *Id.* at 170–179.
[143] *Id.* at 179.
[144] *Id.* at 180–81.
[145] *Id.* at 169–170.
[146] *Id.* at 186.
[147] *Id.* at 184.
[148] *Id.* at 184, 190.
[149] *Id.* at 191. Invisible labor refers to devalued labor imposed as expectations on women of color in academia to serve—not only as professors—but as mentors and guides to the racial conscience of institutions and students of color. *See* Patricia A. Matthew, *What is Faculty Diversity Worth to a University?*, THE ATLANTIC (Nov. 23, 2016), https://www.theatlantic.com/education/archive/2016/11/what-is-faculty-diversity-worth-to-a-university/508334/; *see also* Michelle A. Holling, May C. Fu & Roe Bubar, *Dis/Jointed Appointments: Solidarity amidst Inequity, Tokenism, and Marginalization*, *in* PRESUMED INCOMPETENT: THE INTERSECTIONS OF RACE AND CLASS FOR WOMEN IN ACADEMIA 250, 255 (Gabriella Gutiérrez y Muhs et al. eds., 2012).
[150] Cruz, et al., *supra* note 16, at 192–93.

based on their position as a public sector employee, a female, and a Latina.[151] Participants reported being looked down upon because they worked in public service.[152] They reported receiving comments regarding why they had not yet left their jobs and implying that public service jobs should only be a "steppingstone."[153] Some reported receiving "compliments" from judges on how well they speak English.[154] They also reported receiving comments from other attorneys implying that their accomplishments were made possible by affirmative action.[155] There was also a wide reporting from participants of being mistaken for support staff.[156]

In addition to incorporating the recommendations from the 2009 HNBA study,[157] the LAPIS study additionally recommended that there be, inter alia, a mentorship program for Latina attorneys in the public sector field, better diversity training, better pay and/or loan repayment options, more support for translation services, and that the stigma that public sector jobs are less prestigious be addressed.[158]

In sum, Latina attorneys in the public sector widely report being highly satisfied with their careers. However, they face unique obstacles, including the stigma that public sector employees are less competent, leadership opportunities equal to men, and that stereotypes such as not speaking English proficiently or being mistaken for support staff. With respect to language proficiency, it is worth noting that not all Latina attorneys are fluent in the Spanish language and any expectation otherwise is driven by an entrenched social structure of racism that operates on a black/white binary, where other groups falling outside of this binary are treated as monolithic.[159] It is also essential to note the

---

[151] *Id.* at 193–95.
[152] *Id.* at 194–95.
[153] *Id.* at 195.
[154] *Id.* at 192–93.
[155] *Id.* at 193.
[156] *Id.* at 195.
[157] Jill L. Cruz & Melinda S. Molina, *Hispanic National Bar Association Commission on the Status of Latinas in the Legal Profession, Few and Far Between: The Reality of Latina Lawyers*, HISPANIC NAT'L BAR ASS'N 9 (Sept. 2009) (recommending mentoring programs for Latina lawyers, increasing representation and visibility of Latina lawyers, conducting early outreach to Latina youth, and encouraging Latina–based support networks, among others).
[158] Cruz, et al., *supra* note 16, at 210–13.
[159] *See* Cleo Hernandez, *Latina Lawyers: Underrepresented and Overqualified*, MICH. J. OF RACE & L. (Mar. 16, 2018), https://mjrl.org/2018/03/16/latina-lawyers-underrepresented-and-overqualified/#_ftn9; *see also* Alfredo Mirandé, *"Light but Not*

social capital that is concomitant with being a light-skinned[160] Latina attorney, who may have different experiences with discrimination based on language than dark-skinned Latina attorneys.

Notwithstanding these challenges, Latina attorneys report wanting to remain in the public sector.

F. There is a Dearth of Research on Women of Color in the Criminal Justice Field but Some Recent Elections Provide Valuable Insights

The studies analyzed in Part II, Sections A through E provide some insights but do not *directly* address hiring, retention, and promotion of women criminal lawyers. With regard to women of color, there are data about their participation in the legal profession generally,[161] but there do not appear to be any that focus exclusively on the criminal justice field.

In the federal government, only seven of the 93 U.S. Attorneys are women, and only two are Black (men).[162] Approximately one-third

White": A Race/Plus Model of Latina/o Subordination, 12 SEATTLE J. FOR SOC. JUST. 947 (2014).

[160] The Author uses the term "light-skinned" here as it is used by the primary source from the LAPIS study. Cruz, et al., *supra* note 18, at 193.

[161] *See* Joan C. Williams, et al., *You Can't Change What You Can't See: Interrupting Racial and Gender Bias in the Legal Profession*, AM. BAR ASS'N (Nov. 1, 2018), https://www.americanbar.org/groups/diversity/women/publications/perspectives/2018/october-november/new-you-cant-change-what-you-cant-see-interrupting-racial—gender-bias-the-legal-profession; Lauren S. Rikleen, *Closing the Gap: A Road Map for Achieving Gender Pay Equity in Law Firm Partner Compensation*, AM. BAR ASS'N (2013), https://www.americanbar.org/content/dam/aba/administrative/women/closing_the_gap.authcheckdam.pdf; Janet E. Gans Epner, *Visible Invisibility: Women of Color in Law Firms*, AM. BAR ASS'N (2006), https://www.americanbar.org/products/ecd/ebk/217591/; *Visible Invisibility: Women of Color in Fortune 500 Legal Departments*, AM. BAR ASS'N (2012), https://nextions.com/wp-content/uploads/2017/05/aba-visible-invisibility-study-legal-departments.pdf. However, there are studies that focus on women of color in the criminal justice system and as victims. *See* Carmen Rios, *Criminal Injustice: 5 Disturbing Facts About Women of Color and the Prison Industrial Complex*, EVERYDAY FEMINISM (Mar. 10, 2015), https://everydayfeminism.com/2015/03/woc-prison-industrial-complex/ (discussing the school-to-prison pipeline and over-sentencing for women of color); *see also* Maya Salam, *Native American Women Are Facing a Crisis*, N.Y. TIMES (Apr. 12, 2019), https://www.nytimes.com/2019/04/12/us/native-american-women-violence.html (discussing the largely ignored issue of missing and murdered indigenous women).

[162] Zoe Tillman, *There are 93 U.S. Attorneys. Seven are Women and only Two are Black*, BUZZFEED NEWS (Jun. 28, 2020, 1:01 PM), https://www.buzzfeednews.com/article/zoetillman/trump-us-attorneys-lack-diversity-

of the Federal Defenders are women.[163] Those are *appointed* leadership positions. In terms of high-level *elected* office, a close look at the experiences of the record numbers of women of color running for and winning high-profile District Attorney races and the greater numbers of women appointed and elected to the federal and state benches, many of whom have criminal dockets, provides more pieces of the puzzle.[164]

To contextualize the amazing feat of running for and serving in elected office as a woman of color, reports of women of color in leadership roles indicate that they experience numerous microaggressions including not being spoken to directly by peers and subordinates and having their ideas ignored during meetings only to see someone else bring up the same ideas and later take credit for them.[165] Challenges range from microagressions to outright death threats.[166]

Even when a person of color obtain a prestigious leadership position, there is a concern among the underrepresented legal community regarding how long they can maintain these positions. A recent article discussed that more women of color are being elected as District Attorneys (DAs) but addressed concerns about how long these women would remain in office.[167] While most DAs are white males, more women of color, like Kim Foxx (the Black State's Attorney in Chicago), are being elected into DA positions. However, it does not appear that the standards are the same.[168] For example, Ms. Foxx recently received public backlash from DA associations for negotiating a plea deal in a media case when this type of commentary is normally reserved for DAs who are convicted

justice-department.

[163] E-mail from Juval Scott, Federal Public Defender for the Western District of Virginia, to author (Dec. 1, 2020, 5:11) (on file with author).

[164] *See* Melba Pearson, *More Women of Color Are Getting Elected as District Attorneys, but Can They Stay There?*, ESSENCE MAG. (Jun. 24, 2019), https://www.essence.com/news/politics/women-of-color-district-attorneys/; *see also* Andrew Schneider, *Meet 'Black Girl Magic,' the 19 African-American Women Elected as Judges in Texas*, NAT'L PUB. RADIO (Jan. 16, 2019, 4:17 PM), https://www.npr.org/2019/01/16/685815783/meet-black-girl-magic-the-19-african-american-women-elected-as-judges-in-texas.

[165] Sanders, *supra* note 84 (explaining hateful behavior toward Kim Foxx, the State's Attorney for Cook County, Illinois).

[166] Karma Allen, *State Attorney Kim Foxx Gets Death Threats After Dropping Jussie Smollett Charges* (Apr. 23, 2019), https://abcnews.go.com/US/state-attorney-kim-foxx-death-threats-dropping-jussie/story?id=62568123.

[167] Pearson, *supra* note 164.

[168] *Id.*

of criminal conduct.[169]

Marilyn Mosby, the Black Baltimore City State's Attorney, received death threats for prosecuting the police for the death of Freddy Gray.[170] In stark contrast, Larry Krasner, a progressive white male and former defense lawyer, ran for Philadelphia District Attorney on a criminal justice reform agenda and was elected by a wide margin.[171] While Krasner has faced some challenges to his reform agenda, they pale in comparison to the serious violent threats received by Black women DAs.[172]

The concern is that implicit bias and overt acts of discrimination and hostility will deter women and women of color from pursuing and remaining in leadership roles, not to mention the role of implicit biases. Kim Foxx recently ran for and was reelected as Cook County's State's Attorney, but Aramis Ayala, the first African-American state attorney in Florida, did not seek re-election in 2020,[173] at least partly due to the vitriolic backlash to her opposition to the death penalty.[174] Nonetheless, Ms. Ayala's service as state attorney was a progressive step for diversity in the office and for legal practice in the state of Florida.[175]

While not focused on women prosecutors, a survey was conducted in 2017 to shed light on the mystery surrounding prosecutorial discretion.[176] The survey aimed to uncover what motivated prosecutors to prosecute certain crimes since prosecutorial discretion is one of the

---

[169] *Id.*

[170] *Id.*

[171] Akela Lacy & Ryan Grim, *Pennsylvania Lawmakers Move to Strip Reformist Prosecutor Larry Krasner of Authority*, INTERCEPT (Jul. 8, 2019, 2:55 PM), https://theintercept.com/2019/07/08/da-larry-krasner-pennsylvania-attorney-general/.

[172] *See* Eli Hager & Nicole Lewis, *Facing Intimidation, Black Women Prosecutors Say: "Enough"*, THE MARSHALL PROJECT (Jan. 16, 2020, 2:00 PM), https://www.themarshallproject.org/2020/01/16/facing-intimidation-black-women-prosecutors-say-enough.

[173] Monivette Corderio & Jeff Weiner, *Aramis Ayala Won't Seek Re-Election as Orange-Osceola State Attorney; Belvin Perry May Enter Race*, ORLANDO SENTINEL (May 28, 2019, 5:40 PM), https://www.orlandosentinel.com/news/breaking-news/os-ne-aramis-ayala-no-re-election-run-orange-osceola-state-attorney-20190528-z65rv7rmqjdqfoyxsd6rp6junu-story.html.

[174] *Id.*

[175] *Id.*

[176] Johanna Wald, *What's Inside the Prosecutorial 'Black Box'?*, THE CRIME REP. (Mar. 22, 2018), https://thecrimereport.org/2018/03/22/whats-inside-the-prosecutorial-black-box/.

driving forces in the prison population increase.[177] Notably, the results indicated that Black prosecutors had a difficult time placing other Black people behind bars, while white prosecutors did not report initial discomfort with racial disparity in prosecutions.[178]

The survey findings implied that this hesitation was not necessarily a bad thing and reported that prosecutors would like to receive better training, including a familiarization with the impact of incarceration on the local community.[179] Many prosecutors reported feeling an expectation to be hard on crime and that this expectation affected their decision-making.[180] The study also suggested that if the prosecutors were not only more in tune with the impact of incarceration on their local community but also were evaluated on more than convictions alone, their personal mental health and job satisfaction would improve.[181] Prosecutors' job satisfaction and positive mental health means sounder exercise of discretion, and communities would benefit from less incarceration.[182] The positive feedback loop would mean prosecutors would have more flexibility in addressing crime in the community.[183] If prosecutors were evaluated less on convictions, and more on holistic justice actions, all prosecutors, including women—especially women of color—might find more breathing room as DAs.

G. Lawsuits Filed by Women Lawyers Illuminate Systemic Issues in Criminal Law

Although the aforementioned findings are helpful for framing women's issues in the profession broadly, the studies did not explain whether/why women were leaving *criminal* law at higher rates than men in the practice and women in other practice areas. However, while it has been difficult to find conclusive studies explaining this flight of women from criminal law, some recent lawsuits alleging gender discrimination have shed some light on why at least some women are leaving.

Women all over the country, including women practicing criminal law, are embracing the "MeToo" and "TimesUp" themes.[184] Undoubtedly

[177] *Id.*
[178] *Id.*
[179] *Id.*
[180] *Id.*
[181] *Id.*
[182] *Id.*
[183] *Id.*
[184] *See* Rebecca Everett, *Women Suing Prosecutor Describe Retaliation, 'Culture of Cronyism and Sexism'*, NJ ADVANCE MEDIA (Jan. 10, 2019),

countless women have contemplated legal action, and some particularly brave women have actually filed discrimination suits.

A major cause of the increase in discrimination suits is the #MeToo movement.[185] The Me Too campaign was founded in 2006 by Tarana Burke as an expression of solidarity by survivors of sexual assault, harassment, and discrimination. In 2006, activist Tarana Burke heard repeated reports of sexual violence in her work with girls through a nonprofit she had co-founded called Just Be Inc.[186] Ms. Burke started the Me Too campaign that year "to spread a message for survivors: You're heard, you're understood."[187] The hashtag #MeToo rose to greater prominence in October 2017 when allegations against film producer Harvey Weinstein went public.[188]

Ai-jen Poo, executive director of the National Domestic Workers Alliance and an award-winning activist, describes the #MeToo movement as one "of survivors and their supporters, powered by courage, determined to end sexual violence and harassment . . . . We prioritize the leadership and healing of survivors, especially the least visible, most vulnerable among us. And we are growing in our power."[189] The #MeToo movement inspired many women to say enough is enough. Created by 300 women in entertainment, #TimesUp and TIME'S UP, Now grew out of the #MeToo movement and support concrete legal and public relations action in favor of gender equality and equity.[190]

One recent lawsuit was filed by a former female shareholder in Ogletree Deakins Nash Smoak & Stewart P.C., a defense-side labor and employment law firm, against the firm, alleging a culture of systematic pay discrimination wherein women are consistently paid less than men

---

https://www.nj.com/news/2019/01/women-suing-prosecutor-describe-toxic-culture-of-discrimination-harassment.html; *see also Duffin et al. V. D'Antonio et al.*, ACLU OF N.M. (last visited Jul. 16, 2020), https://www.aclu-nm.org/en/cases/duffin-et-al-v-dantonio-et-al.

185 Susan Saltzstein & Jocelyn Strauber, *#MeToo Litigation: The Changing Landscape, A Year Later*, N.Y.C. L.J. (Mar. 27, 2020), https://www.law.com/newyorklawjournal/2020/03/27/metoo-litigation-the-changing-landscape-a-year-later/.

186 *Id.*

187 *Id.*

188 Anna North, *The #MeToo Movement and its Evolution, Explained,* VOX (Oct. 11, 2018), https://www.vox.com/identities/2018/10/9/17933746/me-too-movement-metoo-brett-kavanaugh-weinstein.

189 *Id.*

190 *Our Story*, TIME'S UP, https://timesupnow.org/about/our-story/ (last visited Dec. 11, 2020) (describing the origins of this new civil rights organization).

and financially punished if they speak out against the discrimination.[191] Women criminal lawyers are also filing discrimination suits across the country.[192]

Another suit was filed on January 10, 2019, by current and former female prosecutors and a female investigator in the Atlantic City Prosecutor's Office against the District Attorney and the Atlantic City Prosecutor's Office ("ACPO"). The plaintiffs' complaint alleges pay inequities and an office culture that "favored men over women, turned a blind eye to instances and reports of sexual harassment and gender discrimination, and permitted retaliation."[193] The complaint further alleges a history of discrimination against women in the ACPO, citing the fact that there have only been male District Attorneys since 1985 and there has never been a Chief Female Detective in the ACPO.[194]

A similar lawsuit was filed in Doña Ana County, New Mexico in April 2019.[195] The complaint alleges that not only were the women in the Doña Ana County DA's office not given equal compensation or job advancement, they were subjected to blatant sexual harassment. One female prosecutor reported that she was told to sit on a highly publicized murder trial because her superiors wanted a "pretty, young prosecutor" sitting at the prosecution table.[196] These lawsuits provide a detailed account of what some women are experiencing in criminal law.

Women are suing some of the most powerful actors in the criminal justice system. Approximately two hundred public defenders in Chicago recently filed suit against the head public defender (a woman named Amy Campanelli)[197] and Sheriff Tom Dart, alleging that their inaction resulted in worsening sexual harassment by male detainees.[198] And they are

[191] Complaint for Penalties and Injunctive Relief at 23-24, Warren v. Ogletree, (Cal. Super. Ct. Jan. 23, 2019) (No. 37-2019-00004519), 2019 WL 329444.

[192] *See* Kate Bieri, *2016 Lawsuit Against DA Alleges Discrimination*, KVIA.COM (Sept. 14, 2017) (describing one such lawsuit).

[193] Plaintiffs' Complaint at 5, Ruberton v. Tyner, No. LCV201959304, (N.J. Super. Ct. Law Div. Jan. 10, 2019).

[194] *Id.* at 12.

[195] *See* Katie Hoeppner, *ACLU Files Lawsuit Against Third Judicial District Attorney's Office for Sex Discrimination, Retaliation, and Violating Female Attorneys' Free Speech Rights*, ACLU OF N.M. (Apr. 29, 2019), https://www.aclu-nm.org/en/press-releases/aclu-files-lawsuit-against-third-judicial-district-attorneys-office-sex.

[196] *See* Plaintiff's Complaint at 18, Duffin v. D'Antonio, No. D-101-CV-201901169 (N.M. Apr. 29, 2019).

[197] It is important to note that women report discrimination not only from men but also from other women.

[198] Megan Crepeau, *Detainees Regularly Expose Themselves to Female Public*

getting results. For example, in 2019, Federal Judge Carlos Murguia was sanctioned by the Judicial Council for the 10th Circuit Court of Appeals for sexual harassment and other offenses.[199]

H. "Push" and "Pull" Factors Explored in Other Male-Dominated Professions

Research from other male-dominated professional fields provides valuable insights. In an article examining what holds women back in business, Harvard Business School professor Robin Ely and Florida State University professor and sociologist Irene Padavic describe "pull" factors and "push" factors.[200] "Pull" factors are a woman's own reasons to lean out of work, such as changing interests or a desire to spend more time at home, among others. "Push" factors might include inadequate work or family accommodations, the pressure to conform to the "masculine style" preferred by employers in dealing with clients, and the poor reputation of highly successful businesswomen who have had children. Professors Ely and Padavic conclude that "[w]hat holds women back at work is not some unique challenge of balancing the demands of work and family but rather a general problem of overwork that prevails in contemporary corporate culture."[201] Of course, Americans in general work longer hours and take less vacation time than workers in peer nations.[202] While a complete normative shift in balancing work and personal life would be beneficial for all women, as described below, the listening sessions indicate that other gender-related challenges still remain in criminal justice careers.

Similar "push" and "pull" factors are driving women to leave the medical field as well. Upwards of 40% of women physicians transition to part-time or leave the field within six years of completing their residencies. This is due primarily to familial commitments in addition to

Defenders, Suit Alleges, CHI. TRIB. (Nov. 9, 2017, 7:04 AM), https://www.chicagotribune.com/news/breaking/ct-met-sex-harassment-public-defenders-lawsuit-20171108-story.html.

199 Joshua Bote, *Kansas Federal Judge Rebuked for Sexual Harassment and Illicit Affair with Convicted Felon*, USA TODAY (Oct. 1, 2019, 5:25 PM), https://www.usatoday.com/story/news/nation/2019/10/01/kansas-federal-judge-reprimanded-sexual-harassment-felon-affair/3828593002/.

200 Robin J. Ely & Irene Padavic, *What's Really Holding Women Back?*, HARV. BUS. REV. (Mar.-Apr. 2020), https://hbr.org/2020/03/whats-really-holding-women-back.

201 *Id.*

202 Derek Thompson, *Workism is Making Americans Miserable*, ATLANTIC (Feb. 24, 2019), https://www.theatlantic.com/ideas/archive/2019/02/religion-workism-making-americans-miserable/583441/.

experiencing discrimination related to pregnancy or breastfeeding.[203] Notably, even if women who leave choose to return to the profession, reentry itself poses additional barriers like exams and evaluations for measuring continued competency.[204]

Realizing there was no definitive relevant literature, TF co-chairs Carla Laroche and Tina Luongo, they designed the TF's work to occur in two stages: first to listen to women who have not been heard before by the ABA and next to gather quantitative data. The next section describes in detail the qualitative data gathered in the listening sessions between November 2018 and June 2020.

III. ABA WCJ TF LISTENING SESSIONS ADD POWERFUL VOICES TO EXISTING LITERATURE

While identifying and reviewing the relevant literature, the author simultaneously collaborated with TF co-chairs and members to host listening sessions. In January 2019, the author created—with input from TF co-chairs and members—a survey based on the questions asked in the CLA and LAPIS studies.[205] The survey questions were designed to prepare women for their "testimony" before the Task Force. Co-chairs Carla and Tina organized an initial pilot listening session in Washington, D.C. during the ABA CJS Fall Institute. Following this, the author coordinated listening sessions across the country with significant assistance from ABA staff, Sila Manahane, Kristen Edwards, and TF members.

The author and TF member Professor Barbara Creel worked together to design the format of the listening sessions. Creating safe and supportive spaces was of utmost importance. TF members worked hard to listen and learn, rather than share and teach. We identified capable and discreet law students to serve as notetakers at each session, both to allow TF members to focus on what they were hearing rather than notetaking and to promote opportunities for mentorship among law students, TF members and participants. The author also took detailed notes, and after each session sent hers and the notetakers' to all TF members.

---

[203] Amy Paturel, *Why Women Leave Medicine*, ASS'N OF AM. MED. COLL. (Oct. 1, 2019), https://www.aamc.org/news-insights/why-women-leave-medicine; *see also* Elena Frank et al., *Gender Disparities in Work and Parental Status Among Early Career Physicians*, JAMA NETWORK (Aug. 2, 2019), https://docs.wixstatic.com/ugd/3fdf20_b47503c5516f4b61b42dc04b94605f15.pdf.

[204] *Id.*

[205] *See infra* Appendix B.

Participants were assured their participation and comments would remain confidential. The author maintained consistent and ongoing contact with participants after their listening sessions. Members of the TF invited participants to various CJS events, including to serve as panelists, to help them feel included in the Section and to bring greater attention to participants' valuable expertise.

The details of these listening sessions were as follows:

Listening Session Details	# of non-TF Participants	Surveys Collected
11/18: ABA CJS Fall Institute, Washington, D.C.	10	N/A[206]
1/19: ABA Midyear Meeting, Las Vegas, NV	17	N/A[207]
3/19: University of New Mexico, Albuquerque, NM	17	10
4/19: ABA CJS Spring Meeting, Nashville, TN	5	N/A[208]
6/19: Seattle University School of Law, Seattle, WA	5	3
6/19: Gonzaga University School of Law, Spokane, WA	19	14
7/19: NBA Annual Convention, New York City, NY	12	0[209]
8/19: UC Hastings College of the Law, San Francisco, CA	20	10

[206] The author, who wrote the survey instrument, had not yet been hired.

[207] The author had just been hired and sent the survey out to participants with little notice.

[208] The format of hearing from these women was to meet in small groups with TF members. The author was unable to be present and did not collect surveys because of the more informal format (supper clubs where TF members met with participants at various local restaurants in small groups).

[209] Almost all the participants in this session were Black judges from around the country and, while surveys were not submitted by any participants, the conversation lasted several hours and included meaningful reflections that were written down by the author.

9/19: HNBA Annual Convention, NYC, NY	3	1
11/19: Howard University School of Law, Washington, D.C.	33	15
3/20: FSU College of Law, Tallahassee, FL	10	4
6/20: Experienced Women, Zoom	13	11
TOTALS	164	68

Listening sessions were closed, invitation-only events whose participants include women and gender non-conforming lawyers with diverse lived and professional experiences who were recognized as leaders in criminal justice. These participants are nominated by Task Force members, CJS leaders, and nominees from local and national lawyers' associations. To better contextualize the sentiments expressed, a brief description overall and description of each session is provided.

Participating women were invited to share information about their backgrounds both in the surveys and during their presentations. Many chose to share their racial, ethnic, and cultural backgrounds, as well as their gender identity and orientation, but some did not. Locations were chosen based on a number of variables, including geographic diversity, presence of a Task Force member or members in the city, ability to find a law school host (inclusion of women law students was important to the TF), whether the ABA CJS had recently held events in the city, and ability to draw diverse participants. In terms of diversity, the ideal locations could attract both urban and rural lawyers, lawyers who are members of underrepresented racial, ethnic, and cultural groups, and lawyers with diverse gender identities and orientations.

The sessions included women working in rural towns in New Mexico and Washington; Native American, Black, and Hispanic judges from all over the country; cisgender and transgender women lawyers and judges; current law students, women who had just graduated from law school and women who have been practicing for nearly fifty years; lesbian and bisexual women; women from religious minorities. These women worked at the county, state, and federal levels as prosecutors, public defenders, private criminal defense lawyers, and judges. Also represented were analysts and advocates working in state and local government, non-profit organizations, and private foundations.

All decisions about where to host sessions were made by the co-chairs and reporter, with input from TF members. Prior to most sessions, the author produced written briefs for TF members on the local and state demographic context. Five sessions[210] were held in conjunction with regular ABA meetings because most Task Force members' travel was covered to those meetings. Two sessions—both in New York City—were held in conjunction with the annual conventions of the largest associations of Black and Latinx lawyers. Lawyers came from around the country and world to attend these conventions.[211] The TF hosted four sessions at law schools to which one or more TF members had connections. Finally, one session was held via Zoom during the COVID-19 pandemic.

A number of common threads emerged from the sessions including the following: challenges relating to salaries, gendered expectations, lack of respect for and devaluing of women, lack of flexibility, stage-of-life issues, allyship, generational challenges, juggling work/life commitments, compassion fatigue/vicarious trauma/burnout, and resilience/survival. Women with intersectional identities reported exacerbated challenges. After a brief summary, the author provides direct quotes from participants that illustrate these themes in their own powerful words. The comments come from younger and older women, women with significant experience and new attorneys, women who are first-generation college graduates and women who grew up with significant resources, and women from different racial and ethnic groups. The fact that women from all different backgrounds shared at least some similar experiences indicates the pervasive sexism in criminal law.

Many of the statements reflect overt mistreatment. Even more frequent than reports of overt mistreatment were reports of microaggressions,[212] such as not having their ideas credited or being

[210] November 2018 in DC, January 2019 in Las Vegas, April 2019 in Nashville, August 2019 in San Francisco, and November 2019 in DC were all held in conjunction with ABA/CJS events.

[211] *94th Annual Convention & Exhibits*, NAT'L BAR ASS'N, https://www.nationalbar.org/NBA/NBA_Annual_Convention.aspx?WebsiteKey=0131bda0-b8d6-42ea-88ce-2447f3c18193 (last visited Jul. 24, 2020); *2019 Annual Convention*, HISPANIC NAT'L BAR ASS'N, https://hnba.com/2019-annual-convention/ (last visited Jul. 24, 2020).

[212] Microaggressions refer to the "everyday slights, indignities, put-downs and insults that members of marginalized groups experience in their day-to-day interactions with

presumed to be the one to sacrifice professionally for their home lives. Recent listening sessions from the Task Force revealed that microaggressions towards women and other underrepresented populations are ubiquitous.

At one listening session, a participant described how being a woman practicing criminal law in a leadership role is challenging because of interactions with peers and clients alike. She described how she was repeatedly told by male colleagues to "calm down" and not be too aggressive. She described this experience as "tone policing." Additionally, she faced sexual harassment by defendant clients who made comments on her body. She also noted that working in criminal defense is challenging for any person, but as a woman she has the additional pressure to "shave yourself down" to fit a particular societal norm.

Other women shared experiences that did not seem to qualify as overt harassment or explicitly discriminatory, but they nonetheless felt disturbed enough to remember the experiences in great detail. The cumulative impact of these disturbing experiences over time seems to tip the scale toward harassment and discrimination. These interactions that women described are examples of microaggressions, implicit bias, stereotyping, and stereotype threat[213] that are well-documented in the literature.[214]

Many women shared experiences of disparate treatment and other negative reactions when it came to parental leave after the arrival of a new baby. Women reported that they were often asked if they were coming back, while men did not appear to be asked this question because it was presumed that they would return. For women who were as committed to their work as their male counterparts, such questions led them to feel devalued.

Further, women were often expected to be the ones to take time off from work. One participant noted that women employed as attorneys in her office often had spouses with similarly demanding jobs, while their

---

individuals who are often unaware that they have engaged in an offensive or demeaning way." Hahna Yoon, *How to Respond to Microaggressions*, N.Y. TIMES (Mar. 3, 2020), https://www.nytimes.com/2020/03/03/smarter-living/how-to-respond-to-microaggressions.html.

[213] Stereotype threat is the risk of confirming a negative stereotype about one's social group. *See* Claude M. Steele & Joshua Aronson, *Stereotype Threat and the Intellectual Test Performance of African Americans*, 69 J. OF PERSONALITY & SOC. PSYCH. 797, 797 (1995).

[214] *See supra* Part II for studies.

male counterparts often had spouses who stayed at home or worked part time.

Particularly poignant are the experiences shared by women from diverse ethnic and racial backgrounds. For example, Native American women shared unique experiences coming from traditionally matriarchal societies on which patriarchy was imposed by Anglo and Spanish colonists. As a traditionally matriarchal society, one woman felt her role as a judge was restoring her cultural traditions to their natural order. This particular judge shared that she too experienced voicing a decision or opinion that went ignored until the very same idea passed through the lips of a white man. Women of color—in particular, Black women—reported a high prevalence of discriminatory treatment from everyone in the criminal justice system, including judges, bailiffs, security guards, opposing counsel, colleagues, and even clients and clients' families. Notably, however, quite a few women of color public defenders reported feeling supported at work by colleagues and supervisors, with a few exceptions. In contrast, many of the white women at the listening sessions shared that *overt* discrimination and harassment is not common, but that it does still occur.

<u>Relatively Low Salaries in Criminal Law Serve as a Challenge, Particularly for Women of Color and First-Generation Lawyers</u>

- "The salaries are low. Many of us don't have trust funds or parents that will pay off our student loans. Our check is not our own. It is also going to someone else. It is the family check. It is hard to live on the salaries."
- "[In my role in hiring,] a woman with three children, very well qualified, declined the prosecutor position. It didn't pay well enough to even cover the childcare."
- "My [immigrant] parents were so upset I went into criminal law."
- "I am 58, and I didn't have loan debts, which were a major factor in deciding what I was going to do."
- "As a supervisor, I know that we lost women lawyers because of salaries. Recently however there was an increase for PDs and DAs, so now their starting salary is $50,000."
- "Everyone runs to me when they need a translation, but my Spanish language skills are not taken into account in my pay."
- "As the executive director of my office and a first-gen Latina lawyer, I know what a supportive work environment looks like.

We have created flexible work schedules [e.g. working from home, even before the COVID-19 pandemic]; salary transparency and a salary ceiling where no one can earn more than 2.5 times what the lowest paid individual in the office makes; we pay all our interns; and we cover 100% of mental health care costs."

Discrimination Based on Gendered Expectations of Women in Criminal Law, Particularly Challenging for Women of Color and LGBTQ Women

- "Very often we [judges] see male attorneys treating female attorneys in a way that is disrespectful and unacceptable in the court system and in society."
- "Men try to intimidate you through intimations of incompetence and sometimes blatant overtures of incivility."
- "I have been called or seen other women called, 'honey,' 'sweetie,' 'eye candy,' 'cutie.'"
- "If women have to work twice as hard as men to be recognized as competent, Black women have to work four times as hard."
- "I am routinely called by my first name when male attorneys are called 'Mr. So-and-so.'"
- "I spent 27 years as a man in my office before transitioning almost five years ago. The horrible things you hear that men say about women actually happen."
- "There's a fine line between aggressive and bitch. I was called a chihuahua by a judge once; management said to 'let it go.'"
- "I get called 'little lady,' and people said, 'people will vote for you [for elected public defender] because you are hot.'"
- "I was introduced by my supervisor to a judge as a 'spicy little Latina.'"
- "I have been told I don't look or act feminine enough."

Lack of Respect for and Devaluation of Women

- "I have been told by more than one judge that I remind him of his daughter."
- "I've had a male judge say to me, 'Counsel, school your features,' when I was frowning at him when he ruled against me."
- "I had a male attorney call a female witness a 'whore for the government.' The female judge just said his name. We have thick skins, but that's not good enough."
- "I asked my office for a mentor and they assigned someone who

was a year older than me, a white man. How could he be my mentor?"

- "Sometimes I feel like an imposter, like I'm not a real attorney. No matter how long I do this, there is some disbelief in me deep down."
- "[I'm so tired of] 'he-peating.'"[215]
- "No one thinks I am the attorney. They assume I'm the secretary or sister or auntie."
- "As women in the profession, we tend to undervalue ourselves."
- "People don't expect Black women to read and write well. God forbid I have a typo because the assumption [is] that it is my intelligence and not the speed of my typing."

Women Are Not Necessarily Other Women's Allies

- "I've had a female judge say, 'When you're in my courtroom I expect you to dress like ladies . . . no skin. If I see skin, you're out.' I've seen female judges being harsher to female attorneys."
- "[Even as a woman, I acknowledge] the elephant in the room is women having babies [and what that means for their productivity]."
- "If it weren't for men who looked out for me along the way, I would not be where I am today."
- "I have benefitted from great men bosses who supported me every step of the way."

"Toughen Up, Buttercup" vs. #TimesUp

- "We need to address the generational problem of entitlement and other generational differences."
- "If you can't eat a bologna sandwich while you're reading an autopsy report, you shouldn't work for me."
- "I have seen a lot in my nearly forty years in the same government agency. I have seen sex discrimination and the problems with "boy's club" behavior (i.e. having to drink, use certain language, partake in the same behavior). I have seen women getting scolded or even demoted for calling out sexism in the office."
- "If my employer can't meet my needs or mistreats me, I will not

[215] This term refers to the phenomenon when a woman voices an idea, which a man repeats without attributing to her, and then he gets credit for the idea.

stick around."

- "The new generation forces us to look in the mirror. I had my two children 14 months apart and was back to work within three days. I have always advocated for and supported women. But when I hired a young associate to work at my small firm who got married shortly after she started and then wanted a three-week honeymoon, I reluctantly said, 'okay.' Then she was pregnant and wanted three months of paid leave [which is not required because of the employer size]. I even more reluctantly said, 'okay.' And then she wanted to talk about *transitioning* back to work, and I nearly lost it because I needed her back full-time. Then she was breastfeeding in the office! The male attorneys had no problem with it. I was the one with the problem, and I realized maybe I wasn't as progressive as I thought and needed to change. She's a good lawyer and employee. I want to keep her."
- "Women who succeeded *in spite* of the many obstacles to their advancement are naturally inclined to tell younger women to suck it up as they did. They may even view their success as deriving in part from their ability to overcome those obstacles. (*See* "What-doesn't-kill-you-makes-you-stronger.") Tempting though this approach is, it is wrong. Simply because women have been impeded in their progress for centuries is no reason to perpetuate the practice. Just because a woman learned to 'deal with' sexual harassment in the workplace is no reason her daughter should have to do so."
- "No one (male or female) leaves law school with a guarantee of professional success or even an ideal work schedule. Ours is a labor-intensive profession … any woman who expects to excel will have to demonstrate her competence. If a woman believes her family responsibilities require a fixed number of hours between certain times of day, after which she is "off the clock," she may find employment, but her choices will be limited, because practicing law is not factory work that ends when the bell rings. If, instead, she wants a more flexible work schedule than most employers now provide, that goal is realistic, achievable, and critical to promoting the ascension of women to positions of authority in the legal profession."

Systemic Obstacles to Juggling Work-Life Commitments and the Need for Greater Flexibility in Criminal Law Jobs

- "When I started out, all the male prosecutors I worked with had stay-at-home wives or were unmarried, so they could stay late, work on weekends, and celebrate victories in court."
- "Our office absolutely will not allow job sharing. When I came back from having my baby, that was all I wanted."
- "I would love to work part-time, but I'm not aware of many part-time opportunities in the public sector."
- "I was lucky to hire an over-qualified woman to work for me as my judicial clerk. After giving birth, her main priority was her child and she said she was tired of working for men who just didn't understand her needs."
- "I literally pumped in the bathroom, with a shower curtain for cover. I should have advocated for myself and the people coming behind me because there's not an adequate space. We have space in the office to have one, but they didn't want to spend the money to have one. They turned the filing cabinet room into the pumping room for the defenders and the prosecutors."
- "I stopped breastfeeding because I knew they didn't have the room ready and I refused to pump in the bathroom."
- "I sometimes don't reveal that I'm a mom. I don't want people to have lower expectations of me."
- "Having to be in court until 5 PM or later means never being able to pick your children up from school."
- "There is no chance of retaining quality women attorneys if there has to be a choice between families or work; families will always be chosen."
- "They say every crisis is an opportunity. The current pandemic is surely the former and should serve as the latter. If we in the legal profession have learned nothing else, it is how much more can be done remotely than anyone thought possible. My hope is that employers, private and public, will internalize these lessons, and that both women and men will use this experience to advocate for flexible work hours that allow them to accommodate the ever competing needs of family maintenance, child rearing, and work."

Stage-of-Life Issues

- "With respect to retention and promotion, [the question] is how you make it there and still have a family . . . what's often overlooked is fertility stuff and IVF and freezing your eggs. I don't want to have children until I've done a homicide."
- "I do not have children. I chose not to have kids. I have never had to explain to someone that I have to leave because I have to pick up my kid. That was indeed a significant factor in my opportunity to make choices."
- "Another problem is menopause. What do you do when you have a hot flash in the courtroom? Or what happens if you can't wait two hours to go to the bathroom?"
- "I feel like I get assigned more work since I'm single to make up for people in my office who have children."

Compassion Fatigue/Vicarious Trauma/Burnout

- "I left criminal law because I couldn't stand seeing so many young black men go to prison."
- "Looking young [and being a minority] has caused . . . [me] to come in overly prepared and organized to be taken seriously. I grew up with a single mom, was the first to go to college. I came in with a different perspective: I've had people in my family incarcerated. I became a prosecutor to help people. However, being one is hard—from all sides: defense says you're too aggressive, victim saying not aggressive enough, cops not wanting to come in."
- "They [men and women] bully and intimidate to evoke anger and then we get labeled as the 'Angry Black Woman.'"
- "We bury these things [sexism, racism] because if we don't, we can't continue to work."
- "This job requires that I have regular therapy."

Resilience/Survival

- "There will always be people in your life who will treat you wrong. Be sure to thank them for making you strong. Tap them on the shoulder and thank them."
- "Failure is very important for your career success. You need to embrace failure as a trial attorney. For those who want to be litigators and as an attorney in general, failure is part of life. You

have to learn how to embrace it."

- "Just because I don't have debt or I didn't have kids, doesn't mean I shouldn't be working to deal with this system and trying to make this system and workplaces better."
- "Lawyers perform. Everywhere you are, you're in a performance space."
- "If we have a platform and seats at the table, we need to use those voices."

The last in-person listening session occurred on March 6, 2020, just days before the pandemic forced widespread shutdown of courthouses and other public spaces. The shutdown and the focus on racial justice in the aftermath of the George Floyd murder have affected the pace of the TF's work, but these conditions have only heightened members' passion for criminal justice. The listening sessions established powerful relationships between the women involved, and many expressed a desire to stay connected to one another and to the TF. The TF is exploring ways to maintain and expand on those new relationships. For example, the widespread use of Zoom invited the opportunity for the TF to pivot from its work for a bit to check in with women who previously presented to see how COVID-19 and calls for racial justice are affecting their work.

IV. SOLUTIONS TO CHALLENGES FACED BY WOMEN CRIMINAL LAWYERS

Since February 2019, the TF has held monthly conference calls and in-person meetings twice a year. During these calls and in-person meetings, members debrief listening sessions and discuss potential remedies. While the final recommendations have not been drafted, potential remedies identified by the TF and indicated in the literature include meaningful mentorship, more flexible workplace policies, better training (particularly in rural and underfunded jurisdictions), more transparency and accountability, and better tracking of relevant data.[216] These remedies are described in greater detail here.

A. Mentorship

To date, mentorship is the most commonly cited remedy in both the literature and the listening sessions to mitigate women leaving criminal law. Many women are hesitant even to apply to some of the

[216] *See* Cruz et al., *supra* note 16, at 200–01; *see also* MADON, *supra* note 101, at 8–9.

senior positions. One woman at the Albuquerque listening session shared that there has never been a female U.S. Attorney in New Mexico and that this phenomenon was a result of women not applying.[217] She expressed that if more women encouraged each other to apply to leadership positions, there would likely be more women in these roles.[218]

Recently retired longtime Alexandria (Virginia) Public Defender Melinda Douglas provides a great example of the power of mentorship.[219] Ms. Douglas is widely regarded as having mentored countless female criminal lawyers by example and by actions. In an in-depth interview upon her retirement, she noted that as a public defender she was free to focus solely on defending her clients, rather than on making money or putting another person in jail or prison.[220] A frequently articulated request by listening session participants was access to mentorship programs that pair new attorneys with persons similar to them who are in some sort of leadership or advanced role to ease feelings of isolation. The ABA offers numerous mentoring opportunities through its various sections, but it is clear that there are tens of thousands of women criminal lawyers and law students who are not ABA members. The TF is thus investigating ways to amplify existing mentoring opportunities through the ABA, local and state bar associations, law schools, and other groups. In the short term, the TF includes mentoring opportunities for law students in our listening sessions, and students report gratitude for these opportunities.[221]

B. More Flexible Workplace Policies May Address Drift and Dissatisfaction

Greater work schedule flexibility also would support women and decrease the likelihood that they decide leave criminal law or, in some cases, law altogether. This issue has been studied in other contexts, particularly in private sector legal jobs. Even in workplaces that allow some flexibility, women and men report a stigma attached to working

[217] Memoranda from Albuquerque Listening Session, Maryam Ahranjani [March 1, 2019] (on file with author).

[218] *Id.*

[219] Rachel Weiner, *'I Defend: It's What I Do.' Public Defender in Virginia Retires Decades After Founding Office*, WASH. POST (Nov. 1, 2019, 10:03 AM), https://www.washingtonpost.com/local/legal-issues/i-defend-its-what-i-do-public-defender-in-virginia-retires-decades-after-founding-office/2019/11/01/5f028a46-fb23-11e9-8906-ab6b60de9124_story.html.

[220] *Id.*

[221] Author's and TF members' notes and emails (on file with the Author).

part-time or alternate schedules.[222] However, in the listening sessions, women expressed—quite emotionally, in some cases—how juggling all their responsibilities was met with a "toughen up, buttercup" mentality, which felt like an affront to their professional identity and personal dignity.

Litigators reported that they would like the opportunity to job share or work from home on non-court days upon return from parental leave, while caring for elderly relatives, or just in general to strike a balance between work and home commitments.[223] Women in the listening sessions talked about how much the opportunity to save the commuting and preparation time (meals, clothing, etc.) by working from home whenever possible would make a significant difference, but they reported that government policies remain largely inflexible.[224]

Advocates of balance programs argue approval for them should come from the highest level of an organization, should be in writing, and information about them should be widely circulated.[225] In addition to top-down support in writing, there should also be support in the form of opportunities offered. That is, those who participate in balance programs should not be penalized by being given low-profile work or denied opportunities for advancement.[226] While this literature addresses some important work-place concerns, it does not address the issues in working in a criminal law environment specifically.

Even pre-COVID, some jurisdictions are exploring systemic change. Proponents of the new rule in Florida argue that it will allow more women to take on lead counsel roles and keep them from being sidelined.[227] While the rule is not limited to criminal law matters, it is predicted to have a positive effect on women in the practice of criminal law as criminal law matters are often adjudicated in court proceedings.

---

222 LIEBENBERG & SCHARF, *supra* note 56; *see also* Joan C. Williams, Aaron Platt & Jessica Lee, UNIV. OF CAL., HASTINGS COLL. OF THE LAW, DISRUPTIVE INNOVATION: NEW MODELS OF LEGAL PRACTICE (2015), https://worklifelaw.org/publications/Disruptive-Innovations-New-Models-of-Legal-Practice-webNEW.pdf.

223 Author's notes from Spokane listening session (on file with the Author).

224 Notes from Albuquerque, Spokane and San Francisco Listening Sessions (on file with the Author).

225 Steven K. Berenson, *Creating Workplace Solutions for Women Attorneys: Report of the Lawyers Club of San Diego Balance Campaign*, 28 T. JEFFERSON L. REV. 449, 468–69 (2005).

226 *Id.* at 471–73.

227 Moline, *supra* note 25.

C. Better Training Opportunities, Particularly for Women in Rural and Under-Resourced Jurisdictions on Wellness, Diversity and Inclusion, Professional Development and Other Challenges

The literature and information gathered in listening sessions indicate a need for creating and amplifying existing training opportunities for employees and law students on a number of challenges. These challenges include the pernicious effects of implicit and explicit bias;[228] vicarious and secondary trauma and burnout;[229] diversity and inclusion; and gender-based and intersectional issues. Better training has been raised as a particular concern by women in rural communities and in places that do not have adequate funding for ongoing training.[230] Many bar associations have recommended addressing these issues by providing awareness training for unconscious bias in law schools and in practice.[231]

Since the #MeToo Movement, many laws have been passed to require diversity and inclusion training.[232] Testimony and other evidence presented to local legislative bodies provide some insight into what underrepresented persons face in the workplace. In her testimony before the Oregon legislature, Maya Raghu, Director of Workplace Equality & Senior Counsel for the National Women's Law Center, expressed that anti-discrimination policies should provide sanctions for those who aid or conceal harassment.[233] Additionally, Ms. Raghu points out that reformed legislation in many states now does not allow for non-disclosure agreements precluding women from speaking out about harassment they suffered.[234] Ms. Raghu co-authored a study providing guidance for developing effective sexual-harassment policies with a focus on prevention.[235] This study suggests that an important element, inter alia, is

---

[228] JUDICIAL DIV., AM. BAR ASS'N, ENHANCING JUSTICE: REDUCING BIAS (Sarah E. Redfield, 2017); Jerry Kang et al., *Implicit Bias in the Courtroom*, 59 UCLA L. REV. 1124 (2012).

[229] *The Vicarious Trauma Toolkit*, OFFICE FOR VICTIMS OF CRIME, https://ovc.ojp.gov/program/vtt/what-is-vicarious-trauma (last visited Jul. 16, 2020).

[230] Notes from Albuquerque and Spokane Listening Sessions (on file with the Author).

[231] *Id.*

[232] *See Workplace Protection Act: Hearing on LC 1170 Before the Senate Workforce Comm.*, 80th Leg. Assemb. (Jan. 22, 2019) (testimony of Maya Raghu Director of Workplace Equality & Senior Counsel National Women's Law Center), https://nwlc.org/wp-content/uploads/2019/02/NWLC-Testimony-on-Oregon-Workplace-Harassment-Legislation.pdf.

[233] *Id.* at 7.

[234] *Id.* at 4.

[235] Maya Raghu & Joanna Suriani, *Workplace Justice #MeTooWhatNext: Strengthening*

being allowed to report misconduct anonymously.[236]

A number of women identified—and TF members agree—that training must start in law school, and it must exist in the mandatory curriculum so that *all* law students know about potential gender-related and intersectional challenges and know how to respond when and if they experience or witness discriminatory behavior.

Such training aligns with the recent attention paid to law student wellness and well-being. The ABA itself has launched a wellness pledge that encourages law schools to commit to certain core principles.[237] Legal scholars Nathalie Martin, R. Lisle Baker, Larry Krieger and others have argued persuasively that more attention must be paid to lawyers' and law students' emotional health, pursuit of happiness, and search for meaning in the profession.[238] Professor Martin's book, *Lawyering from the Inside Out* inspires law students to develop a professional identity as a lawyer through mindfulness and emotional intelligence practices. Professor Baker offers a convincing case for developing a positive psychology course for lawyers and law students with the goal of helping law students to develop skills such as resilience, character, positive values, and enhancing relationships, in order to buttress the emotionally taxing work of lawyering.

The author suggests developing a brief guidance document to send to all law school deans and associate deans for curriculum that could be embedded in required 1L criminal law courses, a course that uses Professor Martin's book or a similar text, a positive psychology course such as the one Professor Baker designed, and any other relevant course. The document would address how bias and trauma affect criminal lawyers and how women and gender nonconforming individuals (especially those with intersectional identities) may experience such challenges. The goal

---

Workplace Sexual Harassment Protections and Accountability, NAT'L WOMEN'S LAW CTR. (Dec. 2017), https://nwlc.org/wp-content/uploads/2017/12/MeToo-Strengthening-Workplace-Sexual-Harassment-Protections.pdf.

236 *Id.*

237 *Working Group to Advance Well-Being in the Legal Profession*, AM. BAR ASS'N, https://www.americanbar.org/groups/lawyer_assistance/well-being-in-the-legal-profession/members/ (last visited Feb. 12, 2020).

238 NATHALIE MARTIN, LAWYERING FROM THE INSIDE OUT: LEARNING PROFESSIONAL DEVELOPMENT THROUGH MINDFULNESS AND EMOTIONAL INTELLIGENCE (Cambridge University Press 2018); R. Lisle Baker, *Designing a Positive Psychology Course for Lawyers*, 51 SUFFOLK U. L. REV. 207 (2018); Lawrence S. Krieger & Kennon M. Sheldon, *What Makes Lawyers Happy? A Data-Driven Prescription to Redefine Professional Success*, 83 GEO. WASH. L. REV. 554 (2015).

of the document would be to specifically describe the rewards and challenges inherent in the practice of criminal law for women and gender nonconforming individuals.

D. Gathering More Data on Hiring, Retention, and Promotion of Women in Criminal Law

Based on the lack of directly relevant literature, the TF plans to collect and recommends ongoing collection of more data to help address the perceived flight of women from the practice of criminal law. Interestingly, such a simple recommendation will not be simple to implement for a number of reasons, including potential backlash[239] and the lack of one governing body to conduct the data gathering. With regard to backlash, which as noted earlier sometimes even comes from women,[240] in a recent piece in the *New York Times*, the writer suggested that it would be less arduous to let equality work itself out naturally.[241] History is replete with instances of powerful people failing to cede power voluntarily to marginalized groups. The piece, however, reflected the "toughen up, buttercup" mentality that certainly occupies space in this conversation.

Collecting data and keeping track of the number of women in various roles seems like a simple first step. The roles of women and women of color in the practice of criminal law have not been widely tracked. Getting more data on what roles women fill and what these women are experiencing is the first step in addressing the perceived flight of women from the practice of criminal law. However, while the Task Force has identified the importance of gathering raw data on the number of women in the practice of law from federal, state, and local agencies, it also has realized what an enormous undertaking that would be given its limited resources and staffing. In an effort to at least begin to collect useful data, over the next year, it will be working with allies—including the ABA's Center for Innovation and the American Bar Foundation—to survey leaders across the field and begin collecting data on the hiring, retention, and promotion of women in criminal justice.

In sum, there is a dearth of information on the perceived flight of women from the practice of criminal law and their lack of representation

---

[239] Katherine Mangu-Ward, *Stop Counting Women: Quotas and Tallies Won't Bring Real Progress on Gender Parity*, N.Y. TIMES (Feb. 23, 2019), https://www.nytimes.com/2019/02/23/opinion/sunday/women-directors-quotas.html.
[240] *See supra* Part III.
[241] *Id.*

in leadership positions in the field. The research that is available indicates that while some women experience overt discrimination, most suffer from regular microaggressions in the workplace that over time are likely to lead to burnout and dropout.

It is clear that system-wide change is needed to retain women—especially women with intersectional identities—in criminal law. Although the TF recognizes all women's experiences, there can be no doubt that women with intersectional identities seem to experience all the challenges to a more intense degree than white middle-to-upper-middle class cisgender women. To that end, we have a special focus on supporting and elevating women with intersectional identities.

CONCLUSION

To the extent that one agrees there are obstacles to equality/equity for women in hiring, promotion, and/or retention in criminal law, there are two polar opposite responses: "Toughen up, buttercup!" and #TimesUp. This article previously described both responses in Parts III.A. and III.G., respectively. The latter view is reflected by some of the DC-area law students with whom the TF met in November 2019 at Howard University Law School. Several young women said they simply would not apply to work somewhere that they hear is a toxic work environment. One woman described setting up an informational interview with a male attorney with the hope that he might lead her to a job prospect, but when he continued hitting on her during the meeting, she left disgusted and completely unwilling to consider any advice or information provided by him.

There may be generational, cultural, experiential, and other differences embedded in the two polar extreme views of the status of women in criminal law. The author recommends recognizing both but also recognizing the space in-between. The space in-between includes supervisors and women criminal lawyers alike being willing to engage in hard conversations, being willing to adapt, standing up for one another whenever possible, and acknowledging that sometimes change happens slowly.

Much work lays ahead for the TF.[242] Balancing a full caseload with the intensive demands of a baby, women like Marta simply are not in the best position to effectively advocate for themselves. TF members

[242] Maryam Ahranjani, *Looking Back, Looking Forward*, CRIM. JUST. MAG. 65–66 (Fall 2020).

feel committed to shining a bright light on Marta's and others' challenges. The TF wrapped up listening sessions in June 2020 and moved into the quantitative data-gathering stage. The global COVID-19 pandemic has caused the TF to slow down its work for the time being since some members have school-age children and other caretaking responsibilities that have intensified. To the maximum extent possible, some aspects of our work continues.

The first effort to gather quantitative data is the administration of a survey based on the survey in Appendix B to women who have testified to memorialize their experiences and hear how COVID-19 has affected them. While the TF has secured valuable assistance from the ABA Center for Innovation to administer this follow-up survey, an important next step will be to engage in the next quantitative data-gathering effort, which will be a multi-state survey administered to all licensed women criminal attorneys within two or more states, again aimed at gathering information about barriers to hiring, retention and promotion. The TF will need significant resources, including funding for a research team, to engage in the multi-state survey.

After qualitative data-gathering is complete, the advocacy stage will begin. This stage will include drafting a resolution related to its findings for the CJS to present to the ABA House of Delegates, the powerful policy-making arm of the ABA.[243] The TF also plans to elevate progressive and responsive policies, laws, and information by creating an online toolkit of resources. For example, a number of influential women criminal lawyers have already volunteered to record trainings on how to run to be a District Attorney, how to get elected to state courts, implicit bias, legal requirements for lactation rooms, etc.

The author and members of the TF have received countless emails and calls from law students, women criminal lawyers, allies, and others thanking us for giving them a platform to reflect and for really *listening* and *hearing* them. Of course, those of us involved in the project feel incredibly hopeful because women are standing up and motivating others to speak and stand up for themselves.

There are reasons for hope. The likelihood for improvements for women in criminal justice is relatively high in the current social climate, including the COVID-19 pandemic and calls for racial and criminal

[243] *ABA House of Delegates*, AM. BAR ASS'N, https://www.americanbar.org/groups/leadership/house_of_delegates/ (last visited Feb. 10, 2020).

justice reform in the wake of George Floyd's death at the hands of Minneapolis police officer Derek Chauvin. Societal values around gender norms, balancing work and personal lives, and overall wellness are changing. The ABA—and the CJS WCJ TF in particular—recognizes those changes and has committed to long-term and systemic reform, so hopefully we are moving in the right direction.

APPENDIX A

Women in Criminal Justice Task Force
American Bar Association Criminal Justice Section

Co-Chairs:

Carla Laroche
Clinical Professor
Director, Gender and Family Justice Clinic
Florida State University College of Law Public Interest Law Center (FL)

Tina Luongo
Attorney-in-Charge of the Criminal Defense Practice of The Legal Aid Society (NY)

Reporter:

Maryam Ahranjani
Associate Professor of Law and Don L. & Mabel F. Dickason Professor, University of New Mexico School of Law (NM)

Members:

Lara Bazelon
Professor of Law
Director of the Criminal & Juvenile Justice and Racial Justice Clinics
University of San Francisco School of Law (CA)

Gloria Ochoa-Bruck
Attorney, Former Director of Local Government and Multi-Cultural Affairs, City of Spokane (WA)

Barbara Creel
Karelitz Professor of Evidence Law and Procedure
University of New Mexico School of Law (NM)

Kim Parker
Immediate Past Chair, ABA Criminal Justice Section (MO)

Melba Pearson
Policy and Programs Director, Center for the Administration of Justice, Florida International University (FL)

Yaamini Rao
Deputy Public Defender, Santa Clara County (CA)

Camelia Valdes
District Attorney, Passaic County (NY)

Ellen Yaroshefsky
Professor of Law, Hofstra Law School (NY)

APPENDIX B

ABA Women in Criminal Justice Task Force (WCJ TF)
Survey for Listening Session Participants

Thank you for helping us gather information to inform our upcoming report on Women in Criminal Justice. Our Task Force has several goals, including to highlight the challenges facing women attorneys practicing in the criminal legal system and the unfortunate trend of women leaving the profession; provide recommendations to address the concerns specific to women in the criminal legal profession; and increase the membership of diverse women practitioners in the Section;, ensure the Section's policies and practices are inclusive; , and raise the influence and profile of women practitioners in the Section.

Please complete and submit this survey to WCJ TF Reporter Maryam Ahranjani at Maryam.Ahranjani@law.unm.edu prior to your participation in the listening session.

The identity of those participants who volunteer for the interview and provide their personal contact information will be only known to the researchers. Data from their interviews may be shared in professional conference presentations or publications, but the identity of those interviewees will not be revealed (a pseudonym will be used instead of the person's name) without express permission.

The questions that follow are designed to help capture relevant information. If you feel comfortable, please provide your contact information (which we will keep confidential if asked) for further follow-up.

Part One:Biographical Information

1. If you feel comfortable sharing your name and contact information, please do so here.
2. If you feel comfortable describing your background (racial/ethnic/gender identity/etc.), please do so here.
3. How long have you been practicing law – broadly defined to include academic, policy, and other work that involves using your law degree – overall?
4. Are you currently employed?
5. Have you practiced criminal law?
6. If so, in what capacity (please explain and list all, including amount of time in each role and location) For example, Public defender, Memphis, 3 years; private criminal defense, Nashville, 4 years; trial court judge, Nashville, 5 years (to present)
7. Are you currently a member of the American Bar Association?
8. If not, have you ever been a member of the ABA?
9. If you previously were an ABA member but are no longer a member, why are you no longer a member?
10. If you have never been an ABA member, would you kindly explain why not?

Part Two: Retention of Women Criminal Lawyers

Please answer these questions only if you are a woman who has practiced or is practicing criminal law.

1. What challenges, if any, have you personally experienced with regard to hiring, retention, and promotion in criminal law-related positions?
2. What challenges have you observed *others* experience?
3. Were the hiring, promotion and retention issues better, worse, or the same as they are in your current location? Please explain.
4. If you currently practice criminal law, do you see yourself staying in practice for the foreseeable future?
5. Why or why not?
6. When gender issues arise in the workplace, do you have a source of support (informal or formal)?
7. If so, to whom do you go for support? We're not asking for specific names as much as roles.

Part Three: Solutions

Please focus on your experience as a criminal law practitioner unless the question indicates otherwise.

1. As a criminal law practitioner, what do you feel you need(ed) to be successful?
2. Have these needs changed as you have progressed in your career? If yes, how so?
3. As a criminal law practitioner, what do you feel you need(ed) to remain in the criminal justice practice?
4. Do you think the need to be successful and remain in the field differed between you and your women colleagues?
5. If you have experience practicing in other areas, during your time in those other field(s), do you think these needs to be successful and remain in the field differed between you and your other women colleagues?
6. As a criminal law practitioner, were you provided with what you needed to be successful and remain in the field? Why or why not?
7. What has or did your employer do to promote retention of female criminal lawyers?
8. Of those policies and practices, how effective did you find them? Were there policies or practices that were more effective than others?
9. What could your employer do or could your employer have done to improve retention of women criminal lawyers?
10. How receptive do you think your employer is or would have been to implementing these recommendations?
11. What would it take for your employer to provide those things?
12. Is there any other information you would like to share regarding women practicing in the criminal justice profession?

APPENDIX C
Pulling Back the Curtain

Maryam Ahranjani

Pulling Back the Curtain: A Follow-Up Report from the ABA Criminal Justice Section Women in Criminal Justice Task Force (TF)

Submitted by Professor Maryam Ahranjani, TF Reporter[1]

"Every crisis is an opportunity...We in the legal profession have learned how much more can be done remotely. My hope is that employers...will internalize these lessons and that both women and men will use this experience to advocate for flexible work hours..."

- ✓ Follow-up survey respondent

SUMMARY

In an era when women's hard-fought and hard-earned participation in the workforce is in peril, the ABA Criminal Justice Section's Women in Criminal Justice Task Force (TF) continues its groundbreaking work of documenting challenges in hiring, retention and promotion of women criminal lawyers. *Pulling Back the Curtain* follows up on the initial findings of the TF. The findings are published in the Berkeley Journal of Criminal Law[2] and the ABA Criminal Justice magazine.[3] This report describes the results of a subsequent survey of diverse criminal lawyers

---

[1] The Task Force extends its thanks to the Criminal Justice Section for its support of all of the TF's work, as well as to American Bar Foundation researchers Professors Ajay Mehrotra and Bob Nelson, who provided valuable advice regarding survey structure. TF Reporter and TF Data Committee Co-Chair Maryam Ahranjani, TF Advisory Board Member and Data Committee Co-Chair Yaamini Rao, and ABA Center for Innovation collaborator Sarah Glassmeyer developed the survey that serves as the basis for this report. TF Co-Chair Carla Laroche, TF members Professor Sarah Redfield and Ann Ratnayake Macy, and Yaamini Rao contributed valuable edits to this report. Nat Saing contributed critical editing and formatting assistance. All TF members are listed at the end of this report.

[2] Maryam Ahranjani, *"Toughen Up, Buttercup" versus #TimesUp: Initial Findings of the ABA Women in Criminal Justice Task Force*, 25 BERKELEY J. CRIM. L. 99 (2020) (providing a thorough background of the history of women in criminal law and presenting initial findings from the listening sessions).

[3] *See* Carla Laroche & Tina Luongo, *Task Force Launches*, CRIMINAL JUSTICE MAGAZINE, https://www.americanbar.org/groups/criminal_justice/publications/criminal-justice-magazine/2019/spring/task-force-launches (Spring 2019). Maryam Ahranjani, *Listening Session Participants Express Feelings of Isolation—and Demonstrate Resilience*, CRIMINAL JUSTICE MAGAZINE (Nov. 1, 2019), https://www.americanbar.org/groups/criminal_justice/publications/criminal-justice-magazine/2019/fall/listening-session-participants-express-feelings-isolation-demonstrate-resilience/; Maria Carmen Hinayon, *Who Needs the Old Boys' Club? Let's Make Our Own—Highlights from the WCJ Bay Area Listening Session*, CRIMINAL JUSTICE MAGAZINE (Jan. 21, 2020), https://www.americanbar.org/groups/criminal_justice/publications/criminal-justice-magazine/2020/winter/who-needs-old-boys-club-lets-make-our-ownhighlights-the-wcj-bay-area-listening-session. Daniela Donoso, *Heavy Purse: A Law Student's Reflection on the CJS Women in Criminal Justice Task Force's NYC Listening Session,* CRIMINAL JUSTICE MAGAZINE (April 20, 2020), https://www.americanbar.org/groups/criminal_justice/publications/criminal-justice-magazine/2020/spring/heavy-purse-law-students-reflection-the-cjs-women-criminal-justice-task-forces-nyc-listening-session/. Maryam Ahranjani, *Looking Back, Looking Forward* CRIMINAL JUSTICE MAGAZINE (OCT. 29, 2020), HTTPS://WWW.AMERICANBAR.ORG/GROUPS/CRIMINAL_JUSTICE/PUBLICATIONS/CRIMINAL-JUSTICE-MAGAZINE/2020/FALL/LOOKING-BACK-LOOKING-FORWARD/. Gloria Ochoa-Bruck, *The Call for the Rise of the Modern Prosecutor*, CRIMINAL JUSTICE MAGAZINE (Jan. 11, 2020), https://www.americanbar.org/groups/criminal_justice/publications/criminal-justice-magazine/2021/winter/the-call-the-rise-the-modern-prosecutor/. Hon. Rachel Pickering, *An Awakening and More: How Being Part of the Women in Criminal Justice Task Force Has Provided Me with a Judicial Awareness*, CRIMINAL JUSTICE MAGAZINE (May 1, 2021), https://www.americanbar.org/groups/criminal_justice/publications/criminal-justice-magazine/2021/spring/awakening-how-being-part-women-criminal-justice-task-force-provided-me-judicial-

and judges conducted at the end of 2020. The survey posed questions related to demographics; barriers related to hiring, retention and promotion; potential solutions; and the impact of the COVID-19 pandemic on work and life.

This report is divided into four sections: a brief review of the TF initial findings; methodology; survey questions and responses; and recommendations and next steps. Concluding that hiring, retention, and, particularly, *promotion* of women in criminal justice continue to be a problem, the follow-up survey also revealed the following serious obstacles: (1) limited flexibility with work schedules (which could be addressed, for example, through job-sharing, part-time work, and working from home), (2) insufficient wellness resources, (3) deficient training opportunities, particularly in state and rural criminal law offices, and (4) short supply of meaningful mentorship. Some employers seem receptive to change but many do not. This report shares high-level takeaways and recommendations to address the barriers faced by women criminal lawyers.

---

awareness/. Joy Applewhite, *Brave, Bold, Booked and Balanced* CRIMINAL JUSTICE MAGAZINE (July 20, 2021), https://www.americanbar.org/groups/criminal_justice/publications/criminal-justice-magazine/2021/summer/brave-bold-booked-and-balanced/. Jessica J. Yeary, *From Sweetie to Sisterhood: A Public Defender's Listening Session Reflection* CRIMINAL JUSTICE MAGAZINE (forthcoming).

TABLE OF CONTENTS

INTRODUCTION

This report follows up on the initial findings of the TF that the Berkeley Journal of Criminal Law published in December, 2020.[4] It describes the results of a subsequent follow-up survey conducted between late October and early December 2020. The title of this report was inspired by the idea that the COVID-19 pandemic created both a stage in which remote workers' lives are on display and a curtain (i.e., computer screen).

Concluding that hiring, retention, and, particularly, *promotion* of women in the criminal justice profession continue to be a problem, the follow-up survey revealed the following challenges: (1) limited flexibility with work schedules (which could be addressed, for example, through job-sharing, part-time work, and working remotely), (2) insufficient wellness resources, (3) deficient training opportunities, particularly in state and rural criminal law offices, and (4) short supply of meaningful mentorship and transparent policy guidance. Some employers seem receptive to change but many do not.

This report is divided into four sections: a review of the TF initial findings; a discussion of the survey methodology; an explanation of the survey questions and responses; and an assessment of recommendations and next steps. The methodology section describes the survey administration and respondents and situates the diversity of respondents within available demographic data. The section on survey questions and responses includes a summary of questions and responses, as well as separate sub-sections on the impact of the COVID-19 pandemic on women criminal lawyers, ABA membership, and miscellaneous important comments. Finally, the conclusion shares high-level takeaways and recommendations.

> *"Practicing criminal law as a woman is like playing tackle football in a dress."*

SUMMARY OF INITIAL FINDINGS

When American Bar Association Criminal Justice Section (CJS) staff member Emily Johnson discovered that only 26% of the approximately 16,000 members of the CJS were women, she wondered whether that number was reflective of the total population of criminal lawyers or merely the CJS membership.[5] She raised her questions with CJS Director Kevin Scruggs and CJS Chair Professor Lucian Dervan.[6]

Considering the ABA's core goal of eliminating bias and enhancing diversity, Professor Dervan created the TF to investigate whether women faced challenged in hiring, retention and promotion in criminal law spaces. He appointed Carla Laroche, then a clinical professor at

---

4 Maryam Ahranjani, *"Toughen Up, Buttercup" versus #TimesUp: Initial Findings of the ABA Women in Criminal Justice Task Force*, 25 BERKELEY J. CRIM. L. 99 (2020).

5 Id.

6 Id.

Florida State College of Law who is currently a tenure-stream assistant clinical professor at Washington and Lee University School of Law, and Tina Luongo, chief defender at the Legal Aid Society of New York City, to co-chair the TF. Laroche and Luongo envisioned and created a vibrant TF of women with incredibly diverse lived and professional experiences to carry out its mission.[7]

Between late 2018 and mid-2020, the TF held listening sessions across the country and heard from nearly 200 diverse people at all stages of their careers (including law students and recent graduates) about their experiences in criminal law.[8]

A number of common threads regarding hiring, retention and promotion emerged from the sessions, providing insight into the question: Why are women, particularly women of color, left out of—choosing to leave—criminal law? The threads are barriers to entry and pressures to exit, explicit and implicit discrimination, and burnout/limited resources.[9]

Challenges Include Barriers to Entry and Pressures to Exit; Discrimination; and Burnout, Resources, and Survival

Relatively low salaries in criminal law serve as an initial and ongoing barrier, particularly for women of color and first-generation lawyers.[10] Other systemic obstacles to juggling work and life commitments can add pressure on women to leave criminal justice work. Similarly, stage-of-life developments that especially affect women—including marriage, childbirth and child rearing, caring for aging relatives, and menopause—are not being adequately addressed by criminal justice employers.

One woman explained, "[In my role in hiring,] a woman with three children, very well qualified, declined the prosecutor position. It didn't pay well enough to even cover the childcare." Another woman with aspirations to be promoted in her office explained that the only way to have a chance at promotion in her public defender office would be to handle a homicide case. "With respect to retention and promotion, [the question] is how you make it there and still have a family . . . what's often overlooked is fertility stuff and IVF and freezing your eggs. I don't want to have children until I've done a homicide [case]."

According to the women who testified before the TF, they face discrimination from all stakeholders in the criminal system (judges, opposing counsel, clients, court staff, corrections staff, etc.) based on gendered expectations. One woman explained, "Men try to intimidate you through intimations of incompetence and sometimes blatant overtures of incivility." This discriminatory treatment is particularly challenging for women of color and LGBTQ+ women. One well-respected prosecutor described how she "was introduced by my supervisor to a judge

[7] Carla Laroche & Tina Luongo, *Task Force Launches*, CRIMINAL JUSTICE MAGAZINE, https://www.americanbar.org/groups/criminal_justice/publications/criminal-justice-magazine/2019/spring/task-force-launches (Spring 2019).

[8] Cite to MA column

[9] [9] *Id. See also* Maryam Ahranjani, *Why Are Women Lawyers Underrepresented in Criminal Justice?* AM. BAR. ASS'N (Apr. 6, 2021), https://www.americanbar.org/groups/young_lawyers/publications/tyl/topics/criminal-law/why-are-women-lawyers-underrepresented-in-criminal-justice.

[10] See also Jill L. Cruz, Melinda S. Molina & Jenny Rivera, *Hispanic National Bar Association Commission on the Status of Latinas in the Legal Profession, Study on Latina Attorneys in the Public Interest Sector, La Voz De La Abogada Latina: Challenges and Rewards in Serving the Public Interest*, 14 CUNY L. REV. 147, 199 (2010).

as a 'spicy little Latina." Several women who identify as lesbian or queer reported that they were repeatedly told they did not "look or act feminine enough." Overall, the listening sessions revealed a lack of respect for and devaluation of women and gender nonconforming individuals.

Many women criminal lawyers, particularly women of color and LGBTQ+ women, face burnout, compassion fatigue, and vicarious trauma.[11] They do not have the resources or support to address these challenges and asked for help to process all the stress and expectations. One lawyer noted:

> "Looking young [and being a minority] has caused . . . [me] to come in overly prepared and organized to be taken seriously. I grew up with a single mom, was the first to go to college. I came in with a different perspective: I've had people in my family incarcerated. I became a prosecutor to help people. However, being one is hard—from all sides: defense says you're too aggressive, victim saying not aggressive enough, cops not wanting to come in."

Women who have remained in the field demonstrate resiliency and strong survival skills. One woman of color explained, "We bury these things [sexism, racism] because if we don't, we can't continue to work." One prosecutor who is a mother of two explained that she wants to have a third child but simply cannot afford it. Between her relatively low salary, high cost of childcare, and "regular therapy required for my job," it simply was not possible. But the costs of enduring these challenges without support are high and many dedicated and competent women seek other legal and nonlegal opportunities as a result. One Black judge explained that she "left criminal law because I couldn't stand seeing so many young black men go to prison."

Based on these findings, the TF proposed several strategies to address these challenges. The strategies include improving access to mentors and allies, increasing flexibility, and providing more resources.

Strategies to Address Challenges Include: Improving Access to Mentors and Allies; Increasing Flexibility; Providing Greater Resources to Training and Support; and Collecting More Data

The clear winner for the most important area for improving women's careers in criminal justice is increasing access to meaningful mentorship—something that was noted as particularly lacking in our sessions. Allyship, similarly, is a critical buffer to gender-based discrimination,

---

[11] These three conditions are interrelated and overlapping, but they can have different causes and symptoms. The U.S. Department of Justice Office for Victims of Crime describes **burnout** as "a state of physical, emotional, and mental exhaustion caused by long-term involvement in emotionally demanding situations. Symptoms may include depression, cynicism, boredom, loss of compassion, and discouragement." Both prosecutors and public defenders reported some burnout throughout the listening sessions and in the follow-up surveys. **Compassion fatigue** is "a combination of physical, emotional, and spiritual depletion associated with caring for others who are in significant emotional pain and physical distress," so public defenders are more likely to experience it. **Vicarious trauma** is "an occupational challenge for people working and volunteering in the fields of victim services, law enforcement, emergency medical services, fire services, and other allied professions, due to their continuous exposure to victims of trauma and violence," so it is more often experienced by prosecutors. "Exposure to the trauma of others has been shown to change the world-view of these responders and can put people and organizations at risk for a range of negative consequences." *Glossary of Terms*, https://ovc.ojp.gov/program/vtt/glossary-terms (Aug. 18, 2021).

and allies sometimes come from unlikely places. Adopting more flexible workplace policies may address drift and dissatisfaction. Based on our sessions, greater flexibility in criminal law jobs will also improve the likelihood of recruiting and retaining talented women. The TF's work so far indicates that women, particularly those in rural and under-resourced jurisdictions, need better training opportunities and resources related to wellness, diversity and inclusion, and professional development.

Based on the qualitative reports during and after the listening sessions, it was clear that the TF needed to gather more quantitative information. Through partnerships with the American Bar Foundation and the ABA Center on Innovation, the TF explored various opportunities to conduct quantitative research. After exploring a number of options and balancing the limitations posed by the pandemic with the interest in continuing to do our work despite limitations, the TF decided to conduct a follow-up survey of women who had already participated in the listening sessions. The idea was that women with whom we already had a connection would be more likely to respond than those hearing from the TF for the first time during the global pandemic while they juggled caregiving responsibilities. Another important outcome of the listening sessions were powerful columns written by women who participated in the listening sessions and TF members.[12]

METHODOLOGY

Goals

The follow-up survey was open between October 29, 2020, and December 1, 2020 (2020 Survey). Targeted respondents included the women criminal lawyers who had participated in TF listening sessions between November 2018 and June 2020. Since the TF already invited the participants to answer many similar questions prior to the listening session, there were two goals for this follow-up survey: (1) to document participants responses to gender equity in hiring, retention, and promotion in the criminal law profession in a more effective way and (2) to seek feedback on how the COVID-19 pandemic has affected their careers. One significant addition compared to the pre-listening session survey was an attempt to assess respondents' commitment to the practice of criminal law. Presumably, feedback from highly committed practitioners as opposed to less committed practitioners is even more weighty.

Who Was in the Survey Pool?

The TF emailed the survey with a Qualtrics link to 144 women who had participated in the TF listening sessions, including 36 women who were law students at the time of their participation. Although the survey was sent to practitioners and law students, the primary goal and expectation was to hear from practitioners. Four emails bounced back and a total of nine autoreplies were received. Two out-of-office replies indicated the women were on reduced schedules due to family care responsibilities. One autoreply was an open-ended reply that the attorney was out of the office indefinitely. Two autoreplies indicated the attorneys were on leave.

[12] Cite to 2020 and 2021 CJ magazine columns by Maryam Ahranjani, Daniela Donoso, Maria Carmen Hinayon, Joy Applewhite, Jessica Yeary, etc.

Who Were the Survey Respondents?

In terms of responses received to the survey, forty-nine women responded, including three who were law students at the time they testified. The overall response rate of 34% (49 out of 144) or almost 43% for practitioners only (46 out of 108) was quite high, especially since survey response rates were down during the COVID-19 pandemic.[13] It is likely that the trust relationship built through the listening sessions and follow-up correspondence contributed to the relatively high response rate.

The forty-nine respondents were diverse in terms of geographic location, criminal law position, graduation year from law school, race, ethnicity, and LGBTQIA+ identification. Respondents live and work all over the country—in rural, urban, and suburban settings. They are based in the Northeast (New York, Pennsylvania, Washington DC), Northwest (Washington State), Midwest (Missouri), Southeast (Florida, Virginia), and Southwest (Arizona, California, New Mexico). Respondents included tribal, state, and federal level prosecutors, public defenders, and judges. Respondents also included law students and women working in private criminal defense and at non-profit organizations dedicated to criminal justice.

Respondents' ages ranged from twenty-three to seventy-seven, and the average age was forty-nine. Law school graduation years ranged from 1971 to 2022.

Forty-eight people responded to the questions about race and ethnicity, and one declined to answer. In terms of race/ethnicity, the survey first asked whether the respondent identified as Hispanic/Latinx. Since people who identify as Hispanic/Latinx may identify as members of various races, respondents were then invited to indicate the race(s) with which they identify. Eleven women (23%) identified as Hispanic/Latinx. In terms of race, five (10.4%) identified as American Indian or Alaskan Native; five (10.4%) as Asian/Southeast Asian/South Asian; four (8.3%) as Black or African American; one (2.1%) as Middle Eastern/North African; twenty-four (50%) as white; four (8.3%) as multiracial or multiethnic; and five (10.4%) as other.

---

[13] Jonathan Rothbaum, *How Does the Pandemic Affect Survey Response: Using Administrative Data to Evaluate Nonresponse in the Current Population Survey Annual Social and Economic Supplement*, U.S. CENSUS BUREAU (Sept. 15, 2020), https://www.census.gov/newsroom/blogs/research-matters/2020/09/pandemic-affect-survey-response.html.

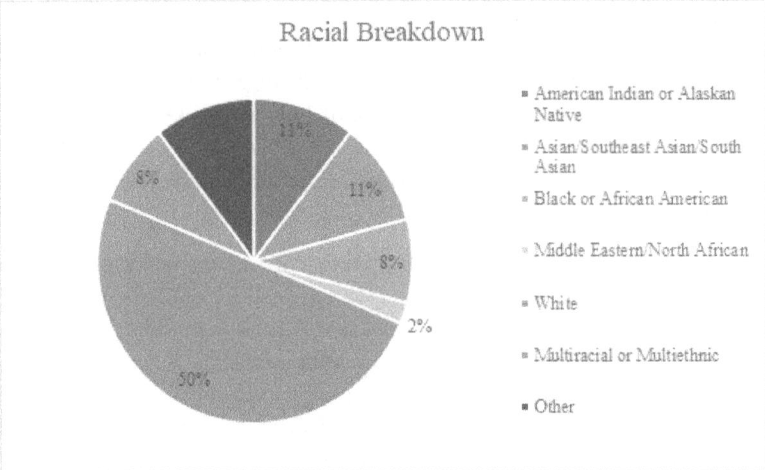

In terms of gender identity, there were forty-nine responses. Forty-five (91.8%) identified as women, two (4.1%) identified as trans women, one (2.04%) identified as a trans man, and one (2.04%) identified as gender non-conforming. Forty-nine people responded to the question about sexual orientation. Forty participants (81.6%) identified as heterosexual, three (6.1%) identified as lesbians, two (4.1%) identified as bisexual, three (6.1%) identified as queer and one (2.04%) preferred not to say.

Situating the Diversity of Respondents

As explained in "Toughen Up, Buttercup" versus #TimesUp: Initial Findings of the Women in Criminal Justice TF,[14] there is no national demographic data on women lawyers, much less women lawyers practicing criminal law. Therefore, it is not possible to compare the demographics of survey respondents to the overall population of women criminal lawyers, or women lawyers in general, for that matter. However, the American Bar Association's 2021 National Lawyer Population Survey provides some self-reported racial demographic information of active lawyers in the United States.[15]

According to that survey, 5% of lawyers identify as African American, 2% Asian, 85% Caucasian/White, less than 1% are Hawaiian/Pacific Islander, 5% Hispanic, 2% multiracial, and less than 1% Native American. The ABA survey considers Hispanic as a race, which is different from the TF's approach, which recognizes that Hispanic Americans may identify with different races. The National Association of Law Placement's (NALP) most recent data also provides some national data, showing that the percentage of lawyers who identify as "LGBT" continues to rise as of 2019, nearly 3% (2.99%) of their survey respondents identify as "LGBT."[16]

---

[14] Ahranjani, *supra* note 2.

[15] AM. BAR. ASS'N, *ABA National Lawyer Population Survey: 2021*, https://www.americanbar.org/content/dam/aba/administrative/market_research/2021-national-lawyer-population-survey.pdf (last visited July 29, 2021).

[16] *LGBT Representation Among Lawyers in 2019*, NAT'L ASS'N FOR LAW PLACEMENT (Jan. 2020), https://www.nalp.org/0120research.

Measured against this data, the respondents to this TF survey were significantly more diverse than the overall population of lawyers. This aligns with the TF's articulated goal of reaching out to and elevating the experiences of traditionally excluded women and gender non-conforming people.

Framing the demographic results more broadly, the percentage of women enrolling in law school has been steadily increasing. Since 2016, women have constituted slightly more than 50% of incoming 1Ls nationally.[17] However, the overall percentage of women *lawyers,* as opposed to law students, is just 37%.[18] The obstacles to hiring, retention and promotion of women criminal lawyers, particularly women of color and women who identify as LGBTQIA+, are important regardless of this trend, but the growing number of women in the profession intensifies the need to understand and eliminate these barriers.

SURVEY QUESTIONS AND RESPONSES

The follow-up survey included questions similar to the ones previously asked of participants,[19] but expanded on personal and observed experiences related to hiring, retention, and promotion in criminal law and included a new section related to the impact of the COVID-19 pandemic on the women's lives. The follow-up survey included a mix of yes/no, multiple choice, and open-ended questions. The four major sections of the survey: 1) demographic information, 2) experiences with hiring, retention and promotion, 3) ideas related to solutions, and 4) impact of COVID-19 pandemic.

Questions and Responses Regarding Hiring, Retention, and Promotion

When asked whether they personally experienced challenges with hiring, retention and promotion, twenty-six people responded. Of the twenty-six, ten (38%) said yes to hiring, fourteen (53%) said yes to retention and twenty-four (92%) said yes to promotion. Respondents were encouraged to explain in a follow-up question, and they shared the following challenges: retaliation for sexual harassment claims and cooperation with investigations, being passed up in favor of older men, difficulty in uprooting their families (which men seemed more able/willing to do), sexism, and discrimination based on religion and national origin.

[17] *Law School Rankings by Female Enrollment (2020)*, ENJURIS, https://www.enjuris.com/students/law-school-women-enrollment-2020.html (last visited July 29, 2021).

[18] AM. BAR ASS'N, *supra* note 6.

[19] Ahranjani, *supra* note 2, at 56.

When asked whether they observed *others* experiencing challenges, twenty-seven responded. Respondents reported even higher numbers: fourteen (51%) said yes to hiring, twenty (74%) said yes to retention, and twenty-four (88%) said yes to promotion. Sixty-five percent of respondents indicated that when hiring, promotion and/or retention were issues, those who were treated negatively were likely to change jobs. Failure to accommodate women with families and intersectionality (race plus gender) were cited as the two most common reasons for making a career switch.

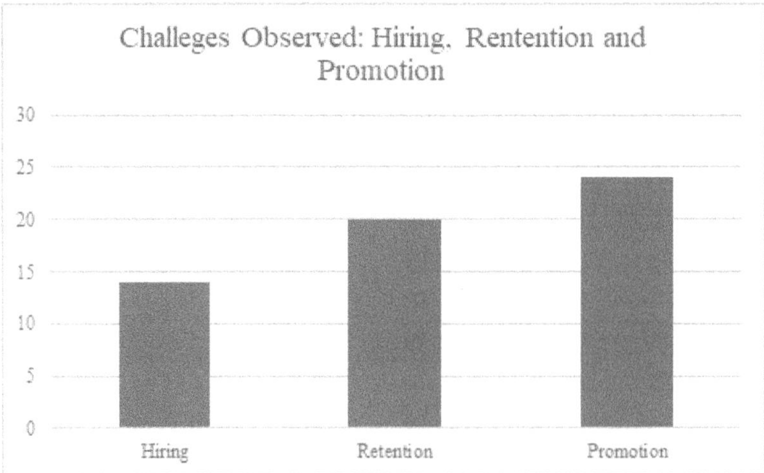

Despite the challenges, 47% respondents plan to stay with their employer for the foreseeable future, and 18% said they may stay. Their reasons for staying include: a love for the work and their colleagues, commitment to their clients who need them, retirement benefits, wanting to serve their people (Native Americans), and autonomy.

When asked whether when gender-related issues arise, they have an informal or formal source of support, thirty-five women provided responses. Ninety-four percent of them responded affirmatively. They were asked to describe sources of support, and the responses included colleagues, friends, women supervisors, men supervisors, HR, law partners, union, and family.

With regard to what women need(ed) to be successful criminal law practitioners, respondents listed a number of items. They include (in no particular order) intelligence, respect, passion, training, grit, creativity, compassion, ability to learn quickly, commitment to hard work, experience, organizational skills, equal playing field, empathy, strong sense of justice, resilience, preparation, determination, idealism, good judgment, mental health support, training, supportive colleagues and others, ability not to back down from lawyers who tend to bully, more funding, equal pay for equal work, active promotion of women, a boss that fights for office needs, an environment that strives to help employees reduce stress and chaos and mentors.

One comment by a respondent sums up the career arc articulated by many women. The respondent observed, "In the beginning, I needed training and mentorship. As my career progressed, I mostly just needed to be left alone." Interestingly, though, when asked, "Have your needs changed as you have progressed in your career?" twenty-two out of the thirty-five respondents (62%) who answered stated, "No." One comment articulates what several women said about needing more support over time because of the complexity of the cases they handle: "Need support in how to handle the gravity and destruction that can be our job." Combining these responses with what participants articulated in the listening sessions, this inconsistency may reflect ambivalence and a sense that while they were tough and did not *need* support at any stage, they certainly would have benefitted from it.

In response to the question prompt, "What do you feel you need(ed) to remain in the criminal justice field?" mental health support and self-care were cited several times. A number of powerful comments by respondents surfaced:

- "I need to not be undermined by individuals who view my success as a threat to them."
- "I am 65 and have been at this for 35 years, pouring heart, soul and body into this. What would it take to keep at it?? A change of pace or a break. A colleague of mine quit after about 3 years, saying she had treated the job as a sprint rather than a marathon. I feel I've been sprinting a marathon."
- "As long as I can help, I need to be here."
- "Systemic racism must be addressed."

Of the thirty-five who provided responses to the question, "How committed are you to remaining in your office?" almost all of them said they were *at least* committed but open to new opportunities. Sixty percent said they are very committed, 14% said they are somewhat committed, and 11% said they are committed but open to other opportunities.

Thirty-five women also responded to the prompt, "Have your employers provided you with what you needed to be successful and remain in the field?" twenty answered "yes" and fifteen answered "no." Women in the federal system seemed more likely to report satisfaction.

Of the seven women who identified as federal prosecutors, public defenders and judges, five responded to the question. Out of those five, four responded, "Yes."

Women were invited to explain what they needed from employers to be successful and remain in the field.[20] The most frequent responses were support, training, flexibility and mentorship. Topics that came up more than once as unmet needs include pay equity and therapy/mental health support. When asked what policies and practices are most effective for retaining women, respondents listed the following concrete items, which have been paraphrased:

- job sharing
- seeing and experiencing promotion to leadership positions (particularly women with children)
- part-time options
- flexibility in general
- flexible work schedules
- better enforcement of workplace harassment policies
- temporary positions
- permitting children to come to the office
- equal and fair pay
- better mentoring
- more training
- listening and being more supportive/encouraging
- exit interviews
- acknowledgement that being flexible does not mean people will be ineffective

In terms of perceptions of employer receptivity to those suggestions, respondents were asked, "How receptive do you think your employer is or would have been to implementing these recommendations?" Out of 20 responses to this question, 20% said extremely positive, 30% said somewhat positive, 15% said neither positive nor negative, 15% said somewhat negative, and 20% said extremely negative.

[20] *See infra* Appendix B for verbatim responses.

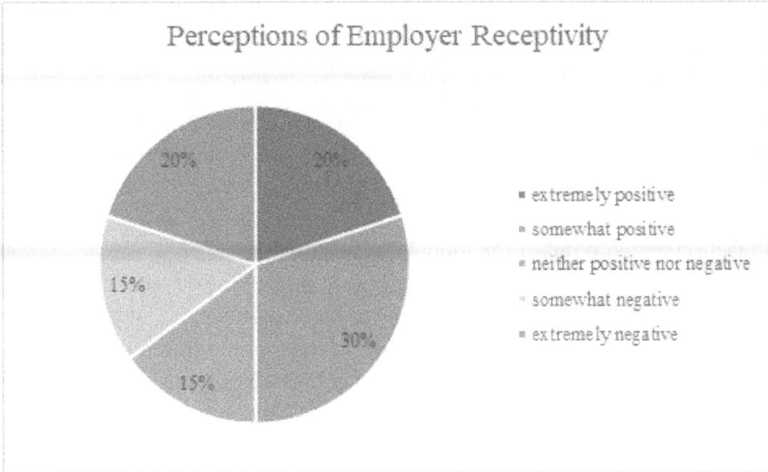

In response to, "What would it take to make changes?" respondents replied: budget changes, management support, adverse civil verdict, mass exodus of women of color/people of color, human resources or union pressure, and willingness to try.

COVID-19-related questions

Based on what we learned during two videoconferences in Summer 2020, the TF sought to capture the ways in which the pandemic affected the work of women in the criminal legal field, and whether they hoped to keep any aspects of the pandemic workday configuration.

When asked which aspects of their lives have been disproportionately affected by COVID-19 and the fact that they are a woman, eight said childcare, four said elder care, thirteen said professional development, twenty-three said quality of life, fifteen said work performance, and four said other.

In response to the question "What other aspects of your life have been affected by the confluence of COVID-19, being a woman, and being in criminal justice?" responses included:

- "No formal coordination with courts, prosecutors and other components of criminal justice system."
- "Everything is harder. I have two teens, both have significant mental health issues and learning challenges. Both are failing many of their classes in online school. My husband also has mental health issues. I am trying to support my family and do my job, and not doing anything as well as I would in non-COVID times."
- "I don't think I've been more affected because I'm a woman. I actually think I probably have less running around to do because my 14-year-old daughter is in virtual school and only has one extra-curricular activity that she can do--swimming every morning with her swim team, socially distanced. She can't see friends or go anywhere. And she's very self-sufficient with her schoolwork, so I don't need to help her with that. I'm lucky I don't have small children."

- "The practice became almost more difficult because of the varied responses by Courts in different counties. It felt as if I was a new lawyer - learning how to navigate every location anew."
- "No quality of life."
- "I butt heads with judges even more now. Unfortunately, our district's chief judge is a misogynist, so those battles have gone . . . poorly."
- "Isolation."
- "One feels even more out of the loop."
- "Specifically I have had to pay for additional childcare for my school age child. In addition to this, any time either one of my children as a minor symptom such as a runny nose, there is a high likelihood that they will be sent home from daycare requiring me to either take off work or work from home. Unfortunately my boss does not understand that this is directly linked to COVID and not just a "sick" child. In fact, in most cases my children are not actually sick, they just are having a symptom that comes with childhood. Currently my boss will not allow us to work from home under these circumstances though he is currently letting three male employees work from home on a scheduled basis. The three young women in the office, who have chosen to pay for daycare rather than schedule work from home are not given any support when they need a day here and there to work from home. Thus we have to use our sick leave or our vacation while our male counterparts are not put in this position."

Finally, when asked "In a post-COVID world, are there any changes you would like to keep?," many women said they hoped some things—greater flexibility in telecommuting/ telework, virtual hearings/settlement conferences, and generally more flexibility in terms of when in the day work could be completed—would remain. One respondent said, "For me personally, there are none."

ABA Membership

Nineteen respondents were current ABA members. For those who were not members, thirteen respondents indicated that membership costs too much (especially relative to benefits), ten indicated they see no benefit to their careers, four said they did not feel they would fit in, and thirteen selected "other." The "other" responses ranged from practicing in tribal courts; ABA not being inclusive of Native American attorneys; already being involved in more salient professional organizations; and serving in a Presidential appointment or judgeship that required resignation from boards, commissions, and advisory councils.

Additional Important Comments by Respondents

Respondents were invited to share additional thoughts related to hiring, retention and promotion of women in criminal law. Here are their comments and observations:

- "STEM-based criminal justice is an area of growth, and it's currently dominated by straight, white men."

- "Practicing in Indian Country requires serious commitment and perhaps someone from that community would be more likely to remain because of family."
- "Women are the best lawyers in the profession. I've been practicing a long time and [have] seen a lot of lawyers working. No question, women are the best lawyers, certainly in criminal law."
- "I think it's always been better for women in criminal law than civil. That Old Boys Club is a lot harder to crack."
- "There is a reason that our profession has such a high level of substance abuse. There is an extreme amount of conflict and stress that we deal with on a regular basis and the profession as a whole needs to address this in a more positive manner. More resources should be provided, employees should have a safe place to check in and voice their frustrations."

PRELIMINARY RECOMMENDATIONS AND NEXT STEPS

This report amplifies the diverse experiences of the people who took the time to respond to this survey. Women criminal lawyers serve a critical role in the promotion of justice. The people who responded to this survey by and large are passionate about their work and are committed to continuing to practice criminal law. However, they identified some major, persistent challenges. Broadly speaking, they include (1) limited flexibility with work schedules (which could be addressed, for example, through job-sharing, part-time work, and working remotely), (2) insufficient wellness resources, (3) deficient training opportunities, particularly in state and rural criminal law offices, and (4) short supply of meaningful mentorship.

These challenges are firmly entrenched and are felt even more profoundly by women with intersectional identities. For example, women of color (particularly Black, Indigenous and Latina women), women from low-income backgrounds, women who have significant educational debt, women with obligations to their extended families and communities, LGBTQ+ people, and others, described the many layers of challenges they face in navigating both workspaces and their personal lives. The high-intensity and emotional nature of criminal law heighten the experience of representing defendants and the state in a system that often seems unfair and imbalanced.

Only systemic solutions will lead to long-term improvements in the hiring, retention and promotion of women criminal lawyers. The chart below describes potential solutions, most of which were identified by the women in the follow-up survey or in the listening sessions:

Challenge	Potential Systemic Solutions for Employers to Implement
Limited flexibility with work schedules	Policies that allow job-sharing, part-time work, and working from home; court schedules that accommodate children's school schedules
Insufficient wellness resources	Creating wellness spaces in offices and courthouses; provide free therapy and other wellness information, policies and programs; meet regularly with attorneys to assess job satisfaction and avoid feelings of invisibility
Deficient training opportunities	Pool resources with other jurisdictions; amplify existing free resources through ABA and state, local, and affinity bars
Short supply of meaningful mentorship	Pool resources with other jurisdictions; amplify existing free resources through ABA and state, local, and affinity bars; create more meaningful mentorship opportunities and incentivize/recognize participation

Employers should view women's drift as a significant problem. The COVID-19 pandemic has both exacerbated and exposed the tightrope on which many working women walk.[21] Women's scars and challenges from the COVID-19 era have affected and will continue to affect their role in the work force and as lawyers.[22] Because of increased caregiving responsibilities, many women have stepped out of the work force and others have reduced their hours.[23]

The pandemic has also provided a window into what greater flexibility could look like, and the responses from our survey indicate hope that some aspects of working remotely will be retained. Such changes must come as a result of open, honest dialogue and culture changes within offices. One judge (who does not have children herself) noted at a listening session, "My observation after years of experience is that women with children make the best criminal lawyers."[24] She described their organizational and time management skills, capacity for empathy, and problem-solving abilities as the top reasons. This anecdote is confirmed by

[21] Jennifer L. Smuts, *Coming Up for Air: Women in Law and Adapting to the Impact of COVID-19*, JD SUPRA, (Mar. 4, 2021), https://www.jdsupra.com/legalnews/coming-up-for-air-women-in-law-and-8541536/; Cynthia L. Cooper, *Work-Life Imbalance: Pandemic Disruption Places New Stresses on Women Lawyers*, AM. BAR ASS'N (Dec. 18, 2020), https://www.americanbar.org/groups/diversity/women/publications/perspectives/2021/december/worklife-imbalance-pandemic-disruption-places-new-stresses-women-lawyers/.

[22] Alexandra Samuel, *How Working From Home Has Changed Employees*, WALL STREET J. (June 12, 2021), https://www.wsj.com/articles/working-from-home-employees-11623463249?st=si1pq9hc2i5lf94&reflink=desktopwebshare_permalink&fbclid=IwAR1WJsSXOrTo91J39RlXbaqZ7HAlgdcB-bFm0p_15McEnCRqZEjdZduvus0.

[23] *Id.*

[24] Notes on file with author.

numerous studies of professional women.[25] In fact, researchers have found that "over the course of a 30-year career, mothers outperformed women without children at almost every stage of the game. In fact, mothers with at least two kids were the most productive of all."[26]

Employers should be concerned not just about retention and promotion of current women criminal lawyers. They also should be aware of demographic changes on the horizon. The enrollment of women in law schools has been steadily climbing in recent years, and, presumably, so too will the number of women who could potentially be hired as criminal lawyers. The combination of the unique features of criminal law—racial and ethnic bias, litigation schedule and related stress, the emotional toll of working in a system that many feel is unjust, and relative lack of resources—with the realities of balancing out-of-work responsibilities of caregiving mean that the profession must adapt, or run the risk of losing highly-skilled, highly qualified women. Sprinting a marathon is simply not sustainable.

With the support of current CJS Chair and TF member April Frazier Camara and incoming CJS Chair Wayne McKenzie, the TF plans to host focus groups in November 2021 and April 2022 with criminal justice stakeholders to share ideas and findings, and to pressure test the TF's suggested remedies. The TF will collect, digest, and reformulate the focus groups' input into further advocacy within CJS and the larger ABA, as well as continue to write about our work.[27] Focus group participants will receive a succinct chart that describes identified challenges and sample solutions.

With their input and the CJS's continued support, the TF seeks to make the criminal legal profession more welcoming and inclusive for all lawyers, especially those who, like the survey respondents, face too many barriers currently.

---

[25] Matthias Krapf, Heinrich W. Ursprung, and Christian Zimmerman, *Parenthood and Productivity of Highly Skilled Labor: Evidence from the Groves of Academe*, Journal of Economic Behavior & Organization (Jan. 2014), https://s3.amazonaws.com/real.stlouisfed.org/wp/2014/2014-001.pdf.

[26] Ylan Q. Mui, Study: Women with more children are more productive at work, WASH. POST (Oct. 30, 2014) https://www.washingtonpost.com/news/wonk/wp/2014/10/30/study-women-with-more-children-are-more-productive-at-work/.

APPENDIX A: ABA Criminal Justice Section Women in Criminal Justice Task Force

Leadership Team

Carla Laroche, Co-Chair
Assistant Clinical Professor of Law
Director, Civil Rights and Racial Justice Clinic
Washington and Lee University School of Law (VA)

Tina Luongo, Co-Chair
Attorney-in-Charge, Criminal
Defense Practice
The Legal Aid Society (NY)

Maryam Ahranjani, Reporter
Associate Professor and Don L. & Mabel F. Dickason, University of New Mexico School of Law (UNMSOL)

Members

Lara Bazelon (Professor of Law, Director of the Criminal & Juvenile Justice and Racial Justice Clinics, University of San Francisco School of Law (CA))

The Honorable Gloria Ochoa-Bruck (Kalispel Tribal Court (WA))

Barbara Creel (Professor of Law and Karelitz Professor of Evidence and Procedure, UNMSOL)

April Frazier Camara (Vice President of Strategic Alliances and Innovation, National Legal Aid and Defender Association (DC))

The Honorable Bernice Donald (U.S. Court of Appeals for the Sixth Circuit (TN))

Daniela Donoso (Equal Justice Works Fellow, Legal Services of North Florida (FL))

Maria Carmen Hinayon (Complaints Resolution Officer, Office for the Prevention of Harassment and Discrimination University of California- San Francisco (CA))

The Honorable Denise Langford-Morris (Oakland County Circuit Court (MI))

Ann Ratnayake Macy (Founder and former Executive Director, National Center for Child Abuse Statistics and Policy (DC))

The Honorable Rachel Pickering (3rd Judicial District (KS))

Sarah Redfield (Professor of Law (emerita), University of New Hampshire School of Law (ME))

Major Susan Upward (U.S. Marine Corps (NC))

APPENDIX B: Responses to Level and Type of Support from Employers

- "There are very little resources for therapy and mental health. This field is full of substance abuse because of the amount of stress and the level of workload we have. My employer specifically also has not recognized the additional stressors that COVID has created in terms of childcare."
- "As a trial lawyer, the office provided little support for logistical issues related to evidence presentation. I was not provided assistance with moving large 65" TVs for closing arguments. I was forced to do so in a skirt suit, with heels, and hurt myself before closing arguments in a child molest case. Certainly, my focus should have been on substantive trial work rather than physical labor that should have been performed my support staff. This gender-neutral policy overlooked the fact that I am 5'1" and 115 lbs and moving a TV of that size was not easy. Further, moving heavy boxes of files to court each day is overwhelming. My male counterparts voiced no complaints, which reflected poorly on me when I did."
- "Promoting competent women to visible positions. Women as supervisors with power to make decisions."
- "I am able to attend trainings and webinars."
- "Sometimes they do and sometimes they don't. It depends on the year."
- "Sexism and dismissive."
- "My work is non-traditional, so most of my work is self-reliant. Prior to COVID, I was able to attend training I requested local and those requiring travel. I also have access to legal databases to conduct research."
- "I am a sole practitioner; I provide what I need."
- "I'm self-employed. I take care of myself."
- "I only had one employer and he and the office were very supportive."
- "Prior to my current role, I did not receive the support I needed and there were fewer opportunities to grow and lead."
- "leeway to grow, leadership opportunity, and ability to make significant decisions and determine direction of the work"
- "They need to pay women equally. That issue is emblematic of a lack of support for the women in this department that has cost us a number of good attorneys."
- "I did not feel supported or mentored necessarily from employers who were focused on my career advancement. However, as my own boss, I am responsible for my own advancement (and the advancement of other women in the practice)."
- "As a program director, it has always been difficult to do this work because of the need for additional resources, i.e., attorneys, advocates and financial. At times, priorities must be juggled to benefit staff and clients."
- "I have always worked with my father as the lead partner of our firm. Therefore, many of these questions are inapplicable to me - such as "policies" or "retention.""
- "They undermine my position as an administrative position instead of legal; even though be essential personnel."
- "Overall, the various U.S. attorneys I worked for supported me and helped me to be successful, or at least didn't stand in my way. Some were more supportive than others. In general, I felt most supported when my supervisors understood my strengths and weaknesses, assigned me cases based on my strengths, and provided training and resources to address weaknesses."

- "I often was alone and isolated. I didn't feel I had someone who had my back or was interested in my growth or development."
- "I've been with the FPD for [many] years - superb training, usually provided with what I need to do my job. Caseload has been for the most part manageable, although right now with compassionate release stuff I feel overloaded. Boss has been great at not micromanaging and yet having our backs."
- "Lack of resources and mentorship."
- "I practice civil law and have worked for civil law firms. They are not equipped to address criminal issues."
- "I have a strong, collaborative relationship with my employer and ask for what I need and generally am able to secure it. Mutual trust is important as is our mutual regard."
- "They have not provided what we need, more humans doing this job, because the county will not provide. Our bosses would if they could."
- "In my current position as a resource attorney I have time flexibility and control my workload. I did not have either when I was at a large public defense agency."
- "My time in federal defender offices has allowed me to develop meaningful mentor relationships, adequate resources, and relevance within the profession."
- "For the most part my employer has provided the basic tools needed to be successful. I was recently promoted to a management position but because of a budget and personnel freeze my ability to do my job effectively has been affected."
- "It has been extremely difficult to obtain additional personnel positions and adequate funding."

APPENDIX D

Sprinting a Marathon

Maryam Ahranjani

Article

Sprinting a Marathon: Next Steps for Gender Equity in Criminal Law Employment

Maryam Ahranjani†

INTRODUCTION

Nearly one year into the pandemic, Samantha was faced with a very difficult decision.[1] She loved her job as a public defender and felt her office made some efforts to be flexible, but the daily grind and stress of juggling her demanding work with being a single parent to a school-age child had become unbearable. Her daily schedule was completely unpredictable. At the beginning of the pandemic, court was online and so was her daughter's school. Hearings could sometimes last up to six hours, during which time her daughter inevitably would need help with online school frustrations, feel hunger, and simply crave attention.

When her daughter's school began to meet in person again, they canceled after school care because of Covid, and sometimes they had to close completely for days or weeks due to positive cases. Childcare, particularly emergency care, was and is scarce and difficult to afford on her salary anyway. Concerned with due process and zealous representation of their clients, the public defender's office and the district attorney's office asked employees to come in person and judges conducted in-person hearings as much as possible. When Samantha's child, too young to stay home alone, was not able to go to school and Samantha was required to be in court (even Zoom court), Samantha was in a serious bind.

With a heavy heart, Samantha quit her dream job and switched to a civil law firm based in a city one hour from her home. Realizing that once that firm returned to in-person work she would again be unable

† She/her/hers. Associate Professor and Don L. & Mabel F. Dickason Professor at the University of New Mexico School of Law; Reporter, ABA Criminal Justice Section Women in Criminal Justice Task Force (TF).

1. Names and identifying information changed to protect anonymity.

to juggle the commute with school drop-off and pick-up, she decided again to make a change and start her own practice. While being her own boss affords the flexibility she needs to be a single parent during Covid, it also means uncertain and unpredictable flow of cases and income. Samantha's story reflects that of women criminal lawyers and other professional women[2] who are primary caregivers.

This Article follows up on a number of other publications related to the work of the ABA Criminal Justice Section Women in Criminal Justice Task Force (TF).[3] As described in Part I, the TF was formed in late 2018 to investigate gender-based barriers to hiring, promotion, and retention in criminal law. Over the past three years, the TF engaged in three major phases of qualitative data-gathering: 1) in-person and remote listening sessions between November 2018 and June 2020; 2) follow-up surveys of listening session participants in late 2020 to assess the impact of the pandemic; and 3) focus group meetings and surveys in November 2021 regarding proposed solutions.

The Berkeley Journal of Criminal Law (BJCL) published the author's analysis of phase one in December 2020,[4] the ABA Criminal Justice magazine published a number of short columns,[5] and the ABA

2. Women doctors are also quitting at higher rates for many of the same reasons described in this Article. Jessica Dudley, Sarah McLaughlin, & Thomas H. Lee, *Why So Many Women Physicians Are Quitting*, HARV. BUS. REV. (Jan. 19, 2022), https://hbr.org/2022/01/why-so-many-women-physicians-are-quitting?utm_source=The+19th&utm_campaign=73dcb407ac-19th-newsletters-daily-0119&utm_medium=email&utm_term=0_a35c3279be-73dcb407ac-360415032&registration=success [https://perma.cc/N8U3-BLT2].

3. The author, on behalf of the TF, extends gratitude to the Criminal Justice Section for its support of all of the TF's work, as well as to American Bar Foundation researchers, Professors Ajay Mehrotra and Bob Nelson, who provided valuable advice regarding survey structure. The author, TF Advisory Board Member and Data Committee Co-Chair Yaamini Rao, and former ABA Center for Innovation collaborator Sarah Glassmeyer developed the survey that serves as the basis for this report. TF Co-Chair Carla Laroche read numerous drafts and provided invaluable feedback. TF members Professor Sarah Redfield, Ann Ratnayake Macy, and Yaamini Rao also contributed valuable edits to an early version. Nat Saing contributed critical editing and formatting assistance. Special thanks to Emilie Keuntjes Erickson and her colleagues at the Minnesota Law Review for their hard work and careful editing. All TF members are listed in Appendix A.

4. Maryam Ahranjani, *"Toughen Up, Buttercup" versus #TimesUp: Initial Findings of the ABA Women in Criminal Justice Task Force*, 25 BERKELEY J. CRIM. L. 99 (2020) (providing a thorough background of the history of women in criminal law and presenting initial findings from the listening sessions).

5. *See* Carla Laroche & Tina Luongo, *Task Force Launches*, CRIM. JUST. MAG. (Spring 2019), https://www.americanbar.org/groups/criminal_justice/publications/criminal-justice-magazine/2019/spring/task-force-launches [https://perma.cc/Z6VD-CCK2]; Maryam Ahranjani, *Listening Session Participants Express*

Criminal Justice Section published a report in October 2021.[6] This Article follows up on the BJCL article by describing and analyzing phases two and three (the results of the follow-up survey conducted between late October and early December 2020, the focus groups conducted on

Feelings of Isolation—and Demonstrate Resilience, CRIM. JUST. MAG. (Nov. 1, 2019), https://www.americanbar.org/groups/criminal_justice/publications/criminal-justice-magazine/2019/fall/listening-session-participants-express-feelings-isolation-demonstrate-resilience [https://perma.cc/LE9A-MWD8] [hereinafter Ahranjani, *Listening Session Takeaways*]; Maria Carmen Hinayon, *Who Needs the Old Boys' Club? Let's Make Our Own—Highlights from the WCJ Bay Area Listening Session*, CRIM. JUST. MAG. (Jan. 21, 2020), https://www.americanbar.org/groups/criminal_justice/publications/criminal-justice-magazine/2020/winter/who-needs-old-boys-club-lets-make-our-ownhighlights-the-wcj-bay-area-listening-session [https://perma.cc/KT6D-YRHH]; Daniela Donoso, *Heavy Purse: A Law Student's Reflection on the CJS Women in Criminal Justice Task Force's NYC Listening Session*, CRIM. JUST. MAG. (Apr. 20, 2020), https://www.americanbar.org/groups/criminal_justice/publications/criminal-justice-magazine/2020/spring/heavy-purse-law-students-reflection-the-cjs-women-criminal-justice-task-forces-nyc-listening-session [https://perma.cc/P9Q9-XTEW]; Lucian E. Dervan, *Undefined Vision: An Ally's Journey*, CRIM. JUST. MAG. (Jul. 15, 2020), https://www.americanbar.org/groups/criminal_justice/publications/criminal-justice-magazine/2020/summer/undefined-vision-allys-journey/ [https://perma.cc/4LE3-3Z7S]; Maryam Ahranjani, *Looking Back, Looking Forward*, CRIM. JUST. MAG. (Oct. 29, 2020), https://www.americanbar.org/groups/criminal_justice/publications/criminal-justice-magazine/2020/fall/looking-back-looking-forward [https://perma.cc/9DSL-266J] [hereinafter Ahranjani, *Looking Back, Looking Forward*]; Hon. Gloria Ochoa-Bruck, *The Call for the Rise of the Modern Prosecutor*, CRIM. JUST. MAG. (Jan. 11, 2021), https://www.americanbar.org/groups/criminal_justice/publications/criminal-justice-magazine/2021/winter/the-call-the-rise-the-modern-prosecutor [https://perma.cc/EF9N-4E8V]; Hon. Rachel Pickering, *An Awakening and More: How Being Part of the Women in Criminal Justice Task Force Has Provided Me with a Judicial Awareness*, CRIM. JUST. MAG. (May 1, 2021), https://www.americanbar.org/groups/criminal_justice/publications/criminal-justice-magazine/2021/spring/awakening-how-being-part-women-criminal-justice-task-force-provided-me-judicial-awareness [https://perma.cc/U4NN-PGNX]; Joy Applewhite, *Brave, Bold, Booked, and Balanced*, CRIM. JUST. MAG. (July 20, 2021), https://www.americanbar.org/groups/criminal_justice/publications/criminal-justice-magazine/2021/summer/brave-bold-booked-and-balanced [https://perma.cc/4XXT-8395]; Jessica J. Yeary, *From Sweetie to Sisterhood: A Public Defender's Listening Session Reflection*, CRIM. JUST. MAG. (Oct. 20, 2021), https://www.americanbar.org/content/dam/aba/publications/criminal_justice_magazine/fall-2021/criminal-justice-v036n03-fall-2021.pdf.authcheckdam [https://perma.cc/N4A2-NJ7E]; Yaamini L. Rao, *Voice Lessons*, CRIM. JUST. MAG. (Jan. 12, 2022), https://www.americanbar.org/groups/criminal_justice/publications/criminal-justice-magazine/2022/winter/voice-lessons/ [https://perma.cc/PAK7-GC55]; Ann Ratnayake Macy, *From Mad Men to Times Up and Beyond: What We Must Do to Ensure Workplace Parity for Women in Criminal Justice*, CRIM. JUST. MAG. (forthcoming 2022).

6. Maryam Ahranjani, *Pulling Back the Curtain: A Follow-Up Report from the ABA Criminal Justice Section Women in Criminal Justice Task Force*, A.B.A https://www.americanbar.org/content/dam/aba/administrative/criminal_justice/tf-women-report.pdf [https://perma.cc/2LBU-EMT5].

November 18, 2021, and the focus group survey administered immediately after the focus groups).

Concluding that hiring, retention, and, particularly, *promotion* of women in the criminal justice profession continue to be a problem, the 2020 follow-up survey revealed the following challenges: (1) limited flexibility with work schedules, (2) insufficient wellness resources, (3) deficient training opportunities, particularly in state and rural criminal law offices, and (4) short supply of meaningful mentorship and transparent policy guidance. Some employers seem receptive to change but many do not. The title of this report came from one of the survey respondents who described her thirty-five-year career in criminal law as a constant sprint—implying a pace that is neither sustainable nor replicable.

Considering the results of the 2020 survey, the author and the TF designed a short summary of challenges and possible solutions.[7] The TF then created a list of diverse criminal justice leaders from public and private employment. These leaders were invited to participate in focus groups held in person in the ABA's Washington, DC office and online on November 18, 2021. The purpose of the focus groups and follow-up survey included pressure-testing proposed solutions and soliciting additional solutions.

This report is divided into five parts. Part I summarizes and reviews the TF initial findings. Part II discusses the 2020 survey methodology, administration, and respondents and situates the diversity of respondents within available demographic data. Part III includes a summary of questions and responses, as well as separate sub-sections on the impact of the COVID-19 pandemic on women criminal lawyers, ABA membership, and miscellaneous important comments. Part IV assesses the TF's preliminary recommendations and proposes potential systemic solutions for employers to implement. Part V reports on feedback from high-level and experienced criminal justice leaders at focus group discussions held in November 2021. Finally, the conclusion shares next steps for the TF to promote systemic reform to create greater gender equity for Samantha and others like her.

I. SUMMARY OF THE TASK FORCE'S INITIAL FINDINGS

When American Bar Association Criminal Justice Section (CJS) staff member Emily Johnson discovered that only 26% of the approximately 16,000 members of the CJS were women, she wondered

7. *See infra* app. D.

whether that number reflected the total population of criminal lawyers or merely the CJS membership.[8] She raised her questions with CJS Director Kevin Scruggs and then-CJS Chair Professor Lucian Dervan.[9]

Considering the ABA's core goal of eliminating bias and enhancing diversity, Dervan created the TF to investigate whether women faced challenges in hiring, retention, and promotion in criminal law spaces.[10] He appointed Carla Laroche, then a clinical professor at Florida State College of Law who is currently a tenure-track assistant clinical professor at Washington and Lee University School of Law, and Tina Luongo, chief defender at the Legal Aid Society of New York City, to co-chair the TF. Laroche and Luongo envisioned and created a vibrant TF of women with incredibly diverse lived and professional experiences to carry out its mission and appointed the author as the reporter.[11]

Between late 2018 and mid-2020, the TF held listening sessions across the country and heard from nearly 200 diverse people at all stages of their careers (including law students and recent graduates) about their experiences in criminal law.[12] A number of common threads regarding hiring, retention, and promotion emerged from the sessions, providing insight into the following question: Why are women, particularly women of color, left out of—and choosing to leave—criminal law? The main threads include barriers to entry and pressures to exit, explicit and implicit discrimination, and burnout/limited resources.[13]

> *"Practicing criminal law as a woman is like playing tackle football in a dress."*

8. *See supra* note 4, at 102.
9. *Id.*
10. Laroche & Luongo, *supra* note 5.
11. *Id.*
12. Ahranjani, *Listening Session Takeaways*, *supra* note 5.
13. *Id.*; *see also* Maryam Ahranjani, *Why Are Women Lawyers Underrepresented in Criminal Justice?*, A.B.A (Apr. 6, 2021), https://www.americanbar.org/groups/young_lawyers/publications/tyl/topics/criminal-law/why-are-women-lawyers-underrepresented-in-criminal-justice [https://perma.cc/YT38-6SUE].

A. UNDERSTANDING THE OBSTACLES

Relatively low salaries in criminal law serve as an initial and ongoing barrier, particularly for women of color and first-generation lawyers.[14] Other systemic obstacles to juggling work and life commitments add pressure on women to leave criminal justice work. Similarly, criminal justice employers are not adequately addressing stage-of-life developments that especially affect women—including marriage, childbirth and child rearing, caring for aging relatives, and menopause.

One woman explained in a listening session, "[in my role in hiring,] a woman with three children, very well qualified, declined the prosecutor position. It didn't pay well enough to even cover the childcare."[15] One prosecutor who is a mother of two explained that she wants to have a third child but simply cannot afford it. Between her relatively low salary, high cost of childcare, and "regular therapy required for my job," it simply was not possible.[16] But the costs of enduring these challenges without support are high, and many dedicated and competent women seek other legal and nonlegal opportunities as a result.[17]

Another woman with aspirations to be promoted in her office explained to the TF in a listening session that the only way to have a chance at promotion in her public defender office would be to handle a homicide case. "With respect to retention and promotion, [the question] is how you make it there and still have a family . . . what's often overlooked is fertility stuff and IVF and freezing your eggs. I don't want to have children until I've done a homicide [case]."[18]

According to the listening session participants, they face discrimination from all stakeholders in the criminal system (judges, opposing counsel, clients, court staff, corrections staff, etc.) based on gendered expectations. One woman explained, "Men try to intimidate you through intimations of incompetence and sometimes blatant overtures of incivility."[19] This discriminatory treatment is particularly challenging for women of color and LGBTQIA+ women. One well-

14. *See also* Jill Lynch Cruz, Melinda S. Molina, & Jenny Rivera, *La Voz De La Abogada Latina: Challenges and Rewards in Serving the Public Interest*, 14 CUNY L. REV. 147, 199 (2010) (presenting the results of a groundbreaking study of Latinas who are public interest lawyers).

15. Notes on file with author.

16. *Id.*

17. *Id.*

18. *Id.*

19. *Id.*

respected prosecutor described how she "was introduced by my supervisor to a judge as a 'spicy little Latina.'"[20] Several women who identify as lesbian or queer reported that they were repeatedly told they did not "look or act feminine enough."[21] Overall, the listening sessions revealed a lack of respect for and devaluation of women and gender non-conforming individuals.

Many women criminal lawyers, particularly women of color and LGBTQIA+ women, face burnout, compassion fatigue, and vicarious trauma.[22] They generally do not have the resources or support to address these challenges and asked for help to process all the stress and expectations. One Black woman judge explained, "[I] left criminal law because [I] couldn't stand seeing so many young Black men go to prison."[23] One lawyer noted:

> Looking young [and being a woman of color] has caused . . . [me] to come in overly prepared and organized to be taken seriously. I grew up with a single mom, was the first to go to college. I came in with a different perspective: I've had people in my family incarcerated. I became a prosecutor to help people. However, being one is hard—from all sides: defense says you're too aggressive, victim saying not aggressive enough, cops not wanting to come in.

Women who have remained in the field demonstrate resiliency and strong survival skills. One woman of color explained, "We bury these things [sexism, racism] because if we don't, we can't continue to work."

---

20. *Id.*

21. *Id.*

22. These three conditions are interrelated and overlapping, but they can have different causes and symptoms. The U.S. Department of Justice Office for Victims of Crime describes burnout as "a state of physical, emotional, and mental exhaustion caused by long-term involvement in emotionally demanding situations. Symptoms may include depression, cynicism, boredom, loss of compassion, and discouragement." *Glossary of Terms*, OFF. FOR VICTIMS OF CRIME, https://ovc.ojp.gov/program/vtt/glossary-terms [https://perma.cc/EHE7-P66Y]. Both prosecutors and public defenders reported some burnout throughout the listening sessions and in the follow-up surveys. Compassion fatigue is "a combination of physical, emotional, and spiritual depletion associated with caring for others who are in significant emotional pain and physical distress," so public defenders are more likely to experience it. *Id.* Vicarious trauma is "an occupational challenge for people working and volunteering in the fields of victim services, law enforcement, emergency medical services, fire services, and other allied professions, due to their continuous exposure to victims of trauma and violence," so it is more often experienced by prosecutors. *Id.* "Exposure to the trauma of others has been shown to change the world-view of these responders and can put people and organizations at risk for a range of negative consequences." *Id.*

23. Notes on file with author.

B. PROPOSED STRATEGIES TO COUNTER THE OBSTACLES

Based on these findings, the TF proposed several strategies to address these challenges. The strategies include improving access to mentors and allies, increasing flexibility, and providing more resources for training and support, which may all fall under an umbrella of culture change. Culture change means systemic shifts toward inclusion and belonging, rather than simply piecemeal performative efforts.[24] Culture change includes increasing access to meaningful mentorship—something that people noted as particularly lacking when testifying in our sessions. The culture change the TF proposes aligns with President Biden's Executive Order on Diversity, Equity, Inclusion and Accessibility in the Federal Workplace.[25]

Allyship, relatedly, is a critical buffer to gender-based discrimination. Allies sometimes come from unlikely places.[26] According to a recent Harvard Business Review article describing evidence-based best practices for allyship, there are a number of ways in which building allyship into work cultures can support more equitable outcomes.[27] The article addresses white men and others occupying spaces of privilege.[28] Professors Mekalu, Beeman, Smith and Johnson explained that allyship includes educating onself, recognizing one's own privilege, accepting feedback, becoming a trusted confidant, insisting that diverse voices be at the table, calling out harmful comments and behavior, sponsoring marginalized coworkers, insisting on diverse candidates for positions, and building a community of allies.[29]

Another aspect of culture change is adopting more flexible workplace policies that may address drift and dissatisfaction. Based on our sessions, greater flexibility in criminal law jobs will also improve the

24. Bryan Walker & Sarah A. Soule, *Changing Company Culture Requires a Movement, Not a Mandate*, HARV. BUS. REV. (June 20, 2017), https://hbr.org/2017/06/changing-company-culture-requires-a-movement-not-a-mandate [https://perma.cc/6HLW-CB8P] (describing how leaders can create meaningful, systemic shifts in work cultures).

25. Exec. Order No. 14035, 86 Fed. Reg. 34593 (June 25, 2021) (defining and prioritizing diversity, equity, inclusion, and accessibility (DEIA) in federal employment such that the federal workforce mirrors the U.S. population, and requiring executive department and agency heads to produce and implement a DEIA Plan).

26. A number of women explained in listening sessions and in the written surveys that women sometimes do not find other women to be allies. Notes on file with author.

27. Tsedale M. Melaku, Angie Beeman, David G. Smith, & W. Brad Johnson, *Be a Better Ally*, HARV. BUS. REV., (Nov. & Dec. 2020), https://hbr.org/2020/11/be-a-better-ally [https://perma.cc/S2RG-BMLS].

28. *Id.*

29. *Id.*

likelihood of recruiting and retaining talented women. The TF's work so far indicates that women, particularly those in rural and under-resourced jurisdictions, need better training opportunities and resources related to wellness, diversity and inclusion, and professional development.

The TF leadership (the author and co-chairs) and members purposefully honored the vulnerability of the participants by nurturing relationships and connecting participants to one another and to various opportunities. The author and TF co-chairs send regular updates and links about our work to participants and facilitated leadership opportunities with the TF and in the ABA Criminal Justice Section. The author and TF co-chairs recruit participants to speak on panels, in classrooms, and on the CJS JustPod podcast[30] and to write about their experiences. Recruited by the TF leadership, a number of TF members and participants wrote powerful columns about the discrimination they have faced and witnesses as judges, prosecutors and defense attorneys.[31]

Based on the qualitative reports during and after the listening sessions, it was clear that the TF needed to gather more quantitative information. Through partnerships with the American Bar Foundation[32] and the ABA Center on Innovation,[33] the author and the TF explored various opportunities to conduct quantitative research. After considering a number of options and balancing the limitations posed by the pandemic with the interest in continuing to do our work despite limitations, the TF decided to conduct a follow-up survey of women who had already participated in the listening sessions. The idea was that women with whom we already had a connection would be more likely to respond than those hearing from the TF for the first time during the global pandemic while they juggled caregiving responsibilities.

30. The JustPod, *Task Force Ops: Initial Findings from the Women in Criminal Justice Task Force*, A.B.A. (Mar. 3, 2021), https://podcasts.apple.com/us/podcast/task-force-ops-initial-findings-from-the-women-in/id1454284972?i=1000511498218 [https://perma.cc/WZY8-EVUU].

31. *See* sources cited *supra* note 5, especially Hinayon, Donoso, Ochoa-Brook, Pickering, Applewhite, Yeary, Rao and Macy.

32. The American Bar Foundation is an independent, nonprofit organization committed to empirical and interdisciplinary research of the study of law. *About*, AM. BAR FOUND., www.americanbarfoundation.org/about/index.html [https://perma.cc/R4NF-UUZQ].

33. The ABA Center on Innovation seeks to encourage innovations that improve the accessibility of legal services. *About Us*, A.B.A., https://www.americanbar.org/groups/centers_commissions/center-for-innovation/AboutUs [https://perma.cc/X8MA-DG4H].

II. METHODOLOGY AND ADMINISTRATION OF THE 2020 SURVEY

The follow-up survey (2020 Survey) was open between October 29, 2020, and December 1, 2020. Targeted respondents included the women criminal lawyers who had participated in TF listening sessions between November 2018 and June 2020. Since the TF already invited the participants to answer many similar questions prior to the listening session, there were two goals for this follow-up survey: (1) to document participants responses to gender equity in hiring, retention, and promotion in the criminal law profession in a more effective way, and (2) to seek feedback on how the COVID-19 pandemic has affected their careers. One significant addition compared to the pre-listening session survey was an attempt to assess respondents' commitment to the practice of criminal law. Presumably, feedback from highly committed practitioners as opposed to less committed practitioners is even more weighty, even though feedback is valuable.

A. Who Was in the Survey Pool?

The TF emailed the survey with a Qualtrics link to 144 women who had participated in the TF listening sessions, including thirty-six women who were law students at the time of their participation. Although the survey was sent to practitioners and law students, the primary goal and expectation was to hear from practitioners. Four emails bounced back and a total of nine autoreplies were received. Two out-of-office replies indicated the women were on reduced schedules due to family care responsibilities. One autoreply was an open-ended reply that the attorney was out of the office indefinitely. Two autoreplies indicated the attorneys were on leave.

B. Who Were the Survey Respondents?

Forty-nine women responded, including three who were law students at the time they testified. The overall response rate of 34% (forty-nine out of 144) or almost 43% for practitioners only (forty-six out of 108) was quite high, especially since survey response rates were down during the COVID-19 pandemic.[34] It is likely that the trust relationship built through the listening sessions and follow-up correspondence contributed to the relatively high response rate.

34. Jonathan Rothbaum, *How Does the Pandemic Affect Survey Response: Using Administrative Data to Evaluate Nonresponse in the Current Population Survey Annual Social and Economic Supplement*, U.S. Census Bureau (Sept. 15, 2020), https://www.census.gov/newsroom/blogs/research-matters/2020/09/pandemic-affect-survey-response.html [https://perma.cc/8KMJ-N4C5].

The forty-nine respondents were diverse in terms of geographic location, criminal law position, graduation year from law school, race, ethnicity, and LGBTQIA+ identification. Respondents live and work all over the country—in rural, urban, and suburban settings. They are based in the Northeast (New York, Pennsylvania, Washington DC), Northwest (Washington State), Midwest (Missouri), Southeast (Florida, Virginia), and Southwest (Arizona, California, New Mexico). Respondents included tribal, state, and federal-level prosecutors, public defenders, and judges. Respondents also included law students and women working in private criminal defense and at non-profit organizations dedicated to criminal justice.

Respondents' ages ranged from twenty-three to seventy-seven, and the average age was forty-nine. Law school graduation years ranged from 1971 to 2022.

Forty-eight people responded to the questions about race and ethnicity, and one declined to answer. In terms of race/ethnicity, the survey first asked whether the respondent identified as Hispanic/Latinx. Since people who identify as Hispanic/Latinx may identify as members of various races, respondents were then invited to indicate the race(s) with which they identify. Eleven women (23%) identified as Hispanic/Latinx. In terms of race, five (10.4%) identified as American Indian or Alaskan Native; five (10.4%) as Asian/Southeast Asian/South Asian; four (8.3%) as Black or African American; one (2.1%) as Middle Eastern/North African; twenty-four (50%) as white; four (8.3%) as multiracial or multiethnic; and five (10.4%) as other.

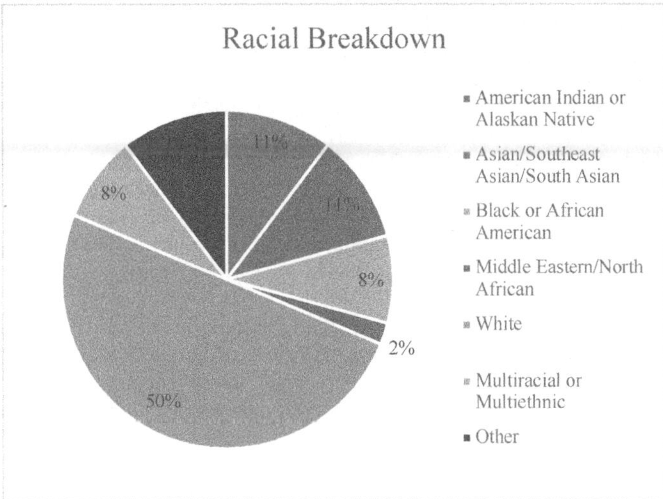

Figure 1. Depicting the racial breakdown of the 2020 Survey respondents.

In terms of gender identity, there were forty-nine responses. Forty-five (91.8%) identified as women, two (4.1%) identified as trans-women, one (2.04%) identified as a trans-man, and one (2.04%) identified as gender non-conforming. Forty-nine people responded to the question about sexual orientation. Forty participants (81.6%) identified as heterosexual, three (6.1%) identified as lesbian, two (4.1%) identified as bisexual, three (6.1%) identified as queer, and one (2.04%) preferred not to say.

C. Situating the Diversity of Respondents

As explained in *"Toughen Up, Buttercup" versus #TimesUp: Initial Findings of the Women in Criminal Justice Task Force*, there is no national demographic data on women lawyers, much less women lawyers practicing criminal law.[35] Therefore, it is not possible to compare the demographics of survey respondents to the overall population of women criminal lawyers, or women lawyers in general, for that matter. The ABA's 2021 National Lawyer Population Survey, however,

35. Ahranjani, *supra* note 4.

provides some self-reported racial demographic information of active lawyers in the United States.[36]

According to that survey, 5% of lawyers identify as African American, 2% Asian, 85% Caucasian/White, less than 1% Hawaiian/Pacific Islander, 5% Hispanic, 2% multiracial, and less than 1% Native American.[37] The ABA survey considers Hispanic as a race, which is different from the TF's approach, which recognizes that Hispanic Americans may identify with different races. The National Association of Law Placement's (NALP) most recent data also provides some national data, showing that the percentage of lawyers who identify as "LGBT" continues to rise as of 2019—nearly 3% (2.99%) of their survey respondents identify as "LGBT."[38]

Measured against this data, the respondents to this TF survey were significantly more diverse than the overall population of lawyers. This aligns with the TF's articulated goal of reaching out to and elevating the experiences of traditionally excluded women and gender non-conforming people.[39]

Framing the demographic results more broadly, the percentage of women enrolling in law school has been steadily increasing. Since 2016, women have constituted slightly more than 50% of incoming 1Ls nationally.[40] However, the overall percentage of women *lawyers,* as opposed to law students, is just 37%.[41] The obstacles to hiring, retention, and promotion of women criminal lawyers, particularly women of color and women who identify as LGBTQIA+, are important regardless of this trend, but the growing number of women in the profession intensifies the need to document and eliminate these barriers.

III. 2020 SURVEY QUESTIONS AND RESPONSES

The 2020 follow-up survey included questions similar to the ones previously asked of participants[42] but expanded on personal and

36. A.B.A., *ABA National Lawyer Population Survey: 2021*, https://www.americanbar.org/content/dam/aba/administrative/market_research/2021-national-lawyer-population-survey.pdf [https://perma.cc/JR34-ZT7A].

37. *Id.*

38. *LGBT Representation Among Lawyers in 2019*, NAT'L ASS'N FOR L. PLACEMENT (Jan. 2020), https://www.nalp.org/0120research [https://perma.cc/9YQS-WUUK].

39. *See* Laroche & Luongo, *supra* note 5.

40. *Law School Rankings by Female Enrollment (2020)*, ENJURIS, https://www.enjuris.com/students/law-school-women-enrollment-2020.html [https://perma.cc/N8KA-YUX3].

41. A.B.A., *supra* note 36, at 4.

42. Ahranjani, *supra* note 4, at 153.

observed experiences related to hiring, retention, and promotion in criminal law and included a new section related to the impact of the COVID-19 pandemic on the women's lives.[43] The follow-up survey included a mix of yes/no, multiple choice, and open-ended questions.[44]

A. Questions and Responses Regarding Hiring, Retention, and Promotion

When asked whether they personally experienced challenges with hiring, retention and promotion, twenty-six people responded. Of the twenty-six, ten (38%) said yes to hiring, fourteen (53%) said yes to retention and twenty-four (92%) said yes to promotion. Respondents were encouraged to explain further, and they shared the following challenges: retaliation for sexual harassment claims and cooperation with investigations, being passed up in favor of older men, difficulty in uprooting their families (which men seemed more able/willing to do), sexism, and discrimination based on religion and national origin.[45]

When asked whether they observed *others* experiencing challenges, twenty-seven responded. Respondents reported even higher numbers: fourteen (51%) said yes to hiring, twenty (74%) said yes to retention, and twenty-four (88%) said yes to promotion. Sixty-five percent of respondents indicated that when hiring, retention, and/or promotion were issues, those who were treated negatively were likely to change jobs. Failure to accommodate women with families and intersectionality (gender plus gender and other personal characteristics)[46] were cited as the two most common reasons for making a career switch.[47]

43. *See infra* app. B.

44. *Id.*

45. *Id.*

46. Columbia Law Professor Kimberlé Crenshaw's intersectionality theory describes how race, class, gender, and other individual characteristics intersect and overlap with one another. *Mapping the Margins: Intersectionality, Identity Politics, and Violence Against Women of Color*, 43 STAN. L. REV. 1241 (1991).

47. Results on file with author.

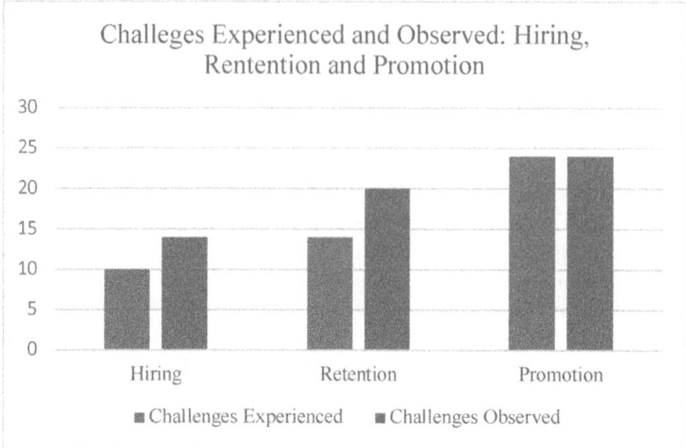

Figure 2. Charting responses to the following questions: whether respondents personally experienced challenges with hiring, retention, and promotion; and whether respondents observed others experiencing challenges with hiring, retention, and promotion.

Despite the challenges, 47% of respondents plan to stay with their employer for the foreseeable future, and another 18% said they may stay. Their reasons for staying include: a love for the work and their colleagues, commitment to their clients who they serve, retirement benefits, wanting to serve their people (Native Americans), and autonomy.

When asked whether they have an informal or formal source of support when gender-related issues arise, thirty-five women provided responses. Ninety-four percent of them responded affirmatively. They were asked to describe sources of support, and the responses included colleagues, friends, supervisors, human resources, law partners, union, and family.[48]

With regard to what women need(ed) to be successful criminal law practitioners, respondents listed a number of items. They include (in no particular order) intelligence, respect, passion, training, grit, creativity, compassion, ability to learn quickly, commitment to hard work, experience, organizational skills, equal playing field, empathy, strong sense of justice, resilience, preparation, determination,

48. *Id.*

idealism, good judgment, mental health support, training, supportive colleagues and others, ability not to back down from lawyers who tend to bully, more funding, equal pay for equal work, active promotion of women, a boss that fights for office needs, mentors, and an environment that strives to help employees reduce stress and chaos.[49]

One comment by a respondent sums up the career arc articulated by many women. The respondent observed, "In the beginning, I needed training and mentorship. As my career progressed, I mostly just needed to be left alone."[50] Interestingly, though, when asked, "Have your needs changed as you have progressed in your career?" twenty-two out of the thirty-five respondents (62%) who answered stated, "No." One comment articulates what several women said about needing more support over time because of the complexity of the cases they handle: "Need support in how to handle the gravity and destruction that can be our job."[51] Combining these responses with what participants articulated in the listening sessions, this inconsistency may reflect ambivalence and a sense that, while they were tough and did not *need* support at any stage, they certainly would have benefitted from it.

> *"I am 65 and have been at this [criminal law] for 35 years, pouring heart, soul and body into this . . . . I feel I've been sprinting a marathon."*

In response to the question prompt "[w]hat do you feel you need(ed) to remain in the criminal justice field?", mental health support and self-care were cited several times. A number of powerful comments by respondents surfaced:[52]

- "I need to not be undermined by individuals who view my success as a threat to them."
- "I am 65 and have been at this for 35 years, pouring heart, soul and body into this. What would it take to keep at it?? A change of pace or a break. A colleague of mine quit after about 3 years, saying she had treated the job as a sprint rather than a marathon. I feel I've been sprinting a marathon."
- "As long as I can help, I need to be here."
- "Systemic racism must be addressed."

49. *Id.*
50. *Id.*
51. *Id.*
52. Quotation information on file with author.

Of the thirty-five who provided responses to the question "[h]ow committed are you to remaining in your office?", almost all of them said they were *at least* committed but open to new opportunities. Sixty percent said they are very committed, 14% said they are somewhat committed, and 11% said they are committed but open to other opportunities.

Thirty-five women also responded to the prompt "[h]ave your employers provided you with what you needed to be successful and remain in the field?" Twenty answered "yes" and fifteen answered "no." Women in the federal system seemed more likely to report satisfaction. Of the seven women who identified as federal prosecutors, public defenders, and judges, five responded to the question. Out of those five, four responded, "Yes."

Women were invited to explain what they needed from employers to be successful and remain in the field. The most frequent responses were support, training, flexibility and mentorship.[53] Topics that came up more than once as unmet needs include pay equity and therapy/mental health support. When asked what policies and practices are most effective for retaining women, respondents listed the following concrete items, which have been paraphrased:

- Job sharing;
- Seeing and experiencing promotion to leadership positions (particularly women with children);
- Part-time options;
- Flexibility in general;
- Flexible work schedules;
- Better enforcement of workplace harassment policies;
- Temporary positions;
- Permitting children to come to the office;
- Equal and fair pay;
- Better mentoring;
- More training;
- Listening and being more supportive/encouraging;
- Exit interviews; and
- Acknowledgement that being flexible does not mean people will be ineffective.

In terms of perceptions of employer receptivity to those suggestions, respondents were asked, "How receptive do you think your employer is or would have been to implementing these

53. *See infra* app. C for verbatim responses.

recommendations?" Out of 20 responses to this question, 20% said extremely positive, 30% said somewhat positive, 15% said neither positive nor negative, 15% said somewhat negative, and 20% said extremely negative.

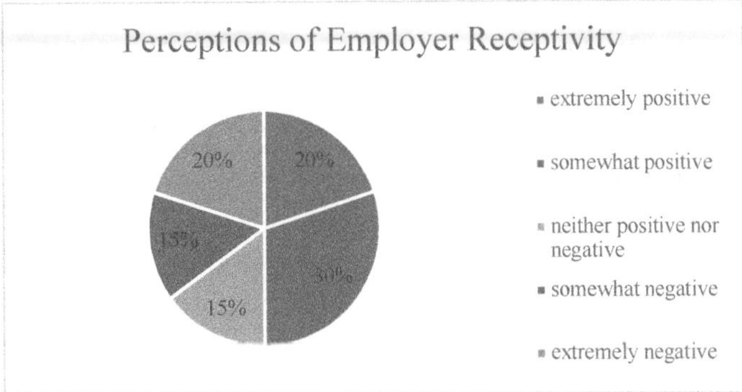

Figure 3. Depicting respondents' perceptions of employer receptivity to implementing policies and practices to retain women criminal law attorneys.

In response to "[w]hat would it take to make changes?", respondents replied: budget changes, management support, adverse civil verdict, mass exodus of women of color/people of color, human resources or union pressure, and willingness to try.

B. COVID-19-Related Questions

Based on information gathered during two videoconferences in Summer 2020, the TF sought to capture the ways in which the pandemic affected the work of women in the criminal legal field, and whether they hoped to keep any aspects of the pandemic workday configuration.

When asked which aspects of their lives have been disproportionately affected by COVID-19 and their gender identity, eight said childcare, four said elder care, thirteen said professional development, twenty-three said quality of life, fifteen said work performance, and four said other.

In response to the question "[w]hat other aspects of your life have been affected by the confluence of COVID-19, being a woman, and being in criminal justice?", responses included:[54]

54. Quotation information on file with author.

- "No formal coordination with courts, prosecutors and other components of criminal justice system."
- "Everything is harder. I have two teens, both have significant mental health issues and learning challenges. Both are failing many of their classes in online school. My husband also has mental health issues. I am trying to support my family and do my job, and not doing anything as well as I would in non-COVID times."
- "I don't think I've been more affected because I'm a woman. I actually think I probably have less running around to do because my 14-year-old daughter is in virtual school and only has one extra-curricular activity that she can do—swimming every morning with her swim team, socially distanced. She can't see friends or go anywhere. And she's very self-sufficient with her schoolwork, so I don't need to help her with that. I'm lucky I don't have small children."
- "The practice became almost more difficult because of the varied responses by Courts in different counties. It felt as if I was a new lawyer - learning how to navigate every location anew."
- "No quality of life."
- "I butt heads with judges even more now. Unfortunately, our district's chief judge is a misogynist, so those battles have gone . . . poorly."
- "Isolation."
- "One feels even more out of the loop."
- "Specifically I have had to pay for additional childcare for my school age child. In addition to this, any time either one of my children as a minor symptom such as a runny nose, there is a high likelihood that they will be sent home from daycare requiring me to either take off work or work from home. Unfortunately my boss does not understand that this is directly linked to COVID and not just a "sick" child. In fact, in most cases my children are not actually sick, they just are having a symptom that comes with childhood. Currently my boss will not allow us to work from home under these circumstances though he is currently letting three male employees work from home on a scheduled basis. The three young women in the office, who have chosen to pay for daycare rather than schedule work from home are not given any support when they need a day here and there to work from home. Thus we have to use our sick leave or our vacation while our male counterparts are not put in this position."

Finally, when asked, "In a post-COVID world, are there any changes you would like to keep?", many women said they hoped some things—greater flexibility in telecommuting/ telework, virtual hearings/settlement conferences, and generally more flexibility in terms of when in the day work could be completed—would remain. One respondent said, "For me personally, there are none."[55]

55. *Id.*

C. ABA Membership

Nineteen respondents were current ABA members. For those who were not members, thirteen respondents indicated that membership costs too much (especially relative to benefits), ten indicated they see no benefit to their careers, four said they did not feel they would fit in, and thirteen selected "other." The "other" responses ranged from practicing in tribal courts; ABA not being inclusive of Native American attorneys; already being involved in more salient professional organizations; and serving in a Presidential appointment or judgeship that required resignation from boards, commissions, and advisory councils.

D. Additional Important Comments by Respondents

Respondents were invited to share additional thoughts related to hiring, retention, and promotion of women in criminal law. Here are their comments and observations:[56]

- "STEM-based criminal justice is an area of growth, and it's currently dominated by straight, white men."
- "Practicing in Indian Country requires serious commitment and perhaps someone from that community would be more likely to remain because of family."
- "Women are the best lawyers in the profession. I've been practicing a long time and [have] seen a lot of lawyers working. No question, women are the best lawyers, certainly in criminal law."
- "I think it's always been better for women in criminal law than civil. That Old Boys Club is a lot harder to crack."
- "There is a reason that our profession has such a high level of substance abuse. There is an extreme amount of conflict and stress that we deal with on a regular basis and the profession as a whole needs to address this in a more positive manner. More resources should be provided, employees should have a safe place to check in and voice their frustrations."

IV. PRELIMINARY RECOMMENDATIONS BASED ON FOLLOW-UP SURVEY

This Article amplifies the diverse experiences of the people who responded to the 2020 survey. Women criminal lawyers serve a critical role in the promotion of justice. The people who responded to this survey by and large are passionate about their work and are committed to continuing to practice criminal law. However, they identified some major, persistent challenges. Broadly speaking, they include (1) limited flexibility with work schedules, (2) insufficient wellness

56. *Id.*

resources, (3) deficient training opportunities, particularly in state and rural criminal law offices, and (4) short supply of meaningful mentorship.

These challenges are firmly entrenched and are felt even more profoundly by women with intersectional identities. For example, women of color (particularly Black, Indigenous and Latina women), women from low-income backgrounds, women who have significant educational debt, women with obligations to their extended families and communities, people who identify as LGBTQIA+, and others, described the many layers of challenges they face in navigating both workspaces and their personal lives. The high-intensity and emotional nature of criminal law heighten the experience of representing defendants and the state in a system that often seems unfair and imbalanced.

Only systemic solutions will lead to long-term improvements in the hiring, retention, and promotion of women criminal lawyers. The author summarized the listening sessions and 2020 survey in the following chart, which describes potential solutions.

Challenge	**Potential Systemic Solutions for Employers to Implement**
Limited flexibility with work schedules	Policies that allow job-sharing, part-time work, and working from home; court schedules that accommodate children's school schedules.
Insufficient wellness resources	Create wellness spaces in offices and courthouses; provide free therapy and other wellness information, policies and programs; meet regularly with attorneys to assess job satisfaction and avoid feelings of invisibility.
Deficient training opportunities	Pool resources with other jurisdictions; amplify existing free resources through ABA and state, local, and affinity bars.
Short supply of meaningful mentorship	Pool resources with other jurisdictions; amplify existing free resources through ABA and state, local, and affinity bars; create more meaningful mentorship opportunities and incentivize/recognize participation.

The TF members digested the findings of the follow-up surveys and decided that the next major step would be to hold in-person focus group meetings. With the support of then-CJS Chair and TF member April Frazier Camara and current CJS Chair Wayne McKenzie, the TF hosted focus groups in November 2021 with criminal justice stakeholders to share ideas and findings, and to pressure test the TF's suggested remedies. The next Part includes the methodology and findings of the focus group meetings and focus group follow-up survey. Throughout the time when the 2020 survey, focus group meetings and 2021 follow-up survey to the focus group meetings occurred, TF members continued to write and speak about our work.[57]

With participants' input and the CJS's continued support, the TF seeks to make the criminal legal profession more welcoming and inclusive for all lawyers, especially those who, like the survey respondents, face too many barriers currently.

V. 2021 FOCUS GROUPS AND FOLLOW-UP SURVEY

On November 18, 2021, the ABA CJS hosted one in-person focus group in Washington, DC and two virtual focus groups with high-level criminal justice leaders who were nominated by the TF members. All three groups consisted of groups of under ten people total, including TF members. The author of this Article trained TF members to facilitate the discussions. The TF leadership team of the author and co-chairs Carla Laroche and Tina Luongo designed a script that included four questions.

Participants included six TF members, the TF co-chairs, the author and sixteen attendees who represented a wide range of criminal justice spaces, including public defenders, prosecutors, private criminal defense, associations and non-profit organizations, judges, and state and federal government. The participants were diverse in terms of geographic location, race, ethnicity, sexual orientation, gender identity, and other characteristics. Several were justice-impacted lawyers, and all are employers and leaders who have the power to implement changes.

Each focus group had approximately three to six TF members and three to seven attendees. Each discussion lasted approximately ninety minutes, although the in-person group lasted closer to 120 minutes. In preparation for the meetings, and in an effort to maximize the limited time, the author sent all confirmed participants a one-page chart that described identified challenges and sample solutions, challenges identified and potential remedies, as well as the TF's two published research papers (*"Toughen Up, Buttercup" versus #TimesUp* and *Pulling Back the Curtain*).[58]

57. *See* sources cited *supra* note 5, especially Donoso, Ahranjani, Ochoa-Bruck, Pickering, Applewhite, Yeary, Rao, and Macy.

58. *See infra* app. D.

In each focus group, TF facilitators asked participants the following questions. The participants' responses to each question are paraphrased.[59]

1. Have you or your organizations implemented anything to facilitate gender equity in hiring, retention, and promotion? If so, please describe.

- Support groups and mentorship programs
- Just because there's a lactation room doesn't mean women should not nurse in public[60]
- Paternity leave
- Work-from-home policies (along with support for work-from-home like laptops, internet coverage, etc.)
- Wellness and substance abuse resources for judges
- Promotion of members' successes since women have trouble self-promoting
- Compressed work weeks (e.g., ten-hour days, four days a week)
- Sabbatical programs
- More training for employers on how to write gender-neutral job postings, be more culturally competent and how to standardize questions
- Microaggression training and bias training
- Providing questions to interviewees in advance so they can prepare
- Mandating a week off each year for self-care

2. Do you have ideas that haven't been implemented? If so, why haven't they been implemented?

- There's no shortage of great ideas; the problem is the criminal justice system is so busy it's hard to find time to implement them.
- Compressed works weeks (e.g., ten-hour days, four days a week, but need to educate judges and encourage them to participate)
- Sabbatical programs (including for judges)
- Better support for imposter syndrome
- Better support for how to handle sticky situations like interviewing while pregnant

3. As the Task Force works to create a toolkit of resources, we would like to know what resources would you and your organizations need to implement greater gender equity?

- Better mentorship for new contracted counsel through the Criminal Justice Act and other attorneys

59. Notes on file with author. Notes were taken in shorthand by a TF member and the author, so verbatim quotes were not available.

60. This point was made by a non-profit leader who was alluding to laws protecting nursing in public.

- Template and how-to videos for leadership skills (especially how to use technology effectively, how to put together a newsletter, how to schedule conference calls, etc.)
- First page of tool kit needs to have an endorsement from the ABA—gender equity is a societal issue, not just a women's issue
- Include list of resources (including National Justice Impact Bar Association and Yale Access to Law School Program)
- Help women learn how to present on Zoom

4. What haven't we thought about that you think we ought to think about?

- ABA could be a real leader in this space
- Legal education could play a critical role in terms of mentorship, training, motivation
- Prosecutors need support too
- There might be unique concerns for people in non-urban areas (but also maybe not)

The focus groups were supposed to be largely in person, but because of ongoing Covid concerns, participants were given the opportunity to request online participation. The format changed from mostly in-person to mostly remote several days before the meetings. The author canceled her own trip to DC because her son was in quarantine due to a Covid exposure. Because of last-minute changes, the limited time in the focus groups and an interest in expanding opportunities for criminal justice leaders to participate, on November 22, 2021, the author sent two separate emails inviting written responses to the four questions. One email went out to those sixteen remote and in-person focus group meeting participants, and another went out to the forty-one other people who had been nominated to participate but who either had not responded or who responded that they were unable to join us. The survey was open between November 22 and December 10 (plus a few extra days for several people who asked). Two reminder emails were sent after the initial request. Fifteen responses were recorded, including ten from attendees and five from non-attendees.

Appendix E contains some of the salient written responses to the questions. Respondents echoed comments made in the focus groups and contributed valuable specific and general feedback to the same four questions asked in the focus groups. Summarizing takeaways from the focus groups and surveys, it is clear that the goal of pressure-testing ideas for gender equity reform gained from phase one and soliciting new ones was met. One likely next step for the TF is to produce a Ten Principles for Gender Equity in Criminal Law.[61] The Ten Principles would be formally endorsed by the ABA and would live on a website with content that would animate the principles of creating healthy, equitable workplaces. The site would house interactive support mechanisms. For example, the site could showcase successful telework programs and outside-the-box ideas like a four-day workweek.[62] The site would also include a robust tool kit to accompany the Ten Principles. The tool kit idea has been on the TF's agenda as an eventual work product, and it became apparent during the focus group meetings with criminal justice leaders that there already is a lot of content that could be compiled[63] and included in the tool kit. One particular tool kit component that was mentioned repeatedly was wellness resources, including model policies for promoting employee wellness.

61. This suggestion by an ally in one of the focus groups was inspired by the ABA's Ten Principles of a Public Defense System, which has been widely adopted by CJ organizations. *See ABA Ten Principles of a Public Defense Delivery System*, A.B.A. (Feb. 2002), https://www.americanbar.org/content/dam/aba/administrative/legal_aid_indigent_defendants/ls_sclaid_def_tenprinciplesbooklet.authcheckdam.pdf [https://perma.cc/R53U-HHVU].

62. Anne Branigin, *Can Four-Day Workweeks Help Women? More Companies Are Trying It Out*, LILY (Dec. 23, 2021), https://www.thelily.com/can-four-day-workweeks-help-women-more-companies-are-trying-it-out/ [https://perma.cc/64UG-NJ28].

63. TF member Lt. Col. Susan Upward suggested incorporating a talent management document used by the Marines. The Diversity Lab and its Mansfield Rule were also mentioned. Grounded in behavioral science, the Mansfield Rule "measures whether law firms have affirmatively considered at least 30 percent women, lawyers of color, LGBTQ+ lawyers, and lawyers with disabilities for leadership and governance roles, equity partner promotions, formal client pitch opportunities, and senior lateral positions." *About the Lab*, DIVERSITY LAB, https://www.diversitylab.com [https://perma.cc/EC34-ENJ8]. The Women's Bar Association of DC (WBA DC) has 600+ resources related to career advancement, including pay equity information. These resources are currently accessible by members only, but the organization is willing to share its relevant content with the TF. The WBA DC also has an anti-racism tool kit, as do other organizations. The Shriver Center on Poverty Law has guidance on trauma-informed lawyering, which the TF heard over and over again was a big challenge, especially for state prosecutors who do not have as much access to training resources and who may be less diverse and connected to the populations with whom they work. *See, e.g.*, *An Antiracist Approach to Trauma-Informed Lawyering*, SHRIVER CTR. ON POVERTY L., (June 29, 2021), https://www.povertylaw.org/article/trauma-informed-lawyering [https://perma.cc/6E7H-4HDC]. Another existing resource is the Association of American Law Schools Best Practices for Recruitment and Retention of Minority Law Faculty manual. *Recruitment & Retention of Minority Law Faculty Members*, ASS'N OF AM. L. SCHS., (Nov. 2012), https://www.aals.org/about/handbook/good-practices/minority-law-faculty-members [https://perma.cc/W332-TDLP].

Another clear need in terms of the tool kits is help in facilitating culture change. Some suggestions for culture change materials included how to assess the current climate in an office—perhaps through external consultants and surveys of stakeholders, review pay scales to make sure lateral and vertical equity exists, identify and articulate clear goals, listen to underrepresented and marginalized people in the office, address changing expectations with regard to work/life balance and advance notice of deadlines, and promote allyship.

Another suggested item for the toolkit is professional development and advancement tools. For example, according to one white collar private defense attorney, women often do not have appropriate set-ups for remote work such as ring lights, microphones, and backgrounds.[64] Since workplaces are likely to continue remote work for some time, it was mentioned that the TF should encourage improvement of online professional development. Another example of professional development was provided by a different private defense attorney who pointed out in a focus group meeting that many people who are underrepresented in leadership have not been taught certain skills—how to set up Zoom meetings, calendaring, polling, etc.—that are essential to being effective managers.[65] Another suggestion was to help women monetize the value of litigation skills gained through criminal prosecution and defense to argue for raises or to change employment.[66]

An important takeaway from the focus groups and written surveys was the need to connect judges to the burdens of the current system and to inspire them to take an active role in changing courtroom schedules and cultures. TF co-chair Tina Luongo pointed out that once judges realized a compressed workweek would benefit them too, they would be more likely to schedule hearings only four instead of five days a week.[67] One TF member who is a judge suggested hosting a judges' conference for judges to learn about gender inequality and heightened challenges for women of color and women with other intersectional identities.

Guided by the qualitative data gathered from the three phases of this work, the final phase for the TF will be to create and promote the Top Ten Principles for Gender Equity in Criminal Law, tool kit, and

64. Notes on file with author.
65. *Id.*
66. *Id.*
67. *Id.*

accompanying web site. As the TF moves through the final phase, we will draw from strong relationships within the judiciary, legal academia, and federal and state criminal law leaders to assist in drafting, supplementing, and promoting our work product.

CONCLUSION

Criminal law employers should view women's drift as a significant problem. The COVID-19 pandemic has both exacerbated and exposed the tightrope on which many working women like Samantha walk.[68] Women's scars and challenges from the COVID-19 era have affected and will continue to affect their role in the work force and as lawyers.[69] Because of increased caregiving responsibilities, many women, especially college-educated women with the option to work remotely, have stepped out of the work force and others have reduced their hours.[70]

> *"They say every crisis is an opportunity. The current pandemic is surely the former and should serve as the latter. If we in the legal profession have learned nothing else, it is how much more can be done remotely than anyone thought possible. My hope is that employers, private and public, will internalize these lessons, and that both women and men will use this experience to advocate for flexible work hours that allow them to accommodate the ever-competing needs of family maintenance, child rearing and work."*

68. Jennifer L. Smuts, *Coming Up for Air: Women in Law and Adapting to the Impact of COVID-19*, JD SUPRA, (Mar. 4, 2021), https://www.jdsupra.com/legalnews/coming-up-for-air-women-in-law-and-8541536 [https://perma.cc/QHM6-W8G6]; Cynthia L. Cooper, *Work-Life Imbalance: Pandemic Disruption Places New Stresses on Women Lawyers*, A.B.A. (Dec. 18, 2020), https://www.americanbar.org/groups/diversity/women/publications/perspectives/2021/december/worklife-imbalance-pandemic-disruption-places-new-stresses-women-lawyers [https://perma.cc/4TWK-JEPN].

69. Alexandra Samuel, *How Working From Home Has Changed Employees*, WALL ST. J. (June 12, 2021), https://www.wsj.com/articles/working-from-home-employees-11623463249?st=si1pq9hc2i5lf94&reflink=desktopwebshare_permalink&fbclid=IwAR1WJsSXOrTo91J39RlXbaqZ7HAlgdcB-bFm0p_15McEnCRqZEjdZduvus0 [https://perma.cc/VM8B-XG3N].

70. *Id.*; Soo Youn, *Remote Work Was Supposed to Help Moms in the Pandemic. Instead, It Hurt Them the Most*, LILY (Nov. 10, 2021), https://www.thelily.com/remote-work-was-supposed-to-help-moms-in-the-pandemic-instead-it-hurt-them-the-most [https://perma.cc/4XM3-CUNA] (describing a study that reports how college-educated women with the option to work remotely were most likely to leave their jobs).

The pandemic has also provided a window into what greater flexibility could look like, and the responses from our surveys and focus groups indicate hope that some aspects of working remotely will be retained. It is important to note, however, that juggling remote work with caregiving is *not* a sustainable solution. All changes and "flexibility" must come as a result of open, honest dialogue and culture changes within offices.

One judge (who does not have children herself) noted at a listening session, "[m]y observation after years of experience is that women with children make the best criminal lawyers."[71] She described their organizational and time management skills, capacity for empathy, and problem-solving abilities as the top reasons. This anecdote is confirmed by numerous studies of professional women.[72] In fact, researchers have found that "over the course of a 30-year career, mothers outperformed women without children at almost every stage of the game. In fact, mothers with at least two kids were the most productive of all."[73]

Employers should be concerned not just about retention and promotion of current women criminal lawyers—they should also be aware of demographic changes on the horizon. The enrollment of women in law schools has been steadily climbing in recent years,[74] and, presumably, so too will the number of women who could potentially be hired as criminal lawyers. The combination of the unique features of criminal law—racial and ethnic bias; intense work with clients and survivors experiencing poverty, racism, homelessness, and other challenges; litigation schedule and related stress; the emotional toll of working in a system that many feel is unjust; and relative lack of resources—with the realities of balancing out-of-work responsibilities of caregiving mean that the profession must adapt or run the risk of losing highly-skilled, highly qualified women.

71. Notes on file with author.

72. Matthias Krapf, Heinrich W. Ursprung, & Christian Zimmermann, *Parenthood and Productivity of Highly Skilled Labor: Evidence from the Groves of Academe*, J. ECON. BEHAV. & ORG. (Jan. 2014), https://s3.amazonaws.com/real.stlouisfed.org/wp/2014/2014-001.pdf [https://perma.cc/XAS8-MLC8].

73. Ylan Q. Mui, *Study: Women with More Children Are More Productive at Work*, WASH. POST (Oct. 30, 2014) https://www.washingtonpost.com/news/wonk/wp/2014/10/30/study-women-with-more-children-are-more-productive-at-work [https://perma.cc/JZ8P-DSTN].

74. *Women in the Legal Profession*, A.B.A., https://www.abalegalprofile.com/women/ [https://perma.cc/V5KH-YYJ8].

For over three years, the TF has collected and elevated the experiences of diverse women and gender non-conforming folk. It is now the TF's charge to develop and implement sustainable changes that guarantee justice, inclusion, and belonging for these practitioners. We deserve, and society needs, a profession that does not require sprinting a marathon.

APPENDIX A

American Bar Association Criminal Justice Section Women in Criminal Justice Task Force

Co-Chairs

Carla Laroche

Assistant Clinical Professor of Law and Director of the Civil Rights and Racial Justice Clinic, Washington and Lee University School of Law (VA)

Tina Luongo

Attorney-in-Charge of the Criminal Defense Practice, The Legal Aid Society (NY

Reporter

Maryam Ahranjani

Associate Professor and Don L. & Mabel F. Dickason, University of New Mexico School of Law (NM)

Members

Lara Bazelon

Professor of Law and Director of the Criminal & Juvenile Justice and Racial Justice Clinics, University of San Francisco School of Law (CA)

Honorable Gloria Ochoa-Bruck

Judge, Spokane Municipal Court (WA)

Barbara Creel

Professor of Law and Karelitz Professor of Evidence and Procedure, University of New Mexico School of Law (NM)

April Frazier Camara

President and CEO, National Legal Aid and Defender Association (DC)

Honorable Bernice Donald

U.S. Court of Appeals for the Sixth Circuit (TN)

Daniela Donoso

Equal Justice Works Fellow, Legal Services of North Florida (FL)

Maria Carmen Hinayon
Complaints Resolution Officer, Office for the Prevention of Harassment and Discrimination, University of California–San Francisco (CA)

Honorable Denise Langford-Morris
Oakland County Circuit Court (MI)

Ann Ratnayake Macy
Founder/Former Executive Director, National Center for Child Abuse Statistics and Policy (DC)

Honorable Rachel Pickering
Third Judicial District (KS)

Sarah Redfield
Professor of Law (emerita), University of New Hampshire School of Law (ME)

Lieutenant Colonel Susan Upward
U.S. Marine Corps (NC)

APPENDIX B

2020 Women in Criminal Justice Survey

Part One: Biographical Information

1. If you feel comfortable sharing your name and contact information, please do so here.
2. Are you of Hispanic/Latino/Spanish origin?
3. How would you best describe yourself? (American Indian or Alaska Native, Asian, Black or African American, Native Hawaiian or Other Pacific Islander, Middle Eastern/North African, White, Multiracial or Multiethnic, Other)
4. If you wish, please elaborate.
5. How do you describe yourself? (Female, Trans Woman/Trans Female, Gender Non-Conforming, Male, Intersex, Other Identity, Prefer not to say)
6. If you wish, please elaborate.
7. Do you consider yourself to be heterosexual/straight, lesbian, bisexual, queer, other, or prefer not to say?
8. If you wish, please elaborate.
9. How old are you (in years)?
10. What year did you graduate law school?
11. How long (in years) have you been practicing law—broadly defined to include academic, policy, and other work that involves using your law degree—overall?
12. Are you currently employed?
13. Have you practiced Criminal Law?
14. How do you primarily identify your professional identity? (prosecution, defense, judiciary, academic, other)
15. Please elaborate.
16. In what capacity have you practiced Criminal Law? Please explain and list all, including amount of time in each role and location). For example, "Public defender, Memphis, 3 years; private criminal defense, Nashville, 4 years; trial court judge, Nashville, 5 years (to present)."
17. Are you currently a member of the American Bar Association?
18. Which answers best describe why you are not a member of the ABA? (Select all that apply: Membership costs too much, I see no benefit to my career or work, I don't feel like I would fit in, Other)
19. Please let us know other reasons that you are not a member of the ABA.

20. If not, have you ever been a member of the ABA?
21. If you previously were an ABA member but are no longer a member, would you kindly share why are you no longer a member?
22. If you have never been an ABA member, would you kindly explain why not?

Part Two: Retention of Women Criminal Lawyers

1. Please answer these questions only if you are a woman who has practiced or is practicing criminal law.
2. What challenges, if any, have you personally experienced with regard to hiring, retention, and promotion in criminal law-related positions?
3. What challenges have you observed others experience?
4. Were the hiring, promotion, and retention issues better, worse, or the same as they are in your current location?
5. Please explain. For example, did you make a conscious career switch due to a gender related issue?
6. If you currently practice criminal law, do you see yourself staying in practice for the foreseeable future?
7. Why or why not?
8. When gender issues arise in the workplace, do you have a source of support (informal or formal)?
9. If so, to whom do you go for support? We're not asking for specific names as much as roles.

Part Three: Solutions

1. Please focus on your experience as a criminal law practitioner unless the question indicates otherwise.
2. As a criminal law practitioner, what do you feel you need(ed) to be successful?
3. Have these needs changed as you have progressed in your career?
4. If yes, how so?
5. As a criminal law practitioner, what do you feel you need(ed) to remain in the criminal justice practice?
6. Do you think the need to be successful and remain in the field differed between you and your women colleagues?
7. If you have experience practicing in other areas, during your time in those other field(s), do you think these needs to be successful and remain in the field differed between you and your other women colleagues?

8. As a criminal law practitioner, were you provided with what you needed to be successful and remain in the field?
9. Could you please explain your answer?
10. What has or did your employer do to promote retention of women criminal lawyers?
11. Of those policies and practices, how effective did you find them?
12. What were the policies or practices that were more effective than others?
13. What could your employer do or could your employer have done to improve retention of women criminal lawyers?
14. How receptive do you think your employer is or would have been to implementing these recommendations?
15. What would it take for your employer to provide those things?
16. Is there any other information you would like to share regarding women practicing in the criminal justice profession?

Part Four: Covid-19 Specific Issues

1. A lot of things have changed in the past year. We'd like to about your experience.
2. Which aspect of your life do you feel has been disproportionately affected by Covid-19 and the fact that you are a woman? (Childcare, Elder care, Professional development, Quality of life, Work performance, Other)
3. Please let us know what other aspects of your life have been affected by joint forces of Covid-19 and being a woman.
4. Covid-19 has caused many changes in the workplace, such as greater flexibility in telecommuting. In a post-Covid world, what changes would you like to keep?
5. Aside from Covid-19, has anything else changed in the year since our initial listening sessions that you'd like us to know about?

APPENDIX C

2020 Follow-Up Survey Responses to Level and Type of Support from Employers[75]

- "There are very little resources for therapy and mental health. This field is full of substance abuse because of the amount of stress and the level of workload we have. My employer specifically also has not recognized the additional stressors that COVID has created in terms of childcare."
- "As a trial lawyer, the office provided little support for logistical issues related to evidence presentation. I was not provided assistance with moving large 65" TVs for closing arguments. I was forced to do so in a skirt suit, with heels, and hurt myself before closing arguments in a child molest case. Certainly, my focus should have been on substantive trial work rather than physical labor that should have been performed my support staff. This gender-neutral policy overlooked the fact that I am 5'1" and 115 lbs and moving a TV of that size was not easy. Further, moving heavy boxes of files to court each day is overwhelming. My male counterparts voiced no complaints, which reflected poorly on my when I did."
- "Promoting competent women to visible positions. Women as supervisors with power to make decisions."
- "I am able to attend trainings and webinars."
- "Sometimes they do and sometimes they don't. It depends on the year."
- "Sexism and dismissive."
- "My work is non-traditional, so most of my work is self-reliant. Prior to COVID, I was able to attend training I requested local and those requiring travel. I also have access to legal databases to conduct research."
- "I am a sole practitioner; I provide what I need."
- "I'm self-employed. I take care of myself."
- "I only had one employer and he and the office were very supportive."
- "Prior to my current role, I did not receive the support I needed and there were fewer opportunities to grow and lead."
- "leeway to grow, leadership opportunity, and ability to make significant decisions and determine direction of the work"

75. Notes on file with author.

- "They need to pay women equally. That issue is emblematic of a lack of support for the women in this department that has cost us a number of good attorneys."
- "I did not feel supported or mentored necessarily from employers who were focused on my career advancement. However, as my own boss, I am responsible for my own advancement (and the advancement of other women in the practice)."
- "As a program director, it has always been difficult to do this work because of the need for additional resources, i.e., attorneys, advocates and financial. At times, priorities must be juggled to benefit staff and clients."
- "I have always worked with my father as the lead partner of our firm. Therefore, many of these questions are inapplicable to me - such as "policies" or "retention."
- "They undermine my position as an administrative position instead of legal; even though be essential personnel."
- "Overall, the various U.S. attorneys I worked for supported me and helped me to be successful, or at least didn't stand in my way. Some were more supportive than others. In general, I felt most supported when my supervisors understood my strengths and weaknesses, assigned me cases based on my strengths, and provided training and resources to address weaknesses."
- "I often was alone and isolated. I didn't feel I had someone who had my back or was interested in my growth or development."
- "I've been with the FPD for [many] years - superb training, usually provided with what I need to do my job. Caseload has been for the most part manageable, although right now with compassionate release stuff I feel overloaded. Boss has been great at not micromanaging and yet having our backs."
- "Lack of resources and mentorship."
- "I practice civil law and have worked for civil law firms. They are not equipped to address criminal issues."
- "I have a strong, collaborative relationship with my employer and ask for what I need and generally am able to secure it. Mutual trust is important as is our mutual regard."
- "They have not provided what we need, more humans doing this job, because the county will not provide. Our bosses would if they could."
- "In my current position as a resource attorney I have time flexibility and control my workload. I did not have either when I was at a large public defense agency."

- "My time in federal defender offices has allowed me to develop meaningful mentor relationships, adequate resources, and relevance within the profession."
- "For the most part my employer has provided the basic tools needed to be successful. I was recently promoted to a management position but because of a budget and personnel freeze my ability to do my job effectively has been affected."
- "It has been extremely difficult to obtain additional personnel positions and adequate funding [from my tribe]."

APPENDIX D

Focus Groups Guiding Document: Recommendations to employers to address major challenges to hiring, retention, and promotion of women criminal lawyers that the TF identified through listening sessions and written surveys between November 2018 and December 2020.

Growth Areas	HIRING	RETENTION	PROMOTION
Culture shift	• Values assessment • Systemic IDEA/DEI racism analysis and plan with focus on gender race ethnicity LGBTQIA+ • Trainings on intersectionality, implicit bias, creating inclusive workplaces that combat feelings of invisibility, and having difficult conversations	• Values assessment with focus on inclusion and equity • Systemic racism analysis and elimination plan • Intersectionality training	• Values assessment • Systemic racism analysis and elimination plan • Intersectionality training • Review promotion practices through an equity lens • Publicize promotion policies
Allyship/mentorship/sponsorship	• Amplify existing in-person and online resources through local, state and national bar associations, CJS, affiliation groups • Create new opportunities • Allyship/mentorship/sponsorship training	• Amplify existing in-person and online resources through local, state and national bar associations, CJS, affiliation groups • Create new opportunities • Allyship/mentorship/sponsorship training	• Amplify existing in-person and online resources through local, state and national bar associations, CJS, affiliation groups • Create new opportunities • Allyship/mentorship/sponsorship training
Flexibility	• Share model part-time, job sharing, remote work schedules • Promote and create policy changes (e.g., aligning court times with school schedules)	• Share model part-time, job sharing, remote work schedules • Promote and create policy changes (e.g., aligning court times with school schedules)	• Share model part-time, job sharing, remote work schedules • Promote and create policy changes (e.g., aligning court times with school schedules)

Support and training	• Lactation space (ABA policy) • Wellness room (NLADA policy) • Compassion fatigue training • Implicit bias training • How to Run a Listening Session • Share model training and promotion manuals • Gender-neutral facilities and respecting pronouns	• Lactation space (ABA policy) • Wellness room (NLADA policy) • Compassion fatigue training • Implicit bias training • How to Run a Listening Session • Share model training and promotion manuals • Gender-neutral facilities and respecting pronouns	• Lactation space (ABA policy) • Wellness room (NLADA policy) • Compassion fatigue training • Implicit bias training • Share model training and promotion manuals • "How to Run for Public Office" webinars (judgeships, DA, PD) • Gender-neutral facilities and respecting pronouns
Legal education	• Train key administrators + faculty on gender equity best practices • Encourage schoolwide discussions about challenges in hiring • Mentorship or network opportunities with local, state, and national bar associations, CJS, affiliation groups • Create a short curriculum about women in criminal law	• Train key administrators + faculty • Host CLEs about/for women criminal lawyers	• Train key administrators and faculty about our findings • Host CLEs about/for women criminal lawyers • Schools promote our webinars/programs/mentoring with their alums

APPENDIX E

Written Responses to Focus Group Follow-Up Survey

Question 1

- "As discussed during the focus group, the WWCDA[76] does extensive internal and external promotion of our members through social media, our list-serve, our website and our newsletter."
- "Yes. Our organization specifically targets and recruits women (transgender and cisgender), nonbinary people, and transgender people (of all genders). We state that this is our mission and explicitly invite and encourage candidates who aren't cisgender men to apply."
- "The organization did external benchmarking. They looked at similarly-situated organizations and their positions and compared them to our organization to see where we measured. What the organization learned is that we have a portion of staff who are not being paid on par with people at comparable organizations and in comparable positions."

Question 2

- "Yes. Some women in management positions and should have increased pay scales but the federal pay bands and hiring and promotion policies and rules have prevented full implementation. It will take time."
- "Published policies that reflect my commitment to equitable hiring practices (e.g., requiring at least one justice-impacted voice per project)."
- "Initiatives to shine light on compensation (either raw numbers and/or metrics) within and across organizations, so that women can better assess whether they are being properly valued. Culturally, it seems people are still reluctant to discuss money."
- "More organizations need standards. My organization has no standard or expected way for advocates to work and no real guidelines. Advocates have no way of measuring their growth, areas for improvement, or knowing what success looks like. It is hard to have equitable promotion and very hard to retain without guideposts."
- "Yes, one of my ideas is to ensure that family leave policies are

76. WOMEN'S WHITE COLLAR CRIM. DEF. ASS'N, https://www.wwcda.org/home [https://perma.cc/5F8P-Y9KF].

gender neutral and that taking advantage of leave is gender neutral. At my last firm we were not able to achieve this at all due to institutional resistance, and I don't have visibility to it at the bigger firm but I very much doubt that people of all genders take leave equally."
- "I think capacity always constrains the totality of our ideas."

Question 3
- "Yes! Please include my organization, the Defender Services Office in the Federal Judiciary."
- "I would like to see the ABA help to promote compensation transparency."
- "Transparency on what success at the organization looks like beyond wins & losses. Flexible work schedules to allow people to work and provide care to family/friends."
- "Resources to advertise the internships in small to medium-sized criminal defense firms and then financial resources to pay all or at least half of the fellowship wages for a summer, for a year and up to two years. Also, it would be good to offer mentorships to new criminal defense lawyers."
- "Tips for empowering women to see themselves as leaders, practical guidance on communication (listening/reading and speaking/writing), a list of orgs who focus on increasing women's representation across many fields (not just legal)."
- "Measures on good screening techniques in hiring to ensure equality and fairness, especially in this virtual world we are now living in."
- "Information on applicable legal compliance to ensure gender equity measures do not create potential liability due to the symmetrical nature of nondiscrimination laws."

Question 4
- "You may have thought of this, but seems like lots of collaboration could happen with gender advocates in the fields of STEM (for example) and maybe even fields where women are overrepresented (nursing, teaching, animal welfare, etc.)"
- "We should also have measures to address the concerns of LGBTQIA+ concerns."
- "Addressing disability representation and inclusion as a matter of gender parity."
- "The added dynamic of being impacted by the so-called justice

system."

- "Oftentimes when we think about leadership, we think about it through the lens of positional authority. However, leaders exist throughout an organization and not all leaders desire positional authority. It is important that those folks are identified and able to develop. Those are the "workers/implementers" and they are key to any leader being able to accomplish their goals. It isn't helpful to have those folks turn over constantly merely because they don't see new ways to grow or make more money without the responsibility of becoming an organizational leader with authority. I think corporate spaces have done this better than non-profit spaces."
- "We had an amazing discussion in our group about formerly incarcerated attorneys and the need to work with state bars on the character and fitness barriers and how these barriers affect minorities and women disproportionately."
- "Role-playing and story-telling from women attorneys on how to handle difficult situations for women when they are practicing law."
- "Gender equity efforts and programs tend to focus most on junior attorneys and leave out the significant population of partner level and more senior women who face the most in terms of endemic gender discrimination and bias particularly when it comes to getting a fair share of origination credit, which is tied to compensation. More efforts and resources should be directed to facilitating an even playing field at the partner level for women to be able to rise up to senior leadership. The pipeline is not the problem, the glass ceiling is and the institutionalized systems that perpetuate that situation are often hidden, unquestioned, and seemingly impossible to change."
- "Addressing disability representation and inclusion as a matter of gender parity."

APPENDIX E
Task Force Launches

Carla Laroche and Tina Luongo

WOMEN IN CRIMINAL JUSTICE

Task Force Launches

Carla Laroche and Tina Luongo

From #MeToo to the Harvey Weinstein indictments, Mama Day Bail Outs and the #SayHerName campaigns, women-focused conversations are occurring. Specifically, women working in criminal legal system are talking, thinking, and feeling.

How many of us watched the Brett Kavanaugh confirmation hearings and felt pulled in opposite directions by what we watched? We have cross-examined complainants like Dr. Christine Blasey Ford at trial. Yet, we watched in, perhaps, angry disbelief as many questioned her credibility.

More telling is, how many of us "old enough to remember" felt the same way when Dr. Anita Hill testified?

What are we advising law students and young lawyers interested in the field of criminal justice about the gendered nature of our work?

Talking about our conflicted feelings and frustration is key to addressing the realities. Recognizing them is critical to understanding recruitment, retention, career satisfaction, and burnout.

Acknowledging that the Criminal Justice Section must take the lead in addressing these issues, Lucian Dervan, current chair of the Criminal Justice Section, launched the Women in Criminal Justice Task Force at the 2018 Fall Meeting in November. The purpose of the Task Force is to publish findings and make policy and practice recommendations that outline the challenges women of diverse backgrounds face in a hard, institutionalized practice such as criminal law and offer cutting-edge solutions that our profession can use to spearhead reform—no small task.

The work of the Task Force will be conducted over three years with the goal to have sustainable and inclusive Section policies, recruitment, and retention plans. The commitment of the Section, the members of the Task Force, and our Advisory Board had to be genuine and invested to give weight to the magnitude of the problems and importance of the solution.

Task Force Membership

The Women in Criminal Justice Task Force sought to ensure that the members reflect the richness of diversity in our criminal justice community. Inclusion has been and will continue to be a key component of the Task Force.

Carla Laroche, my fellow co-chair, and I are honored to introduce the members of the Women in Criminal Justice Task Force. As one can see below, our members are respected leaders in our profession and in their communities and jurisdictions. From Tennessee to Michigan, Maine to Kansas, New York City, California, and the District of Columbia, members are diverse racially, in gender identity and expression, sexual orientation, age, and abilities. Members have worked or served in urban and coastal areas, rural and tribal jurisdictions, the defense bar—both white collar and public defense, the prosecution, the judiciary— both state and federal court, the armed services, and academia.

Lara Bazelon, associate professor at the University of San Francisco School of Law; director of the Criminal & Juvenile Justice and Racial Justice Clinics (CA)

Gloria Ochoa Bruck, City of Spokane, director of Local Government and Multi-Cultural Affairs (WA);

Barbara Creel, professor of law and director of the Southwest Indian Law Clinic, University of New Mexico School of Law (NM;)

The Honorable Bernice Donald, US Court of Appeals for the Sixth Circuit (TN);

Daniela Donoso, law student at the Florida State University College of Law (FL);

Maria Carmen Hinayon, founder and principal attorney at the Law Office of Maria Carmen Hinayon (CA);

The Honorable Denise Langford-Morris, Oakland County Circuit Court (MI);

Carla Laroche, visiting clinical professor and director of the Gender and Family Justice Clinic at the Florida State University College of Law Public Interest Law Center (FL);

Tina Luongo, attorney-in-charge of the Criminal Defense Practice of The Legal Aid Society (NY);

Rachel Pickering, assistant solicitor general in the Office of the Kansas Attorney General (KS);

Sarah Redfield, professor of law at the University of New Hampshire School of Law (ME);

Mara Senn, senior investigator and senior litigation specialist in the Integrity Vice Presidency at the World Bank (DC); and

Major Susan Upward, senior defense counsel, US Marine Corps (CA).

In addition to the esteemed members of this Task Force, Kim Parker, incoming chair of the Criminal Justice Section and Prosecutor Coordinator with the Kansas County & District Attorneys Association, will lead an advisor board of members that will help guide our work.

To guide the Task Force's approach and discussions, we are thrilled to have Professor Maryam Ahranjani join us as the Task Force reporter. Maryam is the Lee and Leon Karelitz Professor in Evidence and Procedure at the University of New Mexico School of Law and is an expert in educational access who has published on topics such as access to education for immigrants and the prisonilzation of America's public schools.

National Listening Tour Begins

The logical first step to the Task Force is to start by listening.

For the first year of the Task Force, we are conducting listening events in several jurisdictions where women practitioners and students can discuss their concerns and challenges in the criminal justice system. We are including places where the Section has not often created the space for conversations and to connect to communities we have not engaged with previously. The agenda of each of the listening sessions will be developed by the Task Force in partnership with local bar associations and law schools in each jurisdiction to address topics critical to the women in those communities who are in our profession.

We held our first listening session during a luncheon at the 2018 Fall Meeting. It allowed us to bring a small group of women together to preview the Task Force's goals and objectives. We had budgeted three hours while wondering how we would keep the conversation going that long.

Well . . . once the conversation began among the women who joined us, it did not stop, and, in fact, we went over the three hours! There was laughter, consensus building, and a healthy bit of debate.

While there was a great amount of frustration about the harsh realities facing women, there was also hope. Many left the luncheon excited about what we just had experienced and what the Task Force would mean for women across the nation. A shared sense of camaraderie and excitement lingered as we met in CLEs during the rest of the Fall Meeting.

That evening as I reflected on the event, I felt as though our first step was a solid one, though not earth-shattering. All of us acknowledged, however, that what we were talking about has been discussed for decades. Many reading this column may be nodding your head in agreement that we have been "here" before. This Task Force, however, brings with it a determination to highlight solutions that will change the conversations, change the way we do things, not only in the Criminal Justice Section, but throughout the profession.

We want to hear from all of you too! We invite you to send us your thoughts and ideas to crimjustice@americanbar.org, with "Women in Criminal Justice" in the subject line.

ENTITY:

CRIMINAL JUSTICE SECTION

TOPIC:

CRIMINAL LAW, CIVIL RIGHTS AND CONSTITUTION

Authors

Carla Laroche

Carla Laroche directs the Gender and Family Justice Clinic as a visiting clinical professor at Florida State University and is co-chair of the Women in Criminal Justice Task Force.

Tina Luongo

Tina Luongo is the attorney in charge of the criminal defense practice of The Legal Aid Society and co-chair of the Women in Criminal Justice Task Force.

APPENDIX F

Listening Session Participants Express Feelings of Isolation—and Demonstrate Resilience

Maryam Ahranjani

November 01, 2019
WOMEN IN CRIMINAL JUSTICE

Listening Session Participants Express Feelings of Isolation—and Demonstrate Resilience

Maryam Ahranjani

Cindy Aragon's voice kept getting cut off because of the spotty cell phone service in the rural area of northwest New Mexico from which she was calling. The listeners were most of the 15 members of the ABA's Women in Criminal Justice Task Force, as well as a room full of women criminal law attorneys from around the state, all of whom convened at the University of New Mexico in Albuquerque on March 1, 2019, to investigate women's experiences in hiring, promotion, and retention. The Task Force members at the event included co-chairs Carla Laroche and Tina Luongo, April Frazier Camara, Barbara Creel, Judge Bernice Donald, Daniela Donoso Garcia, Maria Carmen Hinayon, Judge Denise Langford Morris, Gloria Ochoa-Bruck, Judge Rachel Pickering, Sarah Redfield, and Major Susan Upward.

Women like Cindy testified with the permission and understanding that the Task Force would use their experiences to shine some light on their experiences. Some felt comfortable using their names and others requested anonymity.

Cindy Aragon serves as the managing attorney of New Mexico Legal Aid's Native American Program. She wanted to attend in person but was unable to do so because of work travel. However, she did not want to pass up the opportunity to share her perspective. Despite an administrative error on my part in setting up the call and a poor connection once I corrected my error, her message was heard loud and clear: Her work with Legal Aid representing criminal defendants across the state makes her feel isolated. She spends many hours in the car on dusty roads just to go see her clients, usually while traveling alone. Traveling back can be especially isolating because she has to sit alone with the struggles faced by her clients. As a contract public defender, she described that she has no colleague support, no co-counsel opportunity, and essentially no network.

Isolation was a theme echoed by Kathleen Bowman, director, Office of the Navajo Public Defender, who described how she singlehandedly built up an office of a whopping seven attorneys that is tasked with representing all qualifying Navajo defendants. She is 72 and worries who will take on her work when she retires.

One Native American tribal court judge who has spent her entire career working in and around tribal communities (first as a Legal Aid attorney, then as a domestic violence prosecutor, and for more than a decade as a judge) described that she hopes she is making a difference in tribal communities. However, she reflected, "As a Native woman, I have faced the challenge that my actions, decisions, and authority in the role as a tribal court judge have been more closely scrutinized compared to the scrutiny that is given to a white, male judge."

Jen Birmingham (Las Cruces) and Deirdre Ewing (Carsbad/Roswell), both supervising attorneys in their respective, rural outposts of the state's Law Office of the Public Defender, talked about how hard it is to recruit great attorneys for their offices because very few people want to live in small towns.

These experiences could cause some people to question their own choices. For example, Deirdre is single and queer, and the dating pool is limited where she lives. Resources—particularly any kind of rehabilitation for their clients—are incredibly limited, if they exist at all.

The women who work in Albuquerque (population 558,000—the largest city in the state) described different unique challenges for women in criminal law. Many of them—particularly those who were more advanced in their careers—explained that because most senior attorneys in management were, and to a lesser extent still are, men, and men with partners who could handle home life so that they could focus on work, simply do not understand the challenges with work/life balance and balancing unique challenges that women face. For example, even women in

Albuquerque and Santa Fe described how hard it can be to find adequate space for pumping and storing breastmilk in work spaces.

Women like Tonie Abeyta who are single and have no children feel a burden to take on more responsibilities to support others who have children and aging parents, and this burden seems to fall more heavily on women than similarly situated men. Women shared how humiliating it is to face harassment from guards, clients, and even co-counsel. In litigation, one woman reported how "chest-thumping in the courtroom" often seems the expected norm. They articulated sometimes being demeaned or talked down to by male judges and opposing counsel. Unfortunately, for women all over the state, there exists a lack of support for secondary trauma. Almost all the women from whom we have heard face hurdles that are unique to women.

Because of rigid rules, the women who testified have not been able to achieve flexibility in ways that would allow them to achieve better balance. Attendees reported that most employers—particularly the federal government—do not permit teleworking or part-time schedules. They say flexibility and more resources to decrease caseloads and increase support for their clients and them would go a long way in improving their retention.

Most of the participants reported finding their work incredibly rewarding. They may not be well compensated, but they feel well respected in their communities, and they know that their clients appreciate them. The women who have been working for 30 years or more in the field report that some things have gotten better with time. There are more women in leadership and supervisory positions. There is less tolerance for sexist remarks and behavior.

But there is still room for improvement. Participants appreciated the Task Force creating an opportunity for them to share their experiences and for us to amplify their experiences with the goal of creating more awareness. The opportunity to be heard cannot be underestimated. As the great Persian poet Jelaluddin Rumi pointed out, a wound begins to heal when light shines on it.

The listening session would not have been possible without the efforts of a group of fantastic organizers and volunteers—including TF member Barbara Creel, Emily Johnson at the ABA, Sila Manahane at the University of New Mexico School of Law, and several law students (Kristen Edwards, Lena Kephardt, Meagan Muñoz, Anne Bruno, and Erin Phillips).

With several formal listening sessions remaining as of the writing of this column, our focus is turning to "what next?" How can we reverse the feelings of isolation and frustration? How can we better track what is happening at various points in the pipeline of a career in criminal law, from entry into law school through retirement?

Having heard from women in Washington, DC; Las Vegas; and Albuquerque, the Task Force has begun to envision some ways to connect listening session participants with one another, to create platforms for ongoing support and dialogue, and to create online toolkits and trainings for women interested in elected and leadership positions in criminal law. The Task Force also has planned sessions in Washington state (Spokane and Seattle), San Francisco, and New York City that will further inform its work.

ENTITY:

CRIMINAL JUSTICE SECTION

TOPIC:

HEALTH, CIVIL RIGHTS AND CONSTITUTION, CRIMINAL LAW

Authors

Maryam Ahranjani

Maryam Ahranjani is reporter for the Women in Criminal Justice Task Force. She is an associate professor of law at the University of New Mexico School of Law, where she adopts a socio-legal approach to teaching criminal law, criminal procedure, constitutional rights, and education policy.

APPENDIX G

Who Needs the Old Boys' Club?

Maria Carmen Hinayon

Who Needs the Old Boys' Club? Let's Make Our Own—Highlights from the WCJ Bay Area Listening Session

by MARIA CARMEN HINAYON

On August 8, 2019, the Women in Criminal Justice (WCJ) Task Force held a listening session at UC Hastings College of the Law in San Francisco, California. One of many listening sessions being conducted around the country, this event highlighted the myriad challenges faced by women criminal justice (CJ) lawyers relating to inclusion, retention, and promotion.

The Bay Area is comprised of nine counties: Alameda, Contra Costa, Marin, Napa, San Mateo, Santa Clara, Solano, Sonoma, and San Francisco. The State Bar reports California's legal profession is still predominantly male and white though women comprise about half of the California population. (*Bar Brief*, St. Bar Cal. (July 17, 2019), https://bit.ly/2XxEcPO.) Disparities are significant especially when race is considered. For example, only 7 percent of attorneys are Hispanic/Latino though they comprise 35 percent of the population, while 68 percent of attorneys are white though they comprise only 41 percent of the population. (*Id.*)

The task force heard testimonies from women CJ practitioners, including prosecutors, defense attorneys, civil rights attorneys, "crimmigration" (intersection of CJ and immigration) attorneys, and CJ reform attorneys, as well as judges. Due to the sensitive and personal information shared, the identities of the participants were kept confidential.

This event did not disappoint in terms of diversity and representation. Women of color and LGBTQ women showed up and amplified their intersectional struggles. Task force member and CJS chair-elect April Frazier-Camara led a session dedicated to black women and the unique challenges they face at the intersection of race and gender.

It is crucial to note the stark difference between the experiences of white women and women of color, especially black women. Though all women face gender-based barriers, this event revealed that such challenges are magnified for women of color as they are compounded by race-based oppression. LGBTQ women endure further oppression based on their sexual orientation and gender identity/expression.

Demeaned, Belittled, and Stereotyped

Participants reported being demeaned, belittled, and stereotyped as sexist comments and name calling are common happenstance. Male attorneys and judges refer to women attorneys as "sweetheart," "babe," "little lady," and "eye candy" in a demeaning and patronizing way. For women of color, the insults are often racialized. A white male judge referred to a former public defender as the "exotic foreigner." Another white male judge repeatedly told a public defender of South Asian descent "you remind me of Gandhi" and "your people are good in math."

Women, especially women of color, are perceived as anything but the attorney in courtrooms, being mistaken as court reporters, interpreters, or legal assistants. A black defense attorney noted how a court staff thought her client, who happened to be wearing a suit, was the attorney, not her.

The testimonies revealed how stereotyping pervades the CJ profession. In court, women who are assertive are perceived as too angry while their male counterparts are viewed as effective. Women who show vulnerability are perceived as too emotional while their male counterparts are viewed as sympathetic.

Stereotyping also affects women's ability to broker fair deals for their clients. A male attorney told a public defender she would not get a good deal because women attorneys defend like a girl. A white male prosecutor refused to offer her client a plea despite his being known in the area as someone who likes to plea down felonies to misdemeanors.

For women of color, the stereotypes are compounded with racist overtones. A black defense attorney recalled having a normal conversation with a white law clerk. A colleague later informed her that the law clerk perceived her as threatening. "As a black woman, there is always that thin line between being perceived as assertive or an angry 'b*tch,'" she noted.

MARIA CARMEN HINAYON is a Bay Area-based Filipina American civil rights attorney, a transgender community advocate, and a Women in Criminal Justice Task Force member.

Stereotyping also impacts advancement and promotion. Prosecutors noted how case assignments seem to be based on gender (and sometimes race). A Latina prosecutor reported being promoted to sex crimes although she really wanted (and prepared for) a career in the gang unit. She believes she was sent to the "women" unit where she can be "touchy feely." And because she is Latina, she was not assigned to the gang unit where she would be prosecuting Latino defendants. For prosecutors, high-profile cases like homicide and gang violence are key to promotion and advancement.

Invisible Women in the Old Boys Club

Participants emphasized the persistence of the "old boys club" in the CJ profession, as they feel like outsiders in courtrooms and chambers among male judges and lawyers. In some cases, the "old boys club" culture impacts fairness. A prosecutor recalled finding out that a male judge and a well-known male defense attorney in the area were having improper ex parte communication about their case.

Participants shared experiences of feeling invisible, as they were dismissed and ignored by male judges and attorneys in the "old boys club." One attorney was falsely accused of being noisy in the courtroom and admonished by a judge. When her male counterpart clarified that it was them, the male lawyers, who were noisy, the male judge praised him for his honesty. Meanwhile, the woman attorney received neither apologies nor acknowledgment despite being shamed in open court for something she did not do.

The "old boys club" exists even in the judiciary. A LGBTQ woman judge noted getting mostly civil and misdemeanor assignments, which impedes advancement, as high-profile criminal cases—often assigned to older white male judges—pave the way for appeals or supreme court appointments.

The Difficult Choice between Career and Motherhood

Testimonies show the unforgiving nature of the CJ profession when it comes to pregnancy and motherhood. A former federal public defender had to make the difficult decision of changing careers when she became a mother. While she navigated workplace barriers with ease before motherhood, continuing a CJ career became insurmountable during and after her pregnancy. Lawyers and judges used to ask her if she was pregnant, but they were more like accusations, not a question.

Another public defender and new mother expressed her dilemma about changing careers. Although being a public defender is her passion, she now feels the need to sacrifice her dream job for the sake of her child, as she emphasized the near-impossible task of balancing a CJ career and family life. "I do not want to be in a position where I have to choose between my client or my child," she explained.

#BlackGirlMagic: Black Women at the Forefront

The #BlackGirlMagic session underscored how black women CJ practitioners bear the brunt of the fight for racial justice and gender equity while navigating the CJ system that is opposed to both their womanhood and blackness.

A defense attorney noted the daily burden of constantly thinking about her tone, appearance, and demeanor to avoid negative stereotypes associated with her race and gender. She practiced in a predominantly white jurisdiction where most of the defendants were black men. As a black woman fighting in a white space, she remembered the emotional toll of advocating for clients who looked like her uncle, brother, or father.

A former prosecutor noted how progressive black women prosecutors face bias compared to their white male counterparts. Progressive white male prosecutors are praised for promoting equity and fairness. Progressive black women prosecutors, on the other hand, are publicly criticized and, in some cases, slapped with politically motivated lawsuits.

"That #BlackGirlMagic comes with black girl fatigue," one defense attorney noted, emphasizing the need to support black women attorneys in the CJ profession as they play a crucial role in advancing racial justice and gender equity.

Moving Forward

Participants presented ideas to the task force moving forward. An attorney emphasized how unionization helped them bargain policies such as time-sharing and flexible work arrangements for pregnant women and new mothers. The need for a comprehensive, mandatory, and regular implicit bias and sensitivity trainings among lawyers and judges was also echoed.

Participants emphasized the role of mentorship and pipelines/pathways, as there is currently a lack of transparency and education in the areas of promotion and advancement, including pathways to judgeship and running for elected positions.

Equally needed are concrete mental health support for CJ practitioners and resources for dealing with secondary trauma. Participants reported seeing colleagues leave due to exhaustion while others succumbed to substance abuse.

Lastly, participants highlighted the need for women to be better advocates for themselves and for each other. As learned from one participant's experience, men will often take credit for the efforts of women; so "toot your own horn!" one attorney exclaimed, and "shine light to each other" in order to elevate each other's work and achievements.

Regarding the "old boys club," one of the participants, a black woman defense lawyer, had the perfect response: "Who needs that? Let's make our own. We do things better anyways." ■

APPENDIX H

Heavy Purse

Daniela M. Donoso

April 20, 2020
WOMEN IN CRIMINAL JUSTICE

Heavy Purse: A Law Student's Reflection on the CJS Women in Criminal Justice Task Force's NYC Listening Session

Daniela M. Donoso

If my Tia sees me tagged in anything important on Facebook, she shares it in the 43-membered Donoso Family WhatsApp group chat. And that is exactly what happened when Florida State University College of Law posted about me being the only law student invited to join the ABA Criminal Justice Section Women in Criminal Justice Task Force. Immediately I got a call from my mom, "Y de que se trate esto?" "What is this all about?" she asks.

I explained that women are leaving the criminal justice field, and I am helping to find out why and what we can do to change that problem. I knew my family was very proud of me, even if they had no idea what the Task Force was. But at this initial starting point, I wasn't sure what I was doing on the Task Force. Of course, I felt honored to be invited, and as any good law student would, I said yes to an opportunity. At the time, however, I was a Deferred Action for Childhood Arrivals recipient, Latina law student who had completed one criminal law class. I worried that I would not have much to offer.

My first conference call as a Task Force member was very intimidating. Reading everyone's bios was jaw-dropping, inspiring, and scary. Okay, now I really felt out of place. No one was expecting me to talk, right? Maybe no one except Carla Laroche, Task Force cochair, my past clinical professor, and my current sponsor. She loves to laugh, and I make weird jokes when I am nervous, so it really made the space feel less heavy on that first call. The Task Force discussed its first-year goals, including listening to women from various pockets across the country about their unique challenges in the criminal justice profession.

Our first official listening session was in Albuquerque, New Mexico. It was an incredible time spent listening to powerful testimonies from women who recounted times they were passed over for a promotion, told they could not handle the work, and/or disrespected by coworkers and opposing counsel. None of us really knew what to expect, but this, this rawness, blew us all away. Then came another powerful piece from the trip: dinner.

I looked around the table and felt safe. Each of us was so different from the person we were sitting next to, and yet, we felt so connected by the vulnerabilities of others. None of us really knew what to expect, but again, we were blown away. The table dynamic felt as if we had all been close friends before. The subject matter we discussed was heavy, yet we were able to share moments of joy together and forge a commitment to the mission of the Task Force.

Identity Intersections

Women in the criminal justice profession face various obstacles including work-life balance, not being taken seriously, and lack of institutional support. Before women enter the criminal legal profession, however, they are law students, and law students are facing similar challenges.

Identity as a Latina Student

"I don't know where I belong."

These words were spoken by a Latina attorney who diagnosed herself with imposter syndrome during one of our listening sessions.

> Imposter syndrome: doubting accomplishment with the fear of being exposed as a fraud.

In September 2019, the Hispanic National Bar Association hosted its Annual Convening in New York City. The Task Force hosted a listening panel for Latina criminal law professionals, traditionally underrepresented in criminal law, to share challenges through an intersectional lens and offer guidance to other Latinas in or planning to be in criminal law.

> As a DACA-mented Latina law student, and as a Task Force member, I am especially interested about intersectionality challenges Latinas are facing in the workplace. This experience would be deeply beneficial to both my professional and personal development as an immigrant woman. This is why I am coming to FSU Law to ask if we've ever sent students to the HNBA Convening, and whether it would be possible to send, not only me, but other Latina students who are interested to this important Task Force event.

(Daniela Donoso to FSU Law Career Center.) My Career Center happily paid for my flight, telling me this was a "great opportunity." The fact that the stipend is what allowed me to be present at this event, was more relevant than I could have known at the time.

Law students across the country are finding it difficult to commit to social justice work when there is no guarantee they will be able to pay their loans. In my conversations with students in Albuquerque, for example, they noted their interest in serving the rural communities surrounding them. Many leave law school, however, and must move to big cities. It is hard in rural communities to gain trust and gain employment somewhere they can advance. It is especially difficult for students with various identities who may be hesitant to live in a rural community under the current political climate.

There is a clear need for higher representation of women, particularly women of color, in the justice system within every community. The structural and institutional lack of support and resources keeps many women from joining the criminal justice profession. Law students need women who look like them to give them support, allies to tell them they can succeed and be role models. When this is lacking, students are more inclined to pursue what everybody else is doing.

I was looking forward to the listening session in NYC and I was itching to ask the panelists about the desire and danger of compartmentalizing who you are in a professional setting. Does being Latina ever feel like a bargaining chip? Is it healthy to go into a profession that wants to prosecute people who look like you?

There was no clear answer to any of these questions. Through their unique experiences the panelists all shared two common denominators: a strong mother and scholarship. They have all faced racism, sexism, failure, self-doubt, and exceptionalism throughout their career. They expressed fear of being vulnerable to verbal and physical hate crimes. One panelist described this fear as, "Just something else to carry. My purse is very heavy."

Despite their professional success being riddled with obstacles and "heavy purses," it was the strong female mentorship and scholarship that helped them get there. For most of them, it was their own mother who told them never to give up. They were confident in telling the younger Latinas in the room to be grounded in what you're passionate about and be true to their non-negotiables. They recognized that their student debt was not as high as students coming out of law school now. Scholarship was a major key for them to have the freedom to pursue the right career goals for themselves. Part of their ambition today is making it possible for younger Latinas to fill roles where the panelists are.

Growing up undocumented, I always felt unsure of my future. It was never clear what opportunities were available to me. I didn't know where I belonged.

> Imposter syndrome: doubting accomplishment with the fear of being exposed as a fraud.

It was necessary for me to seek out scholarships for college and law school. At times that imposter syndrome feels truer to me than anything else. I hear the rhetoric that I should not even be allowed in this country, let alone allowed to pursue a law degree. Just like the panelists, two common denominators have helped me get to here, right now: my mother, who has sacrificed everything to make my dreams reality, and the scholarships I have received that now give me the freedom to pursue a career in social justice work.

Looking Ahead

The Task Force is envisioning ways to create platforms for ongoing support for women in criminal law. Law students specifically need the support from their schools, from scholarships, and from sponsors. Law school culture must change from the inside. Students need to be encouraged by their Career Centers to pursue scholarship opportunities.

Sponsors are people in your life who are ready to propel you forward. They make space for you, recommend you, and elevate your confidence. I would not be on this Task Force if it were not for Carla Laroche's invitation. She saw a passion from adversity in my story and thought my perspective as a DACA-mented Latina woman and student with a strong commitment to social justice work was too important not to have at the table.

The commitment I made to this Task Force did not come from agreeing to a contract or having my name called on a roll sheet. The commitment I made was fostered through the relationships bonded over the Task Force dinner table. What we are investigating and tackling together is important. As a law student, the powerful part of being on this Task Force for me is being surrounded by diverse, professional women who want me and others like me to succeed, without having to carry a heavy purse tomorrow.

ENTITY:

CRIMINAL JUSTICE SECTION

TOPIC:

DIVERSITY AND INCLUSION, CRIMINAL LAW

Authors

APPENDIX I
Undefined Vision

Lucian E. Dervan

July 15, 2020

WOMEN IN CRIMINAL JUSTICE

Undefined Vision: An Ally's Journey

Lucian E. Dervan

Share this:

I remember the telephone conversation well. It occurred in the summer of 2018 as I prepared to assume my duties as chair of the American Bar Association Criminal Justice Section. Over the preceding months, Kevin Scruggs, executive director of the Section, and I had discussed various issues related to my term and the goals I had identified for the Section during the next year. Many of those topics were of a familiar sort—increasing membership; addressing particular pressing issues in the criminal justice system, such as the dominance of plea bargaining; increasing the role of committees; finding new leadership opportunities for our younger members, etc. But one idea that stemmed from those conversations was quite different and held the possibility of having a fundamental impact on the profession more broadly.

During some of those transition calls in the spring of 2018, Kevin and I had discussed the challenges faced by women in the criminal justice community. Several reports had been issued in the preceding years regarding the number of women leaving practice, and we were beginning to see impacts from this decline in the diversity of the Criminal Justice Section's membership. It is from these conversations that the idea to create a Task Force sprang, and Kevin and I knew immediately who we should contact to be this idea's powerful steward.

When Tina Luongo joined that telephone call in the summer of 2018, I'm not sure what she was expecting. I suspect, however, that what I said was somewhat out of the ordinary. Typically, when the chair of the Criminal Justice Section creates a Task Force, it is for a well-developed topic and comes with an extremely detailed charge regarding the direction and objectives of the group. My telephone call with Tina, by comparison, contained almost no detail and no significant guidance. I recall simply telling her that we needed a group to begin addressing these vitally important issues and that she was the person we felt could best lead this effort. The challenges experienced by women in the profession are not the challenges I have faced. As such, I would not presume to claim that I have the same understanding as those who have lived these challenges or, therefore, that I know how best to address them. I trusted Tina, an experienced public defender, and the Task Force she would create to be the leaders in determining the focus and the course of this work. For me, that initial telephone call was not about creating a definitive outline of what lay ahead. Rather, my goal was to ensure that Tina knew how important these issues were to me and the Criminal Justice Section and that she had the full support of the Section in taking this Task Force in whatever directions were necessary for success. At the time of this conversation with Tina, I certainly had no unique insights into how to be a good ally, but I did know that allies work to create opportunities for change and strive to ensure that those leading such efforts on all of our behalves know that they are fully supported.

It was several months later when the first telephone call occurred among the founding members of what is now called the Women in Criminal Justice Task Force, a diverse array of women in criminal justice who embraced the opportunity to come together in addressing these issues. By this time, Tina had brought on her co-chair, Carla Laroche, another strong voice and advocate whose passion was instrumental in bringing life to this idea. I did not plan to regularly attend meetings of the Task Force, but I did want to be present on this initial planning call so that I and the Section might once again show our full support for the work of the group. In opening the call, I offered that support and then simply said that I was only present to listen, not to participate. As I noted above, I was not qualified to make decisions about the direction of this group, and, therefore, I did not think it appropriate to add my voice to the early discussions of this Task Force in deciding how to move forward. But I could listen, in hopes that I might understand more and use those insights to find ways to further support this undertaking. Listening, I knew, was another important element of being an ally because through listening comes knowledge, and through knowledge comes the opportunity to be a more effective supporter.

In addition to listening to and supporting the work of others, however, allies need to eventually move from these more passive roles to the more active roles of contributing and engaging in the conversations. While supporting and listening are vital aspects of being an ally as we start down the path of change, only when everyone fully engages in this work can change truly take root. The Women in Criminal Justice Task Force recognized this reality early in mapping out its journey. In the first year, the Task Force traveled around the country, hearing from women about their unique and diverse experiences during listening sessions. The Task Force continues this work, gathering new information every time they have the opportunity to hear from someone whose voice has not yet been captured. In the spring of 2019, however, just before the start of the Criminal Justice Section's spring meeting in Nashville, Tennessee, the Task Force engaged in a new and different type of discussion. The Task Force held the first Women in Criminal Justice Symposium and encouraged participation by both women and men. Though my duties as chair prevented me from attending the entire day, the portions I was able to attend solidified to me the importance of this third pillar of being an ally. During open forum discussions, I heard from women and men, each sharing his or her experiences and challenges and each supporting one another as we move forward together. And this, I believe, is the key regarding allies. While these journeys often begin alone, with allies in the wings listening and supporting, the journey cannot end alone. To truly succeed, we will all need to be in the room together, supporting and respecting one another's diversity, by the end. So I look forward to what comes next for the Women in Criminal Justice Task Force's work, as the group continues to hold symposia that create spaces for allies to come into the room to listen, support, engage, contribute, and hold each other accountable.

The work of the Women in Criminal Justice Task Force is vitally important to our profession. We all benefit from a criminal justice community that is more diverse, equitable, and inclusive. This group is working hard to identify and better understand the barriers that impede women in the profession and, through this knowledge, find solutions for a better future. Under the leadership of Tina and Carla and with the support of our current and future chairs, Kim Parker, April Frazier-Camara, and Wayne McKenzie, I know there will be many exciting developments in the future as this Task Force continues to take an undefined vision and make it into an inspired initiative that is bringing real positive change to the profession we all call our own.

ENTITY:

CRIMINAL JUSTICE SECTION

TOPIC:

CRIMINAL LAW, DIVERSITY AND INCLUSION

Authors

Lucian E. Dervan

-

Lucian E. Dervan is a professor of law and director of Criminal Justice Studies at Belmont University College of Law in Nashville, Tennessee. He is the immediate past chair of the ABA Criminal Justice Section and the current chair of the ABA Commission on the American Jury. You can follow his work on twitter @LucianDervan.

APPENDIX J

Looking Back, Looking Forward

Maryan Ahranjani

October 26, 2020

WOMEN IN CRIMINAL JUSTICE

Looking Back, Looking Forward

Maryam Ahranjani

Share this:

Since the Criminal Justice Section's Women in Criminal Justice Task Force launched in November 2018, we have heard from women in criminal law around the country about their experiences with (1) hiring, (2) retention, and (3) promotion of women in criminal justice. We set many goals for ourselves, including hosting listening sessions, publishing columns, and collecting data, and we are proud of all we have accomplished over the past nearly two years.

First, we held 12 listening sessions around the country in person and virtually after the COVID-19 pandemic made in-person meetings impossible. To highlight a few, in July 2019, Task Force members Judges Bernice Donald and Denise Langford Morris convened a listening session with Black women judges at the National Bar Association Annual Convention. In November 2019, Howard University School of Law hosted a listening session with law students from five DC-area law schools. We purposely tried to meet with women from different identity groups to ensure our work supported diverse perspectives. In total, the Task Force members have formally heard from over 160 women who are diverse in terms of racial and ethnic background, age, LGBTQ status, stage of career, and political ideology.

During the one-day listening sessions, women often shared raw and painful stories. The Task Force wants the trust created during those sessions to be just the starting point of meaningful and supportive relationships. We stay connected with the brave women who participated in listening sessions in several ways. For example, we pivoted to hold an open listening session online in May 2020, for all women who testified, as well as Task Force and Advisory Board members. With the open listening session, we sought to provide a space for reflection and support on how the COVID-19 pandemic has affected women personally and professionally. Approximately 30 women came together to listen and share. Its success confirmed our need to create a long-term platform for connection.

The Task Force members left the May session with a renewed sense of connection and a hopefulness about the possibilities of Zoom. In fact, despite some initial reservations about whether women would feel comfortable sharing personal experiences online rather than in person, we used Zoom to host our next listening session for women with significant practice experience on June 23, 2020. High-level women from around the country enthusiastically answered invitations to participate, and we realized that Zoom in fact allowed us to get women in the "room" in a way that would have been nearly impossible to do in person.

In addition to hosting listening sessions, our next accomplishment has been reporting about the brave women we have met and powerful stories we have heard. As we conducted our listening sessions, we have thus far written several *Criminal Justice* magazine columns, including one by Co-Chairs Carla Laroche and Tina Luongo, Task Force members Maria Carmen Hinayon and Daniela

Donoso, me, Gloria Ochoa-Bruck and former CJS Chair Lucian Dervan. Carla and Tina wrote about the establishment of the Task Force, I wrote about our Albuquerque listening session, Maria wrote about the listening session we held in San Francisco in August 2019, and Daniela wrote about our listening session for Latina women in late September 2019. Lucian wrote most recently about the importance of allyship. Gloria's article forthcoming article explores the role of women prosecutors.

Third, I wrote a law review article called *"Toughen Up, Buttercup" versus #TimesUp: Identifying Challenges and Next Steps for Women Criminal Lawyers*. The article summarizes relevant research and describes our findings in great detail. Currently in the editing stages, the *Berkeley Journal of Criminal Law* will publish the article in late 2020. Some of the major themes described in the article include:

- Relatively low salaries in criminal law serve as a challenge and barrier, particularly for women of color and first-generation college/law school graduates who may have greater debt loads and more pressure to support family members.
- Discrimination based on gendered expectations impedes the success of women in criminal law.
- Women in criminal law experience a lack of respect and devaluation by judges, opposing counsel, court staff, and even clients.
- Most criminal law jobs lack flexibility (part time, flextime, job sharing, working from home, etc.).
- It is extremely challenging to juggle work/life commitments (flexibility to pick up children and go to school events, care for elderly relatives, etc.) in criminal law jobs.
- Certain stage-of-life issues (i.e., pregnancy, lactation, menopause, caregiving for children, and caregiving for older relatives) disproportionality affect women more than men and yet employers do not formally discuss or acknowledge how workplaces may accommodate these stage-of-life issues.
- Women of different generations may have distinct workplace expectations (hence, "Toughen Up, Buttercup" versus #TimesUp).
- Many women (particularly Black and brown women) experience compassion fatigue, vicarious trauma, and burnout but feel too isolated to seek support.
- Intersectional challenges (for women of color, LGBTQ and gender nonconforming people, women serving rural communities, etc.) intensify most, if not all, of the challenges faced by white women.

Finally, at our meeting in March 2020 at the Florida State University College of Law, in Tallahassee, Florida, the Task Force created four committees—strategic planning, work product, communications, and data analysis and collection—to propel us into our next phase. Task Force and/or Advisory Board members chair the committees, which meet monthly and report to the full Task Force during monthly meetings.

Looking forward, we have our work cut out for us, but we are even more determined to succeed. The national commitment to racial and criminal justice in the wake of George Floyd's murder spotlights the importance our work. Our next phase is developing work product (best practices, policies, training materials, mentoring resources, etc.) to address the challenges in hiring, retention, and promotion we heard from women at our listening sessions. One important piece of work product will be the collection of quantitative data by creating and administering a survey to women criminal lawyers in representative states. Working with the ABA Center for Innovation and hopefully other partners, the data committee will engage in comprehensive data gathering over the coming months.

We are grateful to the many women who shared their experiences with the Task Force and to the past and current chairs of the Criminal Justice Section, particularly Lucian, Kim Parker, April Frazier Camara (currently also a Task Force member), and the Section's Council members, for their support. As described, we have accomplished much, and we look forward to continuing the Task Force's momentum.

We invite you to reach out should you want more information about the Task Force and its work. You may email the Criminal Justice Section at crimjustice@americanbar.org with "Women in Criminal Justice" in the subject line.

ENTITY:

CRIMINAL JUSTICE SECTION

TOPIC:

CRIMINAL LAW, DIVERSITY AND INCLUSION

Authors

Maryam Ahranjani

-

Maryam Ahranjani is an associate professor, University of New Mexico School of Law (Albuquerque, New Mexico) and the Reporter, ABA Women in Criminal Justice Task Force.

APPENDIX K

The Call for the Rise of the Modern Prosecutor

Hon. Gloria Ochoa-Bruck

January 11, 2021
WOMEN IN CRIMINAL JUSTICE

The Call for the Rise of the Modern Prosecutor

Gloria Ochoa-Bruck

My first job out of law school was as a deputy prosecutor for the Benton County Prosecuting Attorney's Office. I had no background or experience in criminal justice and my undergraduate degree in business administration provided no education or background in understanding what caused someone to become involved in the criminal justice system. It was widely believed by my colleagues, and at the time myself, that every person that came through was there wholly due to a matter of personal choice. As a prosecutor, our job was to uphold the law, and if facts supported filing charges, we filed charges.

I had two children after graduating from law school and decided to go into private practice as it would afford greatly flexibility for raising a young family. A short time into my transition into criminal defense, a 19-year-old girl I will call Sara and her mother scheduled a consultation. Sara grew up in a small rural town and was homeschooled. After she graduated from high school, she moved to attend community college and got a part-time job at a hardware store as a cashier to assist with her living expenses. Sara had been sheltered in her small community and had little life experience. Sara met a young man who became her first boyfriend. He worked in construction and convinced Sara to scan an inexpensive tool when he came through her checkout stand but not scan an $800 tool set.

Sara made a very poor decision and was immediately caught by loss prevention, who recorded the transaction on video. Sara made a full and tearful confession and provided her boyfriend's contact information. He was eventually tracked down, but the tool kit was never recovered. He hired private counsel, paid the hardware store full restitution, and had his charges amended to a misdemeanor.

Sara was charged with felony theft. She could not afford a private attorney and was appointed a public defender. Her attorney met with her for the first time in court at her pre-trial hearing and explained that the prosecutor's office had a policy that if an employee was involved in a theft, they would not offer a reduction. Given her confession and overwhelming evidence, she would be found guilty and the prosecutor would ask for jail time. Sara pled guilty to felony theft and her sentencing hearing was scheduled in three weeks.

Sara called her mom and told her she pled guilty. Sara's long-term goal was to complete her associate of arts degree and transfer to a four-year university. Her mother quickly realized a felony conviction would derail her daughter's educational and career aspirations and her future. Sara was finishing her first year of community college and had earned excellent grades.

I was retained to file a motion to vacate the guilty plea. The prosecutor assigned to the case would not stipulate to a withdrawal of the plea. Having been a prosecutor, I understood that to them, the facts were clear and met each and every element of the statute, and the guilty plea on the record was knowingly, willingly, and intelligently made. The law does not account for the fact it was made by a 19 year old who had no prior involvement in the criminal justice system.

Having been a prosecutor, I understood clearly that for most prosecutors, the resolution of every case must ensure that a victim is made whole whenever possible, that the defendant is held accountable for their actions, and that the impact of the consequences motivate a defendant not to re-offend. What I came to learn both as a prosecuting attorney and then as defense counsel was that there exists a wide range of philosophical beliefs by prosecuting attorneys of how much weight, consideration, and deference, if any, the resolution of a case should take into account justice as to the defendant and the trajectory of their life.

After losing the motion, I approached the chief criminal deputy and explained that the ex-boyfriend had pled to a misdemeanor. We legally understood the court's reasoning. We also understood the spirit of the policy of addressing an employee's breach of trust and fiduciary duty to their employer. I explained Sara took full responsibility for her actions and understood she needed to be held accountable. However, being held accountable should not result in completely derailing her future. The chief deputy listened and agreed to vacate the guilty plea and amended the charge, and Sara pled guilty to misdemeanor theft. Sara would not face entering adulthood as a convicted felon.

This article is solely focused on nonviolent crime, first-time offenders, and nonviolent crime connected to substance abuse and mental health disorders where an individual is amenable to treatment and services. Most advocates of criminal justice reform, myself included, acknowledge that there are certain individuals who are a danger to the safety of the community or are chronic offenders with criminological traits for whom incarceration is often the only viable option.

Elected and appointed prosecuting attorneys have the authority and the discretion to either enact strictly punitive charging policies or be forward thinking and thoughtfully and strategically enact policies, practices, and initiatives that focus on aggressively targeting violent crime and chronic offenders that is balanced with connecting with their communities and establishing alternative options that focus on accountability and rehabilitation, and taking a leadership role in building thriving and safe communities.

Nancy Parr, the elected Commonwealth's Attorney for the City of Chesapeake, and current president of the National District Attorneys Association, is one of those prosecutors.

Nancy graduated from the University of Richmond, T.C. Williams School of Law, in 1983 and immediately went to work for a law firm representing condominium associations. She quickly realized this was not fulfilling work and wanted to pursue trial practice.

She was hired by the City of Suffolk Commonwealth's Attorney's Office. She worked in the City of Suffolk for 10 years, where she worked mostly on domestic violence, child abuse, and sexual assault cases and was promoted to Chief Deputy Commonwealth's Attorney.

After her children grew up and graduated high school, and after working as Chief Deputy Commonwealth's Attorney for the City of Chesapeake, she moved to the City of Chesapeake and ran for elected office with the support of the prior elected prosecutor, who left office to assume the bench, and her colleagues. She is the first woman elected in her city and has been serving the City of Chesapeake since 2005.

Nancy started community outreach efforts in 2005 because she didn't want community members, whether they be victims of crime, defendants, or the defendant's family, to meet her in the courtroom for the first time. She wanted to know what the community wanted her to know about them and their neighborhoods.

Nancy began concentrated community outreach initiatives and programs that include a basketball tournament with a focus on "playing on the right team" that involves participation from her office, the police department, sheriff's office, and firefighters. The Boys Leadership Conference and the Girl's Empowerment Conference include both young teens and their parents to learn about topics such as financial literacy, Internet safety, and other related topics aimed at empowering families and youth as well as connecting families to community resources.

Nancy wholly funds these programs and others, including Traveling the Road to Success, Graffiti Be Gone, and Every 15 Minutes programs, with financial support from businesses and community leaders in the community. The focus of all these programs is to go upstream and prevent people from becoming involved in the criminal justice system. Nancy expressed that when people are exposed to opportunities, resources, and alternatives, they have more options and can make better decisions that keep them out of the criminal justice system.

Kristine Hamann, Executive Director of the Prosecutor's Center for Excellence (PCE), and a career prosecutor, says the innovative initiatives and programs Nancy is organizing in the City of Chesapeake are not an isolated incident and prosecutors across the country are enacting a variety of programs and initiatives in communities that represent a wide range of sizes, geographic locations, and demographics. Kristine spent three decades serving as a prosecutor in the Manhattan District Attorney's Office in New York City before taking on the role of Executive Director of the PCE. Her career has been focused on prosecution, and she has firsthand experience and knowledge of the impact the role of the prosecutor can have in the criminal justice system.

The PCE provides technical assistance, training, and resources to prosecuting attorneys who are interested in transcending beyond the traditional role of having a limited and relatively passive role of processing police reports and evaluating arrests made by the police and screening them for prosecution. Prosecutors are getting involved and recognizing there is a need for "more complex solutions that not only seek positive outcomes for victims, but also strategies that strive for long-term solutions for defendants, potential defendants, and the community at large. Over the last forty years, there has been a dramatic transformation and expansion of the prosecutors' mission, to not only vigorously prosecute criminal cases, but also to engage in crime prevention, problem solving and engage in community partnerships."

Kristine and her team at the PCE are currently working with prosecuting attorney's offices across the country providing assessments, technical assistance, and training focused on shifting from the traditional role of the prosecutor to a more proactive and engaged role in building safer communities through better outcomes for those involved in criminal justice. *See* www.pceinc.org.

The following are two of the many programs and initiatives for which the PCE provides technical assistance, consultation, and support to prosecuting attorney's offices:

Crime Strategies Units Intelligence (CSUs) across the country have significantly broadened the prosecutor's traditional focus to include analyzing community concerns about crime, identifying crime trends and the people who are the crime-drivers, and coordinating with other prosecutors, the community, and law enforcement partners. This broader knowledge is used to prioritize prosecution efforts and to develop targeted solutions, addressing the underlying problems that lead to criminality.

Statewide prosecutor-led Best Practices Committees have formed in 20 states over the past few years, with more under consideration. They are made up of head prosecutors, senior prosecutors, and prosecution coordinators, from all regions of the state, and provide a process for collaborative policy work. *See* https://pceinc.org/services/#map.

The PCE summarizes best the emerging role of the modern prosecutor. "Although the prosecutor's core mission will always be case-focused due to the nature of the work and the profession, the responsibilities of the modern prosecutor will require the expansion of initiatives and programs that are focused on crime prevention strategies, rehabilitation of offenders, and community engagement.

Prosecutors from around the country who are embracing this broader vision are enhancing public safety and significantly benefiting the men, women and children in the communities that they serve."

About a year later, I received a thank you card from Sara that read, in part, "I just wanted to say thank you one last time. Thanks to you I am moving forward in life. I just got a job offer in Florida and I graduate in August. I appreciate what you did for me."

Although I appreciate the card from Sara and other clients I have received throughout the years I have practiced criminal defense, the expressions of appreciation should rightfully go to all of the prosecuting attorneys in each and every one of those cases that exercised their prosecutorial discretion to ensure that the pursuit of justice included the defendant in cases where it was merited. The time has come for prosecuting attorneys to look beyond conviction rates being the traditional measure of success and examine the impact they are having in the communities they serve. There is a call for the rise of the modern prosecutor.

ENTITY:

CRIMINAL JUSTICE SECTION

TOPIC:

CRIMINAL LAW

Authors

APPENDIX L
An Awakening and More

Hon. Rachel L. Pickering

May 01, 2021
WOMEN IN CRIMINAL JUSTICE

An Awakening and More: How Being Part of the Women in Criminal Justice Task Force Has Provided Me with a Judicial Awareness

Hon. Rachel L. Pickering

Share:

So often in life we begin a project with one perspective, only to have our viewpoint change. And if we are lucky, the new perspective that emerges guides us in our future actions. The first two words of this column's title—an awakening—convey the product of my experience on the Women in Criminal Justice Task Force.

As a bit of background, in late 2018, the Task Force was formed in part to address and discuss the many challenges that women attorneys have in criminal justice practice. We set out to investigate the specific issues that affect the employment, retention, and advancement of women with criminal justice careers.

When I initially joined the Task Force, I thought my contributions would only stem from my prosecution and criminal defense background in trial and appellate work. I was eager to join the project but presumed my role would remain narrow: to assist in preparation of the Task Force's reported findings with limited adjustments to my own thinking. That would soon change.

In 2019 and early 2020, our Task Force visited several locations throughout the country to hold listening sessions and conduct in-depth reviews of women attorneys' experiences. To facilitate this, the Task Force invited women practicing in different areas of criminal justice to come and speak about the challenges they encounter in workplaces and in courtrooms.

With support from the ABA, the Task Force was able to provide the ideal setting for effective listening sessions: a safe place for women attorneys to tell their stories and to be heard. For many, this was the first time they were able to speak about their experiences in the criminal justice field. And more importantly, they were able to talk to an audience that cared about what they shared. Without judgment or disagreement, the Task Force listened and focused on their stories.

We heard of the many challenges that women criminal justice practitioners face in the practice of law. The testimonials provided firsthand information on the numerous obstacles that can hamper or delay a successful career. Many discussed the difficult experience of seeking work/life balance while striving for career advancement. For some, they told of struggles of being new ers and ongoing challenges with childcare while practicing criminal law. For others, it was recalling past experiences in the room that had presented hardships unique to women. At times, the testimonials were hard to hear. Further, these stories were similar throughout our cross-county listening sessions. While there were some experiences that were different across rural and urban areas, many of the same themes emerged.

Specifically, the stories underscored the fact that women practitioners will likely encounter microaggressions, both intentional and unintentional, as they practice law. The more I listened, the more it became clear that all must be afforded respect and support from our legal community.

With my fall 2019 appointment to the bench, I was determined to apply this new awareness. As a new appointee, I sought to consciously and purposely create an environment that respects all in the courtroom. Of course, like all of us, I have stumbled in this effort, but I continue to work towards this goal.

Importantly, I have come to learn that it is the little things that a judge can do that make an impact. For example, given the pandemic, it is helpful to be understanding when attorneys are only able to appear virtually from their homes. Many are facilitating online learning for children, and thus they may not always be able to make it to the courthouse. Some may need to drop children off at school or take parents or other relatives to doctor's appointments, and they may be unable to attend early morning or late afternoon hearings.

In other words, by recognizing that many skilled attorneys are juggling a lot right now, given family and other personal responsibilities, we can create a productive setting that supports a person's dual roles as both an attorney and caretaker. I believe that much of the flexibility that the pandemic has required should remain after the virus has run its course. Additionally, we have all become more attentive and considerate as we have learned to adapt to the stresses associated with the pandemic, and it would be a benefit to all if such consideration were to continue.

By no means am I advocating a lowering of judicial and legal standards. Consideration and thoughtfulness, and supportive courthouse environments, should improve the legal process. Attorneys who are allowed some flexibility to meet work/life demands and are consistently treated with respect should be able to thrive and provide better advocacy for their clients. When they are valued and treated with consideration, they are better able to focus on substance over form. Clients benefit because they see that their representation is held in high regard, giving confidence that the best case is being made on their behalf. All of this bolsters public perceptions of the local courthouse and the legal system. In a sense, when attorneys do not have to sweat the small stuff, they may flourish and the legal process as a whole may benefit.

And yes, as noted above, I have been far from perfect in my efforts to create a considerate and flexible courtroom. For example, I have had to work on being more accommodating when scheduling hearings, learning to have patience with attorneys as they have difficulty appearing virtually, and correcting myself when I have not been as courteous as I would prefer.

But our listening sessions have made it clear that judges have an important role to play in fostering support and improving the legal process. I approach the small part that I can play in this process with a quote from Justice Ruth Bader Ginsburg in mind. She observed that "Real change, enduring change, happens one step at a time." A small step towards real change can be made by providing a supportive setting where all are heard and valued.

As the Task Force has completed its listening sessions and its second year, my initial perspective has indeed changed. These experiences have widened my once-narrow views. The listening sessions bestowed an awareness upon me: As attorneys and judges, we all have a vital role to play. And thus, going forward both individually and collectively, we can take steps to have a positive impact on the practice of law.

ENTITY:

NAL JUSTICE SECTION

TOPIC:

CIVIL RIGHTS AND CONSTITUTION, CRIMINAL LAW

Authors

APPENDIX M

Brave, Bold, Booked, and Balanced

Joy Applewhite

July 20, 2021
WOMEN IN CRIMINAL JUSTICE

Brave, Bold, Booked, and Balanced

Joy Applewhite

Share:

Coined by the motivational speaker Rickey Thompson, the trending term "booked and busy" describes millennials and other generations as they handle multiple roles, often going from one activity to the next. As a 2L at American University Washington College of Law, once I caught wind of the term, I knew it fit my lifestyle. I was taking a 15-hour credit load, interning a few hours a week at the Office of the Public Defender for Arlington County and the City of Falls Church, serving as a Teaching Fellow for the Marshall-Brennan Constitutional Literacy Project, and serving as the president of the Black Law Students Association at the Washington College of Law.

"Booked and busy" kept me running day-to-day between classes, meetings, and tasks that I appreciated because it allowed me to serve others and have a life beyond classes. Oftentimes, I would find myself tired from the daily hustles and would have to take time to pour back into me through self-care activities. But some days, I would find myself sacrificing my needs to pour energy into others. I found myself struggling with imposter syndrome and negative self-talk that would include thoughts like, "Am I doing enough? Did I approach that situation properly? Should I be more involved in this project despite it not being my responsibility?"

Reflecting back, I realize that I would say "yes" at times, not because I wanted to but because I felt like I had to and needed to feel satisfied with who I was as a student, as a leader, as an intern. I internally wanted to satisfy others. In the words of my professor Judge Tanya Jones Bosier, people pleasing others "for their benefit was [becoming] my detriment." I knew this was occurring, but I did not actively start the beginning stages to combat it until a couple of things happened. First, I attended weeks of therapy that I forced myself to go to because I knew it would be good for my well-being given the challenges of being a student and in leadership but just human and a Black woman in her 20 somethings. Second, I attended the ABA Women in Criminal Justice Task Force Law Student Listening Session at Howard University School of Law.

Before entering law school, I was convinced I wanted to work in public defense to help marginalized communities that ranged from Black and Brown people to the poor to individuals with physical and mental disabilities. My "why" was the foundation of my personal statements to law schools, and the thing that encouraged me as I thought of the immense amount of debt that I would have to take on to serve in this sector of the legal profession. I worked to keep an open mind, attending various law firm open houses, but did not feel any passion as I moved around the room, listening to conversations about mergers and acquisitions and other matters that seemed so mundane. When moments would arise that criminal law would be brought up, my ears would perk up and my heart
[illegible]d get excited to talk about something I was passionate about.

Becoming involved in the ABA Criminal Justice Section as a 1L during the annual Criminal Justice Institute in the fall of 2018 solidified that this was the sector of law I wanted to practice in. Having the opportunity to meet practitioners in the field that included the woman trailblazer the Honorable Bernice Donald was an inspiring experience. I made various connections through the Criminal Justice Institute, so when my then-professor, Professor Angela Davis, for the unprecedented Criminal Justice Ethics course at American University Washington College of Law, shared the opportunity to attend the ABA Women in Criminal Justice Task Force Listening Session, I thought I had to attend to hear perspectives about being a woman in the criminal legal sector and share my perspectives about my experiences in law school as a student and interest in criminal law.

Knowing I wanted to enter criminal law did not negate the fact that I would face challenges as a woman practicing in criminal defense. Adding the extra identity I have as a Black person in America, there were various concerns that I had prior to law school, such as student loan debt and family/community expectations about income when I would be entering the public service sector. Before law school, I went to Alcorn State University, a land-grant historically Black college and university. Making the transition to American was an experience in itself that caused me to experience anxiety and imposter syndrome that was new, stressful, and intense. Throughout law school, my concerns intensified as I had internship opportunities in offices where there were no Black women attorneys. I needed to have a safe and brave space where I could discuss gender-related, race-related, and stress-related concerns about entering this profession, so I could determine ways to combat feelings of inadequacy, microaggressions, and stress and anxiety. The visionary I am, I also was beginning to think of what being in this sector would be like when I decide I want to get married and have a family while also pursuing my other passions while practicing law.

Attending the listening session, I met and listened to women who may have faced similar issues that I had and learned how they handled them. Learning that the workplace is improving for women when it comes to being a mother and a lawyer was encouraging. But hearing the stories of how women are still viewed differently when it comes to being a caretaker who has to care for a newborn in those first few months and being the one sometimes who has to do the errands for the children and the household reminded me that we still have a long way to go. To have to choose whether to be a mother or a professional is lessening, but the traditional ways of thinking still persist. If it were not for women, where would the world be?

Now, as I transition into the legal world from law student to practitioner to be, I am visualizing where my career trajectory will go. Although I am interested in criminal defense, Judge Rachel Pickering shared valuable information with my table as someone who did defense work and prosecution. She encouraged us to consider prosecution because people who want to change the system need to be in various positions to make it happen. Bringing that advice to where we are today, the system can only change when the people want to change their mindsets, their values, and ideologies that are rooted in systemic racism and classism. The true change occurs when we speak out against injustice rather than standing still. Although I may not be interested in prosecution, Judge Pickering is correct that we need diversity in all of these spaces. That diversity need not be superficial but immersive, not exclusive but inclusive, and not a moment but a movement.

Women are meant to exist in every space. Our ideas, our words, and our actions have value. Until that is crystal clear, we will continue to break ceilings and be firsts.

ENTITY:

CRIMINAL JUSTICE SECTION

TOPIC:

CRIMINAL LAW

Authors

APPENDIX N

From Sweetie to Sisterhood

Jessica Yeary

From Sweetie to Sisterhood: A Public Defender's Listening Session Reflection

by JESSICA YEARY

Oftentimes, after learning that I am a criminal defense attorney, people will ask if it is scary or if I ever feel threatened by my clients. The truth is no—representing clients has never been as scary as navigating the legal profession as a woman.

In our office and in our courtrooms, I have received many offensive remarks from lawyers and judges, including:

"That b**** walks around here like she owns the place."

"Why can't you just have the baby and come right back to working like those field women do?"

"You have to stop challenging me and then I'll stop yelling at you."

"You're standing here working while pregnant; why can't your client?"

But it's not just the disrespectful and clueless comments. Nothing has ever been as difficult as defending a client's freedom and liberty while balancing a newborn's cluster feeds or an infant's sleep regression. I have never felt as threatened by a client as I have by a male boss who screamed and slammed the desk and cursed at me. I have never been more traumatized than watching mothers being physically peeled away from their babies as they are arrested and sentenced. It's not the clients that scare me. It's trying to stop this system from ruining families while also trying to raise one of my own.

I did not realize how much I needed the ABA's Criminal Justice Section Women in Criminal Justice Task Force listening session until I attended one in Tallahassee in 2020. To be surrounded by so many brilliant advocates from so many different backgrounds, ages, and ethnicities was an amazing experience. To hear every story of courage, bravery, and struggle and see the success and empowerment on the other end was incredibly inspiring.

The shared experiences of the women on the panel brought us together in a profound way. Sisterhood and solidarity in such a niche area of the law—criminal defense, indigent criminal defense at that—highlighted not only how important our work was, but, also, how hard everyone was working to fix this broken criminal legal system.

We shared the standard experiences—ones that most female attorneys endure in the courtroom and the office: sexual harassment, dismissiveness, dirty jokes, questions about our competency, personal attacks, etc. When we thought the comments could not get any worse, someone else would speak up and we would all shake our heads in disgust.

We also saw how everyone pressed on because of their duty to their clients and the respect they have for our work. We took every snarky comment from opposing counsel and turned it into a winning closing argument. We stood up for our deserved pay raise and advocated for the promotion. For some of us, we took a terrifying leap to run for office, and we made it thanks to the support of friends and colleagues who cheered for us along the way. The listening session was not only a glimpse into what we have all gone through, but also how we have all succeeded in spite of the challenges.

We also spoke openly about personal struggles outside of the courtroom. How do you hold sobbing mothers as their children are taken away and then get in the car to go pick up your own? How do you explain the injustice and disparity in our system to your children? What lessons do you teach your kids about their interactions with law enforcement? How do you show up for clients every day and do your very best work when you are literally functioning on four hours of sleep? How do you defend clients accused of sexually motivated crimes

JESSICA YEARY is the Public Defender of the Second Judicial Circuit of Florida. She is board certified in criminal trial law and served two terms as president of the Tallahassee Chapter of the Florida Association of Criminal Defense Lawyers.

while also advocating for women's rights and protections?

These struggles are the reality for so many of us in this practice, and it was powerful to have a safe space to share our stories. But what was truly incredible were the solutions that everyone proposed—the action steps we could, and would, all take to make things better.

We took huge leaps together. We sit among courageous women who challenged incumbents and won, who overturned laws that were unjust and prejudicial, who became the youngest person of color to earn a circuit judgeship, who created nursing rooms in courthouses and offices, and who led entire legal aid organizations committed to zealous representation. We are raising our children to be kind and accepting, but also to be leaders who challenge the status quo.

One of the most frustrating things we had all been told when suggesting new ideas or different strategies was, "Well, this is the way it's always been done." Every single woman in our sessions answered loudly with, "Well, not anymore."

Do not call us honey or sweetie—call us Your Honor, call us Madame Public Defender, call us esteemed Counsel for the Defense. And, most importantly, to each other now, we can call one another our sisters.■

Book Review

continued from pg 48

to dismiss or suppress evidence, but their lawyers refused, often deeming them to be frivolous. The kinds of relationships that disadvantaged defendants have with their lawyers are often full of mistrust and disagreement about the ultimate goals of the court process, as well as the steps to realize those goals.

For middle-class and white working-class defendants, attorney-client relationships are characterized by trust and delegation to a lawyer's expertise. While middle-class defendants are often shocked by the court process (and are far less likely to have prior experience in the courts), they experience many privileges as they make their way through the courts shielded by lawyers they can trust. They often feel heard by lawyers (who are often privately retained). Unlike disadvantaged defendants, privileged defendants rarely feel that they were unjustly treated by police or the courts, making it easier for them to defer to the court's authority. Moreover, they feel respected by judges and prosecutors who afford them opportunities for rehabilitation, treatment, and second chances because they are perceived to be compliant.

Ultimately, I conclude that these processes are a form of institutional discrimination. I show how lawyers differentiate between clients based on the ways they present themselves in the attorney-client relationship. Disadvantaged defendants' understandable mistrust and resistance are punished, whereas privileged defendants' trust, inexperience, and deference are rewarded.

If you were to address an audience of criminal defense attorneys, what would you recommend they do for their clients based upon your research?
In the conclusion of the book, I offer several suggestions for change at three levels—the level of the attorney-client relationship, the level of the institutional norms of the court, and the level of broader society. I think most practicing criminal defense attorneys will find the first level of solutions most useful in their everyday practice. I suggest ways to cultivate trust in relationships with disadvantaged defendants, to experiment with client choice in attorney assignment, and to challenge trial court judges' deference to police accounts of events. But I recognize that the attorney-client relationship is embedded within a web of other relationships and institutional constraints. Many defense attorneys are aware of the pressures they face from prosecutors and judges. But beyond that, defense attorneys can work alongside broader movements for racial and social justice that seek to reduce the number of people processed in criminal courts by investing in housing, education, health care, violence interruption, and harm reduction. My colleague Amanda Woog and I have an article forthcoming in the *California Law Review* called "Courts and the Abolition Movement." In it, we extend on some of the conclusions of the book and offer practical steps for lawyers seeking to work alongside the movement to abolish the prison-industrial complex.■

APPENDIX O

Voice Lessons

Yaamini L. Rao

January 12, 2022
WOMEN IN CRIMINAL JUSTICE

Voice Lessons

Yaamini L. Rao

No one has ever accused me of having a quiet voice. I was born with the kind of volume that resulted in repeated requests to keep my voice down from preschool through, well, yesterday. My biggest pet peeve is being "shushed"; it makes me irate and ashamed at the same time. I am loud, yes, but that has always been my superpower.

Yet, as a woman of color and a criminal defense attorney for the past 10 years, I have found myself unable to use my superpower when advocating for myself. When a judge compared me to Gandhi in open court and proceeded to tell me I must be good at math because "my people were good at math," I silently nodded hoping my cringeworthy fake smile would not harm my client seated next to me. When a court reporter told me in a full courtroom she could not understand me because of my "accent," I murmured a quiet apology rather than snap back that I did not realize it was so hard to understand people who speak "Valley Girl."

When you are a deputy public defender, your sole job is to zealously advocate for the client seated next to you. I take pride in that role. Time and time again, however, I have remained silent at these slights in open court because I feared doing otherwise would harm my clients' interests. Protecting my clients' needs meant ignoring my own. Admittedly, it can be exhausting and overwhelming at times; it is also not at all unique to the experiences of many women and women of color who navigate these spaces.

That is why in 2019 when I was asked by the ABA Women in Criminal Justice Task Force to provide testimony on my experience as a woman of color in the criminal legal field at one of the Listening Sessions in San Francisco, I leapt at the chance. However, I decided (with the help of extremely wise counsel from my mother) that this was not a time for me to "air my grievances." It was time to use this platform I had been given to provide the data to back my working hypothesis—that as a woman and a woman of color in the criminal legal field, I could hardly be alone in feeling frustrated at being silenced.

To confirm my hypothesis, I decided to invite other women in my office to share their experiences because if I harnessed the collective voices of the women and women of color, we could all be heard. We could bring our truths to light and be given the stage they deserved. It was time to give each woman in my office an opportunity to speak up about these microaggressions, both inside the courtroom and sometimes with our own colleagues.

With the help of my scientist sister, I created an internal online survey for my colleagues that asked a range of questions about their ...ghts on recruitment, retention, and promotion of women and women of color and about their experiences in the courtroom ...ffice navigating the complexities of being women criminal defense attorneys. The survey was multiple choice with the option to provide longer answers if a participant wished. When I sent out the survey, I was worried no one would respond—but a whopping 65 percent replied. Each person shared their candid responses about their experiences.

After the survey closed, I conducted a follow-up focus group. I invited participants to lunch and asked questions based on the survey responses. The women who attended shared openly their concerns about career mobility, balancing demanding trial-oriented careers they loved with family obligations, and the common experience by some of feeling sidelined and silenced based upon their status as women and women of color. As I listened to my colleagues, I noticed that the forum allowed them to have what we all needed: space to have their voices heard and validation that their experiences mattered.

With the permission of my office leadership, who openly encouraged me to do so, I took my "study" to the ABA listening session. When it was my turn to speak, I pulled a huge black binder filled with tabbed pages out of my bag and placed it on the table. It was my turn to amplify the voices of my colleagues who were waiting to be heard.

I began reporting the data and giving anecdotes about our collective experiences as women and women of color defenders. I shared the strong voices of my colleagues by using my own. It felt freeing in a way that I had not ever experienced. My voice grew louder and back to the volume that I have come to love and own. As one of the participants in my "study" stated, "[J]ust listen to us—we have something to say, and it has value."

I have not looked back since that August 2019 listening session. After that session, I met with leadership in my office to discuss my results and talk about ways to continue to open paths for women and women of color in our office. The ABA Women in Criminal Justice Task Force invited me to join their Advisory Board and co-chair the Data Committee. Along with three other incredible women of color defense attorneys I met at the listening sessions, I co-founded the Women of Color Defender Network where women of color defense attorneys from all over California come together monthly in support and solidarity.

By harnessing the collective voices of my colleagues and giving them the audience they deserved, I regained my own voice in the process. It is loud, it is powerful, and it is here to stay.

ENTITY:

CRIMINAL JUSTICE SECTION

TOPIC:

CIVIL RIGHTS AND CONSTITUTION, CRIMINAL LAW

Authors

APPENDIX P

From Mad Men to Times Up

Ann Ratnayake Macy

May 04, 2022

FEATURE

From Mad Men to Times Up: What We Must Do to Ensure Workplace Parity for Women in Criminal Justice—A Women in Criminal Justice Taskforce Member's Perspective

Ann Ratnayake Macy

A working woman from the 1950s tells her granddaughter, "'Women's bosses . . . expected certain favors for their jobs—and they were usually sexual favors. They rarely valued women as human beings, or as workers. Nothing was expected of us, except cooking, cleaning, and bearing children. We were trophy wives; we weren't supposed to have a brain. If I voiced an opinion, they looked at me like, "who are you?"' To be a working woman in the 50s . . . was to be 'underpaid and undervalued.'" Mia Jacobs, *Living "Mad Men": A Woman at Work in the 1950s*, Nat'l Women's Law Cent. (Sept. 4, 2014). A question the Women in Criminal Justice Task Force (TF) asked is how much has changed and how much still has to change. The TF is a task force created by the Criminal Justice Section of the American Bar Association (ABA).

Women's labor-force participation after the mid-1970s accelerated. Eileen Appelbaum, Heather Boushey & John Schmitt, *The Economic Importance of Women's Rising Hours of Work* 3–7(Ctr. for Am. Progress Apr. 2014). From 1970 to 2000, workforce participation rates for women ages 25 to 44 increased from 47 percent to 76 percent, where it held steady until before the COVID epidemic. *Id.* However, how much of our grandmother's world still exists that holds women back from reaching the highest level of success—particularly in the criminal justice field—is one the TF seeks to answer. The answer is disturbing.

The TF heard the testimony of 168 female leaders in the criminal justice field which was followed-up by a quantitative survey. The data illuminated four broad themes posing challenges to women in the workplace: (1) gender discrimination, lack of respect, and devaluation; (2) caregiving, motherhood, and systemic obstacles to juggling work–life expectations; (3) the need for sponsorship and allies; and (4) special issues related to the criminal justice field in terms of low salaries and vicarious trauma.

Why are these issues important? When women are left behind, organizations and society lose. The research is robust and very clear –the most gender-diverse organizations are likely to significantly outperform the least gender-diverse organizations. McKenzie & Co., *Diversity Wins: How Inclusion Matters* (May 19, 2020). In the criminal justice field, the presence of female leaders provides more actual justice and more procedural justice. Women's leadership correlates with reduced corruption. Maryam Ahranjani, *"Toughen Up, Buttercup" versus #TimesUp: Initial Findings of the ABA Women in Criminal Justice Task Force*, 25 Berkeley J. Crim. L. 99, 103–04 (2020) [hereinafter Ahranjani, *Initial Findings*]. Victims, defendants, and jurors from marginalized groups are more likely to perceive the system in a positive way if attorneys have similar identities and can understand their experiences and empathize with them. *Id.* Correspondingly, the most marginalized of all victims, child victims have expressed more comfort with female attorneys. *Id.* In order to improve the criminal justice system, ensuring female leaders is imperative.

This was the case when the CJS Women's Task Force began its work, and it is equally true, and very much more difficult, today. The COVID-19 crisis disproportionately impacted women. Tyler Boesch et al., *Pandemic Pushes Mothers of Young Children Out of the Workforce*, Minneapolis Fed. Rsrv. Bank (Feb. 2, 2021). Because ingrained gender expectations manifest as mothers bearing more of the unpaid work related to children, and the COVID crisis mandated children be taught from home, as many as three million women left the workforce because of the lack of bandwidth. *Id.* Women are 1.3 times more likely than men to have considered stepping out of the workforce or slowing down their careers—particularly mothers, senior women, and Black women. McKenzie & Co., *The Pandemic's Gender Effect: Women Are Disproportionately Affected by the COVID-19 Crisis. Here's How to Help*, McKinsey Q.: Five Fifty (2020). A TF survey respondent explains how this can potentially manifest in the criminal justice field. "I pay for additional childcare for my school age child. Any time either one of my children has a minor symptom such as a runny nose, there is a high likelihood that they will be sent home from daycare requiring me to either take off work or work from home. Unfortunately, my boss does not understand that this is directly linked to COVID and not just a 'sick' child." *See* Ahranjani, *Initial Findings, supra.*

The COVID crisis in addition to four broad themes of (1) gender discrimination; (2) systemic obstacles to juggling work–life expectations; (3) the need for sponsorship and allies; and (4) special issues related to the criminal justice field exacerbates women's challenges in the criminal justice workplace. The COVID crisis presents both an impediment to female workforce participation and significant opportunities related to flexibility and restructuring office policies. Suggested strategies to improve the hiring, retention, and promotion of female leaders in the criminal justice field are (1) training ourselves and others to be aware of our biases, challenge them, and track our progress; (2) working to restructure office policies in order to create parity and hold ourselves accountable by collecting data; (3) becoming an ally—or aligning yourself—with women and women of color and other intersectionalities in particular; and (4) educating practitioners on strategies for dealing with vicarious trauma and traumatic stress.

The Women in Criminal Justice Task Force

Emily Johnson, a communications specialist with the Criminal Justice Section of the ABA, asked section leaders why only 26 percent of the section's members are women. The TF came to fruition from these discussions and the support of Section Director Kevin Scruggs, Section Chair Lucian Dervan, and subsequent Section chairs. Twelve women with diverse life, racial, and demographic experiences are members of the TF. Co-chairs Tina Luongo and Carla Laroche, and reporter Maryam Ahranjani lead the TF. The advisory group of experienced practitioners also helps guide the project. The author of this article is a member of the TF.

The TF first listened to women testify regarding their experiences in the workplace. Local and national bar associations, taskforce members, and criminal justice leaders nominated diverse female leaders in the field to give testimony on their experiences in the workplace. From November 2018 to March 2020, the TF crisscrossed the nation from Washington, D.C., to Washington State holding 12 listening sessions to hear 168 women testify. Ahranjani, *Initial Findings, supra.* The TF conducted a follow-up quantitative survey from October to December 2020. Maryam Ahranjani, *Pulling Back the Curtain: A Follow-Up Report from the TF* (Am. Bar Ass'n 2021).

During the listening sessions and survey, some common themes emerged from the radically diverse women and locations that shed light on the challenges in hiring, retention, and promotion that women recounted. Women of varying life experiences described similar challenges relating to the four broad themes that were discovered as a result of the survey mentioned above.

Gender Discrimination, Lack of Respect for and Devaluation of Women (Particularly LGBTQ Women and Women of Color)

The Problem

Men's and women's achievements are recognized and evaluated differently. Virginia Valien, *Gender and Evaluation in Extending Justice: Reducing Bias* (Bernice B. Donald & Sarah Redfield eds. 2021). Negative gender and intersectional stereotypes influence both male and female evaluators when valuing the same performance. Naomi Ellemers, *Gender Stereotypes*, 69 Ann. Rev. Psychol. 275, 278–79 (2018). Women are less likely than men to be selected for promotions and prestigious positions. *Id.* For instance, female professors were less likely than male professors to be awarded an endowed chair despite the lack of difference in academic publications, citations, years into career, or number of children. *Id.* A meta-analysis of almost 100 empirical studies conducted among 378,850 employees in different industries documents the broad undervaluing of women's performance across all sectors. Aparna Joshi, *When Can Women Close the Gap? A Meta-Analytic Test of Sex Differences in Performance and Rewards*, 58 Acad. Mgmt. J. (2014). Furthermore, the same meta-analysis found that gender differences in fiscal rewards—bonus, raises, and promotions—are 14 times larger than the already undervalued performance ratings would indicate. *Id.* Similarly, in private practice within the legal field, only 19.5% of people on the equity partner trajectory in large law firms were women. Cynthia L. Cooper, *Broken Rungs on the Career Ladder: A New Analysis of Problems Encountered by Women Lawyers in Private Practice* (Am. Bar Ass'n Jan. 21, 2020).

The differences in perception and treatment translates to differences in financial compensation. As of 2018, women's median earnings are still lower than men's in nearly all occupations, surprisingly even in those predominately dominated by women. Inst. for Women's Pol'y Rsch., *Fact Sheet: The Gender and Wage Gap by Occupation 2018, and by Race and Ethnicity* 1 (Apr. 2019). Based on statistical analysis that controls for other factors, nearly 40% of the gap is unaccounted for, leading researchers to conclude discrimination and unconscious bias continue to impact women's wages. *Id.* This wage gap is firmly entrenched in the American workplace and more profound for women with certain intersectional identities. In 2018, white females earned 78.6% of the median salaries of their white male counterparts, Hispanic females earned 55.5%, African American females earned 58.9%, and Asian females earned 84.3%. *Id.* Some women who testified at the TF listening sessions acknowledged intentionally working to dispel negative stereotypes that might adversely impact perceptions of their job performance. Unfortunately, intersections of race and gender magnify these challenges.

Examples of the types of comments voiced at the listening sessions illuminating negative gender and/or intersectionality discrimination in the criminal justice field are below.

- "No one thinks I am the attorney. They assume I'm the secretary or sister or auntie."
- "I am routinely called by my first name when male attorneys are called 'Mr. So-and-so.'"
- "I get called 'little lady,' and people said, 'people will vote for you [for elected public defender] because you are hot.'"
- "There's a fine line between aggressive and bitch. I was called a chihuahua by a judge once; management said to 'let it go.'"
- "I have been told I don't look or act feminine enough."
- "I've had a male judge say to me, 'Counsel, school your features,' when I was frowning at him when he ruled against me."
- "I had a male attorney call a female witness a 'whore for the government.' The female judge just said his name. We have thick skins, but that's not good enough."
- "People don't expect Black women to read and write well. God forbid I have a typo because the assumption [is] that it is my intelligence and not the speed of my typing."
- "They [men and women] bully and intimidate to evoke anger and then we get labeled as the 'Angry Black Woman.'"
- "I was introduced by my supervisor to a judge as a 'spicy little Latina.'"
- "We bury these things [sexism, racism] because if we don't, we can't continue to work."

- "I have seen a lot in my nearly 40 years in the same government agency. I have seen sex discrimination and the problems with 'boy's club' behavior (i.e., having to drink, use certain language, partake in the same behavior). I have seen women getting scolded or even demoted for calling out sexism in the office."

See Ahranjani, *Initial Findings, supra.*

Potential Solutions

Creating and amplifying evidence-based programs on the effects of implicit and explicit bias—regarding gender stereotyping coupled with other intersectionalities—will help create meaningful change. Organizations can mandate an implicit bias curriculum so that all employees know how to respond when they experience or witness discriminatory or biased behavior.

The bias training must not only increase the awareness that biases are involuntary and widespread, but also provide guidance on how to manage bias, change behavior, and track progress. Francesca Gino & Katherine Coffman, *Unconscious Bias Training That Works*, Harv. Bus. Rev., Sept.–Oct. 2021. Otherwise, training that only increases awareness regarding reflexive and widespread nature of implicit bias may actually increase discrimination—if people think its unavoidable. *Id.*

Recommended programs go beyond just raising awareness. *Id.* They ask participants to take implicit bias tests that provide feedback on levels of implicit bias and teach strategies for overcoming that bias. Studies demonstrate this type of training works to encourage people not only to eliminate bias within themselves, but also to call it out in others. *Id.*

Creating a meaningful antidote to gender and intersectional discrimination is not just a single education session. It requires changes to policies such as the standardizing the hiring process, the eliminating self-assessments from performance reviews, making the promotion process transparent, and instituting incentives for improving workplace parity. *Id.* Organizations should also track representation and hiring and promotion outcomes—not only for women, but also women of color and other marginalized intersectionalities. LeanIn.Org & McKenzie & Co., *2021 Women in the Workplace* 39 (2021). Organizations should determine whether managers are hiring and promoting women and women of color at similar rates to other employees. If the analysis finds gaps, the organization must double down on best practices. *Id.*

Caregiving, Motherhood, and Systemic Obstacles to Juggling Work–Life Commitments

The Problem

Reforms to rigid "in office" policies, and systemic access to childcare and family-friendly policies are needed. The out-of-date rigid workplace and societal framework is a principal impediment to finding parity for women in the workplace in general and for women in the criminal justice field in particular. US Congress Joint Economic Committee, Invest in Women Invest in America: A Comprehensive Review of Women in the US Economy 6 (US Congress 2010).

Women have entered the workplace, but typically they still assume significantly more of the household tasks such as laundry, meal preparation, dishwashing, cleaning, childcare, and eldercare. Megan Brenan, *Women Still Handle Main Household Tasks in U.S.*, Gallup (Jan. 29, 2019). In particular, childcare negatively impacts women's careers. For example, a 2019 study found 95% of fathers in heterosexual couples who could not find childcare continued to work, compared to 77% of mothers. Leila Schochet, *The Child Care Crisis Is Keeping Women Out of the Workforce*, Ctr. for Am. Progress (Mar. 28, 2019). Research also suggests organizations are less likely to hire mothers for jobs, to perceive them as competent, or to pay mothers as much as male colleagues with the same qualifications. Claire Cain Miller, *The Motherhood Penalty v. Fatherhood Bonus*, N.Y. Times, Sept. 16, 2014.

Below are comments from women who testified in front of the TF that illustrate this issue.

- "I sometimes don't reveal that I'm a mom. I don't want people to have lower expectations of me."
- "Having to be in court until 5 PM or later means never being able to pick your children up from school."
- "There is no chance of retaining quality women attorneys if there has to be a choice between families or work; families will always be chosen."
- "With respect to retention and promotion, [the question] is how you make it there and still have a family.

- "I do not have children. I chose not to have kids. I have never had to explain to someone that I have to leave because I have to pick up my kid. That was indeed a significant factor in my opportunity to make choices."
- "When I started out, all the male prosecutors I worked with had stay-at-home wives or were unmarried, so they could stay late, work on weekends, and celebrate victories in court."
- "Our office absolutely will not allow job sharing. When I came back from having my baby, that was all I wanted."
- "I would love to work part-time, but I'm not aware of many part-time opportunities in the public sector."
- "I was lucky to hire an over-qualified woman to work for me as my judicial clerk. After giving birth, her main priority was her child and she said she was tired of working for men who just didn't understand her needs."

See Ahranjani, *Initial Findings, supra.*

Potential Solutions

In addition to implicit bias training, greater work schedule flexibility supports women. Even in workplaces that allow some flexibility, women and men report a stigma attached to working nonstandard schedules. *Id.* at 144–45.

The COVID crisis forced organizations to embrace flexibility. LeanIn.Org & McKenzie & Co., *supra*, at 46. Allowing employees to work from home and having flexible hours are two of the most effective things organizations report they have done to improve employee well-being. *Id.* Employees with more flexibility to step away from work are much less likely to be burned out. *Id.* Fewer employees are concerned that requesting flexible work arrangements has impacted their opportunity to advance. *Id.* This experience has disproved many of the previously held stereotypes in terms of productivity and responsibility. It's important, particularly for women, that these flexible reforms remain in place, even as the COVID crisis ebbs.

Leaders in organizations and criminal justice should embrace the opportunity COVID presents to restructure the workforce to create improved parity for women. Supporting access to childcare and family leave policies and allowing for more flexibility in the "8-5 be at your desk mentality," will help women in today's society find parity in the workplace.

The Need for Mentorship, Sponsorship, and Allies

The Problem

A lack of sponsorship may be preventing women from advancing into leadership. A sponsor is someone who promotes a subordinate's skills and helps advance the subordinate's career; in turn, the sponsor reaps the benefits tied to the subordinate's performance. Benefits of sponsorship have tended to accrue more often to men than to women. Herminia Ibarra, *A Lack of Sponsorship Is Keeping Women from Advancing into Leadership*, Harv. Bus. Rev. Online (Aug. 2019).

Powerful men may be more likely to sponsor other men when leadership opportunities arise given people's tendency to gravitate to those who are like them. *Id.* Furthermore, women may fail to cultivate a sponsorship relationship because it can often be misconstrued as sexual interest, and/or perceptions that getting ahead through connections is inappropriate. Sylvia Ann Hewlett et al., Ctr. for Work-Life Policy, *The Sponsor Effect: Breaking Through the Last Glass Ceiling* (2010).

In addition, the TF's efforts noted dynamics in the field from more experienced, powerful women who not only fail to sponsor female subordinates but are more critical of female than male subordinates. The latest research suggests that being more critical of female subordinates is a way that some powerful female leaders internalize gender discrimination they have faced in their own career. Kim Eleseller, *Queen Bees Still Exist, But It is Not the Women We Need to Fix*, Forbes (Aug. 30, 2021). Lastly, women who succeeded *in spite* of the many obstacles to their advancement are naturally inclined to tell younger women to suck it up as they did. *Id.* They may even view their success as deriving in part from their ability to overcome those obstacles, explained by the "What-doesn't-kill-you-makes-you-stronger" or "Toughen Up Butter Cup" mentality. *Id.*

Examples of testimony given at listening sessions illustrating these phenomena are below.

- I've had a female judge say, 'When you're in my courtroom I expect you to dress like ladies: no skin. If I see skin, you're out.' I've seen female judges being harsher to female attorneys."
- "[Even as a woman, I acknowledge] the elephant in the room is women having babies [and what that means for their productivity]."

- "If it weren't for men who looked out for me along the way, I would not be where I am today."
- "We need to address the generational problem of entitlement and other generational differences."
- "The new generation forces us to look in the mirror. I had my two children 14 months apart and was back to work within three days. I have always advocated for and supported women. But when I hired a young associate to work at my small firm who got married shortly after she started and then wanted a three-week honeymoon, I reluctantly said, 'okay.' Then she was pregnant and wanted three months of paid leave [which is not required because of the employer size]. I even more reluctantly said, 'okay.' And then she wanted to talk about *transitioning* back to work, and I nearly lost it because I needed her back full-time. Then she was breastfeeding in the office! The male attorneys had no problem with it. I was the one with the problem, and I realized maybe I wasn't as progressive as I thought and needed to change. She is a good lawyer and employee. I want to keep her."

See Ahranjani, *Initial Findings*, *supra*.

While the TF recorded accounts of this surprising phenomenon, a newer generation of female leaders are rising to the challenge of creating parity in the workforce, rather than reinforcing impediments. The *2021 Women in the Workplace* study found female managers spend twice as much time as men on diversity and inclusion work that falls outside of their formal job responsibilities. LeanIn.org & McKenzie & Co., *supra*.

Potential Solutions

In addition to evidence-based anti-bias training and workforce policy changes, having programs that help cultivate allies for women that may eventually lead to sponsorship will help move talented women forward to leadership positions. Allies can be mentors, strategizers, connectors, opportunity givers, or sponsors. Ibarra, *supra*. A mentor provides personal advice and support privately. *Id*. A strategizer shares insider knowledge about how to advance in the organization and how to fill any developmental gaps that may hinder progress. *Id*. A connector makes introductions to influential people within his or her network. *Id*. An opportunity giver secures a high-visibility project or promotion within his or her control on behalf of the individual. *Id*. A sponsor advocates for the individual in succession for multiple opportunities with his or her reputation at stake. *Id*. Sponsorship has the potential to make or break a career. *Id*. Leaders must intentionally become allies of high-performing women, and particularly women of color and other marginalized intersectionalities, to create parity in the workplace. *Id.*

Low Salaries in Criminal Law Serve as a Challenge, Especially to Attorneys Who Face Intersectionalities

The Problem

In addition to the general wage gap that women face, attorneys that practice public sector criminal law are paid less than any other types of attorneys given the hours criminal trial attorneys work. For example, the national average entry salary in 2021 for public defenders and prosecutors is $65,939 and $66,802, respectively. *National Survey of Public Defender Salaries 2021*, Big Law Investor (last visited Nov 22, 2021); *National Survey of District Attorney Salaries 2021*, Big Law Investor (last visited Nov 22, 2021).

- "The salaries are low. Many of us don't have trust funds or parents that will pay off our student loans."
- "Our check is not our own. It is also going to someone else. It is the family check. It is hard to live on the salaries."
- "[In my role in hiring,] a woman with three children, very well qualified, declined the prosecutor position. It didn't pay well enough to even cover the childcare."

Potential Solutions

In 2021, an ABA survey documented students graduated from law school with an average of $160,000 in debt. Am. Bar Ass'n & AccessLex Inst., *Student Debt: The Holistic Impact on Today's Young Lawyer* ii (2021). More than half of respondents felt financially insecure either a portion of or all the time. While most young lawyers could find $1,000 to cover a financial emergency, Black, Hispanic/Latino, and indigenous respondents were less confident in their ability to do so. *Id.* Low salaries combined with high student debt for lawyers makes it difficult for attorneys to enter and stay in the criminal justice field, especially women, who often must compare childcare cost to salary. Moving forward, the Public Student Loan Forgiveness Program (PSLF) may help solve some of the discrepancies between law school debt and salaries for public sector criminal law attorneys. In 2021, the Department of Education began the first wave of student loan forgiveness under

PSLF, and the expectation is that the program will continue into the future. Additionally, organizations should increase pay when possible.

Compassion Fatigue, Vicarious Trauma, Burnout, and Traumatic Stress

The Problem

In the criminal justice field in particular, the jobs require exposure to the most heinous of human actions. Listening to individual clients recount their victimization, looking at videos of people raping children, reviewing case files of homicide, hearing about or responding to the aftermath of violence and other traumatic events day after day, and responding to mass violence incidents that have resulted in numerous injuries and deaths can cause vicarious trauma and traumatic stress. *The Vicarious Trauma Toolkit*, Off. for Victims of Crime (last visited Nov. 22, 2021). Traumatic stress comes from direct exposure to traumatic experiences. *Id.* Traumatic stress can result in extreme emotionality or absence of emotion, fearful-jumpy-exaggerated startle response, and flashbacks. *Id.* Vicarious traumatization results from indirect exposure to trauma. *Id.* Vicarious trauma can involve avoidance of victim/survivor, hypervigilance and fear for one's own safety, intrusive thoughts and images, or nightmares from victims' stories. *Id.*

Examples of comments from the listening sessions are below.

- "I left criminal law because I couldn't stand seeing so many young [B]lack men go to prison."
- "If you can't eat a bologna sandwich while you're reading an autopsy report, you shouldn't work for me."
- "This job requires that I have regular therapy."

See Ahranjani, *Initial Findings*, *supra*.

Potential Solution

Vicarious trauma and traumatic stress are an occupational challenge for those working in the criminal justice field. Criminal justice organizations have an ethical "duty to train," wherein workers are taught about the potential negative effects of the work and how to deal with it. *Vicarious Trauma for Law Enforcement PowerPoint Presentation*, US Dep't of Just., Off. for Victims of Crime (2015). Trauma-informed organizations recognize these challenges and assume the responsibility for proactively addressing the impact of vicarious and direct trauma through policies, procedures, practices, and programs that help process trauma. *Id.* Criminal justice systems and organizations that work within them must become trauma-informed to retain their best workforce. In criminal justice, addressing vicarious trauma is important for women and for men, and magnified for those with intersectionality.

Conclusion

While the criminal justice field also has specialized issues that hamper the hiring, retention, and promotion of women, the TF found gender discrimination entrenched in work practices and cultural norms similar to other fields. While in some ways we have moved past our grandmother's workplace of unbridled discrimination, we must do better for our daughters. Leaders in organizations must restructure rigid archaic workplace processes and systems to provide pathways to success. Authentic "buy-in" and demonstrative actions from the top are essential to create needed change. We must also each (1) train ourselves and others to be aware of our biases, challenge them, and track our progress; (2) work to restructure office policies to create parity; (3) ally with women and women of color and other intersectionalities in particular; and (4) educate practitioners on strategies for dealing with vicarious trauma and traumatic stress. The future can be bright, but it is upon all of us to create the change.

ENTITY:

CRIMINAL JUSTICE SECTION

Authors

Ann Ratnayake Macy

-

Ann R. Macy is an adjunct professor at American University in Washington, DC. Ann specializes in issues related prosecuting violence against women and children.

Special thanks to all of the members of The Women in Criminal Justice Taskforce, as well as, Professor Sarah Redfield, Professor Carla Laroche, Allie Phillips, and Candace Mosely.

APPENDIX Q

Task Force Concludes Research Phase and Moves into Action

Maryam Ahranjani

July 25, 2022
WOMEN IN CRIMINAL JUSTICE

Task Force Concludes Research Phase and Moves into Action

Maryam Ahranjani

The ABA Criminal Justice Section's Women in Criminal Justice Task Force (TF) continues its groundbreaking work of documenting and addressing challenges in hiring, retention, and promotion of women criminal lawyers. The TF was formed by then-CJS Chair Lucian Dervan in late 2018 to investigate gender-based barriers to hiring, promotion, and retention in criminal law. Over the past three and a half years, the TF engaged in three major phases of qualitative data-gathering: (1) in-person and remote listening sessions between November 2018 and June 2020; (2) follow-up surveys of listening session participants in late 2020; and (3) focus group meetings and surveys in November 2021 regarding proposed solutions.

The TF's work has appeared in many spaces—law review articles, this magazine, blogs, and podcasts. The Berkeley Journal of Criminal Law (BJCL) published *"Toughen Up, Buttercup" versus #TimesUp*, which described existing literature and shared the findings of phase one. This magazine published quarterly columns by TF members and listening session participants. The CJS published a report called *Pulling Back the Curtain* in October 2021. Most recently, the Minnesota Law Review published *Sprinting a Marathon*, analyzing and describing phases two and three (the results of the survey conducted between late October and early December 2020; the focus groups conducted on November 18, 2021; and the focus group survey administered immediately after the focus groups).

Concluding that hiring, retention, and, particularly, *promotion* of women in the criminal justice profession continue to be a problem, the 2020 follow-up survey identified the following challenges: (1) limited flexibility with work schedules; (2) insufficient wellness resources; (3) deficient training opportunities, particularly in state and rural criminal law offices; and (4) short supply of meaningful mentorship and transparent policy guidance. Some employers seem receptive to change, but many do not. The title *Sprinting a Marathon* came from one of the survey respondents who described her 35-year career in criminal law as a constant sprint—implying a pace that is not easily sustainable or replicable. It also aptly describes the TF's work to attempt to untangle systemic gender-based challenges.

Considering the results of the 2020 survey, the TF designed a short summary of challenges and possible solutions. The TF then created a list of diverse criminal justice leaders from public and private employment, state and federal government, nonprofit organizations, and law schools and invited them to participate in focus groups held in person in the ABA's Washington, DC, office and online on November 18, 2021. The purpose of the focus groups included pressure-testing proposed solutions and soliciting additional solutions. Those who were invited but unable to attend the focus groups were invited to participate via an online survey. The article summarizes the focus group and survey responses to four key questions. The four questions asked in each of the focus group meetings and in the online survey were:

1. Have you or your organizations implemented anything to facilitate gender equity in hiring, retention, and promotion? If so, please describe.
2. Do you have ideas that haven't been implemented? If so, why haven't they been implemented?
3. As the Task Force works to create a toolkit of resources, we would like to know what resources would you and your organization need to implement greater gender equity?
4. What haven't we thought about that you think we ought to think about?

As described in *Sprinting a Marathon*, after hearing from the focus group participants, the TF started 2022 with the goal of creating Ten Principles for Gender Equity in Criminal Law Employment, first within the CJS, then the ABA House of Delegates, and then among the larger justice community. The Ten Principles will include a tool kit with animating information, example policies and programs, and other resources for implementation. In the coming months, the TF will work with various ABA Sections and individuals to seek input and support. Stay tuned for our column next quarter to learn more about the Ten Principles.

ENTITY:

CRIMINAL JUSTICE SECTION

TOPIC:

CIVIL RIGHTS AND CONSTITUTION, CRIMINAL LAW

Authors

APPENDIX R
#NoRetreat

Lieutenant Colonel Susan E. Upward, USMC

April 19, 2023

WOMEN IN CRIMINAL JUSTICE

#NoRetreat – The Women in Criminal Justice Task Force Takes the Road Less Traveled to the ABA House of Delegates

Lieutenant Colonel Susan E. Upward, USMC

Share:

At one of the first meetings of the Women in Criminal Justice Task Force in early 2019, an accomplished female attorney passionately told us the story of how she had tried for years to get a nomination to become a judge, only to be repeatedly marginalized and overlooked for other candidates, the vast majority of whom were white males. She got emotional as she told her story, wondering out loud whether her goal was all worth it and if she should keep going.

My response to her was immediate, visceral, and perhaps a little loud—as the only military member in the room, I instinctively blurted out, "We are *not* retreating. We can regroup, but no retreat." Little did I know that "#NoRetreat" would become the Task Force's unofficial motto as we soldiered on in our mission: investigate gender-based barriers to hiring, promotion, and retention in criminal law, and report on the status of women in this field.

Over a period of 18 months, we conducted 12 listening sessions across the United States and online. We intentionally sought participation and input from professionals in rural and underfunded areas in an attempt to collect qualitative and quantitative data from every nook and cranny of the criminal law profession. Task Force members and participants alike participated in podcasts and volunteered to write a regular column in this magazine. Maryam Ahranjani, our brilliantly accomplished reporter, penned two law review articles documenting our research. Maryam Ahranjani, *Sprinting a Marathon: Next Steps for Gender Equity in Criminal Legal Employment*, 106 Minn. L. Rev. 228 (2022); Maryam Ahranjani, *"Toughen Up, Buttercup" versus #TimesUp: Initial Findings of the ABA Women in Criminal Justice Task Force*, 25 Berkeley J. Crim. L. 99 (2020).

Of course, the Task Force experienced challenges, well beyond COVID-19 and the inherent difficulties in conducting listening sessions of such a sensitive and personal nature online. We struggled with the narrow scope of our mandate and had to be actively conscious to avoid mission creep. Although we were focused on women in the criminal law profession, we quickly realized the issues we discussed applied broadly to women across the entire spectrum of legal services—women in civil practice or other areas of law are also experiencing a lack of opportunities for professional development and advancement, among other challenges. *See* Patricia Lee Refo, *Making Strides Towards Gender Equality in the Legal Profession*, ABA Bus. & Corp. Litig. Comm. Newsl., Spring 2019.

We also saw the disproportionate effect amplified when considering the intersection of gender with other demographics, including women of color, women in rural areas, members of the LGBTQ+ community, etc. *See* Matt Reynolds, *Slow Going: Despite Diversity Gains, Some Law Firm Leaders Bemoan Lack of Progress*, ABA J., Dec. 2022. Moreover, while the issues we identified disproportionally affect women, some areas also affect men—they too can suffer from the negative consequences of the flexibility stigma or the vicarious trauma from handling criminal cases. *See* Roberta D. Liebenberg & Stephanie A. Scharf, *Where Does the Legal Profession Go from Here?*, ABA Practice Forward Rep. (2022).

Along the way, there were also naysayers. As our participants and our own experience told us, there were categories of cynics along the lines of "gender equity is no longer a problem," "gender equity is not a big problem," and "even if gender equity is a problem, it's not *my* problem." Moreover, we found that while many employers are not receptive to change, some are but do not know where to start. Such sentiments only reiterated the importance of our work and motivated us to press on, but they also uncovered a bigger challenge: What do we do with the bevy of information we gathered, and how do we promulgate that information in a comprehensive form that provides a realistic path toward gender equity?

At a focus group meeting in November 2021, Jonathan Wroblewski, Director of the Department of Justice Office of Policy and Legislation and a former Criminal Justice Section (CJS) council member, suggested we model our product after the ABA Ten Principles of a Public Defense Delivery System. Approved by the ABA House of Delegates in 2002, that document had already achieved what we sought to accomplish with our work—create a practical guide that reflected research findings and was actually being adopted and implemented widely.

As a result, the Task Force produced a report entitled *Ten Principles to Achieve Gender Equity in the Criminal Legal Profession*. The principles are based on the Task Force's extensive data collection and offer recommendations to promote gender equity in four areas of interest to employers (hiring, retention, promotion, and equitable practice). They are:

1. Create culture change.
2. Acknowledge and address intersectional challenges.
3. Implement diversity, equity, and inclusion training.
4. Create transparent policies and opportunities for professional development.
5. Eliminate the flexibility stigma.
6. Offer multilayered, individualized support.
7. Provide low- or no-cost therapeutic support.
8. Provide private spaces.
9. Support caretaking.
10. Continual evaluation and adjustment.

The accompanying commentary to the principles defines terms like "allyship" and "flexibility stigma," and the report also provides animating information, illustrative sample policies and programs, and other resources for implementation. While our goal was to promote gender equity, the implementation of these principles will provide workplaces that are diverse, inclusive, and equitable for *all*, and ensure that we collectively do a better job of serving clients, communities, and the justice system at large.

On November 19, 2022, the CJS Counsel unanimously voted in favor of adopting the Task Force's Report. The Resolution will next be presented for adoption to the full House of Delegates as early as the 2023 Midyear Meeting in New Orleans.

But the work cannot stop there. For decades, the ABA has adopted other resolutions to advance the goal of gender equity, but this is the first resolution that specifically addresses and provides steps for lawyers in the criminal legal system. Yet, as the Task Force has come to more fully document over our journey, gender issues continue to persist both in and out of the criminal justice space. For example, the *ABA Profile of the Legal Profession 2022* shows quantitively the number of women in senior leadership roles at large firms does not correspond to the growing number of women in the profession, which also struggles to retain female attorneys. Just a month before the CJS Council's adoption of the Task Force's report, the ABA announced its collaboration with the Association of Law Firm Diversity Professionals to increase data collection to assess and advance diversity, equity, and inclusion among law firms. Even the day before the CJS Council's vote, the ABA's Council of the Section of Legal Education and Admission to the Bar voted to eliminate the LSAT to increase diversity in law schools, which disproportionately affects women and particularly minorities; the House of Delegates will consider this change in the future. *See* William C. Kidder, *Portia Denied: Unmasking Gender Bias on the LSAT and Its Relationship to Racial Diversity in Legal Education*, 12 Yale J.L. & Feminism 1 (2020).

Clearly, there is still work to be done, and the Task Force's Resolution is just a small piece of a larger puzzle. But what it does represent is more than just words: the report and the principles represent each and every voice that we heard during listening sessions across the United States—each person who responded to our request to come and testify, to tell us their stories and their experiences, and to share with us their heartfelt concerns and deepest fears.

Moreover, #NoRetreat is not just a mantra—it represents the two ideals that should permeate this issue moving forward. First, no woman should feel like she does not have a support network. The Task Force is working with the CJS Women in Criminal Justice Committee and other committees across the ABA. We seek to encourage and promote the women who do incredible work in this space, especially those with intersectional identities, in underrepresented areas, and without the support network that usually accompanies larger urban areas. Second, we refuse to accept the status quo simply because it might be the path of least resistance. We must continue to discuss the hard issues and continue to do the hard things to advance the talented women who play such a critical role in the criminal justice system.

Our friend, whose story I told at the beginning of this article, was elected as a judge earlier this year after pouring her heart and soul into the campaign. Her story shows that the road has been a long one, but the journey is not over. Retreat is simply not an option.

ENTITY:

CRIMINAL JUSTICE SECTION

TOPIC:

CRIMINAL LAW

Authors

Lieutenant Colonel Susan E. Upward, USMC

-

Lieutenant Colonel Susan E. Upward, USMC is an active-duty Marine judge advocate currently stationed at Marine Corps Air Station Cherry Point, North Carolina. She is a published author and speaker on implicit bias, recently contributing a chapter entitled "Ducks Pick Ducks—The Military's Institutionalized Unconscious Bias Challenge" in *Extending Justice: Reducing Bias* (Bernice B. Donald & Sarah E. Redfield eds., Carolina Academic Press 2022). She is a member of the Women in Criminal Justice Task Force and several other ABA committees. The views presented are those of the author and do not necessarily represent the views of the Department of Defense or the US Marine Corps.

APPENDIX S
Reflections by a Sister in Law

Hon. Denise Langford Morris

July 15, 2023
WOMEN IN CRIMINAL JUSTICE

Reflections by a Sister in Law: 40 Years in Practice and Counting

Denise Langford Morris

Once upon a time, I was a brand-new attorney hoping to be employed at the Oakland County Prosecuting Attorney's office in Michigan. I shall never forget stopping by my mom's house, thrilled about finally capturing a job interview in the heat of the early 1980s recession. Times were tough, no place was hiring, and I was ecstatic at the possibility of finally working as a lawyer. I had been licensed to practice for over a year and had continued to work as an investigative child abuse social worker in Wayne County Juvenile Court. Oakland County was and is the wealthiest county in Michigan and L. Brooks Patterson, one of the state's toughest prosecutors, was at its helm.

Well, I was excited until my well-informed, socially conscious, and intelligent mom, who always seemed to know everything, shared the following, "L. Brooks Patterson? Anti-busing? I know you're not going out there to work!!!" My heart sank immediately, and I felt as if I had just swallowed a ton of ... you know what.

The anti-busing activism that catapulted Patterson to beat his former boss in an upset election for prosecutor, and drew attention to Pontiac, MI, ultimately resulted in the late great Judge Damon J. Keith's decision to allow busing in the north and was refused review by the Supreme Court. Boycotts, violence, racial incidence, and nightmares spilled over from Oakland County, throughout the region and the country. I was unaware of what had transpired with anti-busing since I hadn't read a newspaper or listened to the news in years and most of this happened when I was a kid. Moreover, I was too busy working full time and going to school full time while obtaining my Bachelor's, Master's, and Law degrees, not to mention being a teen mom.

My mom's words were ringing in my ears, but my interview was in two hours. I had no one to call or consult with on what I should do about this dilemma. Plus, I knew I was determined to be a dang lawyer, and this interview was my opportunity to do so. I buckled up and drove what seemed like a million miles and a lifetime to Pontiac, in Oakland County, Michigan. Please understand that Oakland County was wealthy and 90 percent white. And I, a Black woman, had never heard of, much less visited, Oakland County until I applied for the interview. Pontiac felt like a foreign land to me. The office had no Black employees at any level—no staff, clerks, or lawyers. Further, it had very few women in positions other than secretary or clerk.

Though the Oakland County Prosecuting Attorney's Office's history and lack of diverse legal staff remained in the forefront of my mind, my overeager desire to be a prosecutor prevailed. Lo and behold, I received a job offer on the spot. Elated as I was to finally be working as a lawyer, I pondered on the long drive home, how would they treat me?

Forty years later and after a rewarding career, I know the answer to that question. Today, the question I have found myself asking after finding myself surrounded by a team of brilliant, diverse members of the American Bar Association Criminal Justice Section Women in Criminal Justice Task Force (Task Force) is, "How are people treating women criminal lawyers across the nation?"

The lawyers, judges, and professors on the Task Force traveled across the country to hold listening sessions with extremely diverse criminal women practitioners, who shared far too many similarities. The stories we heard from too many women about the challenges they faced because of their identities only bolstered what we already knew based on our own life stories and the strength we gained from one another given our varied perspectives.

Task Force members truly bonded and have become sisters in the law over the past 4.5 years of listening, learning, and sharing personal goals, dinners, and our favorite beverages on occasion. Together, we represented a desire to support one another and to encourage new opportunities for the women who come behind us. Our goals were to listen, observe, and meditate on what we could do to assess the apoplectic anger, feelings of disadvantage, sadness, despair, and grief that many of our participants never realized they felt until they began to share. We were on a mission.

Having had the privilege of serving as a trial judge for 30 years, I thought I was a pretty good listener. With a Master's degree in Guidance and Counseling and as a former social worker, assistant prosecutor, assistant U.S. attorney (civil division), and a trial judge, I knew I had heard a lot. I have held the closest secrets at my vest while facilitating settlements on the eve of trial and had lawyers and colleagues ask for help when faced with disciplinary investigations. But the listening sessions were different, as I realized that I had not been challenged as a woman lawyer the way that many of my sisters had.

My view after 40 years as a lawyer, including 30 years as a busy trial judge, is that there is no doubt in my mind that we as women still have a long way to go. Have we made progress? Yes, we have. When I started practicing, one of my friends shared she was called a "bitch" in open court and neither the judge nor the lawyer said a word. My friend was hurt and disgusted, but she had no place to turn. All I could do was listen, allow her to vent, and share her bottle of wine.

Like my conversation with my friend, the Task Force unlocked secrets and truths during our listening sessions. We heard blended realities of the journeys that sisters in the law endure daily. We also uncovered hope and aspiration for the future. We must forge ahead together by supporting, mentoring, and caring about one another.

As the criminal legal profession works towards eliminating bias based on gender, race, and other characteristics in the workplace, the Task Force worked to develop guidance and pathways to help our sisters in law. With the words of those who testified before us as our guide, we developed Resolution 501: Ten Principles to Achieve Gender Equity in the Criminal Legal Profession. We presented it to the House of Delegates (HOD) at the American Bar Association 2023 Midyear Meeting in New Orleans, Louisiana, and the HOD unanimously adopted it.

While the Task Force is proud of this feat, stay tuned, for there is truly more to come. The Task Force co-chairs Professor Carla Laroche and Criminal Justice Section Chair-Elect Tina Luongo, our fearless Task Force reporter Professor Maryam Ahranjani, along with all the other Task Force members want nothing less than to stamp out the discrimination that hinders women in the criminal law profession. The goals of diversity, equity, inclusion, and belonging for women and people of color in the field of law include setting forth the tools that will assist in training, monitoring, allowing transparency in the workplace, and securing the goal of helping women lawyers and all lawyers enjoy and succeed in the practice of law.

The sisters in the law on the Task Force have been privileged to serve and have great admiration and gratitude to all of the participants in every listening session heard and felt. It has been a great honor to join my sisters in the process as we continue to strategize an amazing future for all sisters in the law.

ENTITY:

CRIMINAL JUSTICE SECTION

TOPIC:

DIVERSITY AND INCLUSION, CIVIL RIGHTS AND CONSTITUTION, CRIMINAL LAW

Author

Denise Langford Morris
ABA CJS Executive Board and Women's Task Force

Judge Denise Langford Morris (Ret.), first woman dean and first African American, served on the Oakland County, Michigan, Circuit Court for 30 years, managing criminal and civil jury trials; mediator, arbitrator, and special master at JAMS Downtown Detroit Resolution Center; serves on the ABA CJS Executive Board and Women's Task Force.

APPENDIX T

Listening Authentically, Extending Inclusion

Sarah Redfield

Criminal Justice Magazine Fall 2023

Listening Authentically, Extending Inclusion

Sarah E Redfield

Oct 01, 2023 6 min read

Summary

- The Task Force has been committed to hearing many voices, including the voices of women who were not always sought or heard.
- Resolution 501 recognized and reflected the groundbreaking work of the Task Force and stellar accomplishment for CJS.
- In defining the problem and making clear its genesis and the contours of its resolution, the Task Force has taken an important and necessary step to get leaders in the field to discuss and own the Ten Principles and put in place structures and practices to bring about real change.

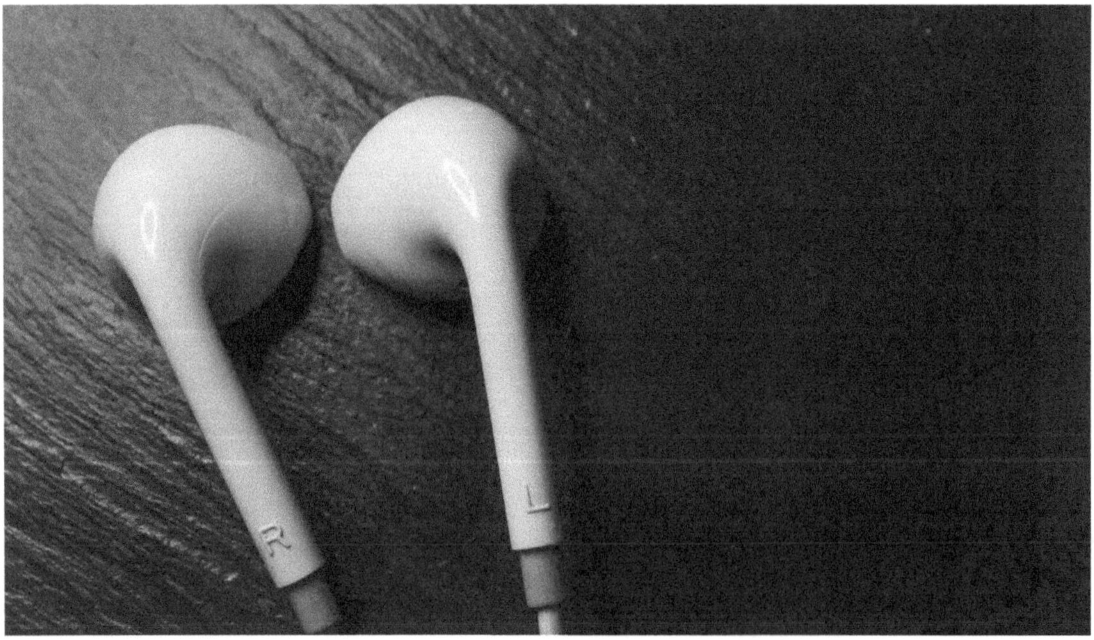

Ar Ducha Misfa'i via Getty Images

Then CJS Chair Lucian Dervan convened the Women's Task Force (Task Force) in late 2018, directing them to investigate gender-based barriers to hiring, promotion, and retention in the practice of criminal law. Consistent with this mission, Lucian appointed members who were diverse in race and ethnicity, age, sexual orientation and gender identity (SOGI), family status, ability, experience, and career paths:

- Carla Laroche (Task Force Co-Chair, Felder-Fayard Associate Professor of Law, Tulane University School of Law)
- Tina Luongo (Task Force Co-Chair, Attorney in Charge, Criminal Defense Practice, The Legal Aid Society of New York City)
- Lara Bazelon (Professor of Law, Director of the Criminal & Juvenile Justice and Racial Justice Clinics, University of San Francisco School of Law)
- April Frazier Camara (President & CEO, National Legal Aid and Defender Association)
- Barbara Creel (Karelitz Professor of Law, University of New Mexico School of Law)
- The Honorable Bernice Donald (U.S. Court of Appeals for the Sixth Circuit, Ret.)
- Daniela Donoso (Program Wide Immigration Attorney, Legal Services of North Florida)
- Maria Carmen Hinayon (Compliance and Policy Investigator, University of California Davis)
- The Honorable Denise Langford-Morris (JAMS Mediator and Arbitrator, Oakland County Circuit Court, Ret.)
- Ann Ratnayake Macy (Adjunct Professorial Lecturer, Department of Justice, Law, and Criminology, American University)
- The Honorable Gloria Ochoa-Bruck (Spokane Municipal Court)
- The Honorable Rachel Pickering (Kansas Court of Appeals)
- Sarah Redfield (Professor of Law, University of New Hampshire School of Law)
- Lieutenant Colonel Susan Upward (Judge Advocate, U.S. Marine Corps)

The Task Force was ably organized and led by our multitalented reporter Maryam Ahranjani (Task Force Reporter, Ronald & Susan Friedman Professor of Law, University of New Mexico School of Law) and supported by an equally talented Advisory Committee.

Listing the charge and members of the group in this way is accurate and might almost be enough given the experience that is represented. But such a description misses what the group became as it proceeded with its work—a committed and cohesive group tremendously dedicated to the task at hand, and, as it turned out, to each other and to the other women we met in the process—and in a larger sense, to all women in criminal justice.

From the very beginning, we were committed to hearing many voices, including—especially including—voices of women who were not always sought or heard. To this end, members of the Task Force and Advisory Committee conducted surveys and focus groups. We traveled across the country for 12 listening sessions deliberately designed to hear from a very diverse spectrum of women. Throughout, we sought to define *diverse* as broadly as possible, including race and ethnicity, gender, SOGI, ability/disability, socioeconomic status, family status, language, work and life experience, and employment and career placement. We heard from people in small and large places, in cities and rural communities. We heard from students just beginning their careers and from those whose careers were now decades in the making. We heard from a wide array of practitioners, professors, and judges from the full spectrum of criminal practices. And, not surprisingly, we heard from those who had left the practice of criminal law to take up different areas of practice or to establish themselves in other occupations.

We listened, and we listened, and we learned. We were touched, influenced, and inspired by what we heard. Depressingly so, as we heard stories about women not being recognized as attorneys, not being paid fairly, not being promoted fairly, and not being given credit for their work. These were stories that had been the same for decades. We cried in some places as we heard stories about women's struggles at different stages in their lives: efforts to find a safe, clean, and private place to breastfeed or pump milk for their babies; efforts to meet the challenges in daycare and education options for their children; efforts to support their parents and other family members—and **still continue to work**. We grieved with others as we heard about the abuse, harassment, and bias in their communities.

As we listened and learned, two points crystallized: one, so clearly a negative; the other so clearly the opposite. Both feel like key and core realities. First, the negative: So many, many of the stories we heard were the same—the same as from others in Task Force sessions—but, even more negatively, they were the same stories that I (and other members of our group) would have told when we started our careers decades ago.

Second, the positive: We learned from each other and supported each other to help us hold on to the view that, although the work for equity was painfully slow, it was happening and, at least in part, it was happening with us. We collectively became a force for change, a much stronger force than any one of us alone had been. That is, as discouraging as it was to continue to bear witness to the intransigence of employers and institutions to advance and sustain authentic inclusion and equity for women, other things also happened, substantively and personally for the Task Force. The substantive work of the Task Force is described in several other articles in CJS and other publications, as are the substantive principles that were distilled from this work to become the basis for a resolution presented by the Criminal Justice Section and adopted by the American Bar Association House of Delegates, Resolution 501, *Ten Principles to Achieve Gender Equity in the Criminal Legal Profession*, and Report (Feb. 6, 2023), https://tinyurl.com/24kp833j (the accompanying Report includes citations to CJS articles and other resources).

The adoption of Resolution 501 recognized and reflected the groundbreaking work of the Task Force and was a stellar accomplishment for CJS. But again, the reporting of this fact does not convey the full message. The facts and reporting miss the human part of the Task Force's work. Without labeling it as such, we were directly addressing one of the problems that so many women face: their loneliness and often their isolation. In contrast, we became friends with each other; we celebrated children and grandchildren, we supported each other through COVID and as parents and others dear to us died. We became coaches, mentors, and sponsors for each other. We celebrated major publications and awards as well as promotions and elections to tenured professorships, judgeships, and one Lieutenant Colonel. Indeed, I'm sure that our support and coaching played some small part in those successes.

Throughout the work, we shared our own lived-experiences and an understanding of how this related to what we heard and learned in the larger circles of our work. We saw our connections among ourselves and to those who worked with us—and their connections with us and with each other. It was as we reflected on this small and then larger group that we understood the meaning of an ingroup, a group that shared cultural experiences even while we were so diverse in so many ways. And it is this last point that I think is the true takeaway for the Task Force: It is important not to allow ourselves to be isolated; it's critical to see our commonality with other women and to find support and offer support to them. It is equally critical not to isolate ourselves from our allies, but rather acknowledge the important sustaining support from Lucian in starting this work and from all of our colleagues who worked to see the Ten Principles become a reality adopted by the ABA as Resolution 501. It is a step we all achieved—the Task Force and all who came together in this work.

In defining the problem and making clear its genesis and the contours of its resolution, we have taken an important and necessary step to get leaders in our field to themselves discuss and own the Ten Principles and put in place structures and practices to bring about real change. But, of course, the even harder work remains. The work of the Task Force to date has incorporated a continuous feedback loop of listening, research, writing, and listening again. The work now needs to continue that loop to a more action-based agenda in the field among our colleagues. We look forward to cooperating to these ends with those we've included so far and all the criminal justice community writ large.

Author

Sarah E Redfield

Professor Sarah E. Redfield Sarah Redfield is Professor Emerita at the University of New Hampshire School of Law and Affiliate Professor at the University of New Hampshire Department of Women's and Gender Studies. Professor...

APPENDIX U

Black, Female, and Elected: The Long Road for Black Women as Top Prosecutors

Melba V. Pearson, Rachel A. Silverthorn, and Tierra Fulwood

Criminal Justice Magazine Fall 2023

Black, Female, and Elected: The Long Road for Black Women as Top Prosecutors

Melba V Pearson, Rachel A. Silverthorn, and Tierra Fulwood

Oct 18, 2023 17 min read

Summary

- Voter perception is a big issue that questions candidate viability, qualifications, and electability.
- Negative media attention is impossible to avoid, but data and facts can counteract the narrative.
- Buy-in starts on the campaign trail by informing and influencing voters.
- Challenges can be addressed through broader education, training opportunities, more robust features about Black female candidates, and effective donor engagement strategies.

Stephen Zeigler via Getty Images

In the wake of recent high-profile cases, the role of the elected prosecutor has taken on new scrutiny and attention. The debate over criminal justice reform, including what reform should look like, continues to be a polarizing topic in many circles. One positive, however, is more diverse candidates putting their hats in the ring for the position of elected prosecutor. Specifically, Black women began successful runs for elected prosecutor positions in the early 2000s. Though there are still very few, the numbers have increased since the 2016 election cycle. As of 2019, 73 percent of elected prosecutors were white men; women of color made up only 2 percent of those elected nationwide—39 of whom are Black women. Reflective Democracy Campaign, *Tipping the Scales: Challengers Take on the Old Boys Club of Elected Prosecutors* (Oct. 2019) [hereinafter *Tipping the Scales*]. That is more Black women than the amount who held elected prosecutor positions in 2014 (17)—but they are still underrepresented compared to the population. Reflective Democracy Campaign, *Justice for All?* (July 2015). More diverse candidates are running for elected prosecutor positions more frequently in recent years, with white women and men of color more likely to win elections than white men. *Tipping the Scales, supra*. Of note, however, is that this does not hold true for women of color; the number of Black women who are successful in winning elections is still low. It bears examining as to the reasons why. In order to get a full picture, it is critical to consider the challenges of running for this office, governing in the current political environment, and what the future may hold for others who seek this path—through the eyes of those who went through the process as candidates or strategists.

Introduction

Elected district attorneys (DAs) face many challenges throughout their tenure as prosecutors. (Prosecutors may be referred to as district, commonwealth, state's, or state attorneys depending on the jurisdiction. For ease of reference, we use the terms DA and SA depending on the title used in the state in which each elected is in office.) As the diversity of prosecutor's offices continues to increase, more people of color and women are running for elected positions. The main issue is the *perception* of whom voters think should be in office as an elected prosecutor. With the majority of elected prosecutors being white men, there is a subtle (and, in some instances, not so subtle) belief that an elected prosecutor should be a white man—or, at the very least, a man. *Tipping the Scales, supra.* To better understand the challenges and criticisms faced by women of color in elected positions, we spoke with several Black female elected prosecutors—focusing on the election process, governing, and the future of the office.

Navigating the Election Process

One of the toughest hurdles for the Black female electeds to overcome in their quest for office was the election process itself. Qualifications were never a real issue on its face; the candidates had a deep history of service to their communities and had been practicing law for significant amounts of time. Lynneice Washington, who became the first female DA in Alabama history, ran in 2016 and won by 299 votes. She encountered sexism firsthand, where many people viewed being an elected prosecutor as a "man's role" and questioned why she would even run. In the primary election, one of her opponents also had the last name of Washington (they were not related). The narrative became "vote for the husband." DA Washington pointed out the flaw in the thinking—"*what sense does that make? Why would we be married and oppose each other in an election?*" The narrative later changed to "they're brother and sister; vote for the brother." Former 9th Judicial Circuit (Orlando, FL, area) SA Aramis Ayala shared a similar experience while running for state attorney in 2016. "*When I ran, it was a time where it was shocking that a Black person, let alone a Black woman, would be running for this position.*" The impression, she felt, was partially due to the belief that Black attorneys work solely in criminal defense. A'shanti Gholar, president of Emerge, an organization that hosts the program "Seated Together" that trains all women to run for office (with an emphasis on the New American Majority, which includes Black women), looks at the issue more pointedly. She notes that the first barrage of questions Black female candidates for elected prosecutor face include "Are you qualified enough? Are you viable? Are you electable?" For her, those are all code words for "straight white man" because "they are who we (society) see as viable."

Viability becomes a topic in terms of how the announcement of a candidacy is received. While politics can be brutal between opponents, there is an additional layer when gender is in the mix. For Sherry Boston, it came in the form of an interview with the incumbent district attorney she was challenging for office. "*The media went to interview the then DA and asked, 'what do you think about Solicitor General Sherry Boston running against you?' and his response was 'Well, she has a very successful husband and a beautiful family.' In that moment, I thought, I've been an elected prosecutor for six years running an office—my current office is bigger than most district attorney's offices (with the exception of his) across the state; and his initial response to my decision to run for DA was that he wanted to compliment me on having a successful husband and a beautiful family. I said to myself, is he not taking me seriously as a lawyer, as an elected, as a prosecutor?*" Contra Costa (CA) DA Diana Becton shared similar stories in terms of how she was received. She felt that the subtle messaging from her opponents (both white) was "*we belong here and you don't. We know how to do this job, and you don't*"—despite her having been a judge in criminal court for 22 years prior to running for office.

The viability discussion spills directly into the struggles of fundraising. If one doesn't believe a Black woman can win or be successful in a position, why donate? All of the candidates struggled, making numerous calls to raise money. Outside funders often sat on the sidelines for fear that the candidates would not succeed. DA Washington spoke fondly of the faithful donors who would come through in a pinch but stated, "*I had to invest in myself. I had to use my own funds.*" SA Kim Foxx observed as well as experienced the fundraising shortage in comparison to white men and considers herself "lucky" to have received $400,000 in seed money from her former boss, which helped her on the path to raising $3 million. She was blatantly told, "*You're not getting traction in a race for less than $1 million.*" In her 2020 re-election campaign, a wealthy white man challenged her and raised $15 million to her $3 million. She was able to succeed despite him outspending her 5 to 1, but it was a challenge despite the power of being an incumbent. Lastly, big donors will sometimes stay out of prosecutor's races because they do not see the benefit, especially in the short term. DA Diana Becton noted one of the biggest challenges is that "*people don't understand what prosecutors do, and there are no promises that can be made as a prosecutor. You have to be fair and can't advocate for special interests or certain donors over others. This keeps large donors out of these* *races.*" For former SA Ayala, the battle was even in the shadows—including a whisper campaign urging donors not to support her, with veiled threats of what could happen to their individual careers if they did support her.

Finally, Black female candidates face being painted with the same brush as national issues. DA Boston found that she was well received in the majority minority district of DeKalb County, Georgia—where there are many Black female elected officials. However, her fights were not local; it was with officials in other parts of Georgia, or out of state altogether. After a recent radio interview about her work at Emerge, A'shanti Gholar shared how the vast majority of callers were white men who said varying themes of "*Black women are not qualified to be in office; women of color and elected office bring too much race into things; Black women mayors are ruining all of the major cities.*" SA Foxx reflected on her historic 2016 three-way race with all female candidates—a Latina incumbent, an African American challenger, and a white woman challenger, where race became the focus rather than gender. She found the pushback to be more subtle—"*you came from a low income background, so will you see crime the same way we do? As if someone from a housing project would not care about crime the way a white person from the suburbs would!*" She found success by centering her experiences as a crime survivor, an attorney, and growing up in an under-resourced community rather than running from it. "*We could all read statute books, but what I brought to this (race) is a Black woman from public housing here in Chicago.*" PA Kym Worthy faced this from another perspective. In 2004, she was elected to serve as Wayne County's Prosecuting Attorney, which is a diverse county that consists of 43 distinct communities leaning predominately white and Democratic. Detroit is the largest city in her jurisdiction, which is predominately Black and Democratic. There are five other communities of color in her jurisdiction. At the time she was first elected, there was only one other Black elected prosecutor—now Vice President Kamala Harris, who was then the San Francisco DA. While running, Prosecuting Attorney Worthy was not liked by the police union as a result of convicting two police officers of murder. Because detractors could not target her on her qualifications, the narrative became that she hated police—which eventually fell flat with voters.

Governing as a Black Woman

Criticisms of DAs come from several avenues. It can come internally from colleagues who do not appreciate new policies or the changes in direction/leadership and externally from the media or other elected officials for potential political gain.

DA Boston faced little criticism on the local level; with her jurisdiction being majority Black and more politically liberal, she had support from the community and other agencies. However, criticism came from the state and national levels regarding her policies, under the guise of combating "woke" or "far left" prosecutors making communities less safe (despite the fact certain types of crime have been on the rise nationally across both progressive and conservative jurisdictions). Former SA Ayala, due to her stance on the death penalty, received nooses in the mail, as well as enduring an employee stating on social media that she should be "tarred, feathered, and hung from a tree."

PA Worthy experienced pushback in 2004 against what would be viewed as mainstream programs today. "*No one else was doing diversion programs or alternatives to incarceration in 2004,*" she shared. "*We were laughed at and ostracized, but now, everyone has similar programs. Jail does not always solve the crime problem. You can walk and chew gum—tough on crime but measured in terms of second chances.*"

On top of other avenues, the media can feed off of negative stories, sometimes exacerbating the problem. SA Foxx spoke about the criticism that comes from how DAs handle high-profile or celebrity cases. SA Foxx found that she was defined by one case, whose resolution was not to the public's satisfaction for two years; meanwhile, she vacated the convictions of over 240 wrongfully convicted Black men and women—which received less media coverage. DA Washington experienced a media nightmare surrounding the case of a pregnant young woman who lost her baby as a result of a gunshot wound during a fight that she initiated. Many people and media outlets used the tragic situation as a means of grandstanding their political platforms regarding women reproductive rights and abortion; DA Washington was confronted with death threats concerning the case before and after her decision to dismiss it. In contrast, DA Cy Vance openly chose not to prosecute high-profile celebrity Harvey Weinstein for very serious felony offenses. The media reaction to Vance's decision was completely different in terms of the criticism at the time, with him only receiving a fraction of the outrage. It was only a decade later and after the advent of the #MeToo movement that Weinstein was finally held accountable for his actions.

Along a similar vein, DA Sherry Boston was heavily criticized for pledging not to prosecute women or providers for abortions. Boston joined 83 other elected officials in their continued fight for women's rights by not prosecuting abortions. Press Release, Fair & Just Prosecution, Joint Statement from Elected Prosecutors (June 24, 2022). A vast majority of the elected district attorneys who signed the open letter pledging not to prosecute abortions were white, yet only DA Boston received widespread negative attention from the media. (While DA Boston faced media backlash, we acknowledge that SA Andrew Warren suffered adverse impacts for signing the same letter through gubernatorial action vs media backlash.)

The clear theme is that because negative media attention is impossible to avoid, having a solid media team who can work to highlight the DA's position with data and facts is highly important. Having data showing real impacts helps, as does building relationships within the community. When DA Becton was accused of not promoting women, the statistics for her office showed not only were women being promoted, but they were also a larger majority of management than ever in the history of the office. Sometimes, the media attention is just about timing—SA Foxx experienced a new level of media attention compared to previous administrations coming into office in the era of the "progressive prosecutor movement" as a Black woman. It may not always be the actual role of the elected DA that generates media attention, but who is in that role. Regardless, the DAs had to put the attention out of their minds. As former SA Ayala puts it, "*the attacks were only distractions from me getting the justice that I had committed to during my campaign*."

As women of color, these elected DAs have a different world view than others might. They each expressed feeling an extra responsibility to the users of the criminal justice system—victims, defendants, witnesses, and communities—because they know what it is like. More than one is a survivor of domestic violence; all personally know people who have been impacted by the system. By bringing their life experiences to the role, they have been able to use their positions as springboards for young people and their communities as a whole through programming including diversion for low-level and first-time offenders, internships for those pursuing law careers, and expansion of diversity in executive positions.

The Future and Sustainability of Change

The reality is that the future is unpredictable, uncontrollable, and uncertain—mainly because new leaders are elected by the people or appointed by the governor. Much like everything else, what people in different communities want can be heavily influenced by media coverage as well as local/national politics. Therefore, many of the prosecutors can only hope for an office that continues with the same goals they have established. "*The hardest part in this journey is being able to walk away from an office and hoping that it can sustain itself*," DA Boston shared.

Many of the prosecutors agree that the key component of future change is expanding the group of Black elected prosecutors. In order to expand this group, the prosecutors believe strongly in the power of being a positive influence. The influence starts long before the prosecutors take office; it starts with getting the buy-in on the campaign trail by informing as well as influencing voters, and it continues once the prosecutors take office through influencing their staff. In doing so, the elected prosecutors hope to inspire collective change. Many hope that their successor will be a Black woman who has been working in their office and believes strongly in the goals and foundation that have been laid. DA

Boston explained the concept of influence in her office as motivating the line prosecutors so that if they leave, they will take with them a desire to be an agent for positive change, building on the lessons learned in her office.

PA Worthy considers another facet of the role of Black female elected prosecutor—expanding the group by intentionally supporting a successor. Often, the communities that these prosecutors serve put their faith and trust in the incumbent, so when a prosecutor decides to leave office, it is likely that they can influence the community as to whom to support as the next person to serve in that role. As the longest-serving Black female elected prosecutor—not just in her jurisdiction, but in the entire country—her interest lies in not just being the first, but ensuring she is not the last Black female in this role.

Former SA Ayala points to transparency as a tool to ensure that changes survive from administration to administration. By engaging with the public and giving them regular updates about new policies—including data around the level of success—the community can feel empowered to demand that effective policies continue beyond the tenure of the currently elected.

Ultimately there is no one right or wrong answer on how to shape the future. Elected prosecutors around the country constantly consider how their present impact can lead to permanent future changes. However, the reality is that even though DAs can make policy changes during their tenure, they can be reversed when the next person is elected. Ultimately, the best solution for future change is to keep the community engaged in what changes are being made and earning their buy-in for continued support of policies that have been implemented.

Storm Clouds Are Brewing

However, there is a disturbing trend emerging in terms of the democratic process. In the majority of jurisdictions, prosecutors are elected. In general, elected prosecutors, as with all elected officials, can be removed for issues surrounding dereliction of duty—which normally has a very narrow construction. It has previously been seen in the context of an elected that is struggling with addiction or other health issues, somehow incapacitated and unable to complete their term. In Florida, we have seen the governor take a far more expensive view; in an unprecedented move, Governor Ron DeSantis removed Tampa area SA Andrew Warren because he disagreed with Warren signing open letters stating he (along with dozens of elected prosecutors across the country) would not prosecute doctors for providing abortions or transgender care. Rebekah Riess & Shaia Shelton, *Florida Supreme Court Rules Against Former Democratic State Attorney Ousted by DeSantis*, CNN (June 23, 2023). While neither scenario played out in terms of an active case before Warren's office (or anywhere in Florida), the governor removed him from office and appointed a conservative attorney in his place. He has threatened to do the same to the Orlando area SA, Monique Worrell (a Black female); the public battle has weighed on prosecutor morale, brought uncertainty to victims of crime whose cases may be in the office, and harmed relations with local law-enforcement. Jennifer Hunt Murty, *State Attorney Worrell Accuses Gov. DeSantis of a "Witch Hunt,"* Ocala Gazette (Apr. 29, 2023). In Georgia, more of the same is percolating, with the conservative Republican legislature passing a new law that broadens the requirements that can be used to remove an elected prosecutor from office. Sam Levine, *Georgia Governor Signs Bill That Allows Removal of District Attorneys*, The Guardian (May 5, 2023). This is seen as a direct attack on Fani Willis, the Fulton County DA and a Black female, who is currently investigating a high-profile case involving the former president of the United States. This follows the Pennsylvania Legislature's attack on Philadelphia DA Larry Krassner in which they attempted to impeach him—despite being duly elected twice by his constituents. Diamy Wang, *Philadelphia DA Larry Krasner Impeachment Trial Indefinitely Halted*, Daily Pennsylvanian (Jan. 17, 2023).

These attacks on prosecutors are a highly problematic threat to the rule of law in the United States. It gives the impression that the will of the voters does not matter and can have the long-term effect of discouraging voters from being at the polls since the person they elected could be removed due to partisan conflicts. There is also a chilling effect with the intent to dissuade elected prosecutors from taking on tough issues or politically charged cases. There is the fear that if you do not do what the majority wants, despite your oath to seek justice, you will be removed from your position. It will disproportionally impact electeds of color, but especially Black female electeds who feel a strong mandate to address systemic issues impacting communities of color in the criminal justice system.

Key Takeaways

Some of the challenges these DAs have faced are no doubt faced by others in the life of an elected DA, but some are unique to Black women in this role. Addressing these challenges can be achieved through a number of means. First, broader education is needed in school and in public discourse about the role as well as the importance of prosecutors. Understanding the role will encourage people to donate the same way they would to a congressional candidate or a presidential candidate. It will also help voters understand what is important to them in a prosecutor and could inform voting decisions. As Aramis Ayala puts it, "*we have to teach people that there can be differing visions of justice*."

Along these lines, changing the narrative about what makes a good leader and that there is no one identity that is successful more than others can open voters to considering people from different backgrounds rather than maintaining the historical idea of what a

DA looks like. More robust media feature stories about female DAs, DAs of color, and female DAs of color around the country focused on the positive work they are doing could do wonders in changing public perception, rather than running solely negative pieces—often in response to a single case. The more commonplace it is to see diverse DAs, the easier it is to support a Black female candidate for DA if that candidate's agenda resonates with the voters.

Better engagement strategies for donors on the importance of supporting prosecutor's races are sorely needed—especially in the wake of new attacks on the independence of prosecutors, as seen in Florida by gubernatorial action and Georgia by way of legislation. Campaign finance reform plays an important role here as well. Capping races at a certain amount of money would allow people with actual experience—such as the line prosecutor who never worked for a big corporation or firm—the same opportunity to compete and run. Often, prosecutor races involve one big-name candidate who arrives with a large campaign budget versus others, who, despite their best efforts, raise pennies on the dollar of their opponent. Until this change happens, DA Washington had some advice for those considering the path of an elected: "*So what I would say to any woman whose successful election would place them into the status of a trailblazer for any elective position is to be passionate, be confident, be ready to fight for the cause, and be prepared to invest in yourself. Large contributors will not believe in you until you win.*"

Finally, there is a need for better training opportunities like Emerge for Black female candidates and Vera's Reshaping Prosecution program to support Black female elected DAs. Such programs can help Black candidates structure their campaigns more efficiently and train them in how to avoid potential media pitfalls and the effective use of data to educate the community on the role of a prosecutor in their daily lives.

DA Washington faced an additional unique election challenge—one hundreds of thousands of women face each year. In a previous run for elected office, she was diagnosed with breast cancer, enduring chemotherapy as well as a double mastectomy. In her reflection of that time, she shared, "*there were many nights that my pillow was wet, but ... I wanted my son to see that in life you're going to have obstacles. You'll have barriers, but don't allow it to stop you. You can go over. You can go under, even maneuver around. If you get tired, just walk in place. You must keep moving, and the best way to give him that lesson was to be a living lesson for him.*"

It is this resilience and perseverance that can serve as a model to other Black women pursuing this path.

Special acknowledgment to the following women for sharing their experiences:

- **Aramis Ayala**, Former State Attorney, 9th Judicial Circuit, Florida; Assistant Professor, University of Central Florida
- **Diana Becton**, District Attorney, Contra Costa County, California
- **Sherry Boston**, District Attorney, DeKalb County, Georgia
- **Kim Foxx**, State's Attorney, Cook County, Illinois
- **A'shanti Gholar**, President, Emerge
- **Lynneice Washington**, District Attorney, Jefferson County, Bessemer Division, Alabama
- **Kym Worthy**, Prosecuting Attorney, Wayne County, Michigan

Authors

Melba V Pearson

MVP Law

Melba V. Pearson is a nationally recognized civil rights and criminal law attorney, policy expert, and advocate for equity in the justice system. She currently serves as Director of Prosecution Projects at Florida...

Tierra Fulwood

...

About the Editor and Authors

All the authors are active members and leaders in the American Bar Association (ABA) Criminal Justice Section, as well as other sections and groups within the ABA.

Maryam Ahranjani is Professor of Law at the University of Nevada Las Vegas William S. Boyd School of Law, where she teaches, writes, and speaks in the areas of criminal law and procedure, constitutional law, and education law.

Joy Applewhite is Assistant Public Defender at Law Offices of the Public Defender in Hobbs, New Mexico.

Justin Bingham is City Prosecutor for the City of Spokane, Washington.

Aubony Burns is Senior Deputy Prosecuting Attorney for the King County (Washington) Prosecuting Attorney's Office.

Bernice Donald is a mediator, arbitrator, court-appointed neutral, neutral evaluator, and temporary judge/judge pro tem for JAMS and retired judge of the U.S. Court of Appeals for the Sixth Circuit, U.S. District Court, and U.S. Bankruptcy Court.

Denise Langford Morris serves as a mediator, arbitrator, and court-appointed neutral at JAMS after a long career as a judge on the Oakland County, Michigan, Circuit Court.

Carla Laroche is the Felder-Fayard Associate Professor of Law at Tulane University Law School and The Murphy Institute, where she teaches, writes, and speaks about voting rights, family law, and racial and gender justice.

Tina Luongo is the Chief Attorney of the Criminal Defense Practice of the New York Legal Aid Society.

Gloria Ochoa-Bruck is a Spokane (Washington) Municipal Court Judge and previously served as Associate Judge for the Kalispel Tribe, along with many other positions in government and private practice.

Rachel Pickering serves on the Kansas Court of Appeals and previously served as a district court judge for the Third Judicial District in Topeka, Kansas.

Sarah Redfield is an expert on implicit bias and is retired from the faculty of the University of New Hampshire Franklin Pierce School of Law.

Susan Upward is a lieutenant colonel and Judge Advocate in the U.S. Marine Corps.

Camelia M. Valdes is County Prosecutor for Passaic County, New Jersey, and previously served as Assistant U.S. Attorney in Newark.